# First Impressions

Yale UNIVERSITY PRESS    NEW HAVEN AND LONDON

Published in cooperation with the
William P. Clements Center for Southwest Studies Southern Methodist University

# First

David J. Weber and William deBuys

# Impressions

*A Reader's Journey to Iconic Places of the American Southwest*

Published with assistance from the foundation established in memory of
Henry Weldon Barnes of the Class of 1882, Yale College.

Yale University Press books may be purchased in quantity for educational,
business, or promotional use. For information, please e-mail sales.press@yale.edu
(U.S. office) or sales@yaleup.co.uk (U.K. office).

Designed by Nancy Ovedovitz and set in Adobe Garamond type by
Tseng Information Systems, Inc.

Printed in the United States of America.

ISBN 978-0-300-21504-5 (hardcover : alk. paper)
Library of Congress Control Number: 2016963030
A catalogue record for this book is available from the British Library.

This paper meets the requirements of ANSI/NISO Z39.48-1992
(Permanence of Paper).

10 9 8 7 6 5 4 3 2 1

To my friend Jim Hopkins,
who mediates all experience through the written word
*David J. Weber*

To the family and memory of David J. Weber
*William deBuys*

# Contents

# Preface

*First Impressions* was conceived as a book by David J. Weber in 2004 or early 2005. His earliest computer files for the project appear to have been created in March of 2005. After that, more files came thick and fast, as Weber collected "impressions" of places he loved in the Southwest and as he whittled down the list of potential sites to the fifteen you see here. In the project's early years, however, *First Impressions* competed for time with other projects. Besides his usual teaching load, Weber was directing the institute he had founded, the Clements Center for Southwest Studies at Southern Methodist University in Dallas. He was also completing one of the most audacious and challenging of his twenty-seven books, *Bárbaros: Spaniards and Their Savages in the Age of Enlightenment.* Once he finished *Bárbaros,* he condensed his magisterial *The Spanish Frontier in North America* to a thinner, more accessible edition. *First Impressions* grew page by page, as time permitted. Unfortunately, there was not enough time. David died on August 20, 2010, in New Mexico. Files and books for *First Impressions* lay on the desk in the study at his home in Ramah.

Ultimately Carol Weber, David's wife of nearly fifty years, asked William deBuys to pick up where David had left off.

Here, let me shift out of the third-person voice. I had been a fellow at the Clements Center in 1999–2000, editing a volume of the explorer John Wesley Powell's major writings. At the beginning of the fellowship year, I knew David mainly as a figure with whom I might chat on the rare occasion that I attended a meeting of the Western History Association. During my year at SMU, however, our friendship deepened. Through both semesters, fall and spring, we had dinner together, just the two of us, every Tuesday night. We met always at the same restaurant and rarely varied the dishes we ordered. The point of our dinners was conversation, not food. We might have missed one or two Tuesdays in the course of the year because of travel or other engagements, but the routine of our regular meetings soon became for me the most salient and enjoyable feature of my time at SMU. Fellows from previous years had told me that the Clements Center was a high-quality operation, and this seemed to be the proof: that the director would take time from his crushing workload to meet one-on-one with a visiting fellow, week after week. Initially, I assumed David gave equal attention to other fellows, or at least to the senior fellows of other years. Gradually, I learned that this was not always the case.

One of the interesting things about our dinners was that we rarely talked shop. We talked a great deal about the Southwest, but not as a subject for the practice of history. Instead we talked of it as home ground and a place to live, a place where the most important events of our lives had and would continue to take place. Many years earlier I had built an adobe cabin on my mountain farm in northern New Mexico. David was then embarking on the construction of his and Carol's home in Ramah, New Mexico, near Zuni and Gallup. We talked about practical matters like siting a house and about the constant puzzle of trying to live in some kind of harmony with the land.

We also talked about writing, not history writing, but the general business of making good sentences, paragraphs, and pages. David was a naturally gifted writer, but he had never talked much with his colleagues about the craft of committing the (historical) stories he told to paper. He seemed to derive pleasure from acquiring names—*arc of a narrative* was one—for concepts and techniques he had long understood instinctively and had employed on a daily basis, but that had somehow escaped being assigned a term among his fellow historians.

After the fellowship year, we stayed in touch. One summer, David and Carol visited my farm in southern Taos County. Another summer, I visited them in Ramah. And with some regularity we corresponded, more frequently after David became ill.

Other writing commitments prevented me from taking up *First Impressions* until 2014, but in that year I was the fortunate recipient of a second (half-year) Clements Center fellowship that enabled me to set about completing David's book.

The result is a book by two authors, who worked on the project not together but sequentially and who were friends of long standing. The discerning reader may detect small differences in style from one passage to the next, but it won't be easy. And certainly no reader will be able to detect any difference between one author's affection for the Southwest and the other's. For both of us, the Southwest has been a source of lifelong fascination, and through the vehicle of this book we hope to share it.

William deBuys
El Valle, New Mexico

# Acknowledgments

David Weber and I cannot write these acknowledgments together, but if we could, one thing would not change: David's wife, Carol Weber, would be preeminent among the people thanked. It was Carol who asked me, with the support of her children, Amy and Scott, to finish David's book. I am deeply grateful for the opportunity to work on this project and for her kind assistance from start to finish.

The good people at SMU's Clements Center for Southwest Studies, which David founded and for many years directed, have also been essential to the creation of *First Impressions*. Ruth Ann Elmore assisted David in the early years of the project, and it was she who helped me make sense of the computer files he left behind. But that is only the beginning, as her efforts in support of this project have continued to the present. It is no exaggeration to say this book might not exist without her. The same is true of Andrew Graybill, who succeeded David as director of the Clements Center—his support and the support of the rest of the center's community, especially including Sherry Smith, have been vital. To those already mentioned, I would like to add the names of my "fellow fellows" at SMU during the spring semester of 2014—Julie Reed, Ben Francis-Fallon, and Max Krochmal: the good cheer at the Clements Center made working there a pleasure.

I spent a lot of that term in SMU's DeGolyer Library, whose marvelous collection provided much of the documentary material and many of the illustrations reproduced here. I am greatly indebted to the entire staff of the library, especially Russell Martin, Pamalla Anderson, Terre Heydari, and Kate Dziminski. I know David would quickly add that his DeGolyer colleagues were invaluable allies for him, too.

Key advisers and friends to David were Bill and Lois Rosenthal, who read early drafts of many chapters. David's notes show that he also wanted to express appreciation to Erika Bsumek at the University of Texas and to his Ramah, New Mexico, friends, Dick Knowles and Tim Amsden. It will surprise no one who knew David that he intended to thank his dear friends Jim Hopkins and Patti LaSalle. Early on, David wrote the dedication to Jim that appears at the front of this book.

Among those who generously responded to my many queries, I would thank in particular John Kessell and Tom Sheridan, both of whom kindly answered an embarrassing number of them, as well as Tom Wolf, Christa Sadler, Greg Woodall, Scott Thybony, Brad Dimock, Klara Kelley, David Scheinbaum, and Bunny Fontana.

My friend Tomas Jaehn, formerly at the Chavez History Library of the Museum of New Mexico, also helped in essential ways, as did his colleagues Hannah Abelbeck and Emily Brock in Photo Archives and Michelle Roberts at the nearby Museum of Fine Arts.

Speaking of museums, Jana Hill and Emily Olson at the Amon Carter Museum were a pleasure to work with.

Many others who helped with permissions and images for the book include Marc Gottlieb, Briony Jones, Daniel Chambers, Mariana Cook, Leif Milliken, Khaleel Saba, Holly Reed, Laura Calderone, Bruce Dinges, Dan LaClair, Todd Jay Welch, and Jonathan Marc Pringle.

At Yale University Press, Laura Davulis, Erica Hanson, Eva Skewes, Seth Ditchik, Phillip King, and Robin DuBlanc all helped bring this book into being.

It has become a welcome habit with each successive project to thank Don Lamm, who once again was essential in getting my work into print. My thanks also extend to Don's superb colleagues at the Fletcher agency, Sylvie Greenberg and Melissa Chinchillo.

Another welcome habit is thanking Deborah Reade, mapmaker extraordinaire. This is our sixth collaboration, and I hope there are more to come.

Undoubtedly, names have been left out here that should have been included. David is not available to be consulted, and my memory is more than fallible. My apologies for any and all omissions.

But finally, I would indulge in the most welcome habit of all, that of thanking Joanna Hurley for her good spirit and companionship throughout the process of making this book.

# First Impressions

# Introduction

The landscapes shaped by narratives are
as real as those sculpted by the action
of wind, waves, and glaciers.
Patricia L. Price, *Dry Place*

Past and present come together more vividly in the hard, dry beauty of the Southwest than in any other part of America. The region's aridity helps preserve historic landmarks, and its sparse vegetation leaves long-abandoned sites in plain view, be they prehistoric dwellings, Spanish missions, forts, mining camps, or ranch houses. It is not by chance that archaeologists have studied the Southwest more intensively than any other region in America.

Travelers often learn about the southwestern past from guidebooks that offer capsule accounts of the region's history. Inquisitive students and general readers who take a step further inform themselves about the region from secondary sources—books and articles written by scholars or popular writers. This book offers another point of entry into the southwestern past: first-hand accounts written by early non-native visitors and residents.

These primary sources, which have come down to us in the form of diaries, letters, and ecclesiastical and government reports, convey the concerns and inflections of earlier generations, and are the building blocks on which modern writers depend. Unfortunately, despite their intrinsic interest and historical value, many are difficult to access, having been published in weighty tomes or hard-to-find books that are housed in special libraries beyond the reach of most general readers. This book brings those sources together in a single volume and quotes from them generously.

The sources also make clear that a book can generally deliver only half of the historical conversation. We know Francisco Vázquez de Coronado's version of events from the first Spanish encounter at Zuni, but we don't know—not with specificity—what the people of Hawikku and its neighboring pueblos thought and felt about that fatal collision of cultures. Although many rich strands of native oral tradition have come down through the centuries, accompanied by an imperishable sense of injury and loss, the time-stamped, site- and author-specific native view of what happened when the starving Spanish host (and its Indian allies) appeared before the stone village of Hawikku can never be fully recovered. And the same is true at Ácoma, Taos, and the Mohave villages. It is true at Canyon de Chelly, where Navajos dwelled among the ruins of the Ancient Ones, and it is also true at Wa:k, the Sobaípuri village that the world came to know as Bac, where Franciscans built the beautiful mission of San Xavier. History is always incomplete, more shadow than light, and nowhere more so than in the first contacts between the Old World and the New. Even as we craft our stories from what we can see, we strain to penetrate the shadows and learn better the shape of what we cannot know.

The Southwest is a big place. Within it, the Navajo Reservation alone is the size of West Virginia. Some scholars define the Southwest as extending from Oklahoma to California. According to the largest definitions, it sweeps northward to take in all of Nevada, Utah, and Colorado, and southward, even more dramatically, ignoring the political division of the international border, to embrace Sonora, Chihuahua, Baja California, and parts of other Mexican states, stretching far toward Mesoamerica. In *First Impressions*, however, it is a smaller Southwest, confined to the U.S. side of the border and unified as much by the habits of the traveling American public as by geography and culture. Every region is a constructed thing, and this one is built from sets of expectations and appetites that find unity under a blazing sun and a brilliant blue sky. The Southwest here might be said to be a state of mind, which many travelers feel most strongly in Arizona, New Mexico, southern Utah, and southern Colorado.

*First Impressions* focuses on fifteen iconic and conspicuous places, each one the subject of a separate chapter. Four sites feature pre-Columbian ruins—Casa Grande, Mesa Verde, Chaco Canyon, and Canyon de Chelly; five are living Native American communities—Ácoma, Mohave, Zuni, Taos, and again we can include Canyon de Chelly; two are Spanish towns—Santa Fe and again Taos; one was an early Spanish fort—Tucson—and one was a Spanish mission—San Xavier del Bac. Three of the sites are spectacular natural wonders—the Grand Canyon, Carlsbad Caverns, and Rainbow Bridge—to which, again, a fourth might be added, the remarkable Canyon de Chelly. Another striking natural feature—El Morro, or Inscription Rock—combines a pre-Columbian ruin with pre- and post-contact graffiti.

The first recorded impressions of most of these places date to Spanish colonial times, but three of the sites were not discovered until the late nineteenth and early twentieth centuries: Mesa Verde, Rainbow Bridge, and Carlsbad Caverns. Given that the Southwest, blessed with extraordinary cultural and scenic richness, is home to a disproportionate number of America's national parks and monuments, it is not surprising that eight of the fifteen sites are included within the national park system. Three are national parks—Carlsbad Caverns, the Grand Canyon, and Mesa Verde; one is a national historical park—Chaco Canyon; and four are national monuments—Canyon de Chelly, Casa Grande, El Morro, and Rainbow Bridge.

✦➤

Those who penned the first descriptions of southwestern places created an influential legacy. Not only did they establish a baseline from which we still measure change in the region's people and places, but they powerfully shaped the impressions of those who followed them. Each generation of observers seems to have read the accounts of those who preceded them—either in the original texts or in paraphrases appearing in other books. As a result, later visitors seldom saw the region with entirely fresh eyes. A U.S. topographical engineer who set out to survey the land west of Zuni in 1851, for example, carried along with his sextant and barometer an account of the earliest European traveler in the region, Coronado, who visited—and

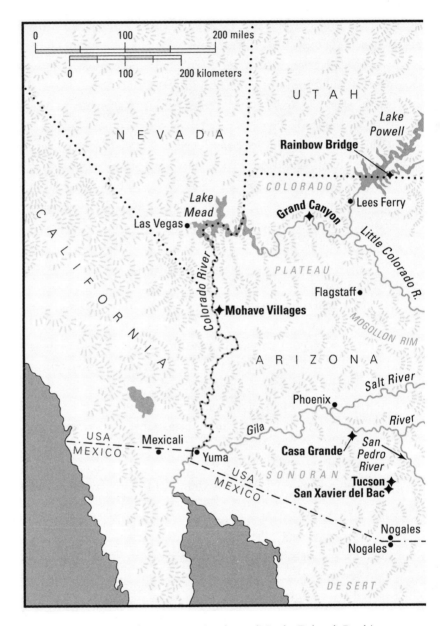

Fifteen Iconic Places in the American Southwest (Map by Deborah Reade)

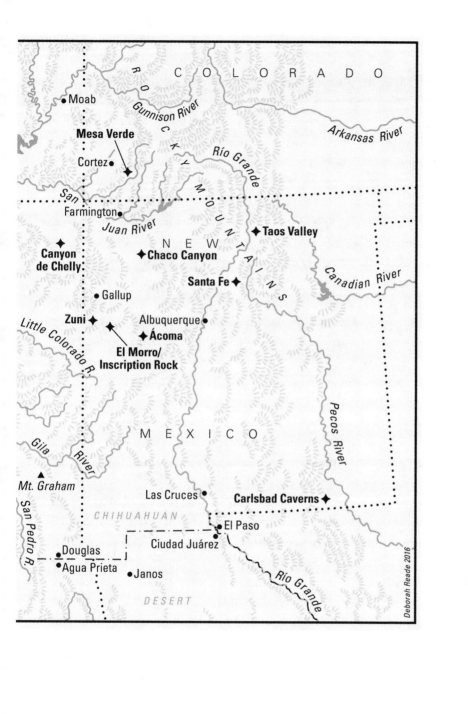

conquered — Zuni in 1540.[1] Today, of course, nearly all of us arrive at well-known southwestern destinations like the Grand Canyon or Santa Fe with our notions of the place built from visual images as well as words.

First impressions are powerful but, despite the conventional wisdom, not necessarily lasting. They are subject to modification. The author of a popular guidebook to the Southwest, for example, noted that on first arriving in New Mexico he had regarded its "box-like" adobes as "an architectural abomination," but "within a week fell eternally in love" with adobe. Knowledge brought understanding, and he, like other visitors, discovered adobe's practical "coolness in summer, warmth in winter, and economy in all seasons."[2]

Observers usually reflect the values of their time and place, and as times change, so do sensibilities. The culturally constructed attitudes of twentieth-century Anglo Americans, for example, differed in important ways from those of their nineteenth-century predecessors. One might say that their cultural lenses had changed, as had the region they focused on.

Until the early nineteenth century, the Southwest remained part of the Spanish Empire, and it was no one's "Southwest" — it was the "North." It comprised a large portion of the northern frontier of the viceroyalty of New Spain, which stretched to present-day Alaska and included much of what would become the American West. Spaniards, led by Francisco Vázquez de Coronado, explored the region as early as 1540, and by 1598 Spain established a permanent colony in New Mexico. A century later, in the late 1600s, Spain began to plant missions in what is today Arizona. Spain maintained its presence in the region until 1821, when Mexico won independence. The lands of present-day Arizona and New Mexico remained part of the northern frontier of an independent Mexico for another quarter century, until the forces of the expansionist United States invaded in 1846.

The treaty of Guadalupe Hidalgo ended the U.S.-Mexico War in 1848, and under its terms Mexico capitulated to the harsh demands of the victor and ceded the northern half of its lands to the United States. With that treaty, and with Mexico's subsequent sale to the United States of portions of New Mexico and Arizona as the Gadsden Purchase in 1853, the Mexican North became the American Southwest.

The international border imposes an arbitrary line of division on what was formerly an ecological and cultural whole. In contemporary politics, the differences between the worlds on either side of that line are, lamentably, emphasized more than the similarities (it was not always so), and this book could easily incorporate iconic sites south of the line, like the ruins of Paquimé (Casas Grandes) or the magnificent Barranca del Cobre (Copper Canyon), both in Chihuahua, but these are sites to which the average visitor north of the border is less likely to find his or her way, and so *First Impressions* accedes to the barrier of the borderline and keeps its focus on U.S. soil.

Having entered the United States as a territory rather than a state in 1850, New Mexico included all of what would become Arizona as well as part of southern Colorado. To the north, Utah also became a territory in 1850, extending eastward to embrace the portion of present-day Colorado that lies west of the Continental Divide. Mineral discoveries and the bitter politics leading to the U.S. Civil War prompted the fracturing of the two oversized territories. In 1861 the U.S. Congress created the territory of Colorado out of chunks of Utah, Kansas, Nebraska, and New Mexico. That same year it fashioned Nevada Territory out of Utah's western extremity. (Nevada became a state in 1863, Colorado in 1876, and Utah in 1896.) In 1863, Congress carved Arizona out of the western half of New Mexico, and in 1912, after long delays owed largely to Anglo American antipathy for the language, ethnicity, and Catholicism of the region's Hispanic people, Arizona and New Mexico became the forty-seventh and forty-eighth states, respectively.

Parallel to the story of shifting imperial fortunes and political change, there existed quieter, subtler, and more anonymous transformations that proved no less powerful in their cultural impacts and that also had the capacity to reorder entire ecologies and rework landscapes. Even before the arrival of the knights of Spain, European illnesses like smallpox, influenza, and whooping cough arrived in native villages with devastating effect, killing large numbers of people. The story is well known: Indians, so long isolated from the microbial portmanteau of Eurasia, had little resistance to the diseases of the "Columbian Exchange." The agents of subsequent changes were the first crops, grasses, unintended weeds, fruit trees, and animals that Spaniards brought up the trail from Mexico. The changes came not one at a time but in a flood. Those wrought by horses, cattle, sheep, and goats brought new challenges as well as blessings. They improved transportation, made animal protein more readily available, and also forced native farmers to guard or fence their cropland against the new herbivores, whose grazing quickly marked the land. Since then, the tides of change have continued to roll across the land, with new people, ideas, and technologies, whether subtly or blatantly, contributing their transformative effect.

Given the variety of changes manifested in the region, individual chapters in this book may contain multiple first impressions—sometimes because the places themselves changed and sometimes because visitors' sensibilities did. Santa Fe, Taos, and Tucson were far different in 1900 from what they had been in 1800, as were the expectations of the travelers who came to them. Indian towns, like Ácoma and Zuni, certainly changed far less, and natural features, such as the Grand Canyon, Rainbow Bridge, and Carlsbad Caverns, may not have changed at all, but people's impressions of those places metamorphosed as each succeeding generation brought new perspectives to them. Usually these new sensibilities reflected society's shifting views toward the entire region, but on occasion they anticipated societal change and helped to shape it.

The plan of the book is to take the reader forward in time, through successive "first impressions," to the point where the present-day aesthetic of each of the fifteen places takes shape—where it begins to become iconic. Our goal is to perform a kind of archaeology by sifting through the first impressions of a given place and capturing those that inform the "sense" of that place today.

➼➤

In our collective imaginations, three characteristics, taken together, make the Southwest a distinctive region of the United States: its arid land and its historic yet still vital Hispanic and Indian presences. Anglo American outsiders initially viewed each of these characteristics with disdain, but ultimately the passage of time produced a reversal, and all three became widely and deeply appreciated.

Today, more Indians live on the lands of their forebears in Arizona and New Mexico than in any other region of the United States. Aridity made tribal lands relatively undesirable to outsiders and, combined with the protections of Spanish law, helped Native Americans retain a land base in the Southwest even as waves of Anglo expansion displaced Indians elsewhere. No less distinctive is the region's Hispanic population, which is highly visible and numerous, making up nearly half the population of New Mexico and almost a third of Arizona's.[3] One encounters reminders of the land's Hispanic heritage at every turn, in the names of place after place, from Agua Caliente to Zorro Creek.

Parts of the Southwest are true deserts that receive less than ten inches of rainfall a year. This is true of the Chihuahuan and Sonoran Deserts of northern Mexico, which ignore the international border and extend deep into New Mexico and Arizona, respectively. One of the iconic places in this book, Carlsbad Caverns, is located in the Chihuahuan Desert, and three are found in the Sonoran Desert on rivers that provide life-sustaining oases—Casa Grande on the Gila, and Tucson and San Xavier del Bac on the Río Santa Cruz. Far to the northwest, another desert, the Mohave, covers the region where Nevada, California, and Arizona converge. The Mohave villages, which also command a chapter in this book, flourished in this region by taking advantage of the waters of the Colorado River, not far from where it exits the Grand Canyon.

North of the Sonoran and Chihuahuan Deserts, above the so-called Mogollon Rim that cuts through eastern Arizona and western New Mexico, the Colorado Plateau rises like "an island in the sky," as one writer has characterized it. Its ubiquitous piñon and juniper notwithstanding, the Colorado Plateau is also a dry place, an "island of high, dry rock" whose waterways have carved the continent's most spectacular canyons.[4] Eight of the places in this book lie in this arid region of sweeping vistas—Ácoma, Canyon de Chelly, Chaco Canyon, Grand Canyon, El Morro, Mesa Verde, Rainbow Bridge, and Zuni. Many of today's visitors find the dry country achingly beautiful and spiritually powerful. For the earliest Spanish and Anglo American visitors, however, these dry lands held no such appeal. Don García López de Cárdenas, who looked into the gaping maw of the Grand Canyon in 1540, would have agreed with Lieutenant Joseph Christmas Ives, who wrote, after penetrating the canyon in April 1858, "The region last explored is, of course, altogether valueless."[5] As recently as a half century ago, many policy makers thought it would be no great loss to put the land under the water of a reservoir, as at Lake Powell behind Glen Canyon Dam, or to use the high desert as a dumping ground for radioactive waste.

It should come as no surprise that from their first encounters with America, the earliest European explorers viewed new lands through a utilitarian lens. After reaching the Mexican mainland, Hernán Cortés wrote to his queen and her teenage son, who had recently been proclaimed king, "so that Your Highnesses may know what land it is, what people live in it, the way in which they live, their rites and ceremonies, religions and customs and *what profit Your Highnesses may gain from it.*"[6] The first Spanish explorers who made their way into the Southwest followed Cortés's example. Their reports focused on the economic potential of plants, animals, mineral resources, and people. If they found beauty in the natural world, they did not reveal it in their laconic descriptions of the land. For Coronado, for example, deserts held no charm and mountains were not scenic; they were dangerous obstacles to be overcome.[7] Like-minded sixteenth-century Europeans and many who came after them believed that beauty resided in the manicured garden and the cultivated field; wilderness existed to be tamed.[8]

Utilitarian values also shaped the first Anglo Americans' impressions of the arid Southwest. Although some writers found a sublime beauty in the dry country, it was the beauty of desolation, chaos, and menace.[9] Most writers, like Lieutenant Ives, simply pronounced it worthless. Lorenzo Sitgreaves, after crossing central Arizona in 1851, noted in his report, "I can add very little to the information afforded by the map [which accompanied his report], almost the entire country traversed being barren and without interest."[10] That same year, John Russell Bartlett surveyed the U.S.-Mexico boundary. In his formal report, published in 1854 after the Gadsden Purchase had added to southern New Mexico and Arizona, Bartlett dismissed the Sonoran Desert as "uninteresting in the extreme. As we toiled across these sterile plains, where no tree offered its friendly shade, the sun glowing fiercely, and the wind hot from the parched earth, cracking the lips and burning the eyes, the thought would keep suggesting itself, Is this the land which we have purchased, and are to survey and keep at such a cost? As far as the eye can see stretches one unbroken waste, barren, wild, and worthless."[11]

The reversal of values from the nineteenth century to the twentieth could hardly have been more dramatic. By 1927, Willa Cather spoke for an increasing number of Americans, while shaping the views of many more, when she described southwestern lands with unstinting praise: "The sky was as full of motion and change as the desert beneath it was monotonous and still,—and there was so much sky, more than at sea, more than any-where else in the world. The plain was there, under one's feet, but what one saw when one looked about was that brilliant blue world of stinging air and moving cloud. Even the mountains were mere ant-hills under it. Elsewhere the sky is the roof of the world; but here the earth was the floor of the sky. The landscape one longed for when one was far away, the thing all about one. The world one actually lived in, was the sky, the sky!"[12]

Looking down at the land instead of up at the sky in 1940, the Albuquerque-born writer Erna Fergusson is also memorably descriptive:

*The arid Southwest has always been too strong, too indomitable for most people. Those who can stand it have had to learn that man does not modify this country; it transforms him, deeply. Perhaps our generation will come to appreciate it as the country God remembered and saved for man's delight when he could mature enough to understand it. God armored it, as the migrating Easterner learned in his anguish, with thorns on the trees, stings and horns on the bugs and beasts. He fortified it with such hazards as no legendary hero ever had to surmount. The Southwest can never be remade into a landscape that produces bread and butter. But it is infinitely productive of the imponderables so much needed by a world weary of getting and spending. It is wilderness where a man may get back to the essentials of being a man. It is magnificence, forever rewarding to a man courageous enough to seek to renew his soul.*[13]

Although the author's use of "man" to mean either men or women may seem old-fashioned, her larger message surely still holds true: that the Southwest remains in certain ways indomitable, that it continues to test and inspire the men and women who explore it, and that, at least for those willing to listen, it encourages a return to essentials. That's why many of the region's residents have chosen it for their home. It is also why so many visitors return again and again, their curiosity and wonder undiminished as they ponder its places, cultures, and lands.

# 1 Ácoma

From its mesa-top perch 360 feet above the valley floor, the pueblo of Old Ácoma has fascinated travelers for more than four and a half centuries. One interpretation of its name is the "place that always was," and Ácoma has some right to that designation.[1] The mesa appears to have been occupied at least as early as the time of Christ. Later, the Keres-speaking people who built the historic pueblo may have been among the many groups who migrated south from the Four Corners region in the thirteenth century. The name Ácoma also denotes Haaku, the place that the gods prepared for the Ácoma people. The name Ácoma might be taken as meaning "the prepared place."

The archaeological record seems to show that by the 1200s, if not before, Keres-speaking people had established a cluster of villages in a wide radius around the present pueblo. Some of them settled atop the mesa for defense and all farmed below it, particularly to the north of the mesa in the valley of the Río San José. Understandably, the mesa-top settlement fascinated the earliest Europeans to arrive at Ácoma, as it has subsequent visitors ever since.

The first written description of Ácoma comes from the military expedition of Francisco Vázquez de Coronado. After learning that the Zuni pueblos failed to possess the wealth claimed for them by Fray Marcos de Niza, a disillusioned Coronado received a delegation of Indians from a populous town of Towa-speaking people far to the east, which Spaniards initially called Cicuique and later Pecos—the name by which we know the abandoned and ruined pueblo today. The Pecos spokesman, whom Spaniards nicknamed Bigotes, for his moustaches, offered to guide Coronado's party to pueblos farther east, and Coronado quickly accepted. Within days he dispatched Captain Hernando de Alvarado with twenty horsemen, a priest, Fray Juan Padilla, and perhaps some Indian allies to show the way.

Setting out, possibly from the conquered Zuni town of Hawikuh, Bigotes led Alvarado's party eastward along a well-worn trail that ascended the Zuni River and the Río Pescado and then crossed the long Ramah and El Morro Valleys, where they noted the ruins of once-sizeable towns, to the area of present-day El Morro National Monument.[2] This area had supported multiple large villages in the late thirteenth and early fourteenth centuries, but by the time Alvarado arrived, its former residents had long since left and reconsolidated their communities in villages, like Hawikuh, at lower altitudes along the Zuni River.[3] From the El Morro Valley, Alvarado's band climbed into a ponderosa forest, crossed the Continental Divide, and picked its way across a formidable expanse of black, lava-strewn badlands, or *malpaís,* which today comprises El Malpais National Monument. The badlands behind them, they continued to Ácoma and thence to the Río Grande and the cluster of Tiwa-speaking pueblos that they called Tiguex. Their ultimate destination was Pecos Pueblo, which they apparently reached a dozen days after their departure from Zuni.

Alvarado's eastward trek from Hawikuh to Pecos produced several descriptions of Ácoma, one from his own pen. While encamped on the Río Grande, Alvarado dispatched a message to Coronado in which he tersely described the ruins of the "cities" he had seen along the way, including the inhabited mesa-top "city" of Ácoma, which he called Acoco—one of several Spanish efforts to spell whatever variant of the name *hák'u* they were hearing.

*We departed from Granada [apparently Hawikuh] on Sunday, the twenty-ninth of August 1540, the day of the beheading of San Juan, [on] the route to Acoco. When two leagues had passed, we encountered an ancient building like a fortress. A league farther on we found another one, and a little farther another one. Farther beyond these we found an ancient* ciudad *[city]. [It was] exceedingly large [and] completely destroyed, although a great part of the perimeter wall was [still] standing, which was probably six* estados *tall [an estado was about five and a half feet]. The outside wall [was] well built of excellent stone, [which was] shaped around its doorways and sewers, as [in] a* ciudad *in Castilla.*

*Half a league beyond this [or] about one league, we found another ruined* ciudad. *The wall of this [one] must have been very good; the first* estado *was made of very large granite stones and from there up of very good cut stone.*

*Here [apparently at the Río Pescado] two routes divide; one to Chia [Zia] and the other to Coco [Ácoma]. We took this [latter] one and arrived at the aforesaid place. It is one of the strongest things that have been seen, because the* ciudad *is located on a very high, steep, rugged hill of rock and its ascent is so difficult that we regretted having climbed up to that place. The houses are three and four stories high. The people are the [same] kind [as those] from the* provincia *of Cíbola. They have an abundance of food: corn, beans, and turkeys [like] those of Nueva España.*[4]

Alvarado's description of Ácoma as "one of the strongest things" echoed through other Spanish accounts. One member of Alvarado's party, whose identity remains unclear, added a bit of hyperbole: "[It is] the strongest place ever seen in the world. . . . They came out to us in peace, although

"Acoma. No. 1." The first visual images of Ácoma did not appear in print until 1848, when the U.S. government published three lithographs based on sketches made by Lieutenant James W. Abert. The first of the three, seen here, provides a view of the mesa from Abert's camp. (From the *Report of Lieut. J. W. Abert of His Examination of New Mexico, in the Years 1846–'47*, 1848; courtesy DeGolyer Library, Southern Methodist University)

they well could have refused to do it and have stayed on their rugged rock without our being able to harm them."[5]

Years later, sometime in the 1560s, Pedro de Castañeda de Nájera penned a detailed account of Alvarado's encounter with Ácoma. Castañeda did not accompany Alvarado, but Alvarado and his men apparently told him their story, which he wove into the fullest and most literary narrative of the Coronado expedition that has come down to us. Castañeda may have embellished the story when he noted that the Ácomas came down from the mesa top ready to fight. Alvarado made no mention of Ácoma bellicosity, and the anonymous account by one of Alvarado's men, quoted above, said that the Ácomas received the Spaniards in peace. Nevertheless, as Castañeda tells it,

*The general ordered that Hernando de Alvarado go with [Bigotes's company] with twenty companions and a commission for eighty days. He was to return to make a report of what they found. This Captain Alvarado [then] pursued his journey. After five days' travel they arrived at a* pueblo *called Acuco which was situated on top of a great rock. It was [a pueblo] of about two hundred warriors, marauders feared throughout the land and region. The* pueblo *was extremely strong because it was [immediately] above the entrance to the rock, which everywhere was sheer stone of such great height that it would take a well-handled arquebus to shoot a ball onto the top. There was only one way up, a stairway cut out by hand. It began at the top of a short, steep incline which that part formed. Near the ground this stairway was wide for about two hundred steps, until it reached the rock [itself]. Then there is another [stairway from that point], narrow and next to the rock, of about one hundred steps. At the top of this they have to climb up on the rock [itself for a distance of] about three times the height of a man by means of cavities into which they insert their toes. And [the same] is done with their hands. At the top is a large, dry-laid stone wall. From there, without exposing themselves, they can knock down so many [people] that no armed force would be strong [enough] to win entrance from them. On top there is space for planting and harvesting a very large amount of corn. And [there are] cisterns for collecting snow and water.*

*These people came out on the plain below [prepared] for war. [Even] the best reasoning was of no avail with them. They marked lines, intending to stop our people from crossing them. When, however, they saw themselves attacked [with]*

*a sudden rush, they immediately surrendered the plaza, I mean came to peace. Before they could be hurt, they performed their peace rituals, which [were] to come up to the horses, take their sweat and smear themselves with it, and form crosses with the fingers of their hands. The surest [guarantee] of peace, though, is to join hands, one with the other. This [promise] these [people] hold inviolate. [The people of Acuco] presented a great many very large roosters with wattles [turkeys], much bread, many cured deer hides,* pinole, *flour, and corn.*[6]

Although Castañeda wrote this account from hearsay, he did visit Ácoma a few months after Alvarado passed that way. Amid heavy snows, he journeyed eastward from Zuni in December of 1540, as Coronado assembled all of his men in the Río Grande Valley for the coming winter. Castañeda later remembered that at the "great, rugged hill of rock" of Ácoma, natives peaceably offered them food. "Many companions [of mine] went up to the top to see [the pueblo] and the stairs in the rock. [They did it] with great difficulty, because they were not accustomed to [the stairs], by which the natives, who bore loads of food supplies, and the women water, went up and down so easily. It appeared that they did not [even] touch [their loads] with their hands. In order to climb up, our people had to pass their weapons from one to another on the ascent."[7]

→>

Although Ácoma powerfully impressed the first Spanish visitors as an impregnable, unconquerable site, history best remembers it for the way it fell to Spanish arms.

In the spring of 1542 Coronado withdrew from New Mexico, discouraged and dishonored. Forty years passed before Spaniards visited Ácoma again.

Drawn north by renewed rumors of profitable lands, as well as by the possibility of pagan souls ripe for saving, two small groups of Spaniards penetrated New Mexico in 1582 and 1583, leaving behind descriptions of Ácoma that add details, if not always clarity, to the accounts of Coronado's expedition. The chronicler of the 1582 expedition, Hernando Gallegos, estimated that Ácoma had "five hundred houses," but the leader of the 1583 expedition, Antonio de Espejo, believed that it housed six thousand people.[8] Where Castañeda had noted that only one flight of stairs led to the citadel, the chronicler of the 1583 expedition correctly observed that four narrow flights of steps led to the top of the mesa, "carved in the very rock, up which only one person can climb at a time."[9]

The Ácomas initially welcomed both parties of Spaniards, offering food and supplies. When Espejo's group returned to Ácoma for a second time in 1583, however, it found the Ácomas "in rebellion," meaning perhaps that they refused to provide the Spaniards with food. Espejo's party responded to the "impudence of the Indians" by attacking those who lived and farmed below the mesa in the valley of Río San José (in the vicinity of present-day Acomita), burning their homes and destroying cornfields.[10] Espejo's group made no attempt to punish the impregnable village on the mesa top, which this new generation of Spanish explorers also described as unassailable: "the best stronghold in existence even among Christians."[11]

Spaniards came and went but established no permanent presence in New Mexico until 1598, when Juan de Oñate settled a group of colonists at the pueblo of Ohkay Owingeh, to which the Spaniards had given the name San Juan, on the Río Grande north of present-day Española. Within a year, the colonists' confrontation with the Ácomas proved a defining moment for the fledgling colony and a monumental tragedy for Ácoma.

A few months after his arrival at Ohkay Owingeh, Juan de Oñate traveled west to the villages of Ácoma, Zuni, and Hopi to demand, as he had at pueblos on the Río Grande, that native leaders swear allegiance to the Spanish church and king. At Ácoma, where he stopped in late October, Indian leaders listened to his interpreter, conferred, and then, according to a formulaic Spanish record, agreed to "render at once obedience and vassalage for themselves and in the name of their nation."[12] A month later, on December 1, a small party of some thirty men, led by Oñate's nephew, Juan de Zaldívar, arrived at Ácoma, hurrying to catch up with Oñate, who was an unknown distance to the west. The Ácomas seemed welcoming and said they would furnish Zaldívar's party with cornmeal. According to the Spanish accounts, when some of the Spaniards ascended to the mesa top on December 4 to collect the corn, Ácomas suddenly attacked them. Stores of food that the Ácomas needed to get through the winter were likely at stake. Whatever the truth of the matter, the Ácomas apparently killed thirteen Spaniards, including Zaldívar. Three Spaniards escaped early in the fighting, and another five, it was said, jumped from the cliffs of the mesa: four of the five, miraculously, lived to tell the tale.[13]

Messengers brought news of the tragedy to Oñate, who was then camped near El Morro on his way back from the Hopi pueblos. Fearing a general uprising, Oñate made his wary way to his headquarters at Ohkay Owingeh, where he presided over lengthy deliberations to determine if the Ácomas' actions justified making war against them. His advisors, Franciscan clergy among them, concluded that they did. Rebellion, in the Spanish legal tradition, was cause for a just war, and the Ácomas had rebelled against the Crown to which they had sworn vassalage. As Oñate would later explain to the viceroy in a letter of March 2, 1599: "Because of failure to exercise as much caution as was necessary, my *maese de campo* [field commander or field marshal] and twelve companions were killed at a fortress pueblo named Ácoma, which must have contained 3,000 Indians, more or less. In punishment of their wickedness and treason to his majesty, to whom they had previously rendered obedience in a public ceremony, and as a warning to the others, I razed and burned their pueblo."[14]

Oñate, however, did not personally carry out this dire retribution. In January 1599, he sent Juan de Zaldívar's younger brother, Vicente, to demand that the Ácomas turn over the rebels who had killed his compatriots and that the entire pueblo submit to Spanish rule or face war with no quarter—war by fire and blood.

Zaldívar rode west to Ácoma in the dead of winter at the head of seventy soldiers. Carnage ensued. In his official account of the fighting, written in the third person and duly notarized in the legalistic Spanish custom of the day, Zaldívar self-righteously asserted that the Indians had brought retribution upon themselves and that he slew the men at Ácoma in order to save the women and children, whom the men were killing rather than surrender them to the Spaniards. The event is so pivotal to the history of Ácoma and so traumatic to its people that period reports deserve to be quoted at length:

*Proceedings at Acoma*

*On the arrival of the captain and chief of the forces, Vicente de Zaldívar, sargento mayor, lieutenant governor and captain general of his majesty's army, at the peñol [large rock] and stronghold of Acoma in the provinces of New Mexico, January 21, 1599, he explained to the Indians of the pueblo through the interpreter, Don Tomás, that he came only to make peace with them and to find out why they had killed the* maese de campo, *Don Juan de Zaldívar, ten captains and soldiers of his company, a mulatto, and an Indian. The Indians were fortified on the peñol, well armed with many bows and arrows, war clubs, stones, swords, and the coats of mail that they had taken from the Spaniards whom they had killed. Refusing to give any satisfaction to these proposals, the Indians all shouted loudly, raised their swords on high, and presented themselves in the coats of mail and other pieces of equipment that they had taken from the dead Spaniards, boasting that they had killed ten Spaniards and two Mexicans, and that we were all a pack of scoundrels and whoremongers.*[15] *At the same time they made a great noise, shot many arrows, and hurled stones and wooden spears at the soldiers. The latter merely dodged the missiles of the Indians, because the lieutenant governor had ordered his men not to fire an harquebus or offend anyone by word or deed despite the fact that the Indians had dug deep holes at the base of the pueblo and had concealed these pitfalls so that the horses and their riders would fall in. The holes were so numerous that although the warning was given and care was exercised, still some soldiers were trapped. Meanwhile the Indians kept shouting that they wanted to fight. To provoke the Spaniards, they displayed many blankets and things of their own and also the swords and the booty that, as has been said, they had taken from the Spaniards. They hurled many insulting words, asking what we had come for, why we were waiting, and why we did not fight, since they were ready for battle and were waiting for nothing but to kill us and then to kill the Queres and the Tiguas and everyone at Zía because they had failed to kill the Spaniards.*

*This was their answer to the peace summons which the lieutenant governor made once, twice, and thrice, and which he asked me, the secretary, to give an affidavit of. In testimony of which I made this one. Witnesses, Contador Alonso Sánchez, Captain Gaspar de Villagrá, Captain and Purveyor General Diego de Zubía, Captain Marcos Farfán de los Godos, and Captain Pablo de Aguilar, Signed,* VICENTE DE ZALDÍVAR. *Before me, and I so certify,* JUAN VELARDE, *secretary.*

*On January 22, 1599, the lieutenant governor and captain general camped a little way from the peñol and stronghold of Ácoma to see if he could reach an understanding with the Indians. The latter spent all that night in huge dances and carousals, shouting, hissing, and making merry, challenging the army to fight. Since the natives would not listen to reason, he ordered some of the horses led to water, whereupon many Indians broke out of a small gully near the rock and began to discharge arrows, killing two horses. Immediately the lieutenant governor and captain general, in view of the impudence and bold determination of the Indians to kill the Spaniards, ordered his men to give battle without quarter, as was authorized in his instructions, and he signed his name. Witnesses, Captain Villagrá, Captain Marcos Farfán, Contador Alonso Sánchez, and Captain Aguilar.* VICENTE DE ZALDÍVAR. *Before me,* JUAN VELARDE, *secretary.*

*On this day, feast day of Saint Vincent, at three o'clock in the afternoon, more or less, the lieutenant governor and captain general began the battle. The fight continued with much obstinacy on the part of the Indians, who would not listen to reason. It lasted until nightfall, when the general ordered the stronghold besieged and the entire army to be on the watch, fully armed, throughout the night, at posts which he assigned them. He so decreed and signed,* VICENTE DE ZALDÍVAR. *Before me,* JUAN VELARDE, *secretary.*

*On the 23rd of this month, San Ildefonso's day, the Indians on the rock continued the battle with determination and fury. The fighting proceeded from early morning, with many Indians killed and wounded. Then the lieutenant governor and captain general spoke to them through Don Tomás, the interpreter, and urged them to consider the number of their dead and not to persist until all were killed, promising that he would do justice to all who surrendered and placed themselves in his care. They replied that they and their women and children wanted only to die, and that the Spaniards were scoundrels. Thereupon they attacked Don Tomás with arrows and stones.*

*In view of their rashness, the battle proceeded until about five o'clock in the afternoon. The Indians, recognizing defeat and that they had no recourse but to die or surrender, as some of their houses were already on fire, asked for peace and for an end to the battle. Accordingly, the lieutenant governor ordered them to cease fighting and to lay down their arms, assuring them that he would do them justice. Witnesses, Captains Villagrá, Gerónimo Márquez, Marcos Farfán, and Pablo de Aguilar.* VICENTE DE ZALDÍVAR. *Before me,* JUAN VELARDE, *secretary.*

*On January 23, 1599, the lieutenant governor and captain general sent for the Indian chiefs and the rest of the people to ask them why they had killed the* maese de campo *and his companions. To do this he had them seized and placed in some estufas [kivas] where these Indians fortified themselves in their prisons and broke away through many tunnels and mines concealed in the estufas and which opened out into adjoining houses. The Indians ran from house to house and killed each other without sparing their children, however small, or their wives. In view of this situation, the lieutenant governor ordered the battle to proceed without quarter, setting fire to all of the houses and even the provisions. He ordered that all Indian women and children who could be found should be taken prisoners to save them from being killed by the Indian warriors. So they rounded up about five hundred of them, young and old, men and women. He sent them all to his Excellency, Don Juan de Oñate, governor and captain general of these kingdoms and provinces.*

*I certify that I was present throughout these proceedings. Witnesses, Captain Villagrán, Contador Alonso Sánchez, Captain Marcos Farfán, and Captain Gerónimo Márquez.* VICENTE DE ZALDÍVAR. *Before me, and I so certify,* JUAN VELARDE, *secretary.*[16]

In this self-protective account, Zaldívar, strangely, neglects to mention the bold military strategy that he employed to scale the mesa top. He sent most of his men to ascend the main trail, drawing the Ácomas to the north side of the mesa while he and a few others, unseen, set about scaling the south side. Reaching the top, Zaldívar and his men gained the advantage of surprise, although that alone seemed insufficient to the Spaniards to explain their victory. It was claimed by at least one of Zaldívar's men that Santiago himself—Saint James, the Moor slayer and eventual patron saint of Spain—arrived on the scene to help the Christians carry the day.

While the Spaniards celebrated the divine intervention that brought them victory, Ácoma's survivors lamented their destroyed village and their dead. Zaldívar marched the captives—some eighty men and five hundred women and children—to Santo Domingo, where Oñate made a lesson of them for other Pueblos. After a show trial, in which a Spanish-appointed defense attorney represented the captives, Oñate pronounced all the adults guilty. He sentenced some two dozen men judged to be over twenty-five to twenty years of personal servitude and to have one foot severed—a sentence that may or may not have been executed fully. He sentenced captives of both sexes between the ages of twelve and twenty-five to twenty years of servitude. He ordered that children under twelve be taken from their parents, the girls placed under the care of Franciscans and the boys under the tutelage of Vicente de Zaldívar.

Oñate's razing of Ácoma and the harsh sentences he delivered have remained central to the story of the pueblo's past, so that the pueblo and the conquistador have become entwined in memory. But where Ácoma might have reminded members of an earlier generation of the audacity of stout-hearted conquistadores, modern Americans are more likely to think of Oñate's brutality.[17] Certainly the trauma of the 1599 battle and its aftermath remains vivid for the people of Ácoma today. One oral account, collected in 2013, holds that Oñate, knowing that "a man prays holding corn pollen in his right hand," directed that the right hands of his male captives be cut off so that they might never again pray correctly.[18]

Oñate's cruel treatment of Ácoma clouds contemporary efforts to honor him for having initiated Spanish settlement in what is today the American Southwest. In El Paso, where Oñate first crossed the Río Grande, sculptor John S. Houser spent years creating the world's largest equestrian bronze statue to commemorate him, but the project met a firestorm of protest along the way. As one Ácoma told the El Paso City Council, "I speak on behalf of Ácoma men who had their feet severed and who were then enslaved for 20 years. It is simply wrong to honor a person who causes so much grief, pain and destruction."[19] In 2003, the El Paso City Council ordered that Houser's three-story statue be renamed *The Equestrian,* thus disassociating it from Oñate. It was installed outside of town at the airport rather than in a midtown sculpture garden.

North of Santa Fe, close by the Río Grande in the tiny community of Alcalde, another bronze equestrian statue commemorates Oñate's first settlement at Ohkay Owingeh, formerly San Juan Pueblo. In 1998—on the four hundredth anniversary of Oñate's arrival in New Mexico—one or more people purporting to act on behalf of Pueblo Indians used a power grinder in the dead of night to amputate the bronze Oñate's right foot. Neither the perpetrator nor the severed metal foot was ever found. This well-publicized moment in protest vandalism brought national attention to the tragic events at Ácoma and derailed efforts in Albuquerque to commemorate Oñate with public statuary.[20]

↦

Despite its grievous woes, the pueblo returned to life. Ácomas gradually reconstructed their village on the mesa top, and by 1640, with guidance from a Franciscan missionary, Juan Ramírez, they appear to have finished building the great church of San Esteban del Rey that stands there today,

"Ácoma. No. 2." This lithograph from Lieutenant J. W. Abert's report is derived from a watercolor he painted (seen in Plate 1). (From the *Report of Lieut. J. W. Abert of His Examination of New Mexico, in the Years 1846–'47*, 1848; courtesy DeGolyer Library, Southern Methodist University)

said by the architectural historian Vincent Scully to be "the noblest in the Southwest."[21]

Ácoma joined other pueblos in the great revolt of 1680, killing its priest and destroying Christian symbols. In the years following, it resisted reconquest. By 1710, however, the mission church was restored and reopened to those Ácomas who accepted Christian baptism. Under frequent attack from Navajos and ravaged by occasional epidemics, Ácoma barely mustered the resources to support a resident priest and in some years had none. As a result, few written records describe isolated Ácoma in the 1700s or early 1800s.

With the American conquest of New Mexico in 1846, during the U.S.-Mexican War, a new wave of visitors encountered the pueblo. The first Anglo American to describe Ácoma in print, twenty-five-year-old Lieutenant J. W. Abert, arrived at Ácoma on October 21, 1846, two months after U.S. forces seized control of Santa Fe. He described Ácoma as a prosperous place that seemed as timeless as it was picturesque (Plate 1.)

*We reached Acoma, and I consider the view of this place to exceed anything I have ever yet beheld. High on a lofty block of hard sandstone whose sides rise perpendicularly from the plain sits the city of Acoma. On the northern side of the rock the sands have been heaped up by the winds so as to form a practicable ascent. For some distance the rest [of the path] is through solid rock. At one place a singular opening is formed like a narrow gateway with huge towers on each side. Then the road becomes so steep that the Indians have placed logs on it to afford footing. We at length reached the plain [at the top] and found an area of 500 yds. square. There is a church and several blocks of buildings containing 50 or 60 houses that are three stories in height and ascended by the means of ladders which the inmates can draw up at pleasure. The place was located and built for defence.*

*The inhabitants are very hospitable. They invited us into their houses and set before [us] broad flat baskets of corncakes which they bake thinner than wafers [apparently guayave, similar to Hopi piki bread] and crumble up into small pieces. They also gave us fruits such as peaches and melons. Wherever we went they would offer us something, saying "Coman! Coman!" ["Eat! Eat!"]. They are well provided with everything and seem to be a happy set of people. They generally wear Navajo blankets such as are marked with broad stripes of black and white. Their pantaloons are very large and baglike and are confined from the knee down by buckskin leggings; many wear long woollen stockings, which they knit most beautifully. The women stuff their leggings with wool, which gives them quite a clumsy appearance.*

*These people cannot have associated much with the Mexicans, for they scarce know a word of their language. They, however, profess the Catholic religion; their houses are ornamented with the crucifix, and a large chapel with its towers and bells is one of the first objects that catches the eye of the visitor.*

*After ascending to the tops of their three-story houses and looking around over the whole country we returned to camp. Here we found many Indians with melons and peaches, some of which were dried; we found the latter fruit very fine. They have large flocks of sheep, herds of cows and horses, and numbers of chickens and turkeys. The neighboring valley is but poorly watered.*[22]

➻

The so-called Beale Wagon Road, surveyed in the late 1850s by Edward Fitzgerald Beale, roughly followed the 35th parallel between Los Angeles and Albuquerque. (In laying out the route, Beale notably experimented with the use of camels in the American Southwest; he found that the camels did well, but their American handlers never liked them.) The Beale

"Acoma. No. 3." Here Abert depicts Ácomas carrying loads along the main trail up the mesa on the north side. At the top of the mesa stands an Ácoma woman with a clay jar on her head, a common sight that later visitors found biblical and picturesque. (From the *Report of Lieut. J. W. Abert of His Examination of New Mexico, in the Years 1846–'47,* 1848; courtesy DeGolyer Library, Southern Methodist University)

Wagon Road ran slightly to the north of Ácoma and brought occasional visitors, but the pueblo remained little changed. A U.S. Indian agent who visited in 1870 counted 124 families with a total of 436 persons, 154 of them children, including four orphans. Among them, only one person could read or write. With the cultural condescension, not to say racism, typical of his time and class, the agent wrote, "No citizens are on their lands, and here is a good field for the teachers and missionary as their minds are blank as the sheet of paper on which I write."[23]

Teachers came, but not to the mesa-top village. After 1879 the new-laid tracks of the Atchison, Topeka, and Santa Fe Railway touched the Ácoma farming villages of Acomita and McCartys. These communities became the sites for churches and schools, from which Protestant missionaries launched concerted efforts to bring their own brand of Christianity and various aspects of the modern world to the pueblo. More than a dozen miles to the south by a dirt road that was alternately dusty and muddy, Old Ácoma languished in relative peace.

Ultimately, Ácoma's isolation proved highly attractive to a new cadre of

Anglo Americans who wished to put distance between themselves and the hurried, industrializing society represented by the railroad. For them, native villages like Ácoma constituted an implicit critique of modern America, and they extolled rather than lamented the isolation of such places, valuing their adherence to tradition and their resistance to the change-hungry pace of the rest of America. Among the early writers and artists espousing this anti-modernist point of view, Charles Fletcher Lummis stood out as one of the most passionate and prolific. He was also one of the most adept at attracting publicity.

Lummis first visited the region when he walked from Ohio to Los Angeles in 1884, writing newspaper dispatches along the way. He claimed to have detoured from the railroad tracks to take the measure of Ácoma. This home of "strange sky-dwellers" he exclaimed, with characteristic exaggeration, was no less than "the most wonderful aboriginal city on earth."[24] Curiously, Lummis never saw Ácoma on that trip, but when he reached California he was apparently so embarrassed at having failed to visit it that he pretended to have been there.[25] Later, however, he would make a trip to the mesa and expand on its virtues as a place so defensible that the military merits of Gibraltar and Quebec paled beside it. His lofty assessment fails to mention that Spaniards scaled the mesa and destroyed Ácoma in 1599, but no matter. Lummis had a spell to cast:

*There is one Acoma. It is in a class by itself. The peer of it is not in the world. I might call it the Quéres [Keres, the language spoken by Ácomas] Gibraltar; but Gibraltar is a pregnable place beside it. It is the Quebec of the Southwest; but Quebec could be stormed in the time an army climbed Acoma unopposed. If as a defensible town there be no standard whereby to measure it, comparison is still more hopeless when we attack its impregnable beauty and picturesqueness. It is the Garden of the Gods multiplied by ten, and with ten equal but other wonders thrown in; plus a human interest, an archaeological value, an atmosphere of romance and mystery. It is a labyrinth of wonders of which no person alive knows all, and of which not six white men have even an adequate conception, though hundreds have seen it in part. The longest visit never wears out its glamour: one feels as in a strange, sweet, unearthly dream—as among scenes and beings more than human, whose very rocks are genii, and whose people swart [swarthy] conjurors. It is spendthrift of beauty. There are half a hundred cattle and sheep cor-*

rals, whose surroundings would be the fortune of as many summer-resorts in the East; and scores of untrodden cliff-sentinelled gorges far grander yet.[26]

As Lummis continues his breathless description, he compares Ácoma not to another Native American community—presumably he felt his Anglo American readers harbored little in the way of romantic sentiment for their predecessors on the continent—but rather conjures images of ancient Babylon, a seat of "oriental" mystery, which in his era epitomized a safe kind of foreignness and exoticism. Lummis wrote that the contour of Ácoma's cliffs

is an endless enchantment. They are broken by scores of marvellous bays, scores of terrific columns and pinnacles, crags and towers. There are dozens of "natural bridges," from one of a fathom's span to one so sublime, so crushing in its savage and enormous grandeur, that the heart fairly stops beating at first sight of it. There are strange standing rocks and balanced rocks, vast potreros [cliff-ringed meadows] and fairy minarets, wonderlands of recesses, and mysterious caves. It is the noblest specimen of fantastic erosion on the continent. Everywhere there is insistent suggestion of Assyrian sculpture in its rocks. One might fancy it a giant Babylon, water-worn to dimness. The peculiar cleavage of its beautiful sandstone has hemmed it with strange top-heavy statues that guard grim chasms. The invariable approach of visitors is to the tamest side of the mesa; and that surpasses what one shall find elsewhere. But to outdo one's wildest dreams of the picturesque, one should explore the whole circumference of the mesa, which not a half a dozen Americans have ever done. No one has ever exhausted Acoma; those who know it best are forever stumbling upon new glories.[27]

For Lummis, the crowning glory of Ácoma was the timeless, peaceful, and otherworldly community atop the mesa: "Upon the bare table-top of this strange stone island of the desert, seven thousand feet above the level of the sea, stands a town of matchless interest—the home of half a thousand quaint lives, and of half a thousand years' romance. How old is that mysterious sky city no man may know."[28]

Lummis and his fellow anti-modernists left readers with a new impression of Ácoma, one saturated with romanticism. This new impression said less about Ácoma, of course, than it did about its observers. Just as it took a new sensibility to discover the "grandness" of the Grand Canyon in the last half of the nineteenth century, so it took a new sensibility to render seemingly impregnable Ácoma, as Lummis put it, a place of "endless enchantment."

Lummis's words lingered in the minds of visitors who followed him. One tourist in the early 1920s, A. Eugene Bartlett, was thrilled to retrace the Spaniards' steps to the mesa top, but it was Lummis's prose rather than the Spaniards' deeds that gave voice to the experience. Atop the mesa, Bartlett saw "the city that Charles F. Lummis has called 'the most beautiful aboriginal city on earth.' As we came upon the summit and stood just beneath the city's wall, we thought of his words—'cliff-built, cloud-swept, matchless.'"[29]

In addition to the striking scenery, Ácoma's residents themselves captivated the anti-modernists. Agnes Laut, a prolific Canadian writer who visited Ácoma around 1912, marveled at the traditional culture of its "700 sky dwellers," of whom, she said, only one spoke English. Laut strolled the pueblo's three streets amid chickens and mules, past the whitewashed walls of multistory houses. She applauded the Ácomas' enduring habit of entering their homes by way of picturesque rooftop ladders rather than through modern doors. Inside the Ácomas' apartments she found everything "spotlessly clean, big ewers of washing water on the floor, fireplaces in the corners with sticks burning upright."[30]

Laut, like Lummis, wrote to persuade Americans that the picturesque charms of their "unknown Southwest" exceeded the attractions of classical Europe, and that they should visit their own "wonderland." Laut deplored the paucity of tourists who visited Ácoma—fewer than one hundred in a year, she said. "The inconvenience of reaching Acoma will effectually prevent it ever being 'toured,'" she announced. "If anything as unique and wonderful as Ácoma existed in Egypt or Japan, it would be featured and visited by thousands of Americans yearly." If Ácoma were in Germany, "they would be diverting the Rhine round that way so you could see it by moonlight."[31]

➜➤

Many of us today, Indian and non-Indian alike, experience contradictory feelings as we weigh the benefits of modernity versus tradition. At present-day Ácoma, the contrast is particularly striking. The mesa-top village remains without electricity or running water. It is home to about forty full-time residents from a dozen families, although the number swells markedly when ceremonies and celebrations bring Ácomas back to their ancestral home, many to dwellings that stand unoccupied the rest of the year. Most of the four thousand residents of the four-hundred-thousand-acre reservation live below the mesa, in the villages of McCartys and Acomita, hard by Interstate 40. Travelers speeding along the interstate seldom venture far from their route to see more of Ácoma than its casino, restaurant, and gas station, which cluster in a modern-looking complex. Those tourists who detour southward to the old Sky City, however, have a rare opportunity to journey back in time to one of the longest-occupied communities in the United States. From a handsome and welcoming museum at the foot of the mesa, a comfortable bus takes them to the top for a guided tour. Those with a historical sensibility know that, as they ascend to the mesa top, they have joined a venerable and centuries-long progression of non-Indian visitors to Ácoma, stretching back to the days of Coronado.

# 2 Canyon de Chelly

Canyon de Chelly would be a hallowed place even if its history had been peaceful. The purity of its silence and the looming verticality of its sandstone walls produce a special quality of stillness and anticipation, as though here a magnificent stage has been set and only the most extraordinary events might occur upon it. The canyon's ghostly cliff houses and abandoned pueblos testify to past dramas that are lost in time, and their haunting presence reinforces the impression that a person's five senses are inadequate to take the measure of the place. Canyon de Chelly intimidates. It also lulls and lures. Its beauty inspires. To see it a first time is to wish to return.

Most authorities agree, although the matter is open to debate, that the ancient corn farmers of the canyon, who on occasion made homes like aeries on the cliff ledges, accepted the colossal inconvenience and omnipresent danger of living on a vertical face of rock because other, worse dangers drove them there.[1] In the general destabilization and evacuation of the Four Corners region beginning in the mid-1200s, one or more waves of refugees passed through Canyon de Chelly, pausing long enough to build homes, even villages, and make a stand. Bad weather in the form of drought was one of the forces that put such people in motion, but social disintegration and conflict were probably no less important. At a time when hungry, desperate people wandered the region, anyone who possessed a home and a cornfield had good reason to fear anyone who did not. A persistent question in the archaeological past of Canyon de Chelly is whether the human predators who drove the canyon's inhabitants literally up the walls or into fortified villages were hunter-gatherer-raiders of markedly different heritage—possibly Shoshonean ancestors of modern Utes—or other corn farmers much like the people they attacked, who might equally merit the ambiguous classification "Ancestral Puebloan."[2]

Ultimately, in the late thirteenth and early fourteenth centuries when the canyon emptied out, some of its emigrants probably journeyed to Hopi, where several clans claim descent from the people of Canyon de Chelly, and others may have migrated to Zuni or to points east along the Río Grande, or even far south to the environs of the Hohokam.[3]

The Navajos came in numbers to Canyon de Chelly in the mid-eighteenth century, although portions of the tribe knew the place well before then. Previously the Dinetah, the tribe's homeland, had centered near the Continental Divide in what is now northwestern New Mexico, but pressure from enemy Comanches and Utes pushed the tribe westward. In Canyon de Chelly they found water, arable soils, defensive shelter and, perhaps not least, beauty. Before the century was out, the canyon would become the new center of the tribe's territory.[4] Because of extensive intermarriage between Navajos and Puebloans over many generations, and especially in the years following the Pueblo Revolt of 1680, when many Pueblo Indians sought refuge in Dinetah, some of the canyon's new residents may well have carried the genes of the builders of its ruins.[5]

Canyon de Chelly drains the Tunicha Mountains at the north end of the aptly named Defiance Plateau. The tribe spread through this area and through the adjacent Chuska and Lukachukai mountain ranges, continuing westward into ever more arid country, past Hopi, to the edge of the Grand Canyon.

*Chelly* derives from *Tségi,* the name the Navajos gave to the canyon at the center of their land. It translates roughly as "rock canyon" or "in a canyon."[6] In Spanish the word became something akin to *dechelli,* and thence migrated into English as *de Chelly,* which is usually pronounced *d'SHAY.* Often, as in the name Canyon de Chelly National Monument, a unit of the national park system consisting entirely of Navajo Reservation land administered cooperatively by the National Park Service, Canyon de Chelly refers to the entire web of canyons that channel the headwaters of Chinle

NAVAJOS.

Balduin Möllhausen, "Navajos." According to William Goetzmann (*Army Exploration in the American West*, 332), Lieutenant Amiel Weeks Whipple, Möllhausen's employer on the Pacific Railroad Exploration and Survey of 1854, was not pleased with this image, for he considered Navajo warriors "bright-eyed and enthusiastic," not the drowsy fellows Möllhausen depicted. (From *Pacific Railroad Reports;* courtesy DeGolyer Library, Southern Methodist University)

Wash. More specifically, Canyon de Chelly is the main southern constituent of the canyon complex. Its northern counterpart acquired the name Canyon de los Muertos in the late nineteenth century, based on human remains archaeologists found in an alcove they named, not surprisingly, Mummy Cave.[7] The name was later shortened to Canyon del Muerto, perhaps simply by usage, but also perhaps the better to incorporate reference to Massacre Cave, farther up the canyon, where Canyon de Chelly's first recorded tragedy of the historic period appears to have occurred.

The year was 1805. For more than two decades Spain's colony of New Mexico had enjoyed relief from Comanche raiding. During that period of relative peace, the colony began to expand in all directions. By 1800, its westward movement had penetrated Navajo territory. The tribe retaliated with fierce attacks on encroaching colonists, particularly at the newly founded village of Cebolleta, east of Mt. Taylor, which in turn triggered violent responses from the Spaniards. The task of punishing the Navajos fell to Lieutenant Colonel Antonio Narbona, who rode north from Sonora to New Mexico at the head of three hundred troops and a company of Opata Indian auxiliaries. Joined by New Mexico citizen militia and Zuni guides, Narbona set out for Canyon de Chelly in December 1804 but was thwarted by a blizzard, managing to reconnoiter only the mouth of the canyon before falling back to Zuni. The following January, he sallied forth again, this time entering the canyon system by dropping into the head of Canyon del Muerto:

*The Cañon de Chelly I scouted from its beginning to its mouth. It is the fort on which the Navajo Indians had based their hopes of making themselves invincible, and as it is inhabited by many people, and fortified by nature with the cliffs that form it, that hope is not without reason, and although on this occasion, I disillusioned them of it, in spite of this I can do no less than make known to you in fulfillment of my obligation and without omitting anything, that if it should be necessary in the future to return to attack it, it would be indispensible that it be with more men than I had and a great supply of ammunition, for that which I brought from my province exceeded ten thousand cartridges, and in order to get out of the said canyon I was forced to use almost all of them.*[8]

Although only stubble marked the winter fields, Narbona made note of the farmlands scattered along the canyon bottom and the stream of water that nourished them: "[The canyon's] center is ample, and in it they have sufficient fields that are made fertile by a regular river that runs through the middle, but this does not impede [i.e., the width of the canyon does not prevent], but that the enemy from the high rocks assault those that go below, and because of this it is necessary that besides those that battle inside [the canyon], there should go two parties over the rims of the canyons to prevent that the enemy unite in ambush and [be] prepared for that eventuality."[9]

Narbona's ominous statement that his army carried approximately ten thousand rounds of ammunition into Canyon de Chelly and used almost all of it suggests a heavy human toll, and indeed his report to New Mexico's governor provides a body count. He says his army killed ninety warriors and twenty-five women and children, while capturing three warriors, eight women, and twenty-two boys and girls, some of whom were wounded and nearly all of whom would be kept as slaves by the victors. Narbona's losses included one officer reported dead from pneumonia and sixty-four wounded. He also destroyed eighty-five of his own horses "because they were worn out," and he could not risk simply abandoning the animals lest they survive the winter, recover, and become assets to the Navajos.[10]

Thus did Narbona officially report, but he may not have told all the truth. An alternate history exists, attested by a great mass of human bones in a deep niche in the canyon wall at the end of a narrow ledge. The archaeologists who studied the place named it Massacre Cave. You get to it by first climbing a steep talus slope and then scaling nearly two hundred feet of sheer rock using faint hand- and footholds cupped into the sandstone.

Through the generations, the Navajos of Canyon de Chelly have told a story that in brief form goes like this: when the Spaniards came to the canyon, a large number of women, children, and old men took refuge in the cave, just as they had done on previous occasions when Utes came raiding. From below, the ledge and niche are invisible, and the people hiding there would have been safe had it not been for the actions of an old woman who had formerly been a slave in the Spanish colony. Thinking the cave impregnable, she called out insults to the soldiers as they passed by.[11] The Spaniards responded by firing wildly at the enemies they could not see, such that thousands of shots ricocheted off the ceiling of the cave, killing and wounding the people huddled in its recesses. Navajo warriors, meanwhile, rained arrows on the flanks of the Spanish force, but the shooting continued until nightfall.

In the morning, the Spaniards completed their assault, led by a young lieutenant. As he gained the ledge, a Navajo woman attacked him and both toppled into the void, giving the name by which Massacre Cave is known in Navajo: Two Who Fell Off.

So it may be that the gallant lieutenant Don Francisco Piri, whom Narbona laments in his report, died not of pneumonia but of a fall down a cliff, perhaps with a knife in his side, and that the "ninety warriors" Narbona claimed to have killed were not all warriors—or even all male. Near the end of his report Narbona noted the grisly proof of his victory that he was submitting to Governor Chacón: "Corporal Baltasar Ribera brings eighty-four pairs of ears of as many warriors and the six that are lacking to complete the ninety of which I told you are not sent to you because the subject that I encharged with them lost them."[12] Whether Antonio Narbona commanded the killing at Massacre Cave may never be known with certainty—no documentary evidence exists to link him to the event, although the circumstantial evidence is considerable. His own offer of proof that his battle in Canyon de Chelly was valorous, meanwhile, is also ambiguous. Human ears, especially when as dry and shriveled as jerky, give no hint as to gender and, with the exception of the ears of small children, neither do they betray age.

The Navajo wars continued, and each new act of violence begot retaliation, which begot more retaliation. When the Mexican War concluded in 1848, the United States inherited Mexico's and formerly Spain's role in the conflict with the tribe. One of the first major undertakings of New Mexico's new territorial government was a show of force against the Navajos intended to demonstrate the superiority of American arms and the ability of the troops of the new regime to penetrate Navajo land to its innermost stronghold: Canyon de Chelly. Commanding the expedition was Lieutenant Colonel John M. Washington, the civil and military governor of the territory. Supporting him and charged with making a "survey" of the lands to be traversed was Lieutenant James H. Simpson of the Army Corps of Topographical Engineers, then thirty-six years old, who in turn recruited the assistance of two civilian brothers, Richard and Edward Kern, twenty-eight and twenty-six years old, respectively.

The task of surveying entailed ambiguity. Mapmaking was part of it, and in the course of the expedition Edward Kern would draft "the first map with any semblance to accuracy that was made of this vital section of New Mexico and present Arizona."[13] But assessing the lay of the land—its features, resources, and qualities—was part of it, too. Toward that end, Lieutenant Simpson compiled a remarkably detailed and informative, if at times acerbic and disapproving, journal of the expedition, and Richard Kern, one of the most talented artists of the early West, sketched and painted a visual record of the lands explored.[14] We will meet this impressive trio again in the discussion of Chaco Canyon, which they closely observed on the expedition's outbound journey. In addition, Simpson and Richard Kern (while Edward remained with Washington and the main force) made a memorable detour to El Morro on the return journey. Few annals of exploration have bequeathed a richer legacy to the future than that of Simpson and the two Kerns.

Prior to the Washington expedition, the only Americans to have approached Canyon de Chelly belonged to a unit of the Army of the West commanded by Captain William Gilpin. As Antonio Narbona had done in his abortive first foray to the canyon, Gilpin and his men struggled through heavy winter snows over the Chuska Mountains and "passed within a few miles of the celebrated strong-hold or presidio of the Navajos, called El Challé."[15] This was in 1846, as Gilpin and his men hurried to rendezvous with their commander Colonel William Alexander Doniphan, who was charged with the unenviable task of making peace with both the Utes and Navajos prior to taking up his principal mission of invading and conquering the Mexican state of Chihuahua. Meeting with a council of Navajo leaders, Doniphan would succeed in effecting what he thought was a treaty, but the agreement would prove to be meaningless. A similar fate awaited the pact John Washington would negotiate, and Simpson and the Kerns would witness, three years later at the mouth of Canyon de Chelly. In Washington's case the proceedings were tainted by events that occurred several days before his arrival at the canyon.

As Washington's expedition approached the Chuskas, he paused to parley with a delegation of Navajo headmen, backed by several hundred others of the tribe. Leading the delegation was a venerable headman, then over eighty years old and much afflicted with arthritis, who curiously and for reasons that appear to have been lost in time bore the same name as the Navajos' oppressor of 1805.[16] This Narbona had led the tribe in a decisive victory in 1835 over a large force of Mexicans at the pass toward which the expedition was heading. The meeting resulted in agreement to hold a larger peace council at the mouth of Canyon de Chelly in a few days' time. As the gathering broke up, a Pueblo Indian in Washington's command claimed to have spotted a horse among the Navajos' mounts that had been stolen from him some considerable time before. A demand that the horse be returned was denied, and the resulting fracas escalated to the point that Washington ordered his men to fire and even to engage their howitzer. When the roar of the fusillade faded away, Narbona (soon to be scalped) and several other Navajos lay dead on the ground.[17]

Two days later, as the expedition labored to convey the cumbersome artillery through the mountain pass, Simpson recorded in his journal that "in honor of the colonel commanding I have, on my map, called it Pass Washington." As one might imagine, the name was never popular with the Navajo people, but so it remained on official maps for almost a century and a half. In 1992, however, in response to a petition brought by a group of Navajo students, the United States Board of Geographic Names voted unanimously to change the name of the place to Narbona Pass, a fitting acknowledgment of local history and an unusual, if not unprecedented, recognition of the wishes of the area's native inhabitants.[18]

By September 7, after three weeks of travel, Washington was finally encamped near the mouth of Canyon de Chelly, somewhat north of where the town of Chinle now stands. There he waited for the Navajo headmen who had been sent for and who would take some days to arrive. Rather than cool his heels, Simpson asked permission to make a reconnaissance of the canyon, and Washington assented. In particular Simpson wished to assess the "Navajo fortress" described by one of the expedition's primary guides, a New Mexican named Carravahal: "This cañon has been for a long time of distinguished reputation among the Mexicans, on account of its great depth and impregnability—the latter being not more due to its inaccessibility than to the fort which it is said to contain. This fort, according to Carravahal, is so high as to require fifteen ladders to scale it, seven of which, as he says, on one occasion he ascended, but not being permitted to go higher he did not see the top of it."[19]

Simpson had read Lieutenant J. W. Abert's report on Ácoma (and he would submit his own reports to Abert's father, Colonel J. J. Abert, the commander of the Corps of Topographical Engineers). He may have envisioned the Navajo fortress as a high redoubt similar to the citadel of Ácoma, moated by unscalable cliffs. What he would discover, however, was that Canyon de Chelly was the inverse of Ácoma. Whereas Ácoma is a nearly impregnable rock, Canyon de Chelly is the absence of rock, a precipice-sided void. As to Carravahal, the guide may have been describing Massacre Cave or another refuge, now actually called Navajo Fortress, at the juncture of Canyon del Muerto and Black Rock Canyon. He may also have embellished his tale by placing himself almost, but not quite, at the scene.

On the morning of September 8, the twenty-third day of the expedition,

"Cañon of Chelly, eight
miles above the mouth—
Sept. 8th," a lithograph based on
a drawing by Richard H. Kern
(From Lieutenant James H.
Simpson's *Journal of a Military
Reconnaissance . . . to the Navajo
Country . . . in 1849;* courtesy
DeGolyer Library, Southern
Methodist University)

Simpson rode into the canyon with the two Kerns, a third assistant, and an
escort of about sixty soldiers. Previously, from a brief descent into the head
of the Canyon del Muerto, he had observed that the canyon "more than
met our expectations—so deep did it appear, so precipitous its rocks, and
so beautiful and regular the stratification. . . . I had not the time to make
the full examination which I would have liked. I saw, however, enough to
assure me that this cañon is not more worthy of the attention of the lover
of nature than it is of the mineralogist and geologist."

   Now Simpson had the time he desired. He begins with investigation of
several side canyons, which only whet his appetite for further reconnaissance:

   *Having got as far up the lateral branches as we could go, and not yet having
   seen the famous fort, we began to believe that in all probability it would turn out
   to be a fable. But still we did not know what the main cañon might yet unfold,*

*and so we returned to explore it above the point or fork at which we had left it. Starting from this point, our general course lay about southeast by east. Half a mile further, or three and a half miles from the mouth of the cañon, on its left escarpment, I noticed a shelving-place where troops (but not pack animals) could ascend and descend. Less than a mile further, I observed, upon a shelf in the left-hand wall, some fifty feet above the bottom of the cañon—unapproachable except by ladders, the wall below being nearly vertical—a small pueblo ruin, of a style and structure similar, to all appearances, to that found in the ruins on the Chaco. I also noticed in it a circular wall, which, in all probability, has been an estufa [or kiva].*

*The width of the cañon at this point is probably from two to three hundred yards wide, the bottom continuing sandy and level. And, what appears to be singular, the sides of the lateral walls are not only as vertical as natural walls can well be conceived to be, but they are perfectly free from a talus of debris, the usual concomitant of rocks of this description. Does this not point to a crack or natural fissure as having given origin to the cañon, rather than to aqueous agents, which, at least at the present period, show an utter inadequacy as a producing cause?*

*About five miles from the mouth, we passed another collection of uninhabited houses, perched on a shelf in the left-hand wall. Near this place, in the bed of the cañon, I noticed the ordinary Navajo hut, (a conical lodge,) and close by it a peach orchard. A mile further, observing several Navajos, high above us on the verge of the north wall, shouting and gesticulating as if they were very glad to see us, what was our astonishment when they commenced tripping down the almost vertical wall before them as nimbly and dexterously as minuet dancers! Indeed, the force of gravity, and their descent upon a steep inclined plane, made such a kind of performance absolutely necessary to insure their equilibrium. All seemed to allow that this was one of the most wonderful feats they had ever witnessed.*

Soon, Simpson and his companions encountered White House Ruin, one of the most picturesque archeological sites in the Southwest. As Simpson rightly observed, its masonry is Chacoan in style, and its occupation was roughly contemporary with the florescence of Chaco in the late eleventh century:

*Seven miles from the mouth, we fell in with some considerable pueblo ruins. These ruins are on the left or north side of the cañon, a portion of them being situated at the foot of the escarpment wall, and the other portion upon a shelf in the wall immediately back of the other portion, some fifty feet above the bed of the cañon. The wall in front of this latter portion being vertical, access to it could only have been obtained by means of ladders. The front of these ruins measures one hundred and forty five feet, and their depth forty five. The style of structure is similar to that of the pueblos found on the Chaco—the building material being of small thin sandstones, from two to four inches thick, imbedded in mud mortar, and chinked in the façade with small stones. The present height of its walls is about eighteen feet. Its rooms are exceedingly small, and the windows only a foot square. One circular estufa was all that was visible. For a sketch of these ruins, with the stupendous rocks in rear and overhanging them, see [the accompanying figure].*

*Half a mile above these ruins, in a re-entering angle of the cañon, on its left side, are a peach orchard and some Navajo lodges. Proceeding still further up the cañon, the walls, which yet preserve their red sandstone character, but which have increased in the magnificence of their proportions, at intervals present façades hundreds of feet in length, and three or four hundred in height, and which are beautifully smooth and vertical. These walls look as if they had been erected by the hand of art—the blocks of stone composing them not unfrequently discovering a length in the wall of hundreds of feet, and a thickness of as much as ten feet, and laid with as much precision, and showing as handsome and well-pointed and regular horizontal joints, as can be seen in the custom-house of the city of New York.*

The parent material of the red sandstone that so impressed Simpson consisted of dunes that formed at the edge of a sea in the Permian epoch more than two hundred million years ago. Interestingly, the sandstone is not actually red but whitish. It was stained red and tan by minerals carried in the waters of the mists, sprays, and pour-overs that periodically bathed the cliffs. "About eight miles from the mouth of the canon, a small rill [a stream], which below this point had lost itself in the sandy bottom of the cañon, appears above ground; and about five hundred yards further, on the right-hand side, is a lateral cañon, in which we saw another peach orchard."

Simpson and his party soon turned around. Had they proceeded a little farther, they would have encountered Spider Rock, a startling, slender monolith several hundred feet high that stands at the juncture of Canyon de Chelly and Monument Canyon.

Senate Ex.doc 1.ᵗ Sess. 31.ᵗ Cong N°64.                    Pl. 53.

R.H. Kern del.                    P.S Duval's Steam lith press Phil

RUINS OF AN OLD PUEBLO
in the Cañon of Chelly – Sept.8ᵗʰ

"Ruins of an Old Pueblo, in the Cañon of Chelly—Sept. 8th." Richard Kern made this first artistic rendering of White House Ruin, a place that would fascinate the many artists who came after him, including Timothy O'Sullivan. (Courtesy DeGolyer Library, Southern Methodist University)

*Having ascended the cañon nine and a half miles, the horses of the Pueblos in company with us not being strong enough for a further exploration, there being no prospect of our seeing the much-talked-of* presidio *or fort of the Navajos, which had all along been represented to us as being near the mouth of the cañon, and the* reconnaissance *having already been conducted further than Colonel Washington had anticipated would be necessary, the expedition returned to camp, highly delighted with what they had seen. We found, however, the further we ascended it the greater became the altitude of its enclosing walls—this altitude, at our point of returning, being (as I ascertained by an indirect measurement) five hundred and two feet. The length of the cañon is probably about twenty-five miles. Its average width, as far as we ascended it, may be estimated at two hundred yards. . . .*

*Both in going up and returning through the cañon, groups of Navajos and single persons were seen by us, high above our heads, gazing upon us from its walls. A fellow upon horseback, relieved as he was sharply against the sky, and*

*scanning us from his elevation, appeared particularly picturesque. Whenever we met them in the cañon, they appeared very friendly—the principal chief, Martinez, joining and accompanying us in our exploration, and the proprietors of the peach orchards bringing out blanket-loads of the fruit (at best but of ordinary quality) for distribution among the troops. Indeed, the chief admonished his people, as they stood gazing upon us from the heights above, to go to their homes and give us no trouble.*

*I noticed the cross, the usual emblem of the Roman Catholic faith, stuck up but in one instance in the cañon; and this is the only one I have seen in the Navajo country.*

*Should it ever be necessary to send troops up this cañon, no obstruction would be found to prevent the passage of artillery along its bottom. And should it at the same time, which is not at all unlikely, be necessary that a force should skirt the heights above to drive off assailants from that quarter, the south bank should be preferred because less interrupted by lateral branch cañons.*

*The mystery of the Cañon of Chelly is now, in all probability, solved. This cañon is, indeed, a wonderful exhibition of nature, and will always command the admiration of its votaries, as it will the attention of geologists. But the hitherto-entertained notion that it contained a high insulated plateau fort near its mouth, to which the Navajos resorted in times of danger, is exploded. That they may have had heights upon the side walls of the cañon, to scale which would require a series of* fourteen ladders, *is indeed probable, for it would require more than this number to surmount the height we measured.*

*I did expect, in ascending the cañon, to find that the Navajos had other and better habitations than the conical pole, brush, and mud lodge which, up to this time, we had only seen. But none other than these, excepting ruined ones, the origin of which they say they know nothing about, did we notice. Indeed, a Mexican who is a member of the command and who was a captive among them, says that they have no other habitation. In the summer, he informs us, they live wherever the cornfields and stock are. In the winter, they take to the mountains, where they can get plenty of wood. As yet, we have not met a single village of them—it appearing to be their habit to live scatteringly, wherever they can find a spot to plant corn or graze stock. The necessity of living more densely, probably, has not heretofore existed, from the feeling which they doubtless have had up to this period that the inaccessibility of their country was a sufficient barrier to the intrusion of an enemy.*

The Navajo expedition under Colonel Washington, which Lieutenant Simpson memorialized in careful detail, was both a reconnaissance and a demonstration of force. Its purpose was to display to the tribe the might of the United States, which had only begun to establish its power in the newly conquered region, and it was hardly a gentle enterprise. Besides the lamentable confrontation that resulted in the killing of Narbona, the U.S. forces routinely grazed their mules and horses in Navajo cornfields, destroying crops and sometimes first helping themselves to the "fine roasting ears" the fields afforded. On the approach to the canyon, apparently at Washington's orders, they also set fire to "the huts of the enemy"—the Navajos' hogans—"one after another springing up into smoke and flame, and their owners scampering off in flight."[20]

Although the negotiations conducted by Washington at the mouth of Canyon de Chelly produced a treaty between the United States and the Navajo tribe, the agreement had negligible influence on the activities of either party. Little more than a decade later, while the fortunes of the rest of the country were being decided in such places as Vicksburg and Gettysburg, Indian conflicts in New Mexico Territory, which then included Arizona and much of Colorado, reached a new crescendo. By 1863 the territorial governor, General James Carleton, resolved to wage full-scale war against the Navajos, and he ordered Colonel Kit Carson to the task. Carson had little but his predecessor Colonel John Washington's experience to draw on when he invaded the canyon in bitter January weather in 1864. His troops rounded up the Navajos they could find, as they had previously gathered members of the tribe from other locations, and marched them, on foot and under guard, into exile at the Bosque Redondo on the Río Pecos, three hundred miles to the east. The tribe's trek of deportation, conducted under harsh conditions and with minimal supplies, became known as the Long Walk. Many died along the way, and over the ensuing years those who survived fared poorly at Bosque Redondo. Ultimately Carleton's successors recognized that the effort to resettle the tribe had failed, and in 1868 the Navajos were allowed to return to their homeland, including Canyon de Chelly. The restoration was of course welcome, but it failed to erase the memory of the Long Walk, which remains vivid and painful for many Navajos today.

→ ﹥

Because of Canyon de Chelly's geographic remoteness, as well as the social and cultural isolation of its inhabitants, the canyon remained little known and rarely visited by outsiders, its grandeur and treasures still hidden from the rest of the world. By 1873, however, this began to change. The U.S. Army returned, this time with a mission of appreciation, not conquest.

In the first half of the nineteenth century, the United States became a continental empire rather suddenly. Events at the close of that period — the Mexican War and the discovery of gold in California, in particular — drove home the need to understand the new western lands and bind them to the rest of the nation with roads, railroads, and a common system of defense. The Civil War (itself a product of that expansion because the acquisition of new territories — and the question of whether slavery should be permitted in them — helped bring on the war) delayed that process, but once the war was over, the business of surveying, mapping, and geographical assessment began in earnest.

One of the most dedicated (if not always effective) acolytes of this process was Lieutenant George Montague Wheeler of the Army Corps of Engineers. In 1871 Wheeler took command of an enterprise that eventually became known as the United States Geographical Surveys Beyond the 100th Meridian. Within two years his forces had grown to such an extent that he deployed them in five widely separated field parties: Lieutenant R. L. Hoxie's detail began the 1873 field season from a base at Salt Lake City, while Lieutenant William Marshall's group operated from Denver. Wheeler divided his own party in two, both setting out from Santa Fe, and he authorized another unit, with photographer Timothy H. O'Sullivan "in Executive charge of the party," to venture forth from Fort Wingate, near the future site of Gallup, New Mexico.[21] O'Sullivan and his companions were headed for Canyon de Chelly.

O'Sullivan's small group bore responsibility for "triangulation," an essential step in accurate surveying and mapmaking, but its greater charge touched on public relations. The American people, including congressmen in Washington who determined the survey's budget, wanted to "see" their new western lands, and if Wheeler was to win their continuing approval, he needed to give them something to look at. Accordingly, O'Sullivan, born in Ireland but raised in New York City, became a trusted member of Wheeler's team. He had won renown during the Civil War, working first for Mathew Brady and later Alexander Gardner and taking some of the most memorable (and horrific) photographs of the aftermath of Gettysburg and other battles. Accompanying O'Sullivan on the journey to Canyon de Chelly was the landscape painter Alexander H. Wyant, already elected a member of the National Academy, who came west to work for Wheeler probably because he needed the money and possibly because he hoped that a season of vigorous outdoor life on the frontier would improve his frail health.[22] In the latter regard, his disappointment would prove greater than he might ever have imagined.

Eleven days out from Fort Wingate, O'Sullivan and Wyant arrived at Canyon de Chelly with their packers, a Navajo guide, and other companions. For the next four days they photographed, sketched, and explored. Their fifth and last day in the canyon found them before the monolithic cliffs and two-tiered ruins of the "White House." Here O'Sullivan would take his most famous photograph, one destined to find a place in the Museum of Modern Art and to become "firmly rooted in the history of photography, its literature, practices, and collections" (Plate 2).[23]

Wyant recorded the day's events in his diary:

*From & between the top of the debris [of the lower tier of ruins]—15 feet high—formed by the lower & main buildings to the foot of the upper there is a space of rock 29 ft high. A fishing line was cast around a pole put there by the navajos, & thus a rope was drawn up by which O'Sullivan, Keasbey [a naturalist] & Conway [a packer] ascended to the abode of the witch,—a Navajo character [believed to dwell in or at least to visit the upper ruins]. They have a ladder by which their witch ascends but we did not hunt for it for fear of getting our guide into trouble. They say that one white man went up there once & died, when or how they didn't state. Conway acts pro tem as our cook. He gathered a few pieces of wood to further his purpose of making supper last evening. While carrying it towards camp he picked up a piece of a human skull; whereupon Jo our indian guide said that the bone cursed the wood at the moment when Conway's hand touched the sacred fragment, & that if supper was cooked with it he—Jo—would have to get his supper with some of his indian friends. He wouldn't mind telling where the ladder was if he had his friends here. O'Sulli-van has made several views of the ruins & I have made a little pencil sketch. The train is being packed & soon we'll be off again.*[24]

In O'Sullivan's exquisite photograph, *Ancient Ruins in the Cañon de Chelle, N. M.,* we see immense, vertically striated sandstone walls loom-ing above the cavernous alcove of the brightly lit upper ruin.[25] The lower pueblo is a scatter of dark walls rising from rubble. The climbing rope is still in place, linking the "typographic," almost imperceptible forms of two men at the upper ruins (presumably Keasbey and Conway, O'Sullivan having climbed down to take the picture) with two others who stand on the lower ruins: "By stretching across the lower rockface lengths of rope, measuring devices in their own right, the figures make it clear that they measure the landscape less by their inherent tininess than by the extent of their ambi-tion, by the lengths that they will go."[26]

In Canyon de Chelly, a limitation of the wet-plate photographic pro-cess on which O'Sullivan relied turned out to be an asset. The wet-plate process was "color-blind": it recorded light only from "the blue region" of the color spectrum. According to the preeminent historian of photography Beaumont Newhall, "This deficiency was most favorable to the rendition of the red rock of the Southwest.... O'Sullivan caught the majestic tonali-ties and, to a surprising degree, the impression of blazing lights. The latter quality is due, again, to the blue-sensitive emulsion; the skies are very light and the feeling of recessive space is most convincing."[27]

Wyant was also present at the White House, and O'Sullivan photo-graphed him, sitting under a parasol, sketching the ruins. Unfortunately, Wyant's sketch from that day has been lost, but that is not the worst thing that happened to him. From Canyon de Chelly, O'Sullivan led the expedi-tion to Lee's Ferry on the Colorado River; thence, still on the east side of the river, he and his men continued upstream past the Colorado's confluence with the San Juan River and then along the south bank of the San Juan. The men stayed close to the river to the extent terrain permitted, seeking a ford that would allow them to cross northward into Utah and ultimately Colorado, where a rendezvous awaited them on the upper Río Grande. But the crossing eluded them. Instead they struggled through tight canyons and dry tablelands, experiencing long stretches with no water, suffering both the desertion of their guide and a blizzard that caused them much hardship. Embattled, demoralized, and all but stalled, they watched their supplies run perilously low. Ultimately, they gave up the quest to cross the San Juan (although the ford at the mouth of Chinle Wash, unknown to them, was not far away) and, subsisting on half rations, retreated back to Fort Wingate. Shortly after arriving in safety, the exhausted Wyant suffered what was probably a stroke, which paralyzed most of his right side. In the years to come, he valiantly taught himself to paint with his left hand, but the progressive debility resulting from his illness would mark the rest of his life.[28]

In 1875, seeking to reach a more influential audience than formal survey reports might find, the Wheeler survey published a booklet of photographs taken in the field by O'Sullivan and a second photographer, William Bell.[29] Decades later, a copy of this publication came to the attention of Albert Bender, a wealthy San Franciscan and patron of the arts. Bender passed the booklet along to his protégé, Ansel Adams, who had emerged as one of America's finest landscape photographers. Adams in turn shared the booklet with Beaumont Newhall, then the librarian at the Museum of Modern Art in New York, with whom Adams was newly acquainted. At the time, Newhall was embarking upon a gigantic task. He was curating an exhibit that would trace the development of photography through its first century. It was to be a landmark event. No one anywhere had attempted such an overview. When *Photography: 1839–1937* opened at MoMA in March 1937, the Wheeler booklet was prominently displayed, opened to the page showing *Ancient Ruins in the Cañon de Chelle, N. M.* At a stroke, Newhall had inserted O'Sullivan's image of White House Ruin into a rapidly intensifying conversation about photography's place among the fine arts and about the range of its past purposes and future possibilities.[30] He further underscored his endorsement of the image by including it in his enormously influential *History of Photography,* which was initially the catalog of the exhibit and has never since been out of print. In such a way did the photograph of an iconic place become an icon of photography.

Sometimes dead ends and nonevents deserve mention. So it is with a series of presumably great photographs of Canyon de Chelly that were lost before even their maker could see them. Timothy O'Sullivan's closest competitor for preeminence in early western photography was William Henry Jackson, who worked for the rival United States Geological and Geographical Survey of the Territories under the direction of Ferdinand Vandeveer Hayden. In 1875, Jackson, who had already documented the wonders of Yellowstone and whom we will meet again at Chaco Canyon and Mesa Verde, led a photographic detail up Chinle Wash from the San Juan River, through the country that had defeated O'Sullivan and debilitated Wyant two years earlier. He passed not far from the mouth of Canyon de Chelly but continued on to Hopi without entering the canyon.[31]

In 1877, quite likely having seen the Wheeler Survey booklet of O'Sullivan's and Bell's photographs, Jackson returned to Canyon de Chelly, making a hurried visit from nearby Fort Defiance. On this occasion, Jackson traveled without the packers and assistants who usually helped him with his cumbersome wet-plate photographic equipment. Instead he chose to experiment with a new process involving material marketed as "Sensitive Negative Tissue," a precursor to the rolled, dry film that George Eastman would soon develop for his Kodak camera. At Canyon de Chelly, Jackson made "trips down to the great White House [Ruin] and other ruins in the neighborhood and up the Canyon del Muerto, where I photographed everything in sight."[32]

Or he thought he did.

Months later in Washington, D.C., when he set about developing his pictures, none came out. The sheets of "Sensitive Negative Tissue" had failed, yielding not a single image. Not only did Jackson lose his work at Canyon de Chelly, but his much more extensive efforts at Chaco Canyon, which he visited a short time later, also came to naught. "I considered the whole summer shot to pieces.... I can never replace those lost pictures," he lamented.[33] O'Sullivan's pioneering work in the canyon remained unchallenged.

➻

Today Canyon de Chelly National Monument is one of the most singular units of the national park system. Its 83,840 acres—131 square miles—include no federal public land but consist entirely of Navajo tribal trust land, subject to the governance of the Navajo Nation, which is headquartered in Window Rock, Arizona. Most parks in the United States are devoid of human settlement. Canyon de Chelly continues to be home to approximately eighty Navajo families for all or part of the year.

President Herbert Hoover proclaimed Canyon de Chelly National Monument on April 1, 1931, following years of years of discussion sparked initially by concern for the security of the ruins. Archaeologists and later tourists protested that erosion threatened important sites, even White House Ruin. Eventually attention turned to the National Park Service as a fitting custodian for the canyon's wonders, and successful negotiations with local Navajos and the Navajo Tribal Council paved the way for declaration of the monument. Since then, agreements between the Park Service and the Navajo Nation have continued to evolve, allowing Canyon de Chelly to be seen and experienced by people from every corner of the world.[34]

# 3 Carlsbad Caverns

Carlsbad Caverns National Park comprises 46,766 acres in the foothills of the Guadalupe Mountains, some twenty miles south of Carlsbad, New Mexico, where the surface of the land is clothed in the spiky, pale-hued garments of the Chihuahuan Desert. Below the surface lies a labyrinth of dark voids. Ninety-three known caves exist within the park, the centerpiece being Carlsbad Cavern itself. Many more caves penetrate the rest of the mountain range, which formed from an uplifted limestone reef laid down in Permian seas. Over the eons, sulfides migrating upward from petroleum and gas deposits below the reef converted to sulfuric acid upon contact with water (or more particularly, the oxygen dissolved in the water). The acid aggressively dissolved the limestone, creating the caves.

The vast chambers of Carlsbad Cavern set it apart from other cave systems. The Big Room alone commands an acreage equivalent to fourteen football fields. These spaces, combined with the cavern's fantastic rock formations, countless stalagmites and stalactites, and illuminated trails, have made it one of America's favorite tourist destinations and a UNESCO World Heritage Site. While seasons aboveground come and go, the climate of the cavern never changes; from January through December its temperature remains a mild fifty-six degrees Fahrenheit.

Native Americans discovered the mouth of the great cavern at Carlsbad and left pictographs at its entrance, but we have no evidence that they penetrated its depths. And if Spanish explorers peered through Carlsbad's door into the underworld, they left no record of it. Later, a few of the early

Anglo Americans who settled in this remote area after the Civil War seem to have discovered the entrance to the cavern and ventured a short distance inside. Indeed, in the twentieth century, as the fame of Carlsbad Cavern spread, a number of old-timers stepped forward to claim they were the first to know the cave.[1] But finding a cave in a Swiss-cheese countryside was hardly noteworthy. Caves were abundant and stories about them common. Accounts of this particular cave gained currency only when they revealed the wonders that lay inside, beyond the gaping entrance. Learning and telling to the world the story of the cave required ingenuity, persistence, and a peculiar kind of courage. To devote oneself to navigating jumbled rockscapes by lantern light, deep in the bowels of the earth, required not just nerve but an appetite for darkness, stale air, and closed spaces. Young Jim White had that appetite, and nerve to spare.

Jim White also had the gift of blarney, but in a paradoxical way. People who knew him described him both as a man of few words and as a storyteller, fond of spinning a tale. Perhaps he only needed prompting for the words to flow, and like many storytellers he refused to let facts get in the way of a good narrative. More than once, he appears to have told two fundamentally different stories about the same event, without bothering to reconcile them.

Born in Texas in 1882, James Larkin White apparently first entered the caverns in 1901, at age nineteen—or perhaps, as he claimed on another occasion, three years earlier in 1898. In any event, in 1930, when the quiet, unassuming, and nearly illiterate former cowboy told his story to the journalist-adventurer Frank Ernest Nicholson, he gave 1901 as the date of his first entry into the cavern, and he repeated it in numerous other recountings. Nicholson added his own literary flourishes to White's story, which he published as a pamphlet in 1932. With its striking photographs, *Jim White's Own Story* has offered countless visitors to Carlsbad a vivid account of "the discovery and history" of Carlsbad Caverns (Plate 3). The booklet, which is still available for purchase today, may not be accurate in every particular, but "there is little reason to dispute the sequence and pattern of the events it recounts."[2]

Of all the iconic places discussed in this book, none has a story of discovery more compact or straightforward than that of Carlsbad Caverns. What follows are the opening pages of White's recollections of the dan-

The
DISCOVERY AND HISTORY
of
CARLSBAD CAVERNS
NEW MEXICO
By
JIM WHITE
THE DISCOVERER OF CARLSBAD CAVERNS

COMPILED FOR JIM WHITE BY
FRANK ERNEST NICHOLSON

COPYRIGHT 1932 BY JIM WHITE AND CHARLEY LEE WHITE

Autographed title page from *Jim White's Own Story: The
Discovery and History of Carlsbad Caverns, New Mexico,* 1932
(Courtesy DeGolyer Library, Southern Methodist University)

ger and drama of his discovery, filtered through the florid prose of the
sensation-seeking Frank Nicholson. The story is certainly truer to White's
sentiments than to his actual statements. We can be sure that White, who
was poorly schooled and often at a loss for words, would not have compared the darkness of Carlsbad to the "blackness of Stygian depths," or
expressed concern lest his fellow cowboys regard him as "a cow-punchin'
Baron Munchausen" (an eighteenth-century German cavalry officer whose
name became associated with fantastic tales of adventure).

*Jim White's Own Story* contains details that diverge from the historical record, but whether they came from White's memory or Nicholson's embellishments is unclear. The pamphlet tells, for example, of White's return to the cave for three days of subterranean exploration with a fifteen-year-old Mexican boy whom White called "the Kid." *Jim White's Own Story* says that this harrowing adventure occurred just five days after White first discovered Carlsbad, but in an earlier interview with the guidebook writer Blanche Grant, White reported that his three days in the cavern with "the Kid" took place in the winter of 1905–6, years after the first discovery.[3] Inconsistencies and hyperbole aside, *Jim White's Own Story* is a superb tale well told.

*Bats ... millions of black little mammals whirling their way upward in a funnel-shaped cloud that grew and grew until the top-most portion seemed to fuse into the hazy clouds of a New Mexico sunset. That was the spectacle which, thirty years ago, led Jim White to discover the colossal Carlsbad Cavern.*

*"I thought it was a volcano," Jim mused, "but, then, I'd never seen a volcano—nor never before had I seen bats swarm, for that matter. During my life on the range I'd seen plenty of prairie whirlwinds—but, this thing didn't move; it remained in one spot, spinning its way upward. I watched it for perhaps a half-hour—until my curiosity got the better of me. Then I began investigating." Thus the explorer began the most romantic tale of adventure this chronicler has ever heard.*

*An adventure fundamentally—but actually an avenue that led Jim White through a twenty year struggle to draw attention to the world's most spectacular underground phenomenon. Twenty years of hard work, of privation—a continuous battle to convince a nation of doubters that the Great Architect had created His greatest subterranean miracle below the cactus-covered soil of Southeastern New Mexico.*

*Jim White was born in Mason County, Texas, on July 11, 1882. Born on a ranch, he grew up in the midst of the cattle business—and his boyhood life was without the benefit of even a grammar school education.*

*"I began riding range when I was ten years old," Jim says, "and even if there had been a little log school house, I would have preferred bustin' broncos to books and blackboards. I worked on ranches in various parts of Texas, until 1892, when I came over into New Mexico and teamed up with John and Dan Lucas, who owned the X-X-X Ranch, which is about three miles from the entrance to*

the cave. *[White would have been ten years old when he "teamed up" with the Lucases.]*

*"Then came the day when I saw the bat flight. I worked my way through the rocks and brush until I found myself gazing into the biggest and blackest hole I had ever seen, out of which the bats seemed literally to boil. Although the bats were a novelty to me, the hole itself was not an unfamiliar sight. I had roamed this part of the country ever since I'd landed in New Mexico, and long before I'd noticed the opening, therefore I, like other rangemen, knew of its existence. And, like them, I also had felt no urge to see what was hiding in the darkness of that great hole.*

*"That is, until this particular day, I had sat for perhaps an hour watching bats fly out. I couldn't estimate the number, but I knew that it must run into millions. The more I thought of it the more I realized that any hole in the ground which could house such a gigantic army of bats must be a whale of a big cave. I crept between cactus until I lay on the brink of the chasm, and looked down. During all the years I'd known of the place, I'd never taken the trouble to do this. There was no bottom in sight! I shall never forget the feeling of aweness it gave me.*

"Cavern entrance as it looked in 1901 when it was first discovered by Jim White" (From *Jim White's Own Story*, 1943 edition; courtesy DeGolyer Library, Southern Methodist University)

"I piled up some dead cactus and built a bonfire. When it was burning good, I took a flaming stalk and pushed it off into the hole. Down, down, down it went until at last the flame went out. Finally I saw the glowing embers strike and sprinkle on the rocks below. As nearly as I could estimate, the drop must have been two hundred feet. I kicked the remainder of the bonfire into the hole, and watched it fall. This seemed to frighten the bats, and for several minutes they ceased their flight. However, as soon as the embers died out, the bats swarmed forth as before.

"I hung around perhaps an hour longer, then went back to camp. A crew of us were camping in the vicinity at the time—building fences. I didn't mention to a soul what I had seen. A couple of days later, though, I gathered up a kerosene lantern, several coils of rope, some wire and a hand axe. I got to the cave about mid-afternoon. The mouth of the cave, you know, faces the West, and the sun was in just the right direction to shine down into the hole, and light it sufficiently for me to see the bottom of the shaft. At the bottom, and toward the right, I could see the opening of a huge tunnel—and my imagination feasted upon thoughts of where the end of that tunnel might lead. I made up my mind to find out.

"I got busy with the hand axe, cutting sticks of wood from the shrub growth nearby. When I had a sizeable pile, I set about building a ladder by utilizing the rope and wire, with the sticks for steps—like a rope ladder. This I then lowered into the entrance, until I felt the end reach what I thought was bottom. Then, without giving thought to any possible unfortunate circumstance, I found myself climbing down, down, deeper and deeper into the blackness of Stygian depths. At last my feet touched something solid. I lighted my lantern, and found that I was perched on a narrow ledge, almost at the end of my rope—literally and figuratively.

"By now I could see into the tunnel—it wasn't much farther down to the floor of it, and that floor looked smooth and level. I decided that with a little exhibition of human-fly stuff, I could hold onto the rough wall and go down another twenty feet to level territory.

"Standing at the entrance of the tunnel I could see ahead of me a darkness so absolutely black it seemed a solid. The light of my lantern was but a sickly glow. Nevertheless, I forged ahead, and with each step the tunnel grew larger, and I felt as though I was wandering into the very core of the Guadalupe Mountains.

"Finally, I reached a chamber—an immense aperture, oval-shaped, and extending ahead several hundred yards to where it curved off sharply to the right, and then began a sharp descent. Toward the left was another immense tunnel, leading in the opposite direction. The floor of the latter appeared to be more level, and somewhat smooth, so I tackled it first. This proved to be the bat cave, and after exploring about in it, I retraced my steps to the larger entrance, and started down the other tunnel.

"I followed on until I found myself in a wilderness of mighty stalagmites. It was the first cave I was ever in, and the first stalagmites I had ever seen, but instinctively I knew, for some intuitive reason, that there was no other scene in the world which could be justly compared with my surroundings.

"By this time I had crept cat-like across a dozen dangerous ledges, and past many tremendous openings that looked as though they went down and down to the very center of the earth. I dropped rocks into them to sound their depth. Into one hole I pushed a large boulder. It was a couple of seconds before it hit—and even then it didn't hit bottom. But it did strike something, and kept rolling and rolling until the sound became an echo.

"I came to more and more stalagmites—each seemingly larger and more beautifully formed than the ones I'd passed. I entered rooms filled with colossal wonders in gleaming onyx. Suspended from the ceilings were mammoth chandeliers—clusters of stalactites in every size and color. Walls that were frozen cascades of glittering flowstone. Jutting rocks that held suspended long, slender formations that rang when I touched them—like a key on the xylophone. Floors were lost under formations of every variety and shape. Through the gloom I could see ghost-like totem poles, tall and graceful, reaching upward into the darkness. I encountered hundreds of pools filled with pure water as clear as glass, their sides lined with crystalline onyx marble. The beauty, the weirdness, the grandeur and the omniscience absolved my mind of all thoughts of a world above—I forgot time, place and distance. Suddenly, however, a situation presented itself which was serious enough to cause me to make a mental come-back to sterner thoughts. The oil in my lantern had given out, and the flame curled up and died. It seemed as though a million tons of black wool descended upon me. The darkness was so dense it seemed smothering—choking me.

"Fortunately, I had brought with me a small canteen of oil for just such an emergency. But the blackness and the loneliness had got to working under my skin, and when I tried to refill the lantern my fingers shook so much that I *fumbled the filler cap and spilled more oil in my lap than I poured into the thing. And I dropped the filler cap when I tried to screw it back on.*

*"All the time I was hearing the strangest noises! Church chimes and sleigh bells and street car gongs—and a sound like someone practicing on a piano! Finally I got the lantern lighted, and looked up. Each stalactite has its own note and tone, and in a particularly large cluster of them I saw a little bat flying in and out among them, striking against one and then another. By that time you could have made me believe that anything was possible!*

*"Before I had gotten far into the cave, I realized the necessity of my leaving some sort of landmarks in order that I could find my way out should my sense of direction fail. So now and then I had broken off stalactites and lain them on top of rocks, with the smaller end pointing the way out. Presently I was being persecuted with the thought that in the dim glow of my lantern that perhaps I would be unable to find these markers I'd left behind. Then I began worrying with the possibility that I might get lost in this wilderness of stone and darkness. No one at camp knew where I had gone, and even if they had known, and I didn't show up, there was hardly a remote chance of their ever finding me.*

*"The whole thing began to get on my nerves. Although the cave is always cool—56 degrees day and night, summer and winter—yet, I could feel the perspiration trickle down my body, and cold chills run up my spine.*

*"Suddenly I was seized with a mad desire to run—to charge like a crazy bull when he finds himself cornered. I began scrambling along the edge of a black abyss. In my foolish haste I rammed my head against the sharp points of a mass of stalactites. I saw a shower of blinding lights, and felt something trickle down my face. The needle-like points of those formations had pierced my hat and cut a few gashes in my scalp. That sort of cooled me off, and I leaned back against the wall and began communing with myself. Cowboys often talk to themselves. Perhaps they do it out of sheer loneliness.*

*"'Here, Jim,' I said to myself, 'don't get in an uproar! It won't get you anywhere! Take it easy!'*

*"Well, you've been in the cavern, and you know how marvelous are the acoustics—how the echo on one's voice reverberates from every corner. No sooner had I spoken than from every side of me came the words: 'Here Jim! Take it easy! Take it easy! Take it easy!' Those echoes alone were enough to drive a man mad.*

*"Perhaps you can appreciate my sense of satisfaction when I'd wormed my*

*way back and could see a shaft of sunlight filtering down through the entrance. I grabbed onto my rope ladder and made my way up to the world above. The familiarity of it warmed me. Presently I turned and stared back into the cave. It had beaten me—driven me out! I stared back at it like one might regard a stubborn broncho [bronco], and resolved that someday I would conquer it!*

*"As I rode back to camp, busy with thoughts of my adventure and prophecying*[4] *as to the extent of that cave, I felt stronger and stronger a desire to see it all. I decided that if I could get someone to go into the place with me, it wouldn't seem so silent, dark and lonely.*

*"The cowboys at camp however, refused to take my story of the bats and the glittering underground palace seriously. The more I would tell, the louder they would guffaw. When finally they found I was serious, they decided that either I had just naturally gone crazy, or else set out to become a cow-punchin' Baron Munchausen—insomuch as lying was concerned. And try as I might, I couldn't find a single cowboy who'd agree to go with me—I couldn't even find one who was the least bit interested!"*[5]

White needed a partner, and soon found an unlikely but reliable one:

*"We had a Mexican kid working at the Lucas Ranch—a boy about fifteen years old. I never did know his real name, or whatever became of him. We just called him the Kid. Well, the Kid couldn't speak much English, but one day he called me aside and made me understand that if I was willing to take him on a trip into the cave, he'd take a chance. I took him up readily enough, because I was growing more and more anxious to explore the rest of it, and since I couldn't find a man who'd go with me, the Mexican kid was a lot better than going alone.*

*"Five days after my first trip into the cave, the Kid and I set out with a couple of crude torches, which we had rigged up, a canteen of water a sack of grub and a can of kerosene. I was afraid the Kid would get cold feet, and back out at the last minute, but he didn't.*

*"Our kerosene torches were a great improvement over the lantern I had taken on the first visit. They gave off sufficient light to enable us to make fairly good progress. By the time we had reached the giant stalagmites, I could see that the Kid was scared stiff—but he was a game little cuss, and never whimpered once. I doubt if any man could have stood up under the strain any better than the Kid.*

*"Well, the Kid and I stayed in the cave for three days—exploring. We covered*

*about the same territory the tourist of today sees. I shan't go into detail as to our difficulties, findings, hazards and thrills. There were plenty of each. You can use your own imagination—it would be impossible to even exaggerate our experiences during those three days."*

*Asked what was his biggest thrill during this exploration, Jim said:*

*"Well, I believe it was during the second—no, it was the third day. Down in one corner of the Big Room I crawled upon a ledge of rock, and sat down to rest. Presently I looked over the other side of the ledge—and what do you suppose I saw? Through the gloom I saw staring back at me the skull of a man! I brought my torch about, and there was his whole skeleton intact! And I was amazed by the magnitude of it. Evidently the man had been about twice as large as the biggest man I had ever seen! His thigh bones were as big as the largest beef shanks. I deducted that he must have been some prehistoric cave-dwelling giant. I attempted to pick up one of the leg bones, but the moment I touched it, it crumbled in my fingers. Then a drop of water falling on my hand cleared up the mystery. For years—no one knows how many—that skeleton had lain under a drip. The mineral water had softened the bones, and impregnated them with lime, softening and swelling them many times their normal size. The skull, however, was in perfect condition—as it was not under the drip. I picked up the skull, and noticed that the Kid shrank from it.*

*"'We'll take it back to camp with us,' I suggested, 'or else we'll never make the boys believe we found a skeleton down here!'*

*"'How'll we get it there?' the Kid asked hesitantly.*

*"'Oh we'll put it in the bag with the groceries, and carry it out,' I replied.*

*"The Kid had been carrying the grub sack, and immediately he spoke up, 'Then you'll have to carry the groceries!' Nevertheless, I carried it out. Sometime later a doctor in Carlsbad borrowed it to examine. He loaned it to someone else, who, in turn, loaned it to someone else, and so on, until I lost trace of it— unfortunately, for today it would perhaps be the most treasured cave souvenir in my museum.*

*"I have always been of the opinion that the skeleton was of some Indian who had wandered into the cave out of curiosity, and who had probably died of starvation when he couldn't find his way out.*

*"He must have been an unusually brave Red Man, though, for it is a known fact that the Indian feared darkness above all else, which doubtlessly explains why there was never found any trace of Indian habitation within the cavern,*

*although tribes of them lived throughout the cavern vicinity. There can still be seen an Indian cooking pit, beside the present flag pole, near the cavern entrance.*

*"That wasn't, however, the only skeleton I found in the cave. At the bottom of the entrance I found a skeleton wrapped in canvas. It was probably some poor guy whom 'Billy the Kid' or one of the other famous Bad Man who roamed this cavern country years ago, took for a ride. I found one other skeleton, too. It was while we were mining guano. We had dug about fifty feet in a guano deposit when we came across it. It takes perhaps a hundred years for a foot of guano to build up—so whoever this man had been, he necessarily must have wandered into the place about five thousand years ago." Jim grinned. "Gosh!" he said, "how little we know of what all has gone on around this cavern country!*

*"Maybe you'd like to know why the Kid and I stayed only three days in the cave. Well, it was the afternoon of the third day. The Kid had a knapsack on his back, in which was our grub. I was carrying the oil for our torches. It was in a gallon can, which in turn was in a gunny sack, slung over my shoulder. Well, the can began leaking, saturated my clothing. It wasn't long until my back grew rather sore and irritated. I decided to stop and fix things as best I could, just as soon as we could get off of a ledge upon which we were crawling. But the Kid, behind me, brought his torch too near my back, with the result that I found my-self hanging onto a narrow shelf of stone, my clothing ablaze, and a gallon can of oil on my back!*

*"If I hung there on the ledge I knew I'd burn to death, and if I let go I knew I'd be dashed to pieces on the rocks far below. If I threw away the can it would leave us without oil, and we had not enough in our torches to light our way out. We were at least three miles from the entrance at the time.*

*"Well, there was but one thing to do. I went scooting across that ledge like a cat after a bird. Upon reaching a level spot I threw down the can and slapped my big cowboy sombrero over it. The Kid had followed me up the ledge, and while I was smothering the flames from the oil can—and hoping that it wouldn't ex-plode, the Kid was fighting the fire on my back. He had sense enough to skin out of his coat and throw it over my shoulders.*

*"To make a long story shorter, we soon had the fire out, and that saved the hide of my back, else it'd have been charred to a crisp. As it was, the heat had gone through the leather vest and blistered me rather badly. The hair was all gone off the back of my head, and the burns on my hands and arms were grow-ing more and more painful. So it was necessary for us to come out and get back to camp where I could have treatment and bandages.*

*"During the two or three following days I tried my best to make the gang at the ranch and camp believe the story I have partially told here. But it was a hopeless task—and the Kid's English was so poor he wasn't very successful in substantiating my tales.*

*"A few days later I went into town. Carlsbad was then called Eddy. I met a friend of mine on the street and told him of the cave. It so happened that he had once visited Mammoth Cave in Kentucky, and he claimed that there couldn't be any hole in the ground bigger than that. The more he told me about Mammoth, the more I told him about my cave. It ended by his taking me to his library, where he drug out encyclopedias and several other volumes that held information about caves. The more I learned and the more pictures I saw the more I was convinced that the cave I had discovered was larger and more beautiful than any cavern on record.*

*"Trying to convince anyone of the real truth was, however, a fruitless task. I talked bats and cave until word went around that Jim White's cave was in his head—and so were the bats.*

*"These events occurred during June of 1901."*

In 1899, White's neighbors changed the name of their town from Eddy to Carlsbad, hoping to attract tourists to a local hot springs by associating them with Karlsbad, a famous spa in central Europe. Ironically, Carlsbad residents failed to take seriously White's description of the cavern that would later put them on the tourist map. Instead of attracting tourists to the cavern, locals mined the bat droppings, or guano, piled deep in one of the chambers, then dried and sold it as fertilizer, most of it exported to the orange groves of southern California.[6]

In March 1903, Abijah Long, a Texan who had come to Carlsbad two years earlier, filed a mining claim covering the site of the cavern at the Eddy County Courthouse. Unable to remove guano through the cave entrance, he sank a shaft directly over the bat cave and used a pulley, rope, and man-size buckets to haul the guano some 170 feet to the surface. Jim White, whom Long hired to manage the operation, later claimed to have guided Long to the site. Long, on the other hand, claimed to have discovered Carlsbad in 1903 with two other companions, independent of White.[7]

Abijah Long failed to profit from the guano operations and soon sold his rights to a larger company. White continued to work for the new owners.

Jim White with "old bucket at top of shaft that took the first tourists into Carlsbad Caverns" (From *Jim White's Own Story,* 1932; courtesy DeGolyer Library, Southern Methodist University)

In his spare time he deepened his knowledge of the caverns, built trails, erected guardrails (sometimes pounding discarded automobile axles into cracks in the rocks), and tried to arouse public interest.[8] In the mid-1910s, he persuaded the owner of a photography studio in Carlsbad, Ray V. Davis, to make the arduous buggy ride out to the cavern and descend in the guano bucket with his photographic equipment. Davis's remarkable photos supported White's verbal descriptions and helped to spark curiosity about the marvels they depicted. In 1922 White led the first tour group to enter the caverns. In 1923, the General Land Office sent Robert Holley to inspect the site, and his wonder-struck description, illustrated with Davis's photos, contributed to the chain of events that led President Calvin Coolidge to proclaim the Carlsbad Caverns a national monument in October 1923, placing it under the management of the National Park Service. The next month, the *New York Times* publicized Carlsbad with a two-page spread of Davis's photographs, and in 1924 and 1925 the *National Geographic* ran a brace of stories, both featuring Davis's photographs, based on a special expedition to the new monument, which Jim White guided.

Jim White stayed on at the new monument, which at 719.22 acres was then one of the smallest units in the national park system. (Its incremental expansion to its present size would proceed over a span of decades.) White worked as a guide and, for a time, as chief ranger. According to one of his companions in those years, "Jim White does not talk much, except to a few, and not very often then. And I have it straight that what he says is not 'windys' invented to entertain the 'dudes.'"9 White took pleasure in the improvements in the cave, which was elevated from the status of a national monument to a national park in 1930. By then the cavern offered "electric lights, trails as smooth and clean as parquet floors, a lunch and steaming coffee at your finger tips when you get hungry; running water and a telephone clear to the back end, and an elevator to carry you up when you get tired from walking." As access to the cavern improved and management of the monument grew more professional, however, White found himself marginalized. His health had deteriorated, leaving him less physically capable of supervising work crews and guiding visitors, and he fought occasional bouts with alcohol. In the spring of 1929 he resigned as chief ranger. "I could see that the job of Chief Ranger was getting a bit too complicated for me with my limited education," he told visitors in his *Own Story*. "You see, even a sixty-million-year old cave can go too modern, too efficient, and out-grow a common old Cowboy."

In ending *Jim White's Own Story* on that note, Frank Nicholson glossed over White's bitter relations with the cavern's new federal owners in the years that followed his resignation. Family tradition has it that White resigned as a park ranger in June 1929 on the promise that he would be appointed to a new position, chief explorer. The documentary record on this, however, is not clear. In any event, the appointment did not materialize despite strong advocacy from several quarters, including New Mexico's governor, R. C. Dillon, and one of its senators, Bronson Cutting. Park Service officials appear to have welcomed White's resignation, and soon after his departure they dismissed a number of his "cronies" so that the ranger and

Jim White with park superintendent Thomas Boles, 1938
(Photographer unknown; courtesy Palace of the Governors
Photo Archives, New Mexico History Museum [NMHM/
DCA], negative no. HP.2007.20.106)

guide force would "meet the requirements of the service." White's drinking was undeniably a factor in his separation from the Park Service, and
agency files mention multiple complaints about his intoxication while at
work or on monument property.[10] Nevertheless, his family has maintained
that "he did not in those days drink to excess. It was not until years later,
years in which his heart and spirit were broken completely, that he really
began to drink."[11]

Unemployed and frustrated, White took a job at the small cluster of
tourist-related businesses that opened near the park entrance, soon to be
known as White City, where Charley Lee White, no relation to Jim White,
operated a cafe and gas station, and rented out cabins. He hired Jim White

to talk to tourists and sell curios. In 1930, Charley Lee persuaded Jim to tell his story to Nicholson, and he funded the publication of *Jim White's Own Story* in exchange for half of the royalties.[12]

In 1937, Jim White's fortunes changed. That year, as his wife Fanny later recalled, the two of them traveled to Santa Fe. They enlisted the aid of Senator Dennis Chávez to persuade the Park Service to give the Whites a concession to sell *Jim White's Own Story* in the cavern itself. Setting up a table in the lunchroom 750 feet below the entrance, White sold his pamphlet to tourists, answered their questions, and posed for pictures. After his death in April 1946, Fanny maintained the concession, periodically fighting with the Park Service to retain her share of proceeds from the sale of the book and, more generally, to prevent the park's interpretive materials and presentations from diminishing her husband's role as the caverns' discoverer. Fanny died in 1964.[13]

By the time of Jim White's death, some 2.5 million people had visited Carlsbad Cavern. The caverns had come a long way since people dismissed White's reports as "the ravings of a nutty cowboy." Today, appropriately, a plaque in the lobby of the visitor's center pays tribute to the memory of the man and his achievement.

The eventual breakdown in relations between the National Park Service and Jim White and his family should not obscure White's remarkable—and largely solitary—role in the discovery and early exploration of the caverns. White was aware that others claimed to have "discovered" the cave on the grounds of having seen the mouth of it before he did, but he characterized the situation aptly in a letter to one of his supporters: "Perhaps others had seen the Cave mouth before I did, but I was the first man to know what was in the Cave itself. To see a cave mouth and to explore a great cave are two different things."[14]

# 4 Casa Grande

In the valley of the Gila River, midway between Phoenix and Tucson, the ruins of a tall, bulky mud structure stand high in the desert. Since 1932, the mud walls of this *casa grande,* or big house, have enjoyed the protection of an improbable hipped roof on stilts designed by Frederick Law Olmsted (Plate 4). For centuries, however, the ruin called Casa Grande stood exposed to the elements, and when Europeans first encountered it, the immense and slowly eroding earthen walls invited the curious to speculate about their purpose and about the people who had built them, who seemed to have vanished.

An Italian-born Jesuit missionary, Eusebio Francisco Kino, was the first non-Indian to see Casa Grande and describe it in writing. Kino was one of the most remarkable men of his era. A mathematician and explorer as well as a cleric, he had come to Mexico in 1681. Six years later, after a failed attempt at mission building in Baja California, he had begun to work among the O'odham people, whom he called Pimas, who lived on both sides of the present U.S.-Mexico border. He built his first O'odham mission on the headwaters of the Río San Miguel in present-day Sonora and named it Dolores for Our Lady of the Sorrows. This outpost served as his headquarters until his death in 1711. From Dolores, he ranged across today's northern Sonora and southern Arizona, a region he called the Pimería Alta—the land of the upper Pimas (thus distinguishing it from the lands of Pimas living farther south in the Pimería Baja). Among the many missions he founded were three in today's Arizona—San Xavier del Bac, Tumacácori, and Guevavi—all in the Santa Cruz Valley south of Tucson. For this, and for his important work as a geographer, Arizonans have remembered him well. His bust represents the state in the National Statuary Hall Collection in the Capitol in Washington, D.C., and an equestrian statue of the hard-riding padre stands prominently on the grounds of the Arizona state capitol complex.

In November 1694, on one of his many ventures into Arizona, Kino set out to investigate O'odham reports of a westward-flowing river and a nearby casa grande, several days' travel to the unexplored north. Led by O'odham guides from the village known to him as Bac, near present-day Tucson, Kino made his way to the banks of the Gila River, which indeed flows west, and to the site of today's Casa Grande Ruins National Monument. A few years later, Kino recorded his first impression:

*The* casa grande *is a four-story building, as large as a castle and equal to the largest church in these lands of Sonora. It is said that the ancestors of Montezuma deserted and depopulated it, and, beset by the neighboring Apaches, left for the east or Casas Grandes, and that from there they turned toward the south and southwest, finally founding the great city and court of Mexico.*[1] *Closer to this* casa grande *there are thirteen smaller houses, somewhat more dilapidated, and the ruins of many others, which make it evident that in ancient times there had been a city here. On this occasion and on later ones I have learned and heard, and at times have seen, that further to the east, north, and west there are seven or eight more of these large ancient houses and the ruins of whole cities, with many broken metates and jars, charcoal, etc. These certainly must be the Seven Cities mentioned by the holy man Fray Marcos de Niza.*[2] *... The guides or interpreters must have given his Reverence the information which he has in his book concerning these Seven Cities, although certainly at that time, and for a long while before, they just have been deserted.*[3]

In another cool November, three years later, Kino returned to Casa Grande. This time he enjoyed the protection of a military escort led by Captain Juan Mateo Manje, who accompanied Kino on a number of his expeditions. The country of the Apaches—the Apachería—was considered to begin on the north side of the Gila, and travel anywhere in the vicinity was dangerous. Kino's party reached Casa Grande, however, without incident, and Manje reported their approach to the ruin:

*On the 18th we continued to the west over an arid plain. After five leagues
[about fifteen miles], we discovered, at the other side of the river, other houses
and buildings. Sergeant Juan Bautista de Escalante with two companions swam
across the river to reconnoiter there. When he returned he told us the houses were
made with walls two* varas *in width [a vara is thirty-three inches, or nearly a
yard], that they were built like great big castles, and that there were other ruins
all around, all of ancient construction.*

*We continued to the west. After four leagues, we arrived at mid-day at* Casas
Grandes, *inside of which Father Kino said mass even though he had traveled
without eating until then. One of the houses was a large building four stories
high with the main room in the center, with walls two* varas *of width made
of strong* argamasa y barro *[cement and clay] and so smooth inside that they
looked liked brushed wood and so polished that they shone like Puebla earthen-
ware. The corners of the windows are square and very straight, without sills or
wooden frames. They must have been made in a mould. The same may be said
of the doors, although these are narrow, and by this they are known to be the
work of Indians. The walls are 36 paces in length and 21 in width. Good architecture is apparent from the foundations up, as shown by the design on the edge
and surface.*

*At a distance of an* arcabuz *shot [an arquebus or musket shot] are seen 12
more houses partly caved in. They have thick walls, and the roofs are burnt with
the exception of one lower room which is built with smooth round beams—
apparently cedar or juniper. On top of these are* otates *[canes, sticks] and over
these a heavy coating of* argamasa *and hard clay has been placed. This room has a
high ceiling of very interesting construction. All around there is evidence of many
other ruins and high mounds for a stretch of two leagues.*[4]

Manje goes on to conjecture about the origin of the ruins, drawing, no
doubt, on oral traditions relayed to him by his O'odham guides:

*There are many pieces of broken pottery, plates and* ollas *[pots] made of fine
clay, painted in various colors similar to the pottery made at Guadalajara, a city
of this New Spain. It is believed that this was a large city or town of political
people with an established government. There is a main canal that flows from
the river over the plain, encircling and leaving the town in the center. It is three
leagues in circumference, 10* varas *wide and four* varas *deep, where, perhaps,
half of the water of the river was diverted to serve as a defensive moat as well as*

*a reservoir to provide water to the suburbs and to irrigate its neighboring fields.*
*The guides said that at a distance of a day's journey towards the north there are*
*other buildings of the same character of construction, and also on the other side*
*of the river there is another* arroyo *[a dry gully or rivulet] which unites with the*
*one they call Verde.*

*All those buildings were built by people whose chief was called* el Siba, *which*
*in their language means "The cruel and bitter man." Because of the bloody wars*
*waged against them by the Apaches and 20 allied nations many were killed on*
*both sides. Some of the Indians left, divided themselves and returned to the*
*north, from whence they had come in previous years; but the majority went to*
*the east and south. From all this information we judge it is likely they are the*
*ancestors of the Mexican nation. This belief is corroborated by like constructions*
*and ruins located at 34 degrees, and those in the vicinity of the Presidio of Janos*
*at 29 degrees—also called Casas Grandes—and by many others, we were told*
*about, which are seen towards 37 and 10 degrees to the north.*[5]

Although in this account Manje echoes Kino's speculation that the
"Mexicas," or Aztecs, built Casa Grande, in another report of the 1697 expedition, which Manje signed and apparently wrote earlier, he expressed
the theory more tentatively: "From this information, as I have said, many
have inferred that these people who went to Mexico were the ancestors
of Moctezuma. Only God knows the truth; everyone may have his opinion, and I withhold my judgment."[6] When Manje revised his manuscript,
however, further reflection apparently led him to drop his reservations and
agree with Kino that Montezuma's ancestors had built Casa Grande.

Kino also recorded his recollections of his 1697 expedition with Manje
to Casa Grande. This time he offered no speculations about the ruin's builders, remarking instead on the irrigation system that had supported it, which
suggested to him that Casa Grande might provide a well-watered site for
a future mission.

*The soldiers were much delighted to see the Casa Grande. We marveled at*
*seeing that it was about a league from the river and without water; but after-*
*ward we saw that it had a large aqueduct with a very great embankment, which*
*must have been three* varas *high and six or seven wide—wider than the cause-*
*way of Guadalupe at Mexico. This very great aqueduct, as is still seen, not only*
*conducted the water from the river to the Casa Grande, but at the same time,*

*making a great turn, it watered and enclosed a champaign [a flat, open coun-
try] many leagues in length and breadth, and of very level and very rich land.
With ease, also, one could now restore and roof the house and repair the great
aqueduct for a very good pueblo, for there are near by six or seven rancherías of
Pimas Sobaipurís all of whom in all places received us very kindly, with crosses
and arches erected and with many of their eatables, and, with great pleasure to
themselves gave us many little ones to baptize. On one occasion when several of
our horses had been scattered and lost, they at once went in search of them, nor
did they give up until they had collected them all for us.[7]*

Kino's Jesuit successors, as well as the Franciscan missionaries who replaced them in Arizona after the Spanish Crown expelled the Jesuits in
1767, never possessed sufficient manpower to realize Kino's vision of establishing a mission community at the site of Casa Grande and converting the
casa itself into a church. Spanish expansion toward the Gila River stalled
in the face of Apache resistance, and after Kino's day, non-Indians seldom
ventured near the casa grande. The few who did visit the site, however,
echoed Kino's theory that the ruins had once housed the ancestors of Montezuma's Aztec nation.

After their conquest by Hernán Cortés, the defeated Aztecs told the
Spaniards that long ago they had migrated south from an indetermi-
nate place in the north to found their great capital at Tenochtitlán, where
Mexico City stands today. It was perfectly logical for Kino and Manje to
connect this familiar story to the strange ruins beside the Gila and to conclude that Casa Grande must have been either the Aztecs' place of origin
or a way station on their southward journey. Reinforced by testimony from
the occasional missionaries who followed Kino and Manje to the Gila, that
theory became part of the "conventional knowledge" of the day.

Jacobo Sedelmayr, a German-born Jesuit, visited Casa Grande in 1743
and copied much of Manje's description into his report, but he abandoned
Manje's restraint: "In my opinion the great Casa Grande was the residence
of Moctezuma, while the buildings on either bank of the Gila were the residences of his governors."[8] In 1764 another German-born Jesuit, Juan Nentvig, who never visited the ruins but who was familiar with Kino's writings,
explained more cautiously: "There is a tradition current among the Indians
and the Spaniards that the Mexicas, on their long trans-migration, rested
there."[9] Pedro Font, a Franciscan who inspected Casa Grande in October

1775 and recorded its physical dimensions, offered the same explanation with a darker twist: "Apparently it was founded by the Mexicans when in their migration they were led by the Devil through various regions until they reached the Promised Land of Mexico, and when during their stops, which were long, they established settlements and erected edifices."[10]

Thus did Kino's and Manje's identification of Casa Grande as an early Aztec site echo from one generation to the next. Such visitors as Father Font, Francisco Garcés, and Juan Bautista de Anza came to know it as the Casa Grande of Montezuma, or the Palace of Montezuma.[11]

The manuscripts of these early visitors to Casa Grande remained unpublished during their lifetimes, but their words nevertheless informed the publications of several generations of scholars. As early as 1781, Francisco Clavijero's ponderous *History of Mexico,* first published in Italian and soon translated into English, told of Aztecs moving southeasterly from Aztlán, their place of origin, then stopping "for some time" on the Gila River, "for at present there are still remains to be seen of the great edifices built by them on the borders of that river."[12] Clavijero did not identify his source, but the great Franciscan chronicler Juan Domingo Arricivita, in his *Crónica apostólica* (1792), paraphrased Pedro Font's description of Casa Grande as an ancient Aztec city. Unfortunately, either Arricivita or the manuscript on which he relied mistook Font's dimensions of the wall around the Casa for the building itself, thus enlarging the structure from Font's 70 by 50 *pies* (a *pie,* or foot, in Castile was about eleven inches) to 420 by 260 *pies.*[13] The German savant Alexander von Humboldt drew on Arricivita's account, including the mistaken measurements, in his *Political Essay on New Spain,* first published in French and English in 1811.[14]

Humboldt's influential map of New Spain, which accompanied his multivolume *Political Essay,* took matters a step further by noting that just north of the Hopi villages lay the "first abode of the Azteques come from Aztlán," an imaginary landmark that subsequent mapmakers copied.[15] Brantz Mayer, however, outdid even Humboldt in his popular *Mexico as It Is and Was,* published in 1844. Mayer apparently relied on Humboldt for his description of Casa Grande, for he repeated the incorrect measurement, but he may have consulted only his imagination when he described Casa Grande as part of a "chain" of "ancient structures" that led from central Mexico into the heart of North America, all the way to the Great Lakes.[16]

Edward King Kingsborough, in his *Antiquities of Mexico,* which appeared in seven volumes in 1831, reproduced much of Pedro Font's account of his visit to Casa Grande, including the correct measurements and Font's sketch of the floor plan.[17] William H. Prescott, in turn, drew on Kingsborough for his widely read *History of the Conquest of Mexico,* which was published in 1843. From Kingsborough, Prescott (who acquired such popularity that Prescott, Arizona, was named for him) borrowed Font's description of Casa Grande, repeating the idea that the ruins were "a supposed station of the Aztecs."[18] First impressions, it is clear, could be enduring impressions even when erroneous.

The idea that the Casa Grande was an Aztec way station harmonized with another theory that put the Aztecs' origins in the Ohio and Mississippi Valleys. Some American scientists argued that the great pre-Columbian earthen mounds found in that region could not be the work of any contemporary tribe or their forebears. They must have been produced by a native civilization capable of monumental achievements—who else but the Aztecs?[19]

When the United States invaded Mexico in 1846, American soldiers were already primed to believe that Casa Grande was an Aztec ruin. "We were now fast approaching the ground where rumor and the maps of the day place the ruins of the so called Aztec towns," Lieutenant William H. Emory noted in his journal as he made his way down the Gila River in

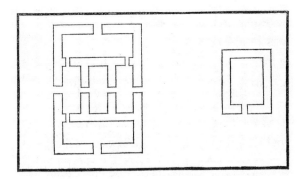

Floor plan of Casa Grande, drawn from measurements made by Fray Pedro Font in 1775 (Published in Edward King Kingsborough, *Antiquities of Mexico,* 1831; courtesy DeGolyer Library, Southern Methodist University)

"Ruins of Pecos, Astek Church." Before he reached Casa Grande, Lieutenant
William H. Emory had already seen "Aztec ruins" elsewhere on his march. This
lithograph focuses on the kiva at Pecos Pueblo, which he visited in August 1846
as he first entered New Mexico with the conquering Army of the West. Repeating
local lore, Emory reported that "the eternal fires of Montezuma" burned within
the underground kiva, or "Astek Church," and he noted how "the remains of the
architecture exhibit, in a prominent manner, the engraftment of the Catholic
church upon the ancient religion of the country." (From William H. Emory,
*Notes of a Military Reconnoissance,* 1848; courtesy DeGolyer Library, Southern
Methodist University)

October 1846, eager to see the "'fabulous' Casa Montezuma."[20] A West
Point–trained member of the Army Corps of Topographical Engineers,
Lieutenant Emory was then en route to the Pacific to help consolidate the
American conquest of California. Two years later, in 1848, Emory's account
of his journey appeared in print as *Notes of a Military Reconnoissance,* and
it contained a lithograph that gave the American reading public its first
printed view of Casa Grande.

In addition to what Emory gleaned from books and maps, he almost
certainly heard tales of the Aztec ruins at Casa Grande from former trappers like Kit Carson and Antoine Robidoux, who guided the U.S. Army
toward California. American "mountain men" had been scouring the Gila

"Ruins of the Casa Grande." Fray Pedro Font's floor plan of Casa Grande had been published in 1831, but this lithograph, based on a sketch by John Mix Stanley, was the first graphic image of the structure to appear in print. (From William H. Emory, *Notes of a Military Reconnoissance*, 1848; courtesy DeGolyer Library, Southern Methodist University)

and its tributaries for beaver since the 1820s. One trapper, Pauline Weaver, had carved his first initial and last name on one of Casa Grande's ancient walls.[21] These trappers left no written description of Casa Grande, but they would have heard legends of the place from local Indians, as did Emory:

> *The Indians here do not know the name Aztec. Montezuma is the outward point in their chronology; and as he is supposed to have lived and reigned for all time preceding his disappearance, so do they speak of every event preceding the Spanish conquest as of the days of Montezuma.*
>
> *The name, at this moment, is as familiar to every Indian, Puebla [Pueblo], Apache, and Navajoe as that of our Saviour or Washington is to us. In the person of Montezuma, they unite both qualities of divinity and patriot.*[22]

If southwestern Indians venerated Montezuma, however, it seems likely that they learned of him from Spaniards or Mexican Indians rather than because they continued an ancient tradition. That was the judgment of Josiah Gregg, whose influential book on New Mexico, *Commerce of the*

*Prairies,* Emory carried with him.[23] It also became the judgment of modern scholars, who see no direct connection between Aztecs and southwestern Indians. In the case of the O'odhams along the Gila, the stories of Montezuma at Casa Grande probably originated with Kino and Manje and their missionary successors.

Lieutenant Emory's arrival at Casa Grande on November 10, 1846, marks an interesting turning point in perception of the site. Although his fellow soldiers, steeped in Prescott's *History of the Conquest of Mexico,* were generally receptive to tales of Aztec glory as they prepared to march to the Halls of the Montezumas, Emory was an independent thinker.[24] By the time he had examined Casa Grande first-hand, he had begun to wonder if the various ruins he had seen along the Gila "may be those of comparatively modern Indians."[25]

On a sweltering day in July 1852, six years after Emory's visit, John Russell Bartlett visited Casa Grande in his capacity as U.S. boundary commissioner and expressed similar doubt. Although Bartlett declared that the site's Aztec origins had become "an acknowledged fact," he reviewed some of the earlier accounts and concluded that "the traditions which give rise to this notion are extremely vague." A studious man, Bartlett, like Emory, examined the facts for himself. "People have got too much in the way of ascribing all ancient remains to the Aztecs," he complained. "We hear of them on the shores of Lake Michigan, where some have located the famous city of Aztlan." The Casa Grande, Bartlett conjectured, might have been used to store corn rather than to house Montezuma.[26]

Later travelers frequently consulted Bartlett's work in particular. Wrote one of his readers, "What race dwelt here? by what people were these crumbling walls put together? . . . modern research has not to this day approached a solution of the mystery."[27]

Nevertheless, the legacy of Kino's first impression enjoyed continued currency. When Kit Carson, who stopped at Casa Grande with Emory in 1846, asked a Pima who built the house, the Pima himself readily identified it as the Casa de Montezuma, then proceeded to describe a miraculously conceived young man who had built it ages ago, along with other nearby dwellings.[28]

Casa Grande was by no means the only southwestern place or ruin attributed to the Aztecs. In Arizona, Anglo Americans named a number
of natural features for Aztecs (Aztec Gulch, Aztec Hills, Aztec Peak, and
Aztec Pass) and for Montezuma in particular (Montezuma Peak, Montezuma's Tanks, Montezuma Head, Montezuma Cave, Montezuma's Chair,
and Montezuma Sleeping). The most popular Aztec-named sites in Arizona, however, are Montezuma Castle and Montezuma Well in the Verde
Valley, both of which are protected within Montezuma Castle National
Monument and are culturally associated with the pre-Columbian Sinagua
people.

Northwestern New Mexico has its analogue in the Aztec Ruins National
Monument, identified as an Aztec site as early as 1861. When English-
speaking Americans settled in the Animas Valley in the 1870s, they not
only assumed that the nearby ruins, which boasted a giant kiva, dated to
the Aztecs, they quickly changed the name of their new town from Wallace
to Aztec.[29] Southwestern Colorado, meanwhile, is home to Montezuma
County, in which lie Montezuma Creek and Montezuma Valley.

At the same time that these names were being adopted, the world of
scholarship began to move in a different direction. In 1889, in his *History of Arizona and New Mexico,* Hubert Howe Bancroft lamented that "it
is also still the custom of most writers to refer to the ruins and relics of
this region as undoubtedly of Aztec origin."[30] By then archaeologists had
begun to excavate portions of Casa Grande and other nearby ruins, and
their investigations led them to reject the notion that migrating Aztecs
had left their imprint on the area. Instead, they came to understand that
the builders of Casa Grande were indigenous to the desert region and had
adapted to its aridity by constructing irrigation systems of extraordinary
sophistication. The resulting "hydraulic" culture, the work of a people now
known as Hohokam, had endured for a thousand years, beginning as early
as 450 CE.[31] It was centered in the basins of the Salt and Gila Rivers and
on certain of their tributaries, including the Verde, Santa Cruz, and San
Pedro Rivers. Emory's speculation that the various ruins along the Gila
"may be those of comparatively modern Indians" was entirely on target,
for archaeologists, as well as contemporary O'odhams themselves, today
point to the O'odhams as being among the Hohokam's descendants.[32] It is
from the O'odhams that archaeologists took the word Hohokam, meaning

"those who are gone" or "used up." The full range of the Hohokam's legacy, however, remains unknown, for although they were apparently "guided by a shared set of beliefs" and also "constructed massive canal networks (up to 22 miles in length) and irrigated extensive tracts of land (up to 70,000 acres)," they may nevertheless have embraced multiple ethnicities and languages.[33]

Today, Casa Grande stands as "the only intact structure of its kind in the Southwest."[34] It may not have sheltered Montezuma, but archaeologists believe that it served vital ritual purposes.[35] It appears to have been built in the early 1300s, during a time when the formerly egalitarian Hohokam society may have become increasingly hierarchical. Building Casa Grande and its extensive irrigation system required a large, highly organized labor force. For the big house alone, large amounts of wood—some 640 beams of juniper, ponderosa pine, and white fir—had to be brought from mountains fifty miles away, and they appear to have been transported overland rather than floated down the Gila. The material for the building, which struck visitors as unusually hard and smooth cement, was caliche. A mixture of clay, sand, and calcium carbonate, caliche was found beneath the surface of the site. Softened with water, it could be kneaded like stiff dough and laid into courses to dry like cement, without forms. The great house is a nearly perfect 3:4 rectangle, oriented to the four winds, as Pedro Font had noted. Openings in the walls probably allowed its inhabitants to track the movement of the sun and may have served as a calendar.

Although archaeologists have rejected the idea that Mesoamericans built Casa Grande, they have found ample evidence of Mesoamerican influence there and at other Hohokam sites, such as Pueblo Grande and the Park of Canals in the Phoenix basin. Evidence ranges from small clay figurines and pyrite-backed mirrors to large public works such as canals, platform mounds, and large oval ball courts, including one at Casa Grande. Most archaeologists believe, however, with support from genetic evidence, that trade goods and ideas moved north from Mexico, not entire peoples.[36] They credit the Hohokam with making their own independent adaptations to a dry land and developing one of the most complex irrigation systems in the Americas.

By the late 1880s, the railroad and a connecting stage had begun to bring both tourists and potential vandals to the Casa Grande, and the need to protect the site became urgent. The impetus to act, however, did not come from within Arizona. Rather, it came from a group of fourteen prominent Bostonians, including historians Francis Parkman and John Fiske, jurist Oliver Wendell Holmes Jr., poet John Greenleaf Whittier, Massachusetts governor Oliver Ames, and the patroness of southwestern archaeology in her day, Mary Hemenway, who apparently galvanized the fourteen to petition Congress to save the ruins. On March 2, 1889, their efforts bore fruit as Congress formally designated Casa Grande as an archaeological reserve—America's first. Congress also appropriated funds to repair and protect the site, and authorized the president to reserve the land on which it stood from sale or settlement.[37] Three years later, in 1892, the executive branch finally fulfilled its congressional mandate when President Benjamin Harrison issued an executive order to purchase 480 acres surrounding the site, creating the Casa Grande Reservation. In 1918, President Woodrow Wilson elevated the reservation to national monument status and put it under the jurisdiction of the National Park Service, where it remains today.[38]

# 5 Chaco Canyon

Chaco Canyon, in the remote San Juan basin of northwestern New Mexico, is the centerpiece of a fifty-three-square-mile reserve, known since 1980 as Chaco Culture National Historical Park. In this brittle land, which receives less than eight inches of rainfall a year, ancestors of modern-day Puebloan people built one of pre-Columbian North America's great urban complexes. Much about Chaco Canyon remains shrouded in mystery. Its engineered roads, its splendid architecture, and its indications of extreme ceremonial complexity, sophisticated astronomical understanding, and cultural influence stretching far beyond the confines of the canyon—all of these qualities bespeak a society and a worldview that we in the present may never fully fathom and that we will never tire of trying to understand.

The physical environment of Chaco Canyon would hardly seem to recommend itself for such a concentration of wonders. Arid, cold in winter, and blisteringly hot in summer, the canyon posed steep challenges for early corn farmers. The growing season was short; building timbers lay scores of miles away in the forests of the Chuska Mountains; and yet, paradoxically, this adversity may have been key to the astounding achievements of Chaco's people. As one scholar has put it, perhaps their success in adapting to so stern an environment "sparked the genius of their culture and then propelled them through centuries of often spectacular growth."[1]

That growth appears to have begun close to the year 850 CE. It extended through the 900s and early–middle 1000s, then faltered under the influence of drought, recovered for several decades, and finally was extinguished. Beginning about 1130 CE, a severe drought gripped the region and did not let go for fifty years. Chacoan society did not survive it, and the magnificent stone great houses, more than a dozen of them rising castle-like along Chaco Wash and on the mesas above it, were surrendered to wind and dust.

By the late eighteenth century, if not before, Spaniards knew of Chaco Canyon and its great houses. Navajos had moved into the area in the early 1700s, and Chaco appears to have lain along a route that Spaniards took into the Navajo country, but those who traveled the route had little to say about it. Chaco appears on a map made by Bernardo Miera y Pacheco in 1778 as Chaca, a name that Miera y Pacheco must have obtained from people familiar with the site since he, although he traveled widely, seems not to have journeyed there. A half century later, in 1823, when New Mexico governor José Antonio Vizcarra led a contingent of fifteen hundred men on a campaign against the Navajos, he traveled through Chaco Canyon and referred to places whose names he or his guides appear to have known. In his sparse journal he noted that he set out on June 21 from Jémez Pueblo, on the edge of the Navajo country, and arrived at the Chaco Wash, which he called La Agua de San Carlos, on June 24, traveling by way of today's Torreon. On June 25, Vizcarra's force entered the canyon. He mentioned only Pueblo Pintado, the easternmost of the great houses, by name, calling it "the first Pueblo de Raton"—apparently Spaniards knew that more than one of the canyon's great houses harbored an abundance of rodents. Of those great houses, Vizcarra merely noted: "During the march the ruins of several pueblos were found, which were of such antiquity that their inhabitants were not known to Europeans."[2]

Chaco Canyon first came to the attention of Anglo Americans through the report of an 1849 military expedition. We have already met the author of the report: Lieutenant James H. Simpson, ably assisted by Richard and Edward Kern, also introduced American readers to Canyon de Chelly. Simpson's report constitutes probably the second published English-language description of pre-Columbian ruins (and certainly the first detailed description) anywhere in the Southwest, the first having been William H. Emory's account of Casa Grande, which Simpson himself cites.[3]

On August 26, ten days after leaving Santa Fe, the expedition "reached the high point of the land dividing the tributaries of the Gulf of Mexico from those of the Pacific." After crossing the Continental Divide, "we commenced gradually descending its western slope—three miles more bringing us to the Rio Chaco, a tributary of the *Rio San Juan;* and five miles more to a point whence could be seen in the distance, on a slight elevation, a conspicuous ruin called, according to some of the Pueblo Indians with us, *Pueblo de Montezuma,* and according to the Mexicans, *Pueblo Colorado.* Hosta [a guide recruited from Jemez Pueblo] calls it *Pueblo de Ratones;* Sandoval, the friendly Navajo chief with us, *Pueblo Grande;* and Carravahal, our Mexican guide, who probably knows more about it than anyone else, *Pueblo Pintado.*"[4]

The expedition camped not far from the ancient stone village. Although Simpson and the Kerns had already traveled a wearying twenty-one and a half miles that day, they soon set out to examine the ruins. From his report, one senses Simpson's enthusiasm. His mission was to give an account of the country through which he passed, and now he had come upon something no American had seen before. He would examine the ruins closely, omitting no significant detail:

*We found them to more than answer our expectations. Forming one structure, and built of tabular pieces of hard, fine-grained compact gray sandstone (a material entirely unknown in the present architecture of New Mexico), to which the atmosphere has imparted a reddish tinge, the layers or beds being not thicker than three inches, and sometimes as thin as one-fourth of an inch, it discovers in the masonry a combination of science and art which can only be referred to a higher stage of civilization and refinement than is discoverable in the works of Mexicans or Pueblos of the present day. Indeed, so beautifully diminutive and true are the details of the structure as to cause it, at a little distance, to have all the appearance of a magnificent piece of mosaic work.*

*In the outer face of the building there are no signs of mortar, the intervals between the beds being chinked with stones of the minutest thinness. The filling and backing are done in rubble masonry, the mortar presenting no indications of the presence of lime. The thickness of the main wall at base is within an inch or two of three feet; higher up, it is less—diminishing every story by retreating jogs on the inside, from bottom to top. Its elevation at its present highest point, is between twenty-five and thirty feet, the series of floor beams indicating that there must have been originally three stories.*

"North West View of the Ruins of the Pueblo Pintado in the Valley of the Rio Chaco," lithograph based on a wash drawing by Richard H. Kern (From James H. Simpson, *Journal of a Military Reconnaissance ... to the Navajo Country ... in 1849;* courtesy DeGolyer Library, Southern Methodist University, David J. Weber Papers)

*The ground plan, including the court, in exterior development is about 403 feet.*[5] *On the ground floor, exclusive of the outbuildings, are fifty-four apartments, some of them as small as five feet square, and the largest about twelve by six feet. These rooms communicate with each other by very small doors, some of them as contracted as two and a half by two and a half feet; and in the case of the inner suite, the doors communicating with the interior court are as small as three and a half by two feet. The principal rooms, or those most in use, were, on account of their having larger doors and windows, most probably those of the second story. The system of flooring seems to have been large transverse unhewn beams, six inches in diameter, laid transversely from wall to wall, and then a number of smaller ones, about three inches in diameter, laid longitudinally upon them. What was placed on these does not appear, but most probably it was brush, bark, or slabs, covered with a layer of mud mortar. The beams show no signs of the saw or axe; on the contrary, they appear to have been hacked off by means of some very imperfect instrument.... At different points about the premises were three circular apartments sunk in the ground, the walls being of masonry. These apartments the Pueblo Indians call* estuffas *[estufas or kivas], or places where the people held their political and religious meetings.*

*The site of the ruins is a knoll, some twenty or thirty feet above the surrounding plain—the Rio Chaco coursing by it two or three hundred yards distant, and no wood being visible within the circuit of a mile.*

If the Río Chaco, dry most of the year, was "coursing by," there must have been heavy thundershowers upstream. Had the showers also fallen in the vicinity of the troops, Simpson would certainly have mentioned the difficulty of travel through the resultant mud, which near Chaco can be a fearsome gumbo. Simpson goes on to reflect, not for the last time, on the origins of the ruins: "Hosta says this pueblo was built by Montezuma and his people when they were on their way from the north towards the south; that, after living here and in the vicinity for a while, they dispersed, some of them going east and settling on the Rio Grande, and others south into Old Mexico."

Early the next day, stealing an hour before the column resumes its march, Simpson and the Kerns return to the ruins:

*Not finishing our examinations at the ruins of* Pueblo Pintado *yesterday afternoon, we again visited them early this morning. On digging about the base of the exterior wall we find that, for at least two feet, (the depth our time would permit us to go,) the same kind of masonry obtains below as above, except that it appears more compact. We could find no signs of the genuine arch about the premises, the lintels of the doors and windows being generally either a number of pieces of wood laid horizontally side by side, a single stone slab laid in this manner, or occasionally a series of smaller ones so placed horizontally upon each other, whilst presenting the form of a sharp angle, in vertical longitudinal section, they would support the weight of the fabric above.... Fragments of pottery lay scattered around, the colors showing taste in their selection and in the style of their arrangement, and being still quite bright. We would gladly, had time permitted, have remained longer to dig among the rubbish of the past; but the troops having already got some miles in advance of us, we were reluctantly obliged to quit.*

The obligation to quit resulted not just from a wish not to be left behind—the trail of the main column would be impossible to lose, and they could easily catch up. More to the point, they were in potentially hostile territory and were few in number. The ruins may have been fascinating, but they did not want to be picked off by a roving band of Navajos or Utes watching for loose horses, forgotten gear, or stragglers separated from the rest of the expedition.

*Thirteen miles from our last camp we came to another old ruin, called by Carravahal Pueblo Weje-gi [Wijiji, in current spelling], built, like Pueblo Pintado, of very thin tabular pieces of compact sandstone. The circuit of the structure, including the court, was near seven hundred feet. The number of apartments on the ground floor, judging from what was distinguishable, was probably ninety-nine. The highest present elevation of the exterior wall is about twenty-five feet. The great mass of rubbish below, however, shows that it must have been higher....*

*The view from these ruins, both up and down the cañon, is fine. Rocks piled upon rocks present themselves on either side, and in such order as to give the idea of two parallel architectural façades, converging at either extremity, at a remote distance. Another and more splendid view burst upon us as we turned an angle of the canon, just before reaching camp. The chief object in the landscape was* Mésa Fachada *[Fajada Butte], a circular mound with tableau top, rising abruptly midway in the cañon to a height of from three hundred to four hundred feet. The combination of this striking and beautiful object with the clear sky beyond, against which it was relieved, in connexion with lesser mounds at its base, the serried tents of the command, the busy scene of moving men and animals in the vicinity, and the curling smoke from the camp fires, made up a picture which it has been seldom my lot to witness.*

*The distance traveled today was 14.86 miles. The road was tolerably good. Scrub cedars, very thinly scattered, were to be seen on the heights; and the* artemisia *[sage] characterized the* flora. *Some patches of good* gramma *grass could occasionally be seen along the Rio Chaco. The country, as usual, on account, doubtless, of constant drought, presented one wide expanse of barren waste. Frequently since we left the Puerco the soil has given indications of containing all the earthy elements of fertility, but the refreshing shower has been wanting to make it productive. The Rio Chaco, near our camp, has a width of eight feet and a depth of one and a half. Its waters, which are of a rich clay color, can only be relied upon with certainty during the wet season.*

The next day, August 28, intent on making further investigation of the ruins within the canyon, Simpson and Richard Kern separate from Colonel Washington and the rest of the command. Edward Kern, responsible for

mapping the main route, stays with Washington. Carravahal, whose familiarity with the canyon is impressive (and raises the question of how he accumulated so much information), accompanies Simpson. Aside from small
variations in spelling, Carravahal's names for the major ruins remain unchanged today.

*Proceeding down the cañon one and a half miles (its general course northwest
by west), we came to an old ruined structure, called by Carravahal* Pueblo Una
Vida. *The circuit of this pueblo we found on measurement to be nine hundred
and ninety-four feet. The structure has been built, like those I have already described, of very thin tabular fine-grained sandstone—the highest present elevation of the main walls being about fifteen feet. Two stories are now discoverable,
but the mass of* debris *at the base of the walls certainly shows that there must
originally have been more. The remains of four circular* estufas *are still apparent....*

*A mile further down the canon, we came to another pueblo in ruins, called by
Carravahal* Hungo Pavie, *which he interprets Crooked Nose. These ruins show
the same nicety in the details of their masonry as those I have already described.
The ground plan shows an extent of exterior development of eight hundred and
seventy-two feet, and a number of rooms upon the ground floor equal to seventy-
two. The structure shows the existence of but one circular* estufa, *and this is
placed in the body of the north portion of the building, midway from either extremity. This estufa differs from the others we have seen in having a number of
interior counterforts....*[6]

*Continuing down the cañon one and three quarter miles further, we came to
another extensive structure in ruins, the name of which, according to the guide,
is* Pueblo Chettro Kettle, *or, as he interprets it, the Rain Pueblo. These ruins
have an extent of exterior circuit, inclusive of the court, of about thirteen hundred feet....*

*In the northwest corner of these ruins we found a room in an almost perfect
state of preservation.... This room is fourteen by seven and a half feet in plan,
and ten feet in elevation. It has an outside doorway, three and a-half feet high
by two and a quarter wide, and one at its west end, leading into the adjoining
room, two feet wide, and at present, on account of rubbish, only two and a half
feet high.*

*The stone walls still have their plaster upon them, in a tolerable state of preser-
vation. On the south wall is a recess, or niche, three feet two inches high by four*

"Interior of a Room in the North Range of the Pueblo Chetho-Kette (The Rain),"
lithograph based on a wash drawing by Richard H. Kern (From James H. Simpson,
*Journal of a Military Reconnaissance … to the Navajo Country … in 1849;* courtesy
DeGolyer Library, Southern Methodist University, David J. Weber Papers)

*feet five inches wide by four feet deep. Its position and size naturally suggested the
idea that it might have been a fireplace; but if so, the smoke must have returned
to the room, as there was no chimney outlet for it. In addition to this large recess, there were three smaller ones in the same wall. The ceiling showed two main
beams, laid transversely; on these, longitudinally, were a number of smaller ones
in juxta position, the ends being tied together by a species of wooden fibre, and
the interstices chinked in with small stones; on these again, transversely, in close
contact, was a kind of lathing of the odor and appearance of cedar—all in a good
state of preservation. Depending from the beams were several short pieces of rope,
a specimen of which I got. The floor of the room is covered with rubbish. A large
quantity of pottery lay strewed about the ruins.*

Simpson's east-to-west exploration of Chaco Canyon progressed from
one massive and magnificent ruin to others still larger and more extraordinary. Now he approaches the most impressive of them all, Pueblo Bonito:

*Two or three hundred yards down the cañon we met another old pueblo in ruins, called Pueblo Bonito. This pueblo, though not so beautiful in the arrangement of the details of its masonry as* Pueblo Pintado, *is yet superior to it in point of preservation. The circuit of its walls is about thirteen hundred feet. Its present elevation shows that it has had at least four stories of apartments. The number of rooms on the ground floor at present discernible is one hundred and thirty-nine. In this enumeration, however, are not included the apartments which are not distinguishable in the east portion of the pueblo, and which would probably swell the number to about two hundred. There, then, having been at least four stories of rooms, and supposing the horizontal depth of the edifice to have been uniform from bottom to top, or, in other words, not of a retreating terrace form on the court side, it is not unreasonable to infer that the original number of rooms was as many as eight hundred. But, as the latter supposition (as will be shown presently) is probably the most tenable, there must be a reduction from this number of one range of rooms for every story after the first; and this would lessen the number to six hundred and forty-one.*

Many others, including the photographer William Henry Jackson in 1877 and generations of archaeologists after him, succeeded Simpson in trying to estimate the total number of rooms in Pueblo Bonito. To this day, no definitive count exists. The National Park Service, which administers Chaco Culture National Historical Park, uses the figure "more than six hundred," placing Simpson's original (and probably hurried) estimate very much on the mark.[7] He is less accurate on other matters, however, and greatly underestimates the number of kivas, or as he calls them, estufas:

*The number of estufas is four—the largest being sixty feet in diameter, showing two stories in height and having a present depth of twelve feet. All of these estufas are, as in the case of the others I have seen, cylindrical in shape, and nicely walled up with thin tabular stone.*

*Among the ruins are several rooms in a very good state of preservation—one of them (near the northwest corner of the north range) being walled up with alternate beds of large and small stones, the regularity of the combination producing a very pleasing effect. The ceiling of this room is also more tasteful than any we have seen—the transverse beams being smaller and more numerous, and the longitudinal pieces which rest upon them only about an inch in diameter, and beautifully regular. These latter have somewhat the appearance of barked willow. The room has a doorway at each end and one at the side, each of them leading into adjacent apartments. The light is let in by a window, two feet by eight inches, on the north side. . . .*

*A few hundred yards further down the canon, we fell in with another pueblo in ruins, called by the guide* Pueblo del Arroyo, *the circuit of which was about one thousand feet. The day, however, being far gone, and the camp of the command doubtless many miles in advance of us, we were obliged reluctantly to forego the critical examination of these ruins which we would have been pleased to give them. . . .*

*All the ruins we have seen to-day, up to this point, have been on the north side of the cañon and within a few feet of its escarpment wall, the sandstone rocks composing it being magnificently amorphous and running up to a height of about one hundred feet. Two miles further down the cañon, but on its left or south bank, we came to another pueblo in ruins, called by the guide* Pueblo de Peñasca Blanca, *the circuit of which I ascertained to be, approximately, one thousand seven hundred feet. This is the largest pueblo in plan we have seen, and differs from others in the arrangement of the stones composing its walls. . . .*

*The question now arises, as we have seen all the ruins in this quarter, What was the form of these buildings?—I mean as regards the continuity or non-continuity of its front and rear walls. Were these walls one plain surface from bottom to top, as in the United States, or were they interrupted each story by a terrace, as is the case with the modern pueblo buildings in New Mexico?*

*The front or exterior walls were evidently one plain surface from bottom to top; because, whenever we found them in their integrity, which we did for as many as four stories in height, we always noticed them to be uninterruptedly plain.*

*The rear walls, however, were in no instance that I recollect of, found to extend higher than the commencement of the second story; and the partition walls were, if my memory is not at fault, correspondingly step-like in their respective altitudes. The idea, then, at once unfolds itself, that in elevation the inner wall must have been a series of retreating surfaces or, what would make this necessary, each story on the inner or court side must have been terraced. This idea also gathers strength from the fact that we saw no indications of any internal mode of ascent from story to story, and therefore that some exterior mode must have been resorted to—such as, probably, ladders, which the terrace form of the sev-*

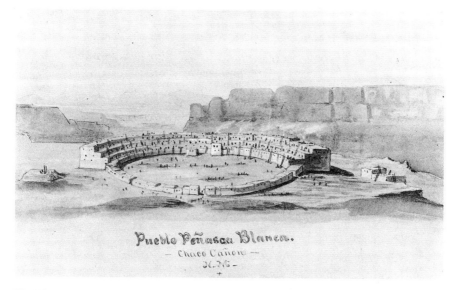

"Pueblo Peñasca Blanca—Chaco Cañon—N.M.," watercolor by Richard H. Kern. Here Kern shows how he and his companions imagined the pueblo, which is now called Peñasco Blanco, to have looked when it was occupied. (Courtesy DeGolyer Library, Southern Methodist University, David J. Weber Papers)

*eral stories would make very convenient. Again, the terrace form of the stories would best conduce to light and ventilation for the interior ranges of apartments. The idea, then, which Mr. R. H. Kern was the first to suggest—that these pueblos were terraced on their inner or court side—is not without strong grounds of probability.*

Simpson reflects on the orientation of the ruins and commences to speculate on the origins of the people who built them:

*In regard to the position of the several structures in respect to the four true cardinal points of the heavens, it deviated in every instance more or less from them; but in no instance was the variation from the* magnetic *cardinal points more than five degrees, except in the case of the* Pueblo Una Vida, *where it was as great as fifteen degrees east. The magnetic variation of the needle from the true pole being, at these localities, about thirteen and [a] half degrees east, the deviation from the four* true *cardinal points, in the case of the* Pueblo Una Vida, *would then be as much as twenty-eight and a half degrees. In the case, however, of all the other pueblos, it was but a very few degrees.*

*In regard to the origin of these remains, there is nothing that I can learn conclusive in relation to it. Hosta, one of the most intelligent Pueblo Indians I have seen, says, as I have before remarked, that they were built by Montezuma and his people, when on their way from the north to the region of the Rio Grande and to Old Mexico. Sandoval, a very intelligent Navaho chief, also says they were built by Montezuma, but further states that the Navajos and all the other Indians were once but one people, and lived in the vicinity of the Silver Mountain;[8] that this mountain is about one hundred miles north of the Chaco ruins; that the Pueblo Indians separated from them, (the Navajos) and built towns on the Rio Grande and its tributaries, but that "their house continues to be the hut made of bushes." Nothing more satisfactory than this have I been able to get from either Indians or Mexicans.*

*On Colton's map of North America, however, I notice that Humboldt is made to locate the residence of the Aztecs, in the twelfth century, between the thirty-sixth and thirty-seventh parallels of north latitude, and the one hundred and ninth and one hundred and twelfth meridians of west longitude; but upon what ground the great explorer has based this hypothesis, I know not, for I have not his works at hand to consult.[9] This thing, however, is certain: the ruins I have described were found upon the Rio Chaco; they are evidently, from the similarity of their style and mode of construction, of a common origin; they discover in the materials of which they are composed, as well as in the grandeur of their design and superiority of their workmanship, a condition of architectural excellence beyond the power of the Indians or New Mexicans of the present day to exhibit; and they are all situated between the thirty-sixth and thirty-seventh parallels of north latitude, and near the one hundred and eight degree of west longitude. It is, then, not at all improbable that they are the identical ruins to which Humboldt has referred.*

Unfortunately, the perspicacious Lieutenant Simpson did not enjoy his circuit of discovery through Navajo country. In contrast to the hundreds of thousands who relish New Mexican cooking today, he remarks near the close of his journey, "I have not yet drunk a cup of coffee or eaten a tortilla of Mexican preparation without its creating in some degree a sensation of nausea at the stomach. There is certainly great room for improvement in the cuisine of this country. The only eatable I have yet partaken of which does not become tainted by their cookery is the egg in its boiled state, and this is doubtless owing to its being protected by the shell."

By September 23, Simpson was back in Santa Fe. In January 1850, he commenced recasting his field notes into a finished draft of his "Journal," which he submitted in mid-April to the commander of the Corps of Topographical Engineers, Colonel J. J. Abert, at the War Department in Washington.[10] It was published later that year. Writing and reflection, however, did nothing to sweeten the sour attitude he bore toward all aspects of the New Mexican frontier:

*Never did I have, nor do I believe anybody can have, a full appreciation of the almost universal barrenness which pervades this country, until they come out, as I did, to "search the land," and behold with their own eyes its general nakedness. … The sedimentary rocks … which are the prevalent formations of the country, have a crude, half made-up appearance … , being almost universally bare of vegetation except that of a sparse, dwarfish, sickening-colored aspect, cannot be regarded … without a sensation of loathing.*

*The face of the country, for the same reason—the general absence of all verdure, and the dead, dull yellow aspect of its soil—has a tendency to create the same disagreeable sensation.*

Chaco's isolation and the difficulty of traversing its often waterless terrain, as well as the risk of encountering hostile Navajos, whose raids the "peace treaty" imposed by Colonel Washington had failed to reduce, discouraged visits by outsiders, and for the next two and a half decades Chaco Canyon remained more a legend than a reality for Anglo Americans entering New Mexico. In 1875, Dr. Oscar Loew, chemist and mineralogist for the Wheeler Survey, briefly examined Pueblo Pintado, which he mistook for Pueblo Bonito, while failing to reach the concentration of great houses in the heart of the canyon.[11]

Two years later the indefatigable photographer William Henry Jackson resolved to visit the canyon. He said he had "no idea of discovering anything new" but wanted to see for himself and compare "the highest development of ancient architectural skill" with the ruins at Mesa Verde and throughout the rest of the San Juan basin that he had documented in 1874 and 1875.[12]

Earlier in 1877 Jackson had visited Canyon de Chelly and wanted to set out directly for Chaco Canyon from that location but, the time being late

April, he found he could recruit neither animals nor guides, "even at five dollars a day," to make the trip.[13] Although "many of the Indians who reside near [Fort] Defiance are familiar with the locality," they "dread to visit it at this time of the year on account of the well-known dearth of water and of grass necessary to sustain their animals."[14]

Having returned to Fort Wingate, Jackson chanced to hear of a Mr. Beaumont living at San Ysidro, near Jemez Pueblo, who might be able to help him. Beaumont, it turned out, knew nothing of the Chaco country, "but what served my purpose even better was his ability as an interpreter in both Spanish and Indian." For a guide, Beaumont recommended that Jackson enlist Hosta, the same ex-governor of Jemez who in his mid-fifties had ably served Washington and Simpson on the expedition of 1849: "We found old Hosta in the midst of his family, a small, thin man. His body was bent under the burden of more than four score years of toil. His eyes were dim with age, and straggling gray hair but thinly covered his head. He declared himself to be as good a man as any of us and ready to guide us over the country he knew so well."[15] Hosta's sole condition was that they take along his grandson, "a lad of twelve or fifteen years . . . merely for the use of his eyes, as his own were failing and he feared he should not be able to recognize distant landmarks."[16]

The four of them set out on muleback, leading one additional mule loaded with all their provisions and gear, including Jackson's camera.[17] Fortunately, heavy rains had recently fallen, freshening the forage for their mules and leaving occasional pools of water in the arroyo bottoms. At the close of the second day they reached Pueblo Pintado, where Hosta pointed out "that the soldiers of Colonel Washington's command and of other scouting parties caused a great deal of the present ruin by pulling out the floor timbers for their camp-fires. He also says he can distinctly remember when there were a number of perfect rooms."[18]

The next day they pressed on to the main part of the canyon, where they made a camp near Pueblo del Arroyo, beside "a few shallow pools of thick, pasty water, the remains of some recent shower."[19] For the next three days they ventured to the ruins of villages up and down the canyon, examining the pueblos (given here in Jackson's spelling) of Weje-gi, Una-Vida, Hungo Pavie, Chettro Kettle, Bonito, del Arroyo, Peñasca Blanca, and two that Jackson identified by numbers: 8 (Kin Kletso) and 9 (Casa Chiquita). Jackson photographed, measured, drew floor plans, and recorded the orientations of each pueblo to magnetic north. He also sketched an accurate map of the canyon and its main features. Although his greatest talents may have lain in photography, he proved himself a shrewd and observant archaeologist, quickly rejecting the notion that the builders of the great houses were related to Montezuma's fabled Aztecs.

He acknowledged that "the masonry, as it is displayed in the construction of the walls, is the most wonderful feature in these ancient habitation[s], and is in striking contrast to the careless and rude methods shown in the dwellings of the present Pueblos."[20] But he did not allow this contrast to divert him as it had others, including Lieutenant Simpson, from a more important insight concerning the "estufas," or kivas, which were so prominent and plentiful among the Chaco ruins. These structures, which also characterized "all the ruins extending southward from the basin of the Rio San Juan, are so identical in their structure, position, and evident uses with the similar ones in the pueblos now inhabited, that they indisputably connect one with the other, and show this region to have been covered at one time with a numerous population, of which the present inhabitants of the pueblos of Moqui [Hopi] and of New Mexico are either the remnants or the descendants."[21]

Three of Jackson's personal discoveries are linked in one of the most popular and visually spectacular hikes available to contemporary visitors to Chaco. While investigating the ruins at Pueblo Peñasco Blanco (as it is spelled nowadays), he scanned the opposite mesa with his field glasses and descried tall ruins piercing the horizon high on the canyon rim a half mile or so behind Pueblo Bonito. Simpson had not reported them, for they were invisible from the canyon floor. Seeking a route to this new find, Jackson explored the side canyon immediately east of Chetro Ketl: "At the far end of this are the ruins of some old structure which had been built upon a low slope of talus, and evidently served as an approach up the bluff"—these were the remains of an earthen ramp now considered to be part of the elaborate and only faintly understood system of Chacoan "roads."

*Continuing around the alcove to its mouth opposite where I entered, I saw some steps and hand-holds cut into the rock that seemed to offer the opportunity I was seeking; climbing up a short distance over a slope of fallen rocks I found in the sides of the crevice an irregular series of stair-like steps hewn into the hard sandstone, each step about 30 inches long and 6 inches deep, the two cut surfaces*

"Ancient Stairway," lithograph based on a drawing by William Henry Jackson. This feature of Chaco Canyon is known today as the Jackson Stairway. (From *Tenth Annual Report of the United States Geological and Geographical Survey of the Territories,* 1878; courtesy New Mexico State Library, Santa Fe)

*at right angles to each other. Upon each side of these steps, in the steepest part of the ascent, are hand-holds so hewn out as to allow the hand to grasp them like the rounds of a ladder; in the other places they are sunken cup-like cavities, just large enough to admit the fingers. Easily gaining the summit, I walked back over the bluffs, ascending by terraces some 200 or 300 feet above the bottom of the cañon.*[22]

Having climbed what is now known as the "Jackson Stairway," he completed his walk to the ruins of the great house he had spied from Peñasco Blanco. This complex he named Pueblo Alto because of its commanding position on a crest of the mesa. In his autobiography, he proudly notes, "It is now regarded as one of the important ruins of the Chaco."[23]

The discovery of wonders continued until his last minutes in the canyon:

*On the morning of our departure from this interesting region I rode from our camp to the foot of the bluff about 200 yards below Pueblo Bonito, to examine*

*some indications of human handiwork which appeared in a crevice, and which
I had not theretofore noticed. Behind an immense bowlder which concealed the
lower part I found a stairway built into a narrow opening running up to the top
of the bluff; some of the steps were hewn in the manner already described, but
there were others formed by sticks of cedar placed side by side wedged firmly in
the crevice. Portions had decayed and fallen out, but enough remained to enable
us to ascend. When once upon the summit we had a splendid bird's-eye view of
Pueblo Bonito, it being almost vertically beneath us.*[24]

Today, by climbing the same route, one accesses a trail that ascends to
Pueblo Alto and returns by the top of the Jackson Stairway before circling
back to the vantage above Pueblo Bonito. The view down the so-called
stairway, incidentally, is not for the faint of heart, and an attempt actually
to descend the stairway would appear to be suicidal. One's admiration for
Jackson's intrepidity soars.

William Henry Jackson's exploration of Chaco Canyon was a tour de
force of rapid, energetic, and intelligent reconnaissance. For him, however,
it proved to be spirit crushing. As mentioned in the chapter on Canyon de
Chelly, his experimental use of "Sensitive Negative Tissue" during the field
season of 1877 ended in the loss of all the photographs he took at both
de Chelly and Chaco. As he wrote in 1940, "The fact that I had compiled
a voluminous first report on the Chaco Canyon ruins—now a National
Monument—didn't comfort me much. My feelings were beyond the repair of Dr. Hayden's praise. They still are. I can never replace those lost
pictures."[25]

In 1907, fifty-seven years after Simpson published his description, President Theodore Roosevelt proclaimed Chaco Canyon a national monument. In 1980 the protective cordon around the ruins was expanded and
the area was redesignated Chaco Cultural National Historical Park. In 1987
Chaco's massive, multistory, finely wrought, stone apartment complexes,
with their many ceremonial kivas, were awarded international recognition
as a UNESCO World Heritage Site. Controversy continues to attach to
Chaco Canyon, however, as energy development on surrounding lands dis-
turbs many outlying sites, and sub-surface vibrations from drilling, frack-
ing, and heavy equipment threaten to destabilize the ancient walls.

# 6 El Morro/Inscription Rock

Prehistoric rock drawings abound in the Southwest, as do (often lamentably) more modern etchings and defacements. No place in the region, however, rivals El Morro for the number of Spanish and Anglo American visitors who carved their names on its walls. Situated near the Continental Divide west of Albuquerque, this striking red sandstone bluff, or *morro,* rises some two hundred feet above the surrounding terrain. Historically, it stood astride a major east–west trail connecting Zuni to Ácoma that extended farther eastward to the Río Grande pueblos, a native route well traveled for centuries, which early Spaniards and Anglos readily adopted. At the foot of El Morro lay a large natural pool, filled by summer rains and winter snowmelt. Its life-sustaining water, well marked by the cliffs towering above it, attracted travelers from far and wide.

As early as 1598, Gaspar Pérez de Villagrá, author of an epic poem about Juan de Oñate's founding of New Mexico, vividly described how the pool, or *estanque,* saved his life when he wandered on foot, lost, cold, and nearly dying of thirst:[1]

> *Until, by great good luck, I reached*
> *The foot of certain lofty cliffs,*
> *At which place I did see there was*
> *A pleasant pool of cold water,*
> *Over whose crystal depths I, almost blind,*
> *Scarcely could conquer the great fury*

*Of that insatiable thirst that all but ended me*
*When, trembling all over, quivering,*
*I forcibly threw up the damp fluid.*
*And, waiting there a little bit,*
*Not free from fear and sweating much,*
*By chance I noticed that nearby there was*
*A little corn which, by some chance,*
*Someone had carelessly left there.*[2]

Spanish soldiers searching for horses scattered by a snowstorm found Villagrá that November and rescued him "near death at Agua de la Peña," the watering place of the rock, as Juan de Oñate termed El Morro.[3] Although Villagrá survived to make his mark as a poet, he seems to have carved nothing on the Peña. But Oñate did. In 1605, on his return from an expedition to the Gulf of California (which he thought was the Pacific Ocean and which Spaniards of his time called the South Sea), Oñate carved—or someone carved for him—the oldest European inscription that remains on El Morro. In Spanish, it memorably begins, *Pasó por aquí:*

*There passed this way the Adelantado Don Juan*
*de Oñate, from the discovery of the South*
*Sea, on the 16th of April, 1605*[4]

Thereafter, many Spaniards passed that way and inscribed their names on the walls of El Morro, but their journals said little about the rock or its Indian petroglyphs until Diego Pérez de Luxán, on March 11, 1682, noted that his party stopped "at a water hole at the foot of a rock. This place we named El Estanque del Peñol."[5] (*Peñol* is an intensification of *peña:* "a big rock.")

Before long, however, the word *morro* began to replace *peñol* and its cognates. A morro is not merely a bluff; the term suggests a headland, especially a rock promontory that marks a coastline for sailors—a navigational aid, as El Morro aided navigation of the land. On November 8, 1692, when Diego de Vargas passed by on an expedition to draw the Ácomas, Zunis, and Hopis back into the Spanish fold following the Pueblo Revolt of 1680, he noted in his journal that he had come to "this place of El Morro," "a very large, extended peñol, at the foot of which is a hollow like an inverted cupola in which rainwater collects."[6] Vargas left his own inscription on the rock, probably on that November day. (On his return to El Morro several weeks later, freezing rain and snow tormented his troop and him.)

*Here was the General Don Diego*
*de Vargas, who conquered*
*for our Holy Faith, and for the Royal*
*Crown, all the New*
*Mexico, at his expense,*
*Year of 1692*[7]

Spaniards continued to inscribe their names on the rock until 1774. Then, for the rest of the Spanish colonial era, none did. Nor, it would appear, did any literate person make an inscription during the period of Mexican control (1821–46). Thus, when Anglo Americans arrived on the scene, the Spanish inscriptions on El Morro appeared as vestiges of a bygone era, and the newcomers marveled at them.

Although El Morro derives its fame from Spanish inscriptions, the first detailed account of the site came from the pen of an American army officer. The ubiquitous Lieutenant James H. Simpson visited El Morro on September 17 and 18, 1849, on the home leg of the expedition into Navajo country that has already guided us to Canyon de Chelly and Chaco Canyon. (We will meet the expedition again when it stops at Zuni.)

As Simpson explained in his journal, a Mr. Lewis met him along the trail and offered to take him to a rock featuring "half an acre of inscriptions" and the ruins of a village on its summit. Lewis, whose identity remains unclear, evidently traded with Navajos in the area and knew the territory. He identified the rock as "the Moro" and the ruins on top of the rock as "the old Pueblo of Moro."[8]

The name El Morro, which appeared on a Spanish map as early as 1778, seems to have found wide enough usage that English speakers adopted it, and certainly Lewis was not the only Anglo American who knew the landmark's location.[9] In August 1849, a month before Simpson's party arrived, a group of forty-niners with a military escort passed by the site en route to California. Two of them left their names on the rock—the first of many English-language inscriptions to come.[10]

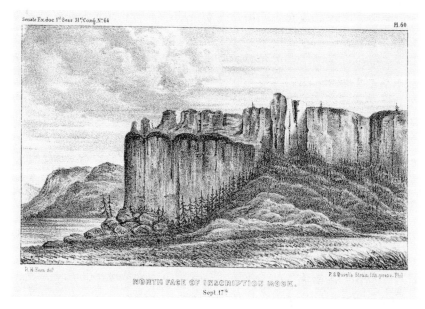

"North Face of Inscription Rock," lithograph based on a wash drawing by Richard H. Kern (From James H. Simpson, *Journal of a Military Reconnaissance . . . to the Navajo Country . . . in 1849;* courtesy DeGolyer Library, Southern Methodist University)

Lieutenant Simpson had no prior knowledge of El Morro, but he accepted Lewis's intriguing invitation to take a side trip to see it. Eight miles west of El Morro, on the banks of a tributary of the Zuni River called the Río Pescado (Simpson's Rio del Pescado), Lieutenant Simpson and Colonel Washington parted company. While Washington led the main army eastward along a trail at the base of the Zuni Mountains, Simpson took a more southerly route paralleling the current state highway that provides access to El Morro. William Bird, Simpson's personal assistant, and the expedition's artist Richard Kern accompanied the lieutenant. At the end of their first long day at El Morro, Simpson wrote:

*We came to a quadrangular mass of sandstone rock, of a pearly whitish aspect, from two hundred to two hundred and fifty feet in height, and strikingly peculiar on account of its massive character and the Egyptian style of its natural buttresses and domes. Skirting this stupendous mass of rock, on its left or north side, for about a mile, the guide, just as we had reached its eastern terminus, was noticed to leave us, and ascend a low mound or ramp at its base, the better, as it appeared, to scan the face of the rock, which he had scarcely reached before he cried out to us to come up. We immediately went up, and, sure enough, here were inscriptions, and some of them very beautiful; and, although, with those which we afterwards examined on the south face of the rock, there could not be said to be half an acre of them, yet the hyperbole was not near as extravagant as I was prepared to find it. The fact then being certain that here were indeed inscriptions of interest, if not of value, one of them dating as far back as 1606, all of them very ancient, and several of them very deeply as well as beautifully engraven, I gave directions for a halt—Bird at once proceeding to get up a meal, and Mr. Kern and myself to the work of making* fac similes *of the inscriptions.*[11] . . .

*It will be noticed that the greater portion of these inscriptions are in Spanish, with some little sprinkling of what appeared to be an attempt at Latin, and the remainder in hieroglyphics, doubtless of Indian origin.*

*The face of the rock, wherever these inscriptions are found, is of a fair plain surface, and vertical in position. The inscriptions, in most instances, have been engraved by persons standing at the base of the rock, and are, therefore, generally not higher than a man's head.*

*The labor of copying the inscriptions having employed us from about noon*

"Inscriptions on South Face of Inscription Rock," lithograph based on Kern's sketch (From James H. Simpson, *Journal of a Military Reconnaissance . . . to the Navajo Country . . . in 1849;* courtesy DeGolyer Library, Southern Methodist University)

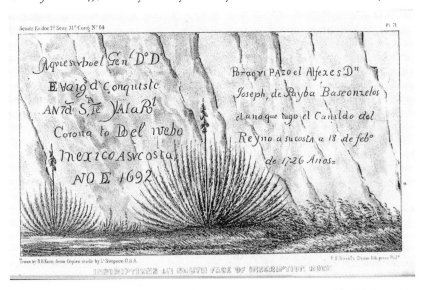

*till near sunset, and there yet being more than enough to keep us at work for the balance of the day, we suspended copying the remainder till the morrow, in order that before dark we might visit the "wonderful ruins" Lewis had assured us we would find on the summit of the rock. So, taking him as our guide, we went around to the south face of the wall, along which we continued until we came to an angle ... where, canopied by some magnificent rocks, and shaded by a few pine trees, the whole forming an exquisite picture, we found a cool and capacious spring—an accessory not more grateful to the lover of the beautiful than refreshing to the way-worn traveler [Plate 5]. Continuing along the east face of the rear projection or spur of the rock a few yards further, we came to an accessible escarpment, up which we commenced our ascent, the guide taking off his shoes to enable him to accomplish it safely. After slipping several times, with some little apprehension of an absolute slide off, and a pause to take breath, we at last reached the summit, to be regaled with a most extensive and pleasing prospect. On the north and east lay stretching from northwest to southeast the Sierra de Zuñi, richly covered with pine and cedar; to the south could be seen gracefully-swelling mounds and distant peaks, beautifully blue on account of remoteness; to the west appeared the horizontal outline of mésa heights, with here and there a break, denoting an intervening cañon or valley; and lying between all these objects and my point of view was a circuit of prairie, beautifully tasty on account of solitary and clustered trees, or sombrously dark on account of low mésas and oblong ridges covered with cedars.*

*This extensive scene sufficiently scanned, we proceeded to examine the ruins which the guide, true to his word, pointed out immediately before us.*[12]

Simpson and his party had arrived at the ruins of the village of A'ts'ina, which today is a major attraction of El Morro National Monument. Between 1250 and 1350, A'ts'ina was the easternmost of six large towns into which the people of the El Morro Valley had gathered for defense. At its peak it may have housed as many as fifteen hundred people. Its residents gradually abandoned A'ts'ina in the late 1300s, relocating to lower altitudes at and near modern-day Zuni. Archaeologist Richard Woodbury, who excavated the ruins in 1954 and 1955, applied the name A'ts'ina to the site, apparently at the suggestion of Zuni workmen who told him the name means "place of writings on the rock."[13] Known among Zunis as Heshoda Yalta, the ruins remain a place of spiritual importance.[14]

Simpson and his men proceeded to make a careful study of A'ts'ina, accurately recording its dimensions and noting its principal features:[15]

*These ruins present, in plan, a rectangle two hundred and six by three hundred and seven feet, the sides conforming to the four cardinal points. The apartments seem to have been chiefly upon the contour of the rectangle, the heaps of rubbish within the court indicating that here there had been some also. There appear to have been two ranges of rooms on the north side, and two on the west. The other two sides are in so ruinous a condition as to make the partition-walls indistinguishable. On the north side was found traceable a room seven feet four inches by eight and a half feet; and on the east side, one eight and a half by seven feet. There was one circular* estuffa *apparent, thirty-one feet in diameter, just in rear of the middle of the north face.... Here, as usual, immense quantities of broken pottery lay scattered around, and of patterns different from any we have hitherto seen. Indeed, it seems to me that, to have caused so much broken pottery, there must have been, at some time or other, a regular sacking of the place; and this, also, may account for this singular phenomenon being a characteristic of the ancient ruins generally in this country. At all events, we see nothing of this kind around the inhabited pueblos of the present day, in which pottery is still much used; and I can see no reason why, if their inhabitants were of their own accord to desert them, they should go to work and destroy the vessels made of this kind of material.*

*To the north and west, about three hundred yards distant, a deep cañon intervening, (see plan of rock, &c., above,) on the summit of the same massive rock upon which the inscriptions are found, we could see another ruined pueblo, in plan and size apparently similar to that I have just described. These ruins, on account of the intervening chasm, and want of time, we were not enabled to visit.*[16]

*What could have possessed the occupants of these villages to perch themselves so high up, and in such inaccessible localities, I cannot conceive, unless it were, as it probably was, from motives of security and defence.*

*The idea has been generally entertained, and I notice [Josiah] Gregg gives currency to it, that a portion of the ruins of this country are "at a great distance from any water, so that the inhabitants must have entirely depended upon rain, as is the case with the* Pueblo of Acoma *at the present day."*[17]

*Near all the ruins I have yet seen in this country, I have most generally found water; and in those cases where there was none, the dry bed of a stream, in con-*

*venient proximity, gave sufficient evidence that even here in time past, there was a supply....*

*But to continue my journal: The shades of evening falling upon us in our labors, we were constrained to retrace our way down to the plain; and it was not long before we were at the base of the rock, hovering over a bivouac fire, eating our suppers, and talking over the events of the day—the grim visage of the stupendous mass behind us occasionally fastening our attention by the sublimity of its appearance in the dim twilight.*

Owing to "the excitement of yesterday's discovery, together with rather a hard pallet, and the howling of the wolves," Simpson slept poorly that night, bivouacked tentless under the stars. He rose at 3:00 a.m., "for the purpose of hastening breakfast, in order that by daylight we might be ready to continue our labors upon the inscriptions." "The day opening beautifully, and the feathered race regaling us—an unusual treat—with their gay twittering, we hastened to the work of finishing the *fac similes*. These completed, and Mr. Kern having engraved as follows upon the rock: 'Lt. J. H. Simpson, U.S.A., and R. H. Kern, artist, visited and copied these inscriptions, September 17, 1849,' we found ourselves ready by 8 o'clock to commence our journey to overtake the command."

The engraving Kern made on that birdsong-filled morning can still be seen on the north face of El Morro. Contrary to Simpson's note, it actually bears two dates, September 18 as well as September 17.[18] Kern's most valuable images, however, were not on the rock but on his drawing pad. He drew the outline of the ruins atop the rock, sketched the potsherds that lay scattered about, recorded some forty inscriptions, nearly all with Spanish names and dates, and sketched views of El Morro from the north and south. And he did this in a mere two days, which included an ascent and descent of El Morro, without the stairways and cleared paths that modern visitors enjoy. Working with lightning speed, Kern made a few errors in transcription, but his drawings of what he called "written rocks" remain irreplaceable, for they reveal inscriptions that have since faded from the soft sandstone or have been destroyed by vandals.[19]

From El Morro, Simpson returned to Santa Fe and Fort Marcy to continue his duties as the chief of Topographical Engineers of the Department of New Mexico. In the first months of 1850 he completed his journal of

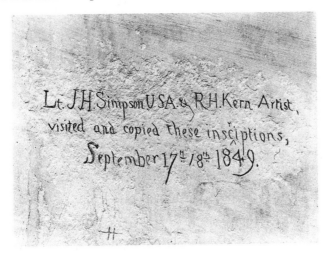

The names of Simpson and Kern, engraved by Kern on the
morning of September 18, 1849, on the north face of El Morro
(Photograph by George Grant, 1929; courtesy United States
National Park Service, Western Archeological and Conservation
Center, Tucson, Arizona, CAT WACC 6720)

the Navajo expedition—his first draft sufficed for the printer. Later that
year the U.S. government published *The Report of Lieutenant J. H. Simpson
of an Expedition into the Navajo Country in 1849,* bringing El Morro to the
attention of the reading public and leading readers to credit Simpson with
discovering the place he called Inscription Rock. Thereafter, the name Inscription Rock, along with El Morro, began to surface in Anglo American
accounts.[20]

Simpson's *Report* included the first visual representations of El Morro
in print. Lithographs of Kern's drawings of the inscriptions, complete with
English translations, appeared on ten plates in the document, which also
reproduced Kern's views of El Morro and the ruins and potsherds atop it.

Simpson remained in Santa Fe until the late summer of 1850, when poor
health forced his departure. He went on to work in Minnesota and Utah,
and by the time of the Civil War, his biographer says, he had "explored and
mapped more of the Far West than any other officer of the Army's Topographical Corps."[21] A New Jersey native, Simpson served the Union in various roles and was brevetted a brigadier general in March 1865. His career
continued after the war, chiefly involving the survey of rivers and harbors.

Richard Kern stayed in New Mexico until the summer of 1851, joining expeditions down the Río Grande and Río Pecos and up the Santa Fe Trail to the Cimarron Crossing. He supported himself, in part, with mapmaking commissions for the army, but he nevertheless had difficulty making ends meet. Ultimately, he joined yet another expedition westward into terra incognita, this one headed by Lorenzo Sitgreaves who, like Simpson, was an officer in the Army Corps of Topographical Engineers. Sitgreaves's orders instructed him to make a reconnaissance westward from Zuni.

On August 30, 1851, a few days after setting out, Sitgreaves, Kern, and their party stopped at El Morro, where Kern inscribed his name on the rock two more times. The party traversed northern Arizona and followed the Big Colorado down to Yuma. Sitgreaves, like Simpson before him, produced a valuable report illustrated by lithographs based on Kern's extraordinary field sketches. Subsequently, Kern accepted a position as topographer and artist on a survey of the 38th parallel, the purpose of which was to discover a feasible route for a transcontinental railroad. Led by Captain John Williams Gunnison, the expedition made its way into the Great Basin in the summer of 1853. There, in what is now west-central Utah, a band of Pahvant Utes, intent on avenging the murder of some of their number by a party of California-bound whites, attacked the surveyors at dawn one morning. Gunnison's body was later found pierced by fifteen arrows. Kern was shot through the heart. Six others also died and four escaped to tell the tale.[22]

Subsequent government explorers who visited El Morro saw no reason to duplicate the work of Simpson and Kern. Amiel Weeks Whipple, exploring the 35th parallel route in 1854, provided only a short description of "'El Moro,' called by Simpson Inscription Rock." He noted that Simpson had described it "minutely," and that "little remains to be added" to Simpson's description of the pueblo ruins atop the rock.[23]

Other visitors in the 1850s chose to elaborate on the emotional impact of El Morro's inscriptions—emotions shared by many visitors today. The German artist H. B. Möllhausen who, as a member of Whipple's expedition, sketched a number of the inscriptions, noted in his diary:

*There is a strange and even solemn feeling in standing thus before these mouldering and half-illegible, but still venerable, relics of past times. There are, indeed, to be seen in many parts of the world more striking memorials of former ages, but they are mostly known, and we have been prepared for the sight of them by historical records. But the impression was more powerful, and we were more immediately carried back in imagination to those long-departed generations, when we stood face to face with these newly-discovered tokens of the presence of the mail-clad Spaniards who also once stood here laboriously carving these inscriptions, and look around us on the objects that have ever since remained untouched, and tried to decipher the characters on which hardly a human eye had since then rested.*[24]

The allure of the past accounts for much of El Morro's impact but not all of it. Some early Anglo American visitors also found themselves stirred by El Morro's dramatic setting. Lieutenant Edward Fitzgerald Beale, traveling eastward in the winter of 1858, had done much and seen more. He'd made significant improvements to a road to California, and the previous summer he had experimented with the use of camels as beasts of burden in the deserts of the Southwest. (As mentioned in the chapter on Ácoma, the camels performed admirably, but the soldiers charged with handling them never lost their preference for mules.) Beale's route took him by way of El Morro, and he made this entry in his journal on February 19: "Up at 3 and off at 5 a.m. One would have to deal in superlatives altogether to describe the beauty of the country through which we have passed this morning. When at 9 a.m. we reached Inscription Rock, I was tired of exclaiming, as every hundred yards opened some new valley, 'how beautiful.' The rock itself seems to be a centre from which radiates valleys in all directions, and of marvelous beauty."[25]

The previous summer, on the outbound journey with the camels (while Beale took a slightly different route), Beale's nineteen-year-old assistant, May Humphreys Stacey, recorded nothing about the historic inscriptions but admired the scene itself. He wrote in his journal: "It was a romantic spot and one we shall all remember, when years have passed, and other scenes will have grown dim in the waters of memory. We parted from the place with regret, after having inscribed on the rock's soft face our names."[26]

✈

In the 1870s the main east-west route through New Mexico shifted from Zuni and El Morro to the north side of the Zuni Mountains, along the path

ALEX. GARDNER, Photographer.                                          3!! Seventh Street, Washington.

ACROSS THE CONTINENT ON THE KANSAS PACIFIC RAILROAD.

(ROUTE OF THE 35TH PARALLEL.)

El Moro, or Inscription Rock, Western New Mexico,
1000 MILES WEST OF MISSOURI RIVER.

"El Moro, or Inscription Rock, Western New Mexico, 1000 Miles West of Missouri
River." The earliest extant photograph of El Morro appears to have been this view,
taken by Alexander Gardner in 1867. At the bottom of his print, Gardner recorded
what he may have regarded as the oldest inscription on the rock: "Por aqui paso el
alferes du Joseph de Payba Basconzelos el ano que tuyo el cauldo del Reyno asucosta
a 18 de Febo de 1526 Anos." This early a date is improbable, yet in 1873 Samuel
Woodworth Cozzens similarly noted a 1526 inscription on the "lower left-hand
corner of El Moro" in *The Marvellous Country; or, Three Years in Arizona and New
Mexico, the Apaches' Home*, 304. (From Alexander Gardner, *Across the Continent on the
Kansas Pacific Railroad;* courtesy DeGolyer Library, Southern Methodist University)

soon followed by the railroad through Grants and Gallup, which would
eventually also accommodate Route 66 and Interstate 40. In his book,
*Some Strange Corners of Our Country,* published in 1892, the great promoter of the Southwest, Charles Lummis, guessed that only a few hundred
Anglo Americans had seen El Morro. With characteristic hyperbole, Lummis pronounced it "the most precious cliff, historically, possessed by any
nation on earth." He went on to lament that it was also, "I am ashamed to
say, the most utterly uncared-for." For Lummis, El Morro was a priceless

"stone autograph-album," and he feared that with "a few more years and a few more vandals . . . nothing will be left of what now makes the rock so precious."[27] He urged the government to take measures to protect El Morro, and, in time, it did. On December 8, 1906, Theodore Roosevelt, one of Lummis's former Harvard classmates, set aside 160 acres around the peñol as El Morro National Monument and prohibited further carving on the rock.[28]

Roosevelt took this action under the authority of the Antiquities Act, which Congress had passed just six months earlier. The act allowed the executive branch to proclaim as national monuments "historic landmarks, historic and prehistoric structures, and other objects of historic or scientific interest that are situated upon the lands owned or controlled by the Government."[29] Devil's Tower, a landmark in Wyoming, was the first national monument created under the act. El Morro, together with two sites in Arizona, the Petrified Forest and Montezuma's Castle, came next. Before Roosevelt left office in 1909, he established a total of eighteen national monuments, several of them in the Southwest: Chaco Canyon and the Gila Cliff Dwellings in New Mexico, and Tonto (an archaeological site), Tuma-cácori (a Spanish colonial mission), and the Grand Canyon in Arizona.

When Charles Lummis wrote about El Morro again in 1925, more than three decades after warning that its inscriptions might be lost, he celebrated that fact that the site "has been fenced, with a locked gate; a railing along the foot of the cliff lets visitors close enough to read the inscriptions, but not to do any autographing of their own; and cactus planted below the rail discourages any crawling under."[30] Lummis credited the part-time custodian of El Morro, Evon Vogt, for the improvements. Paid $10 a month to look after the monument, Vogt kept watch from his ranch nine miles to the west, near Ramah. A trickle of tourists had begun to come to El Morro after the Fred Harvey Company opened its El Navajo Hotel in Gallup in 1918, and they had to pass Vogt's ranch to get there.[31] Although woefully underpaid for what the government defined as part-time work, Vogt took his responsibilities seriously. Lummis expressed satisfaction that Vogt "has placed in water-proof frames by each historic inscription my transliteration and translation; and has supervised the sandstoning-out of intrusive names. It is comforting that after three-quarters of a century of neglect and vandalism the most interesting and important 'Inscription Rock' in the world is at last safeguarded."[32]

Thanks both to accident and design, El Morro's inscriptions and remarkable setting remain largely intact. The first written impressions of it have also endured. As one early twentieth-century guidebook put it, "You will be a dry-as-dust indeed if you do not feel an odd sort of thrill as you put your finger tips upon the chiseled autographs of the men who won for Spain an empire and held it dauntlessly.... Then there is the enjoyment of the place itself—the sunny solitude, and the glorious extended views, the long blue line of the Zuñi Mountains, the pale spires of La Puerta de los Gigantes."[33]

Mary Austin, whose many books enjoyed a wide audience during her lifetime, found El Morro so compelling that she chose it as the place where her spirit would dwell forever, the place she would "haunt." As she wrote in 1924, ten years before her death, "You of a hundred years from now, if when you visit the Rock, you see the cupped silken wings of the argemone [a desert flower] burst and float apart when there is no wind; or if, when all around is still, a sudden stir in the short-leaved pines, or fresh eagle feathers blown upon the shrine, that will be I, making known in such fashion as I may the land's undying quality."[34]

In the second decade of the twenty-first century, El Morro, still splendidly isolated, remains one of the Southwest's most iconic places. Indeed, as one of the leading interpreters of the region has suggested, it may be the very heart of the Southwest.[35]

# 7 Grand Canyon

Nearly 280 miles long, a mile deep, and 5 to 18 miles across, the Grand Canyon is an American icon and a UNESCO World Heritage Site. Thanks to innumerable images in film, print, and electronic media, the nearly 5 million tourists who visit it every year have a notion of what they will see long before they see it. They know that once they reach the canyon's edge, they will behold one of the planet's most spectacular geographies. By contrast, the first Europeans to encounter the Grand Canyon—members of Coronado's epic expedition of 1540—had no such expectations. The enormity of the canyon came as a colossal surprise. Having never before seen anything comparable, they struggled to make sense of the scene and ultimately strained to describe it to others. For a certainty, they were unable to extract meaning from the canyon's revelation of geological time, which lies at the center of our modern understanding of its grandeur.

A week after taking violent possession of the Zuni pueblo of Hawikku and crestfallen that none of the stone villages in the vicinity possessed the riches they were endowed with in legend, Francisco Vázquez de Coronado sent a detachment westward to investigate rumors of other, more prosperous towns. Led by Indian guides, perhaps from Hawikku, Pedro de Tovar set out on July 15 (on the Julian calendar, not our present Gregorian calendar) along a well-worn trail following a succession of waterholes: Jacob's Well, Navajo Springs, Tanner Springs, Greasewood Springs, and White Cone Springs. Tovar's journey, however, gained the invaders only more disappointment, for the Hopi pueblos, or Tusayán to the Spaniards, proved no more inviting or prosperous than the Zuni villages.

But at Tusayán, Tovar heard mention of a great river lying still farther to the west. Tovar's report interested Coronado intensely. Like other sixteenth-century Spaniards, he believed the North American continent to be much narrower than it actually is. He and his patron, Viceroy Antonio de Mendoza, had planned to resupply his New Mexico expedition by sending vessels up the Gulf of California and into a great river the Spaniards had recently discovered but not yet entered or named. Perhaps Coronado could find that river by sending men farther west, beyond the Hopi villages, and thus strengthen his expedition and perhaps one day establish a colony by the sea.

Setting out on August 25, 1540, with a dozen men, field marshal (*maestre de campo*) García López de Cárdenas, a nobleman from Madrid and a relative of the viceroy, retraced Tovar's path to Tusayán. From there, this most trusted of Coronado's lieutenants engaged Hopi guides to lead him westward to what we know today as the south rim of the Grand Canyon. They followed one of several likely Indian trails across plains and mesas that the Spaniards described as an uninhabited desert.[1] Some twenty years later, Pedro de Castañeda de Nájera recounted the story:

*When they had walked for twenty days [leagues?] they arrived at the canyons of the river.[2] When [the company] was camped at its edge it appeared that it was more than three or four leagues through the air to the opposite edge.[3] It is an elevated land covered by forests of short, gnarled pines. [It is] very cold to the north. Even though it was [then] the hot season, it was not possible to live at this canyon because of the cold. For three days they searched for the way down to the river.*

*From that height the stream appeared to be one* braza *[about six feet] across, but from the reports of the Indians it stretched half a league wide. Descent [to the river] was impossible, because at the end of three days the most agile [men] set themselves to climbing down at a place that seemed to them the least difficult. [They were] Captain [Pablo de] Melgosa, a Juan Galeras, and another companion. They descended a long time in view of those [who remained] above, until their forms were lost from sight. Because of the height, [one] was unable to see them. They returned at the hour of four in the afternoon. They did not complete the descent, because of great obstacles they found. What from above seemed easy was not, but rather very rugged and rough. They said that they had descended a third of the way. From where they had reached, the river appeared to be very large. In accordance with what they saw, what the Indians said about its width was true. From the top they had distinguished several smallish blocks broken off from the cliff, apparently the height of a man. The [men] who climbed down swore that when they got to them, they were larger than the principal [church] tower in Sevilla.*[4]

What an experience! In the immense, deceptive distances of the Grand Canyon, a creek that had appeared six feet across turned out to be hundreds of yards in width, and boulders that at first seemed the size of a man had proved to be larger than one of the grandest structures existing in all of Spain. Most Spaniards taking ship to the New World passed through Seville to embark from nearby Cádiz. They were sure to have seen the tower of the cathedral of Seville (a former minaret known as La Giralda). It rose 250 feet high and seemed to soar above the rest of the city.[5] Coronado and every one of his compatriots in New Spain would have understood that the boulders being compared to the tower were indeed of fabulous size.

Still, having established that the canyon was immense, what more need be reported of it? From the Spaniards' point of view there was nothing of value or use in all of its vast, if chromatic, desolation, and the lands of the rim were equally inhospitable, as they were almost wholly bereft of water: "Until that point, every day in the late afternoon they had made a side trip of one or two leagues into the interior in search of streams. When they had traveled another four days the guides said it was impossible to go on because there was no water in [the next] three or four days of travel. Because of that, when [the Indians themselves] traveled that way, they brought women along loaded with water in gourd jars. They buried the gourd jars of water for their return. [They also said] that the distance our people traveled in two days they traveled in one."

Putting aside the intimation that the natives used their women as pack animals for carrying water, one element missing in this account is any consideration that the Hopi guides might be holding back information. The Hopis knew the canyon well. Then, as now, they revered important sacred sites in the canyon, made pilgrimages, and collected plants and minerals there. They could have shown the Spaniards trails that led to the river, but they chose not to. They may have wanted to get the Spaniards lost, and then abandon them to die in waterless terrain. At the least, they wanted the Spaniards to find nothing of interest, nothing that might induce them to stay longer or, once they left, to return.

This episode presents an excellent example of the one-sidedness of the historical record. Castañeda's account, written twenty years after the fact, is shot through with ambiguity and omissions—what actually happened when Tovar and his men accosted the Hopi? At which village did this take place? And did Cárdenas never suspect that his so-called guides were duping him? Scores more such questions might be asked, yet in the absence of an account of events from a Hopi point of view, the Spanish version of this pivotal moment in history remains preeminent. Interestingly, a countervailing account has recently appeared. In *Moquis and Kastiilam: Hopis, Spaniards, and the Trauma of History,* Thomas E. Sheridan and no fewer than six Hopi and Anglo coeditors have drawn on Hopi oral tradition, as well as the historical and archaeological record, to suggest that Tovar's initial encounter with the Hopis, evidently at the village of Kawayka'a, may have been as destructive as Coronado's before Hawikku, that members of Cárdenas's command may have perished in the Grand Canyon, and that Hopi subterfuge was indeed deliberate and well planned.[6] There can be little doubt that they intended to drive the Spaniards away, if not kill them outright. The details of the past may never be known, but the available "facts" now shed new light on a momentous encounter.

The expedition to the canyon's rim yielded neither wealth nor opportunity, but it did contribute to one great insight. In the aftermath of Cárdenas's exploration, by comparing the reports of multiple explorers, Spanish authorities correctly deduced that the river glinting far away at the bottom of the canyon was in fact the same great stream that debouched into the Gulf of California. Castañeda eventually wrote:

*This river was the [Río] del Tizón [Firebrand River], much closer to its source than at the place beyond which Melchior Díaz and his company did not pass.[7] According to what was later apparent, these Indians were at the same level [of society as the Indians contacted by Díaz]. [López de Cárdenas's company] turned around at that point, so that trip had no further result. En route they saw a string of beads [made by] water that fell from a great rock. They learned from the guides that some of the clusters that hung like crystal breasts were salt. They went [up] to it and gathered a quantity, which they brought back and distributed when they reached Cíbola. There they gave a written report of what they had seen to their general, because one Pedro de Sotomayor had gone with don García López ... as chronicler of the expedition.*

Unfortunately, Sotomayor's record of the journey to the Grand Canyon and back appears to have been lost. We have only Castañeda's retrospective summary and a second account by an anonymous writer who, like Castañeda, did not make the journey but who might have seen Sotomayor's report or heard López de Cárdenas and his companions describe what they saw.[8] As a result, the first written impressions of the canyon are decidedly secondhand.

Several years later, under arrest in Spain and accused of crimes against Pueblo Indians that included unleashing murderous dogs and permitting rapes, burnings, and robbery, López de Cárdenas penned an account of his journey to the Colorado River, but the Grand Canyon itself had made so little impression on him that he failed to mention it.[9] Coronado, too, omitted mention of the canyon in his reports. For them the canyon was strictly an obstacle—not an opportunity and certainly not a revelation.

Over the next two centuries, Spaniards had little reason to penetrate the environs of the Grand Canyon. As far as was known, its lands contained neither precious metals nor exploitable Indians and possessed no strategic importance. Nonetheless, a few Spaniards eventually approached the canyon in the course of other work. On November 7, 1776, two intrepid Franciscans, Francisco Atanasio Domínguez, whom we will meet again in the chapters on Santa Fe and Taos, and Silvestre Vélez de Escalante, crossed the Colorado River upstream from the Grand Canyon at a ford that was thereafter known as the Crossing of the Fathers, a place now lying beneath the waters of Lake Powell. Domínguez and Escalante, with a small party that included the talented cartographer Bernardo de Miera y Pacheco, had set out from New Mexico the previous July in search of a route to California. Their wanderings took them on a perilous and bewildering journey through southwestern Colorado and across much of the

Great Basin. Cold weather having set in, they abandoned hope of reaching California and turned back for New Mexico, soon finding themselves in a maze of canyons and vertical scarps beside the Colorado River near the present-day Arizona-Utah border. For days they hunted in vain for a path down to the river and then for a ford. When finally, after much travail, they successfully crossed to the eastern side, they celebrated wildly, "praising God our Lord and firing off some muskets in demonstration of the great joy we all felt in having overcome so great a problem."[10]

In June 1776, unbeknownst to Domínguez and Escalante and a month before they departed New Mexico, yet another Franciscan, equally courageous and peripatetic, had reached the rim of the actual Grand Canyon. Francisco Tomás Hermenegildo Garcés was also seeking a route between New Mexico and California, but he set out traveling west to east, starting from the Mohave villages on the Colorado River, where it divides Arizona from California. Eager to contact the natives of the region as well as to understand its geography, he journeyed with only a few native guides, who eventually led him into the labyrinthine canyon where dwelled the people whose name he rendered as Jabesúa and which modern English gives as Havasupai. This was Havasu or Cataract Canyon, a side branch of the Grand Canyon, part of which lies in Grand Canyon National Park and the rest within the Havasupai Reservation.

The descent into the canyon was perilous, but Garcés informs us only that the way was "difficult," especially where it threaded along a "lofty cliff" with a "horrible abyss" at its side.[11] His route then grew worse, and Garcés was obliged to leave his mule behind and proceed on foot, finally climbing down a sheer face of rock by means of a long ladder. Having safely descended, he continued to Supai, the canyon-wrapped village of the Jabesúas. He stayed there five days, during which he may well have descended the canyon still farther and glimpsed the Colorado River, where the blue waters of Havasu Creek flow into it. The laconic Garcés, however, makes no mention of how he spent his time with the Jabesúas, except that they fed him well.

Having come to Havasu from the west, he now departed to the east, bound for Hopi, or, as the Spanish then called it, Moqui. His route may have climbed to the plateau by way of the logically named Moqui Trail

Canyon. Soon he experienced the full splendor of the main canyon. Where exactly Garcés gazed into the void is open to debate. The traditional interpretation places him between the well-known South Rim lookouts of Moran Point and Desert View, close to where Cárdenas had presumably beheld the canyon more than two centuries earlier. A strong case, however, can also be made for placing Garcés much farther west and somewhat north, near Yuma Point.[12] Either way, the Havasupais guiding Garcés would have led him along branches of the well-established trail linking Supai and Hopi, so that in all likelihood he eventually trod the same route along which Hopi guides would have brought Cárdenas, coming from the opposite direction.

Garcés may have failed to record his exact location, but he did not neglect to make note of his impressions. His first English translator, the renowned ornithologist Elliott Coues, believed that in the following passage Garcés refers to the canyon steeps as a "sierra," and cites instances of his applying the term to other canyon scarps. Garcés was enough awed by what he saw that he bestowed a name on the gaping crack in the earth that stretched before him. He called the portion of the Grand Canyon he surveyed the Puerto de Bucareli in honor of Antonio María de Bucareli, then the viceroy of New Spain. If indeed he stood where tradition places him, the Puerto de Bucareli would be the portion of the canyon downstream from the entry of the Little Colorado River. The name would linger long enough to appear on a map that Alexander von Humboldt published in 1811.[13] The Garcés diary entry for June 26, 1776, begins:

*I traveled four leagues southeast, and south, and turning to the east; and halted at the sight of the most profound* caxones *[cañones or canyons] which ever onward continue (que aun todavia siguen); and within these flows the Rio Colorado. There is seen (vése) a very great sierra, which in the distance (looks) blue; and there runs from southeast to northwest a pass open to the very base, as if the sierra were cut artificially to give entrance to the Rio Colorado into these lands. I named this singular (pass) Puerto de Bucaréli, and though to all appearances would not seem to be very great the difficulty of reaching thereunto, I considered this to be impossible in consequence of the difficult caxones which intervened. From this position the pass bore eastnortheast. Also were there seen on the north some smokes, which my companions said were those of the Indians whom they name Payuches [Paiutes], who live on the other side of the river. I am astonished at the roughness of this country, and at the barrier which nature has fixed therein.*[14]

For Garcés, as for Cárdenas, the canyon was an obstacle, yet his experience at its edge was different from his predecessor's. He never seriously suffered for water, and in high summer he and his guides journeyed without trial across the same ground where, according to the information Cárdenas received, cached pots of water were necessary. The reason was simple. Garcés treated his Indian companions with kindness and respect, and so he benefited fully from their knowledge of the land.[15]

Nevertheless, Garcés viewed the canyon through a narrow intellectual lens. In order for people to appreciate more fully the Grand Canyon, the knowledge and values that framed their understanding would have to change in fundamental ways.

In a marvelous and thrifty book titled *How the Canyon Became Grand* historian Stephen J. Pyne posits that three broad revolutions ultimately enabled people to grapple with the significance of the Grand Canyon.[16] The first was the Romantic revolution, a key element of which was a new aesthetics that attributed high value not just to that which was pretty and well composed, but to scenes and phenomena that were powerful and emotionally moving, even frightening, but that somehow revealed the deeper forces of the world. This was the quality of the sublime, and its elevation to the highest realm of aesthetic appreciation opened the door for people to see nature in a fundamentally new way.

The second revolution involved the scientific discovery of "deep time." When Garcés roved the Southwest, the existence of the world, of planet Earth, was considered by "civilized" people to have endured for no more than six thousand years.[17] Over the next century and a half, in one of the greatest conceptual revolutions in human history, that calculation would extend by nearly six powers of ten, to 4.6 billion years. Viewed in the context of deep time, the layered stratigraphy of the vertical faces of the walls of the Grand Canyon becomes profoundly awe-inspiring. It tells us of the immensity and antiquity of our earthly home and of the cosmos that contains it. It teaches us our place within time and space. But without the perspective of deep time, the walls and the erosional forces that sculpted them remain merely baffling.

The third revolution was political. The *grandness* of Grand Canyon resides partly in the sense that it belongs to the people, not to a lord or oligarch. It is a *national* park. It is even supranational in that it is a World Heritage Site, a place visited and valued by people from around the globe. In late June 1776, when Garcés peered into its bluing distances, the spark of political revolution was nine days from bursting into flame in Philadelphia, two thousand miles to the east. As though yoked together, Western culture's aesthetic and scientific revolutions were also gaining momentum, fed by the inquiries and sensibilities of Europe's Age of Enlightenment.

It would take time for the implications of these revolutions to develop, but at each step of the way, they would inform the world's growing appreciation of the Grand Canyon, and the story of the canyon, to a significant degree, would reflect not so much how the canyon changed, but how people changed their way of seeing it.

In 1861, the U.S. government published reports by two explorers: First Lieutenant Joseph Christmas Ives, a Yale- and West Point–trained scientist and officer of the Army Corps of Topographical Engineers, and John Strong Newberry, the pioneering geologist who accompanied him. These were the first descriptions of the canyon to appear in print in English. Engravings based on sketches by two German-born artist-explorers, Balduin Möllhausen and Friedrich W. von Egloffstein, illustrated the reports and gave Americans their first graphic images of the Grand Canyon.

A few years earlier, the War Department, responding to continued restlessness in the Mormon enclave of Utah, resolved to learn how supplies might be delivered to the region should the army be obliged to quell a rebellion. Accordingly, Lieutenant Ives received orders to explore the Colorado River by boat to assess the river's navigability above Fort Yuma.[18] Ives brought valuable experience to this assignment, for in 1853 and '54 he had crossed the Southwest as a member of Lieutenant A. W. Whipple's survey of the 35th parallel route. In Philadelphia Ives oversaw the fabrication of a special steel-hulled, stern-wheeled steamship, which he named *Explorer*. He then directed that the crated and unassembled parts of *Explorer* be shipped around South America and delivered to the mouth of the Colorado River, where he and his crew bolted it together on the mosquito-plagued mud-flats of the delta. At last, on Christmas Day (his birthday and the source of his middle name) 1857, Ives and his men began to steam upriver. He was twenty-eight years old.

Over the next two months *Explorer* chugged northward past Fort Yuma and through the Chemehuevi and Mohave Valleys. At the mouth of Black Canyon, just below the site of modern Hoover Dam, the ship collided with a submerged rock, which brought both the vessel and its upstream journey to an abrupt halt.

After determining that *Explorer* could go no farther, Ives continued up-stream by skiff for another thirty miles. He found the going perilous but enchanting. Ives had drunk deeply of the Romantic sensibility, and his account of the canyon (which is now inundated by Lake Mead) is a celebration of the sublime: "No description can convey an idea of the varied and majestic grandeur of this peerless water-way. Wherever the river makes a turn the entire panorama changes, and one startling novelty after another appears and disappears with bewildering rapidity. Stately facades, august cathedrals, amphitheaters, rotundas, castellated walls, and rows of time-stained ruins, surmounted by every form of tower, minaret, dome, and spire, have been moulded from the cyclopean masses of rock that form the mighty defile. The solitude, the stillness, the subdued light, and the vastness of every surrounding object, produce an impression of awe that ultimately becomes almost painful."[19]

Having confirmed that they had reached the head of navigation, Ives and his party sailed the repaired *Explorer* downstream to the Mohave villages, where they rendezvoused with Lieutenant John Tipton and a train of more than one hundred pack mules bearing supplies from Yuma. While *Explorer* returned to Yuma, Ives, Newberry, Tipton, the German artists, and a troop of soldiers headed eastward over a new wagon road into the high-lands of the Colorado Plateau. They were guided by three Mohaves, including an exceptional individual, Ireteba, whom Ives had met on the Whipple expedition in 1854.[20] Eventually recruiting additional guides from among the Hualapais, whose domain they had entered, the Americans approached the western end of the Grand Canyon by way of Diamond Creek Canyon, which descends northward to the Colorado River from Peach Springs, the

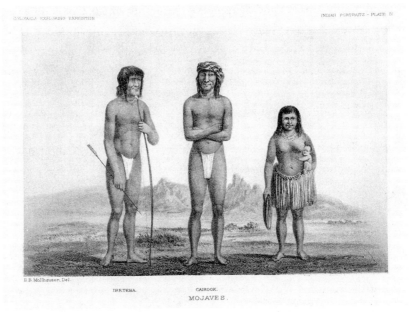

"Mojaves," toned lithograph (black with red and gold). Joseph Ives knew well the
two Mohaves who had guided the Whipple expedition in 1854—"They were noble
specimens of their race, and rendered the party invaluable service" (Ives, *Report upon
the Colorado River,* 68)—and he sought them out to guide him a second time in 1858.
Ireteba appears at the left and Cairook in the center (the identities of the woman
and child on the right are not known). Cairook died in prison in Yuma the year
after this portrait was made, having offered himself as a hostage to assure peace with
U.S. forces. Ireteba would become the major spokesperson for his people, visiting
Washington, D.C., and meeting with President Lincoln during the Civil War. The
image is based on a sketch by Möllhausen, reworked for the lithographer, perhaps by
John James Young. (From Joseph Ives, *Report upon the Colorado River,* 1861; courtesy
DeGolyer Library, Southern Methodist University)

most important source of water for many a mile. One writer has characterized Ives's descent of Diamond Creek as "the first journey from rim to
river" made by a non-Indian (although Garcés, having failed to mention it
in his diary, may have preceded Ives).[21]

Ives saw himself in the mold of the heroic geographer and explorer Alexander von Humboldt, whose global fame in the early nineteenth century
was exceeded only by Napoleon's. In the Grand Canyon Ives would measure and evaluate a hitherto unknown domain and, like Humboldt, he
would also interpret his experiences in emotional terms for the appreciation

of an attentive world. In his account the trip down Diamond Creek and into the Grand Canyon becomes a journey into hell:

*Our guides . . . plunged into a narrow and precipitous ravine that opened at our feet, and we followed as well as we could, stumbling along a rough and rocky pathway. The Hualpais [Hualapais] were now of great assistance, for the ravines crossed and forked in intricate confusion; even Ireteba, who had hitherto led the train, became at a loss how to proceed, and had to put the little Haulpais in front. The latter, being perfectly at home, conducted us rapidly down the declivity. The descent was great and the trail blind and circuitous. A few miles of difficult travelling brought us to a narrow valley flanked by steep and high slopes; a sparkling stream crossed its centre, a gurgling in some tall grass near by announced the presence of a spring. The water was delicious. The grass in the neighborhood was sparse, but of good quality.*

*This morning we left the valley and followed the course of a creek down a ravine, in the bed of which the water at intervals sank and rose for two or three miles, when it altogether disappeared. The ravine soon attained the proportions of a cañon. The bottom was rocky and irregular, and there were some jump-offs over which it was hard to make the pack animals pass. The vegetation began to disappear, leaving only a few stunted cedars projecting from the sides of the rugged bluffs. The place grew wilder and grander. The sides of the tortuous cañon became loftier, and before long we were hemmed in by walls two thousand feet high. The scenery much resembled that in the Black cañon, excepting that the rapid descent, the increasing magnitude of the collossal piles that blocked the end of the vista, and the corresponding depth and gloom of the gaping chasms into which we were plunging, imparted an unearthly character to a way that might have resembled the portals of the infernal regions. Harsh screams issuing from aerial recesses in the cañon sides, and apparitions of goblin-like figures perched in the rifts and hollows of the impending cliffs, gave an odd reality to this impression. At short distances other avenues of equally magnificent proportions came in from one side or the other; and no trail being left on the rocky pathway, the idea suggested itself that were the guides to desert us our experience might further resemble that of the dwellers in the unblest abodes — in the difficulty of getting out.*

*Huts of the rudest construction, visible here and there in some sheltered niche or beneath a projecting rock, and the sight of a hideous old squaw, staggering under a bundle of fuel, showed that we had penetrated into the domestic retreats of the Hualpais nation. Our party being, in all probability, the first company of whites that had ever been seen by them, we had anticipated producing a great effect, and were a little chagrined when the old woman, and two or three others of both sexes that were met, went by without taking the slightest notice of us. If pack-trains had been in the habit of passing twenty times a day they could not have manifested a more complete indifference.*

*Seventeen miles of this strange travel had now been accomplished. The road was becoming more difficult, and we looked ahead distrustfully into the dark and apparently interminable windings, and wondered where we were to find a camping place. At last we struck a wide branch cañon coming in from the south, and saw with joyful surprise a beautiful and brilliantly clear stream of water gushing over a pebbly bed in the centre, and shooting from between the rocks in sparkling jets and miniature cascades. On either side was an oasis of verdure— young willow and a patch of grass. Camp was speedily formed, and men and mules have had a welcome rest after their fatiguing journey.*

*A hundred yards below the camp the cañon takes a turn; but as it was becoming very dark, all further examinations were postponed till to-morrow. In the course of the evening Ireteba came into my tent, and I asked him how far we had still to travel before reaching the great river. To my surprise he informed me that the mouth of the creek is only a few yards below the turn, and that we are now camped just on the verge of the Big Cañon of the Colorado.*[22]

The next morning, April 5, revealed the great river:

*A short walk down the bed of Diamond river, on the morning after we had reached it, verified the statement of Ireteba, and disclosed the famous Colorado cañon. The view from the ridge, beyond the creek to which the Hualpais had first conducted us, had shown that the plateaus further north and east were several thousand feet higher than that through which the Colorado cuts at this point, and the cañons proportionally deeper; but the scene was sufficiently grand to well repay for the labor of the descent. The cañon was similar in character to others that have been mentioned, but on a larger scale, and thus far unrivalled in grandeur. Mr. Mollhausen has taken a sketch, which gives a better idea of it than any description. The course of the river could be traced for only a hundred yards above or below, but what had been seen from the table-land showed that we were at the apex of a great southern land. The walls on either side, rose directly out of the water. The river was about fifty yards wide. The channel was studded with rocks, and the torrent rushed through like a mill-race. [Plate 6]*

*The day was spent in examination of the localities. Dr. Newberry has had opportunities for observation seldom afforded to the geologist. This plateau formation has been undisturbed by volcanic action, and the sides of the cañons exhibit all of the series that compose the table-lands of New Mexico, presenting, perhaps the most splendid exposure of stratified rocks that there is in the world.*[23]

After a few days of exploration, Ireteba and the other Mohaves having departed on a difficult homeward journey, the rest of the party climbed out of the canyon and, intent on striking the river at a second place in hopes of finding a crossing, resumed their eastward trek over the plateau of the South Rim. Soon they saw their opportunity. Following the same path previously trod by Father Garcés, they descended Cataract or Havasu Canyon, where the expedition's cartographer, the Bavarian topographer and artist Friederich W. von Egloffstein, made a nearly fatal attempt to reach the river. Ives told the story in his report:

*Camp 73, Colorado Plateau, April 14.—Lieutenant Tipton, Mr. Egloffstein, Mr. Peacock, and myself, with a dozen men, formed the party to explore the cañon. It was about five miles to the precipice. The descent of the latter was accomplished without serious trouble.... Every few moments, low falls and ledges, which we had to jump or slide down, were met with, till there had accumulated a formidable number of obstacles to be encountered in returning. Like other cañons, it was circuitous, and at each turn we were impatient to find something novel or interesting. We were deeper in the bowels of the earth than we had ever been before, and surrounded by walls and towers of such imposing dimensions that it would be useless to attempt describing them; but the effects of magnitude had begun to pall, and the walk from the foot of the precipice was monotonously dull; no sign of life could be discerned above or below. At the end of thirteen miles from the precipice an obstacle presented itself that there seemed to be no possibility of overcoming. A stone slab, reaching from one side of the cañon to the other, terminated the plane which we were descending. Looking over the edge it appeared that the level was forty feet below. This time there was no trail along the side bluffs, for these were smooth and perpendicular. A spring of water rose from the bed of the cañon not far above, and trickled over the ledge, forming*

CAMP — COLORADO PLATEAU

"Camp—Colorado Plateau," on April 10, when a light snow fell. A toned lithograph (black with gray), based on a sketch by Möllhausen, redrawn by John James Young. (From Joseph Ives, *Report upon the Colorado River*, 1861; courtesy DeGolyer Library, Southern Methodist University)

*a pretty cascade. It was supposed that the Indians must have come to this point merely to procure water, but this theory was not altogether satisfactory, and we sat down upon the rocks to discuss the matter.*

*Mr. Egloffstein lay down by the side of the creek, and projecting his head over the ledge to watch the cascade, discovered a solution to the mystery. Below the shelving rock, and hidden by it and the fall, stood a crazy looking ladder, made of rough sticks bound together with thongs of bark.*[24]

This was the same location at which Garcés had encountered a ladder in 1776. Although it was probably not the self-same one Garcés had used, it nevertheless was hardly in the peak of condition.[25] This ladder

*was almost perpendicular, and rested upon a bed of angular stones. The rounds had become rotten from the incessant flow of water. Mr. Egloffstein, anxious to have the first view of what was below, scrambled over the ledge and got his feet upon the upper round. Being a solid weight, he was too much for the inse-*

J. J. YOUNG from a sketch by F. W. EGLOFFSTEIN

BIG CAÑON.

"Big Cañon," lithograph by John James Young based on a sketch by
Friedrich W. von Egloffstein. Ives wrote: "A sketch taken upon the
spot by Mr. Egloffstein does better justice than any description can do
to the marvelous scene" (110). Egloffstein's work was less realistic than
Möllhausen's and merits Wallace Stegner's criticism that it arose from
a "stunned imagination" (*Beyond the Hundredth Meridian,* caption to a
reproduction of this image following p. 92). (From Joseph Ives, *Report
upon the Colorado River,* 1861; courtesy DeGolyer Library, Southern
Methodist University)

*cure fabric, which commenced giving way. One side fortunately stood firm, and holding on to this with a tight grip, he made a precipitate descent. The other side and all the rounds broke loose and accompanied him to the bottom in a general crash, effectually cutting off all communication. Leaving us to devise means of getting him back he ran to the bend to explore. The bottom of the cañon had been reached. He found that he was at the edge of a stream ten or fifteen yards wide, fringed with cottonwoods and willows. The walls of the cañon spread out for a short distance, leaving room for a narrow belt of bottom land, on which were fields of corn and a few scattered huts.... The cañon Mr. Egloffstein saw could not be followed far; there were cascades just below. He perceived, however, that he was very near to its mouth, though perhaps a thousand feet greater altitude, and an Indian pointed out the exact spot where it united with the cañon of the Rio Colorado.*[26]

Egloffstein's nerve should earn our admiration. Having narrowly survived a slide down a disintegrating ladder, he was cut off from his companions, and yet he proceeded to perform a reconnaissance. Ives continues, "Having looked at all that was to be seen, it now remained to get Mr. Egloffstein back. The slings upon the soldiers' muskets were taken off and knotted together, and a line thus made which reached to the bottom. Whether it would support his weight was a matter of experiment. The general impression was that it would not, but of the two evils—breaking his neck or remaining among the Yampais [Havasupais]—he preferred the former, and fastened the strap around his shoulders. It was a hard straight lift. The ladder pole was left, and rendered great assistance to both us and the rope, and the ascent was safely accomplished."[27]

Egloffstein having been rescued, the party continued eastward, skirting the northern slopes of the Bill Williams and San Francisco mountains and continuing to the Little Colorado River, which the men crossed on May 1 in a portable raft near the modern town of Leupp. Here Ives split his party, sending Lieutenant Tipton, the supply train, and Möllhausen, who knew the route, to Zuni and Fort Defiance. Ives, meanwhile, led a smaller group, which included Newberry, Egloffstein, and a few soldiers, northward across the Painted Desert to the Hopi pueblos, intending to employ guides to take them to a ford on the Colorado by which they might cross to the eastern side of the "Big Canyon." But the Hopis wanted nothing to do with Ives or his expedition. Failing to find willing guides, and failing also to reach the canyon on their own, the Americans ultimately turned eastward to Fort Defiance and Santa Fe. After a brief rest, Ives took bone-jolting stage-coaches south to El Paso and west to San Diego. Ever in motion, he then made his way back to Fort Yuma, sold *Explorer,* and returned to San Diego to take passage on vessels that would carry him to San Francisco and finally New York.[28]

Born in New York and raised in New Haven, Ives was unusual among officers with northern roots. He declined an offered captaincy in 1861 and joined the Confederate army, serving as an aide-de-camp to President Jefferson Davis, with whom he had enjoyed a friendship before the outbreak of war.

With the publication of Ives's description in 1861, the Big Cañon was on its way toward becoming the *Grand* Canyon. Having read Pedro de Castañeda's account of López de Cárdenas's adventure and having heard American trappers' stories of a "big canyon," Ives had come to the region prepared for what he would see.[29] Even more, he fully possessed the sensibility and vocabulary of his Romantic age, and he explored the canyon at a time when nationalistic Americans regarded their seemingly God-given, sublime landscapes as competitive with, if not superior to, the man-made monuments of Europe.

Ives's companion John Strong Newberry, whose geological essay accompanied Ives's report, agreed on all counts. Newberry was the first to note the scientific value of the canyon, and he also commented on the aesthetic qualities of the "stupendous chasm." Near the Diamond River, where he first entered the canyon, Newberry wrote of the cliffs that towered a mile above the river in "a series of pinnacles and pyramids, frequently standing entirely isolated, forming some of the most striking and remarkable objects seen on our expedition. Many of these buttes exhibit a singular resemblance to the spires and pyramids which form the architectural ornaments of the cities of civilized nations, except that the scale of magnitude of all these imitative forms is such as to render the grandest monuments of human art insignificant in comparison with them."[30]

After emerging from the canyon and regaining the vantage of the Colorado Plateau, which he judged to be some seven thousand feet above sea level, Newberry exclaimed: "From this point the view toward the north was particularly grand; the course of the Colorado was visible for nearly a hundred miles, and the series of Cyclopean walls into which the mesas of different elevations have been cut by that stream and its tributaries formed a scene of which the sublime features deeply impressed each member of our party."[31]

Sublime the country may have been, but harsh it was as well. Ives put the matter succinctly at the beginning of his report: "The region explored after leaving the navigable portion of the Colorado—though, in a scientific point of view, of the highest interest, and presenting natural features whose strange sublimity is perhaps unparalleled in any part of the world—is not of much value. Most of it is uninhabitable, and a great deal of it is impassable."[32]

Indeed, on April 18, while the party was still moving eastward across the Colorado Plateau, Ives famously predicted that few would follow him:

*An excellent view was had of the Big cañon. The barometric observations upon the surface of the plateau, and at the mouths of Diamond and Cataract rivers, showed that the walls of this portion of the cañon were over a mile high. The formation of the ground was such that the eye could not follow them the whole distance to the bottom, but as far down as they could be traced they appeared almost vertical. A sketch taken upon the spot by Mr. Egloffstein does better justice than any description can do to the marvelous scene.*

*Our reconnoitering parties have now been out in all directions, and everywhere have been headed off by impassable obstacles. The positions of the main water-courses have been determined with considerable accuracy. The region last explored is, of course, altogether valueless. It can be approached only from the south, and after entering it there is nothing to do but to leave. Ours has been the first, and will doubtless be the last, party of whites to visit this profitless locality. It seems intended by nature that the Colorado river, along the greater portion of its lonely and majestic way, shall be forever unvisited and undisturbed. The handful of Indians that inhabit the sequestered retreats where we discovered them have probably remained in the same condition, and of the same number, for centuries. The country could not support a large population, and by some provision of nature they have ceased to multiply. The deer, the antelope, the birds, even the smaller reptiles, all of which frequent the adjacent territory,*

UPPER CATARACT CREEK NEAR BIG CAÑON

"Upper Cataract Creek Near Big Cañon," lithograph by John James Young from a sketch by Friedrich W. von Egloffstein. More evidence of the "stunned imagination." Perhaps this image reflects the fear Egloffstein felt after he crashed down the Havasupai ladder and found himself awaiting rescue by his companions on Upper Cataract Creek, better known as Havasu Creek. (From Joseph Ives, *Report upon the Colorado River*, 1861; courtesy DeGolyer Library, Southern Methodist University)

*have deserted this uninhabitable district. Excepting when the melting snows send their annual torrents through the avenues to the Colorado, conveying with them sound and motion, these dismal abysses, and the arid table-lands that enclose them, are left, as they have been for ages, in unbroken solitude and silence. The lagoons by the side of which we are encamped furnish, as far as we have been able to discover, the only accessible watering place west of the mouth of Dia-mond river. During the summer it is probable they are dry, and that no water exists upon the whole of the Colorado plateau. We start for the south with some anxiety, not knowing how long it may be before water will be again met with.*[33]

Ives and Newberry had painted the "Big Cañon" in the colors of the sublime and both had praised its potential for scientific research, Newberry to the point of calling the Colorado Plateau, which he named, "a paradise" for the geologist.[34] Both of these perceptions would be carried further forward by the explorer whose name is most closely associated with the Grand Canyon: John Wesley Powell. The Major, as he was widely called, was an ambitious, self-trained geologist and one-armed veteran of the Civil War who determined to explore the Colorado River by boat in 1869. At the time, the core of the Colorado watershed, from Wyoming to the limit of Ives's investigations in Arizona, constituted the greatest remaining blank spot on the map of the United States, exclusive of Alaska. Powell's explorations would make him a national hero and elevate the canyon in both romantic and scientific terms. He would also provide America its first view of the canyon not down from the rim, but looking up from the water.

Powell set out from Green River, Wyoming, on May 24, 1869, with four wooden boats and nine men. Nine hundred miles and fifteen weeks later, Powell reached the Mormon settlements at the mouth of the Virgin River, downstream of the Grand Canyon, with two boats and five men (one member of the expedition had left in Utah; three others abandoned the expedition in the last miles of the Grand Canyon and died trying to walk overland to the settlements). With the publication of Powell's vivid and enduring account of the journey six years later, "the Colorado River and its gorges had found their poet laureate."[35]

No passage in Powell's record of the expedition is more memorable than his entry for August 13, 1869, when he and his companions broke camp near the confluence of the Little Colorado River and the main stem of the big river. At this point Powell and his men had been nearly three months on the river and were preparing to enter what, by then, they and others had begun to call the Grand Canyon:[36]

*August 13. — We are now ready to start on our way down the Great Unknown. Our boats, tied to a common stake, are chafing each other, as they are tossed by the fretful river. They ride high and buoyant, for their loads are lighter than we could desire. We have but a month's rations remaining. The flour has been resifted through the mosquito net sieve; the spoiled bacon has been dried, and the worst of it boiled; the few pounds of dried apples have been spread in the sun, and reshrunken to their normal bulk; the sugar has all melted, and gone on its way down the river; but we have a large sack of coffee. The lightening of the boats has this advantage: they will ride the waves better, and we shall have but little to carry when we make a portage.*

*We are three quarters of a mile in the depths of the earth, and the great river shrinks into insignificance, as it dashes its angry waves against the walls and cliffs, that rise to the world above; the waves are but puny ripples, and we but pigmies, running up and down the sands, or lost among the boulders.*

*We have an unknown distance yet to run; an unknown river to explore. What falls there are, we know not; what rocks beset the channel, we know not; what walls rise over the river, we know not. Ah, well! We may conjecture many things. The men talk as cheerfully as ever; jests are bandied about freely this morning; but to me the cheer is somber and the jests are ghastly.*

*With some eagerness and some anxiety, and some misgiving, we enter the cañon below, and are carried along by the swift water through walls which rise from its very edge. They have the same structure that we noticed yesterday—tiers of irregular shelves below, and, above these, steep slopes to the foot of marble cliffs. We run six miles in a little more than half an hour, and emerge into a more open portion of the cañon, where high hills and ledges of rock intervene between the river and the distant walls.... On we go, gliding by hills and ledges, with distant walls in view; sweeping past sharp angles of rock; stopping at a few points to examine rapids, which we find can be run, until we have made another five miles, when we land for dinner.*

*Then we let down with lines over a long rapid and start again. Once more the walls close in, and we find ourselves in a narrow gorge, the water again filling the channel, and being very swift. With great care, and constant watchfulness, we proceed, making about four miles this afternoon, and camp in a cave.*

*August 14.—At daybreak we walk down the bank of the river, on a little sandy beach, to take a view of a new feature in the cañon. Heretofore, hard rocks have given us bad river; soft rocks, smooth water; and a series of rocks harder than any we have experienced sets in. The river enters the granite!*

*We can see but a little way into the granite gorge, but it looks threatening.*

*After breakfast we enter on the waves. At the very introduction, it inspires awe. The cañon is narrower than we have ever before seen it; the water is swifter; there are but few broken rocks in the channel; but the walls are set, on either side, with pinnacles and crags; and sharp, angular buttresses, bristling with wind and wave polished spires, extend far out into the river....*

*About eleven o'clock we hear a great roar ahead, and approach it very cautiously. The sound grows louder and louder as we run, and at last we find ourselves above a long, broken fall, with ledges and pinnacles of rock obstructing the river. There is a descent of, perhaps, seventy five or eighty feet in a third of a mile, and the rushing waters break into great waves on the rocks, and lash themselves into a mad, white foam. We can land just above, but there is no foot-hold on either side by which we can make a portage. It is nearly a thousand feet to the top of the granite, so it will be impossible to carry our boats around, though we can climb to the summit up a side gulch, and, passing along a mile or two, can descend to the river. This we find on examination; but such a portage would be impracticable for us, and we must run the rapid, or abandon the river.*[37] *There is no hesitation. We step into our boats, push off and away we go, first on smooth but swift water, then we strike a glassy wave and ride to its top, down again into the trough, up again on a higher wave, and down and up on waves higher and still higher until we strike one just as it curls back, and a breaker rolls over our little boat. Still, on we speed, shooting past projecting rocks, till the little boat is caught in a whirlpool, and spun around several times. At last we pull out again into the stream. And now the other boats have passed us. The open compartment of the "Emma Dean" is filled with water and every breaker rolls over us. Hurled back from a rock, now on this side, now on that, we are carried into an eddy, in which we struggle for a few minutes, and are then out again, the breakers still rolling over us. Our boat is unmanageable, but she cannot sink, and we drift down another hundred yards through breakers; how, we scarcely know. We find the other boats have turned into an eddy at the foot of the fall, and are waiting to catch us as we come, for the men have seen that our boat is swamped. They push out as we come near, and pull us in against the wall. We bail our boat, and on we go again.*

*The walls, now, are more than a mile in height—a vertical distance difficult to appreciate. Stand on the south steps of the Treasury building, in Washington, and look down Pennsylvania Avenue to the Capitol Park; measure this distance overhead, and imagine cliffs to extend to that altitude, and you will understand what I mean; or, stand at Canal Street, in New York, and look up Broadway to Grace Church, and you have about the distance; or stand at Lake Street bridge, in Chicago, and look down to the Central Depot, and you have it again.*[38]

Rations dwindling, their nerves frayed, and their clothing drenched and ragged, the men of Powell's little party continued to navigate the canyon's frightening whitewater for two harrowing weeks. On August 28, three of the men decided it would be suicide to attempt the next stretch of rapids— the worst they had seen. With Powell's permission, they climbed out of the canyon, hoping to reach the Mormon outpost of St. George. Powell, who spent a sleepless night trying to decide whether to scuttle the expedition or continue, pressed on. A day and a half later, on August 29, Powell notes triumphantly in his diary, "The river still continues swift, but we have no serious difficulty, and at twelve o'clock emerge from the Grand Canyon of the Colorado."[39]

By his estimate, he had covered 217.5 miles since entering the "Great Unknown" at the Little Colorado on August 13.[40] The three men who walked out of the canyon, William Dunn and the Howland brothers, Oramel and Seneca, died at the hands of Paiute Indians who mistook them for prospectors who had killed a Hualapai woman.[41]

Powell's story of his descent of the Colorado River, published in 1875, became an American epic and the source of much of his fame and influence. A polymath, he went on to publish studies on a remarkable number of subjects, including his visionary *Report on the Lands of the Arid Region of the United States* (1878). An administrator and institution builder as well as a scholar, Powell headed the United States Geological Survey from 1881 to 1894 and directed the Bureau of American Ethnology at the Smithsonian Institution from its founding in 1879 until his death in 1902.

Powell's associates recognized that the Major was particularly adept at recognizing the talents of others and supporting their development. Among the gifted individuals who worked closely with Powell and contributed to the emergence of the canyon's "grandness," four especially stand out: the artists Thomas Moran and William Henry Holmes and the geologists Grove Carl Gilbert and Clarence Dutton. Interestingly, Holmes also became one of the nation's foremost anthropologists and succeeded Powell as director of the Bureau of American Ethnology. His atlas for Dutton's *Tertiary History of the Grand Canyon District* is considered a masterpiece of scientific illustration. Dutton was as much an aesthetician as a scientist. In *Tertiary History* he alternates chapters on geology with chapters that, for want of a better word, interpret the "spirit" of the place. While Gilbert tied the canyon firmly to the era's rapid advances in geological understanding (via pioneering studies of fluvialism, mountain building, and geomorphology), it was Dutton who taught the world how to "see" the canyon.[42]

Moran, for his part, helped complete the aesthetic and scientific work of the others with a singular contribution in the political arena. His operatic paintings of the Yellowstone country helped persuade Congress to create the first national park in 1872, and his many depictions of the Grand Canyon undoubtedly contributed to the canyon's gradual elevation to similar status, finally joining Yellowstone as the nation's seventeenth national park in 1919.[43]

The canyon's journey to national icon depended on iron rails. When Powell set off down the Colorado in May 1869, he started from the trestle bridge in western Wyoming that carried the transcontinental railroad across the Green River. The railroad had allowed Powell to transport his four wooden boats and seven thousand pounds of supplies to the river's edge.[44] Just as the railroad contributed to Powell's pioneering navigation of the Grand Canyon, it also made possible a new way of seeing the canyon. When the Atchison, Topeka, and Santa Fe Railway pushed across central Arizona in the 1880s, it brought tourists near enough to the canyon that a twenty-one-mile stagecoach ride could complete their trip to the South Rim. In 1901 the railroad company built a spur line to replace the stagecoach, and tourists began to visit the Grand Canyon in substantial numbers. A few years later, the railroad company opened the El Tovar Hotel for the comfort of its better-heeled travelers.

With the flow of tourists, the tide began to shift in the familiar struggle between conservationists and those who wished to leave land in the public domain so that its resources could be exploited and eventually privatized. Over the sometimes fierce opposition of hunters, miners, loggers, ranchers, and entrepreneurs, portions of the Grand Canyon became a forest reserve in 1893, a national game preserve in 1906, a national monument in 1908, and a national park, finally, eleven years later.[45]

The Grand Canyon had failed to captivate López de Cárdenas, and even in the early twentieth century there remained a few who failed to respond to its charms. "It is no place for a gentleman, sir!" a valet reportedly informed his master.[46] For most Americans, however, the Grand Canyon has become, as President Theodore Roosevelt presciently proclaimed in 1903, "one of the great sights which every American, if he can travel at all, should see." On that occasion Roosevelt also famously observed that the Grand Canyon should be left inviolate: "The ages have been at work on it, and man can only mar it."[47]

# 8 Mesa Verde

Mesa Verde—the "green tableland"—rises from the Colorado Plateau in southwestern Colorado and enjoys a reputation as "the nation's most outstanding preserve devoted to the works of ancient man."[1] In 1906 the federal government brought the remarkable mesa into the national park system. With other protected archaeological sites in the national park system classed as national monuments or national historical parks, Mesa Verde remains the only national park in America created solely to preserve archaeological resources. Today the park encompasses more than fifty-two thousand acres on which archaeologists have discovered some four thousand pre-Columbian sites, including six hundred cliff dwellings. It ranks among the wonders of America and the world. In 1978 it became one of the first two locations in the United States (the other is Yellowstone National Park) that UNESCO selected as a World Cultural Heritage Site.[2]

The green tableland of Mesa Verde is not flat but slopes considerably to the south, ranging from eighty-five hundred feet in elevation down to six thousand. Sharp-walled canyons, eight hundred to a thousand feet deep, dissect it, making its surface highly irregular. The canyons follow the mesa's slope and drain south and east into the valley of the Mancos River, which swings past the southern extremity of the mesa and runs westward through the Ute Mountain Tribal Park to the San Juan River. As the canyons slice through Mesa Verde, they create smaller mesas, which bear such names as Wetherill and Chapin.

Mesa Verde National Park stands at the heart of a large zone rich in pre-

MESA VERDE FROM MANCOS.

"Mesa Verde from Mancos." The cluster of homes and ranches along the Mancos River was the starting point for discovery of Mesa Verde's treasures. (From Frederick H. Chapin, *The Land of the Cliff-Dwellers,* 1892; courtesy DeGolyer Library, Southern Methodist University)

historic ruins that some archaeologists call the Mesa Verde culture area. By that they mean a portion of the Colorado Plateau north of the San Juan River that includes parts of northeastern Arizona, northwestern New Mexico, southwestern Colorado, and southeastern Utah as far as the Colorado River. In this usage, the archaeologists' Mesa Verde extends far beyond the boundaries of the national park to include much of today's Four Corners area. Many prehistoric sites in the Mesa Verde culture area remain on private or tribal land, but the federal government has put some of the most spectacular under its protection. In 1919 President Woodrow Wilson set aside Yucca House National Monument near a prominent local landmark, Sleeping Ute Mountain; in 1923 President Warren G. Harding designated six prominent sites in the western sector of the Mesa Verde culture area as part of the far-flung Hovenweep National Monument, and he also created Aztec Ruins National Monument in New Mexico on the east side of the culture area; in June 2000, President Bill Clinton designated 164,000

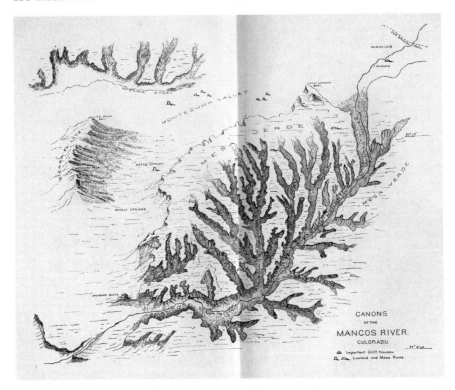

"Canyons of the Mancos River, Colorado." Frederick H. Chapin, the creator of this map, noted that his sketch "is based upon that published in Hayden's Reports, and upon the beautiful panoramic views of Mr. William H. Holmes." (From Frederick H. Chapin, *The Land of the Cliff-Dwellers*, 1892; courtesy DeGolyer Library, Southern Methodist University)

more acres of federal land between Hovenweep and Cortez, Colorado, as Canyons of the Ancients National Monument. South of the San Juan River one enters the Chaco cultural area, but a porous line separates these archaeological zones. Chacoan influences can be found well inside the Mesa Verde cultural zone, and vice versa.

Archaeologists tell us that people hunted, gathered, and farmed in the Mesa Verde cultural area for centuries, coming and going as the seasons and rainfall permitted. In the 900s and early 1000s, for example, drought drove many of the residents southward, and wetter years brought them back around 1050. Over time the dwellings of the Mesa Verdeans evolved from pit houses to surface houses, constructed first of poles and mud and then of more permanent masonry. Meanwhile, their technology evolved from finely wrought baskets to pottery, which enabled them to cook over an open fire and store food and water for long periods. While the household equipment of these ancient people was eminently useful, many of their baskets and pots were also graced by handsome designs and decoration that testify to a refined, even exquisite, aesthetic sensibility.

Atop Mesa Verde, defense against enemies (external if not internal) apparently forced residents to seek safer quarters in the early 1200s. Many moved down from the open mesa tops to occupy hard-to-reach ledges under the arched alcoves of the canyon walls. Here they built row houses, storage rooms, and watchtowers, while still tending their fields of corn, beans, and squash atop the mesa.

Less than a century later, however, everyone had left, driven away, it appears, by prolonged drought (1276 to 1299), unpredictable rainfall, possibly colder temperatures, and wildfires that raged across the dry woodlands. No less influential were the social conflict and warfare that usually accompany an era of diminishing resources. Hungry and quite likely traumatized, people fled the Mesa Verde region, scattering southward in search of better-watered land and safer surroundings.[3] Remarkably—and for reasons that tree rings, potshards, or other archaeological evidence cannot explain—they never returned.

By the time Europeans began to explore the San Juan basin, the once-flourishing communities of the Mesa Verde area had lain in ruins for more than four centuries. The first Europeans probably came in the last half of the 1700s as small Spanish trading and slaving expeditions struck out from Santa Fe for the Great Basin. They could not have missed seeing ruins as they passed through this archaeologically rich region, but only official exploring parties left written records, and these are terse, at best. In 1765 Juan María Antonio de Rivera stumbled upon what he described as a "pueblo in a canyon so expansive and large that it would appear to be two times larger than the village of Santa Fe."[4] In 1776, Don Bernardo de Miera y Pacheco, cartographer for the Franciscans, Francisco Atanasio Domínguez and Silvestre Vélez de Escalante, mentioned in the previous chapter, passed by the junction of the Animas and San Juan Rivers, the site of today's grossly misnamed Aztec Ruins National Monument, and noted on his map, "Here are the ruins of great settlements of ancient Indians."[5] Later, when camped in a meadow on the Dolores River not far from the present-day town of

Dolores, Colorado, the Franciscans merely noted in their journal: "There was in ancient times a small settlement of the same type as those of the Indians of New Mexico, as the ruins which we purposely inspected show."[6]

Anglo Americans began to pass through the region in the 1820s but, like their Spanish predecessors, almost none left written descriptions of ruins. The exception was William Becknell, best known as the "father" of the Santa Fe Trail, who endured a freezing camp in the area in the winter of 1824–25. He later told a Missouri newspaper: "I discovered old diggings and the remains of furnaces [perhaps evidence of Spanish prospectors]. There are also in this neighborhood the remains of many small stone houses, some of which have one story beneath the surface of the earth. There is likewise an abundance of broken pottery here, well baked and neatly painted. This was probably the scite [site] of a town where the ancient Mexican Indians resided, as the Spaniards, who seldom visit this part of the country, can give no account of it."[7]

Becknell's notion that "ancient Mexican Indians" had inhabited the area surfaces repeatedly among early Anglo Americans who came to southwest Colorado. Settlers apply the name Montezuma Valley to the large, fertile swath of land north and west of Mesa Verde, and they found a town in 1886 that they will call Cortez, after the conquistador who vanquished Montezuma. Soon enough, Cortez is declared the seat of Montezuma County. A few of the early settlers may actually have seen the Aztec ruins of central Mexico, having marched there as part of the invading U.S. Army in 1846–47. Even more of them would have read William Prescott's 1843 classic, *The History of the Conquest of Mexico,* which was a best seller in its day. Prescott's romantic evocation of the Aztecs made that group of Native Americans far more attractive to the Anglo imagination than any of the comparatively poverty-stricken Puebloans, Hopis, Navajos, or Utes then inhabiting the greater region of which Mesa Verde was a part.

If any early Anglo visitors climbed to the top of Mesa Verde, they failed to note it. First to record an ascent was geologist John S. Newberry, whom we met in the Grand Canyon and who, again, was serving as a naturalist on a military exploratory expedition. Newberry climbed the north face in 1859. Near the promontory today called Point Lookout, he enjoyed a spectacular view but missed seeing ruins and cliff dwellings. Credit for discovering the cliff houses on Mesa Verde's canyon walls has usually gone to two local ranchers, Richard Wetherill and his brother-in-law, Charlie Mason. It was they who spotted the most spectacular of the Mesa Verde cliff houses in December 1888 and quickly brought them to public attention. Three years later, in the summer of 1891, a young, well-connected Swedish scientist, Gustaf Nordenskiöld, worked at Mesa Verde and is credited with producing "the first true scientific work on some of Mesa Verde's finest cliff dwellings."[8]

Nearly a decade and a half before Wetherill and Mason made their discoveries, however, two small groups of explorers associated with a government-sponsored survey had visited and described the ancient ruins on and around Mesa Verde and published painstaking reports of their findings. They produced the first detailed impression of the ruins at Mesa Verde—those on open ground as well as those on cliff sides, and it was they, as one scholar has observed, who "established the term Cliff Dwellers in both the archaeological and popular literature and art of the Southwest."[9] Their work, however, has merited only passing attention because they missed seeing such spectacular sites as Cliff Palace, Spruce Tree House, and Square Tower House, which are the principal attractions for visitors today.

Thirty-one-year-old William Henry Jackson headed the first of these parties, a small group charged, in 1874, with documenting the region in photographs. Jackson had scarcely begun his long, illustrious career as a photographer and artist of the West, but he had already won considerable praise as a photographer for the U.S. Geological and Geographical Survey of the Territories headed by geology professor Ferdinand Vandeveer Hayden. Hayden's survey had begun in the Yellowstone country in the summers of 1871 and 1872, moved to Colorado in 1873, and was in its fourth season in 1874 when Jackson explored the Mesa Verde area. In Denver early that summer, Hayden divided his men and resources, putting Jackson at the head of a seven-man photographic unit. The group included Ernest Ingersoll, a naturalist and correspondent for Horace Greeley's *New York Tribune* who would become Jackson's life-long friend (which is saying something: Jackson lived to the age of ninety-nine, and he died before Ingersoll). Filling out the team were two "expert packers"—Steve Stevens and Bob Mitchell, a cook named Charlie, and two teenagers "who were expected to make themselves generally useful." Foremost among the baggage was a heavy wet-plate camera, together with its cumbersome glass plates, chemicals, and associated equipment.[10]

With Jackson astride a white mule named Dolly, the group photographed its way through the central Rockies in July and August before dropping down to the San Juan Mountains of southwestern Colorado as summer drew to a close. In early September the men reached the mining town of Silverton, descended the canyon of the Animas River to the future site of Durango (over the route covered today by the popular narrow gauge railroad), then turned westward to the mining camp of Parrott City, in La Plata Canyon to the northeast of Mesa Verde. There, chance brought the party into contact with John Moss, an erstwhile prospector and friend to the local Utes, who amiably offered to lead Jackson to some of the remarkable Indian ruins that Jackson's party had heard about even before leaving Denver.[11]

John Moss, who claimed the title of captain, had explored in the area for years. Jackson described him as fluent in Spanish and in local Indian languages, as well as "a great man among both whites and Indians, & I think the pioneer mover in all that is going on in this region."[12] Moss knew many of the ranchers, farmers, and prospectors who had begun to move into the Mesa Verde area after the U.S. Civil War. Besides discovering silver-bearing veins in the mountains, newcomers like Moss had encountered prehistoric ruins in the valleys below Mesa Verde and had sighted ancient dwellings in the cliffs that rose above Mancos Canyon.

Lured by Moss's stories, Jackson and Ingersoll took the party's two packers and headed into the Mancos Valley on September 8, stopping for the night at a ranch at the site of the future town of Mancos. This was Ute territory, and they made their way warily. Just days before, Jackson later recalled, perhaps embellishing a good story to make it better, a Ute had warned him that "this country, regardless of treaties and boundaries, was owned by his people; it would be dangerous for us to proceed farther with my strange box of bad medicine," namely, his camera.[13] Jackson's experience, however, was the reverse: the only Utes he encountered helped him retrieve some lost mules and merely laughed at him for his interest in photographing ruins.

On the party's first full day in Mancos Canyon, the first of the promised ruins came into sight. Jackson and Ingersoll retold the story of that thrilling day on many occasions, but here is what Jackson wrote in his diary:

WEDNESDAY 9th. *All hands up early. Got breakfast by the first call.... While Steve [Stevens] & Bob [Mitchell] were packing up, the Capt. [John Moss], Ingersol & myself started down the trail ahead to prospect. Ten or 12 miles away the square outlines of the mesa land were in view & between us lay a beautiful valley land with fine groves of cottonwood scattered here and there. The Mancos is a stream, or creek rather, about a rod wide & a foot deep, clear & limpid until it strikes the beaver Dams just above & thru the Cañon. Five or six miles below the ranch the Capt. noticed little grass covered knolls on the opposite side, and said they were sites of old ruined towns. Crossed over to examine. Found the mounds scarcely definable as to shape. There were no stones remaining but the foundations were in some instances tolerably well defined. There were however about every such mound large quantities of broken pottery in very small pieces, rarely larger than a half dollar piece and most of it painted in fancy designs. The ground was generally white with black designs. Found some red, & on others traces of other colors that were evidently faded. Visited the sites of three or four settlements, collecting pieces of the pottery, & then struck down into the [Mancos] canon. Coming into a trail over which about a 100 Indians had just passed with lodge poles and goats. Proceeding down two or 3 miles, we found the first stone ruins a portion of a rock main city in two instances almost entirely covered by debris which evidently hide the foundations to some depth. The stone did not appear to be dressed & the mortar or cement, if it was any, was entirely worn out & its walls altho perfectly true & plumb appeared as tho dry laid. All about were scattered the remnants of crockery. Mounds which indicated former walls with dimensions in the cubic that appeared like inlay or underground excavations. Each one was small, about 10 × 10 & contained singularly, & covering probably a space 100 yds square. The stone is from the cliffs which rise up from the cañon, a light yellow & brownish sand stone & in the ruins evidently much washed away. One would describe many met within our days ride.*[14]

Jackson had encountered the room blocks and abandoned villages of the Mancos Valley. Soon they glimpsed other structures perched on the mesa sides:

*About 8 or 10 m. [miles] below the mouth of the cañon we began to find evidences of those inhabiting the bluffs. All along we had been scanning the cliffs closely without discerning anything. At one place the trail was forced up some way over a slope of debris from the walls of the cañon, & upon a ledge that it approached we found small sections of walls, enclosing small spaces, generally narrow & long, about 5 × 10 or even narrower, little square oven like pieces of masonry were left up on little ledges or in crevices, the rest of the structure having evidently fallen away from them. Some were queer looking niche like structures that would be [hard] to give the use of. [These were probably granaries for storing corn.] Everything about these remains were extremely dilapidated & afforded but little clue or satisfaction in regard to their former inmates....*

*As evening approached we made our camp under a little bunch of cedars & beneath the highest walls of the cañon. Had found nothing that really came up to my idea of the grand or picturesque for photo's & began to feel a little doubtful & discouraged. All hands pitched in to prepare supper. The Capt. taking an active part & proving a general helpmate. After disposing of what sowb. [sowbelly, or salt pork] & bread we had & as all hands were backed up warming their backs legs & spinal columns, we com. [commenced] joking Steve upon the prospect of having to assist in carrying the boxes to the top of the mesa, to photo some houses, not dreaming ourselves that any were really there. He asked us to point out the spot. The Capt. pointed at random. "Gee," says he, "I see it." I beheld upon my close observation there was something that appeared very like a house, the doors and windows could be seen. We all started at once to investigate. The side of the cañon was formed of successive tables or benches of sandstone rising perpendicularly one above the other to a total height of about 800 feet. One house was upon the last one & below it the precipice was fully 100 feet above the narrow bench at its foot. Half way up the others, with the exception of Mr. Ingersol & myself were satisfied & did not care to go any farther as they were afraid of darkness overtaking them before they could get back. We determined to see all there was to be seen that night so as to know how to approach it on the morrow. Found a tree and series of crevices by which, with a little trouble, we reached the plateau upon which the houses stood. Then perched away in a crevice like a swallow's or bat's nest, it was, a marvel & a puzzle. Its total height was about 12 or 14 feet, divided into two stories, and each floor into two rooms. But the photo will better explain all this. The material was a sandstone, the same as the rocks among which it nestled. It had been truly dressed, and upon the outward wing, covered with a plaster or kind of stucco. Inside the walls had been plastered and colored red, with a lighter colored margin about the edges. All about on this same bench, as far as we had time to investigate, were bits of wall, odd corners here and there, showing that the whole bluff line had been once inhabited. But we had no time to see more as it was already growing dark. We got down easily & guided by the glimmering camp fire soon reached our compadres.*[15]

The following morning, Jackson repeated the climb to what he called Two-Story House with his heavy equipment and, in the morning light, took the first photograph of a cliff dwelling. The site is in today's Ute Mountain Tribal Park, which is part of the reservation of the Ute Mountain Utes, the capital of which is Towaoc, Colorado.

Jackson's small party moved quickly down Mancos Canyon over the next two days, finding more ruins and spotting cliff houses but not taking the time to explore them. On the second day, September 11, Jackson noted

William Henry Jackson, *Ancient Ruins, Cañons of the Mancos, Colorado,* the first photograph of a cliff dwelling in the region, showing Two-Story House, September 9, 1874. Captain Moss is standing at left. The nine-room ruin of Two-Story House stands on the east end of Moccasin Mesa in today's Ute Mountain Tribal Park. (Photograph by William Henry Jackson, courtesy Palace of the Governors Photo Archives, New Mexico History Museum [NMHM/DCA], negative no. 049787)

in his diary the jagged profile of the mesa, which was dissected by "deep broad side gashes which left great promontories like bluffs jutting out on the line of the main valley." Near midday, on one of these promontories,

*we accidentally descried, away up so far as to be almost indistinguishable, two smaller houses, plastered back against a perpendicular wall fully 200 feet straight up, & on a ledge so narrow that a mountain rat could not have passed it. It was too novel to pass: so we lunched & while [it was] preparing Capt. Moss & Bob ran around to the rear of the bluff to try & reach the houses from above. The Cap succeeded, but it was nearly at the peril of his life. The ledge which led to the door of the little house was so narrow & the over hanging rock came so close down upon it, that it was extreme & most difficult that he got out after once getting by. Bob came out some ways above on a ledge so narrow & frail that it looked to us as if it must crumble under his feet.*[16]

Later, Jackson fought his way alone through thick creek-side thickets and across the steep-banked Mancos River to investigate an especially large site: "A mile or two below the last mentioned point we saw a town upon the opposite side of the creek. Attempted in one or two places to cross, and then the others gave it up, got over myself after a while.... Riding over to the town I found it to be the best ruin seen yet, tho, only single. Stood about 20 feet in height, with two square foundations at its feet equidistant upon either hand, diameter about 8 feet. See photo. Had an extremely difficult time recrossing & the [pack] train had got a long ways ahead before I emerged from the jungle."[17]

Exiting Mancos Canyon, the party picked up what Jackson later understood to be "the old Spanish trail from Santa Fé to Salt Lake," and late in the day reached Aztec Springs, west of Mesa Verde at the base of Sleeping Ute Mountain.[18] Here they came upon another massive ruin—the future site of Yucca House National Monument (established in 1919). They hoped to camp there for the night, but the springs were dry so, as Jackson notes in his diary, the rest of the party went ahead while he, Captain Moss, and Ingersoll stayed behind to explore still more ruins. Moss and Jackson "got into camp just a little after sun down. The boys had hardly got unpacked. No wood but grease wood & sage brush & no water but that in little pools & sinks in the bed of the creek. All hands gathered the brush. Cap. baked bread & we soon had satisfied stomachs."[19]

Continuing to the west of Mesa Verde, the party explored ruin-rich McElmo Canyon and sites in the future Hovenweep National Monument. Moss knew the way, for he had visited these places before, and Jackson later credited Moss with "much of the success of the trip; for it enabled us to make every day count, and no false moves." Looping around to the north of Mesa Verde through Montezuma Valley, on September 14 they returned to the ranch on the Mancos where they had begun just six days before. Jackson's party had circled Mesa Verde on this lightning trip, but had not ventured deeply into its canyons or explored the mesa top and so missed the most spectacular ruins—those that Richard Wetherill and Charlie Mason would find fourteen years later. Those they did see, however, were a remarkable novelty that Jackson and Ingersoll brought to national attention. They had gone in "quest of the picturesque," as Jackson put it, "and we found it."[20]

Ingersoll published his account of the discovery before Jackson did. It appeared on November 3, 1874, in the *New York Tribune,* giving American readers their first impression of these exotic ruins.[21] As one would expect, Ingersoll's lengthy piece is richer in description and more artfully narrated than the hurried entries that Jackson made in his diary. After explaining the geography of southwestern Colorado to his readers, and tracing the party's journey "across high, rugged, volcanic mountains, wild and picturesque and full of grizzlies," Ingersoll took his readers into the Mancos Valley and to the discovery of Two-Story House:

*The Sandstone House of Former Times*

*Proceeding west 15 miles and descending some 2,000 feet, we struck the Rio Mancos a few miles down where we began to come upon mounds of earth which had accumulated over fallen houses, and about which were strewn an abundance of fragments of pottery variously painted in colors, often glazed within, and impressed in various designs without. Then the perpendicular walls that hemmed in the valley began to contract, and for the next ten miles the trail led over rocks which were anything but easy to traverse. That night we camped under some forlorn cedars, just beneath a bluff a thousand or so feet high, which for the upper half was absolutely vertical. This was the edge of the table-land, or* mesa, *which stretches over hundreds of square miles hereabouts, and is cleft by these great cracks or cañons through which the drainage of the country finds its way into the great Colorado. In wandering about after supper we thought we saw something like a house away up on the face of this bluff, and two of us running the risk of being overtaken by darkness, clambered over the talus of loose débris, across a great stratum of pure coal, and, by dint of much pushing and hauling up to the ledge upon which it stood, we came down abundantly satisfied, and next morning carried up our photographic kit and got some superb negatives. There, 700 measured feet above the valley, perched on a little ledge only just large enough to hold it, was a two-story house made of finely-cut sandstone, each block about 14 × 6 inches, accurately fitted and set in mortar now harder than the stone itself. The floor was the ledge upon which it rested, and the roof the overhanging rock. There were three rooms upon the ground floor, each one 6 by 9 feet, with partition walls of faced stone. Between the stories was originally a wood floor, traces of which still remained, as did also the cedar sticks set in the wall over the windows and door.... Each of the stories was six feet in height, and all the rooms, up stairs and down, were nicely plastered and painted what now looks a dull brick-red color, with a white band along the floor like a baseboard. There was a low doorway from the ledge into the lower story, and another above, showing that the upper chamber was entered from without. The windows were large, square apertures, with no indication of any glazing or shutters. They commanded a view of the whole valley for many miles. Near the house several convenient little niches in the rock were built into better shape, as though they had been used as cupboards or caches; and behind it a semi-circular wall inclosing the angle of the house and cliff formed a water-reservoir holding two and a half hogsheads. The water was taken out of this from a window of the upper room, and the outer wall was carried up high, so as to protect one so engaged from enemies from below.[22]*

Ingersoll, continuing, did his best to describe his adventure in terms his New York City readers would understand:

*A Street a Thousand Feet Deep*

*We were now getting fairly away from the mountains and approaching the great, sandy, alkaline plains of the San Juan River. Our Valley of the Mancos was gradually widening, but still on either side rose the perpendicular sides of the mesa, composed of horizontal strata of red and white sandstone shaped by the weather into rugged ledges and prominences, indented by great bays or side cañons, and banked up at the foot by taluses of the gray marl which lay beneath it. Imagine East River 1,000 or 1,200 feet deep, and drained dry, the piers and slips on both sides made of red sandstone and extending down to that depth, and yourself at the bottom, gazing up for human habitations far above you. In such a picture you would have a tolerable idea of the Cañon of the Mancos.*

He milked Moss's perilous venture along "a ledge so narrow that a mountain rat could not have passed" for all the drama it was worth:

*One of us espied what he thought to be a house on the face of a particularly high and smooth portion of the precipice.... Fired with the hope of finding some valuable relics of household furniture, the Captain and Bob started for the top and disappeared behind the rocks while we busied ourselves in getting ready the photographic apparatus. After a while an inarticulate sound floated down to us, and looking up we beheld the Captain, diminished to the size of a cricket, creeping on hands and knees along what seemed to us a perfectly smooth vertical face of rock. He had got where he could not retreat, and it seemed equally impossible to go ahead.*

*A Tragic Incident*
*There was a moment of suspense, then came a cry that stopped the beating of our hearts as we watched with bated breath a dark object, no larger than a cricket, whirling, spinning, dropping through the awful space, growing larger as it neared the earth, till it fell with muffled thud on the cruel sharp rocks below. But ere we could reach it, another object seemed to fall backward from the highest point and reeled down through the flooding sunshine, casting its flying shadow on the brilliant bluff, gathering dreadful momentum with which to dash its poor self dead on the dentless stones beneath.*

*The Captain had thrown down his boots.*

*He was still there, crawling carefully along, clinging to the wall like a lizard, till finally a broader ledge was reached; and, having the nerve of an athlete, he got safely to the house. He found it perfect, almost semicircular in shape, of the finest workmanship yet seen, all the stones cut true.*

Ingersoll's account of the discovery reached a large popular readership in New York. Jackson's account, based on his diary and written in clinical prose that betrayed no sense of emotion or wonder, appeared in the reports of the Hayden Expedition, and reached a smaller, scholarly group of readers.[23] The U.S. Government Printing Office, which published these re-

ports, reproduced none of Jackson's photographs, but it did include drawings—some based on the photos. These depictions gave Americans their
first visual images of cliff dwellings.

Jackson's report of unique ruins in southwestern Colorado prompted an
enthusiastic Hayden to send two teams into the area the next year. Jackson
led one of the groups, with a different guide and accompanied by a different correspondent/naturalist from the previous summer. Hayden assigned
Jackson to pick up where he had left off the previous year, at a canyon
Jackson had named Hovenweep, and to determine how far ruins extended
across the region.[24] Jackson's photographic reconnaissance would take him
past Mesa Verde again, this time in the temporary company of William
Henry Holmes, a trained artist and budding archaeologist, whose instructions were to lead a second party in a detailed examination of the ruins
Jackson had hurriedly surveyed the summer before. Jackson and the rest of
his photographic detail, meanwhile, would explore the greater Hovenweep
area in southeastern Utah and then make their way south, following Chinle
Wash upstream (and southward) to the mouth of Canyon de Chelly, and
thence southwest along a well-worn trail to Hopi.[25]

Holmes, like Jackson, was a remarkable talent. (The previous chapter
mentioned his stunning atlas for Clarence Dutton's *Tertiary Geology of the
Grand Canyon District*.) Over the course of a long and varied career, he
would make his mark as an explorer, artist, archaeologist, geologist, anthropologist, mapmaker, agency head (the Bureau of American Ethnology), and museum director (the National Gallery of Art). In 1875 in the
environs of Mesa Verde Holmes skillfully drew ground plans of a number of multiroom, open-ground compounds, with their kivas, courtyards,
and towers. Like Jackson, he also described and named a cliff dwelling—
Sixteen-Window House in Greasewood Canyon above the Mancos River,
within the bounds of today's national park. His reports, which included
sketches of tools, pottery, baskets, petroglyphs, and skeletal remains, appeared, like Jackson's, in official reports of the Hayden expedition.[26]

Notwithstanding the government publications they authored, Jackson
and Holmes probably reached their largest public audience at the 1876
Philadelphia Centennial Exposition, where Jackson curated a large exhibit
displaying the work of the Hayden Survey. Many of Jackson's photographs
graced the walls of the exhibit, and various specimens of minerals, plants,

Plate III.

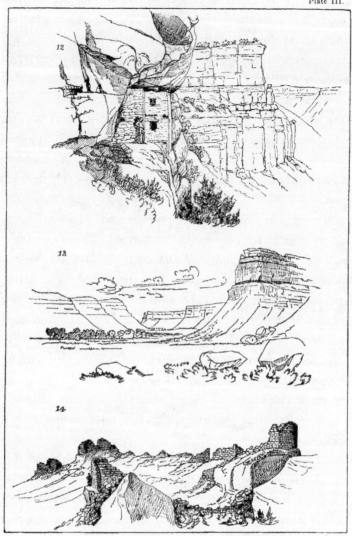

"Ancient Ruins in Southwestern Colorado." Although field photography had made great advances by the 1870s, Jackson's splendid photographs did not appear in the official reports of the Hayden Survey. Rather, in the interest of economy, Hayden illustrated Jackson's report with woodcuts and line drawings. Americans first saw Two-Story House in the sketch at the top of this image, accompanied by a view of Mancos Canyon (middle) and an example of ruins that were not expressly "cliff dwellings" (bottom). (William Henry Jackson, "Ancient Ruins," in *Annual Report of the United States Geological and Geographical Survey of the Territories ... for the Year 1874;* courtesy DeGolyer Library, Southern Methodist University)

and animals were presented for public perusal, but the pièce de résistance consisted of scale models of ruins from southwestern Colorado that Jackson and Holmes painstakingly designed and built together. These may have been, as one historian has suggested, the first three-dimensional representations of western scenes viewed in the East.[27] As Jackson later recalled with pride: "When the fair opened, this display attracted more attention than the many photographs and all the rocks and relics of Dr. Hayden's career. It drew almost as many visitors as Dr. Alexander Graham Bell's improbable telephone, and, had a Gallup Poll existed at the time, I am confident that nine persons out of ten would have voted my models the better chance of enduring."[28]

As authors of the first scientific reports on the Mesa Verde area, Jackson and Holmes broke new ground in correctly identifying the people who built the ancient communities. Jackson told his readers that he would not "speculate either upon the age of these ruins or of the ancestry of the builders," yet he implied that ancestors of the Hopis had built them.[29] He pointed to a "legend" that Hopis had lived in the Mesa Verde area before their enemies drove them south to their mesa-top locations in Arizona. That "legend," an oral tradition, comports well with present-day archaeological knowledge.[30] In his diary, Jackson noted that local Utes referred to the ruins as Hopi houses ("Moqui houses"), although, Jackson added, "they have no knowledge whatever of their former occupants. Not even traditions."[31]

Holmes offered a more explicit theory that went beyond the Hopi connection. He did not believe that ancestors of the "nomadic savages" who still lived in the region, such as Utes or Navajos, had the capacity to build the structures that lay in ruins around him, but he theorized that nomads had driven agriculturalists to take up their defensive positions in the cliffs and eventually forced them to abandon their homes and flee south and east. Thus, Holmes concluded, "the ancient peoples of the San Juan country were doubtless the ancestors of the present pueblo tribes of New Mexico and Arizona."[32] The idea quickly gained an audience beyond the scientific community. In 1878 *Scribner's Monthly* ran a piece called "The Cliff-Dwellers" that summarized Jackson's and Holmes's reports, reproduced some of their illustrations, and reported that "the present Pueblo Indians of New Mexico and Arizona are believed to be the remnant of the descendants of the . . . cliff men."[33] Pueblo elders from many tribes, meanwhile, would have emphatically agreed, but they were rarely consulted.

In Anglo American society the theory that the ancestors of present-day Pueblos built the Mesa Verde dwellings competed with the idea that Aztecs built them. The latter possibility was sufficiently widespread that one guidebook referred to the San Juan River area as the location of "the dead cities of the ancient Aztecs," and some members of the scientific community embraced the notion.[34] In 1878, the same year Holmes published his final report, Lewis Henry Morgan, one of the nation's most honored scholars in the emerging field of anthropology, made a summertime inspection of ruins in the Animas Valley and McElmo Canyon, while his grand-nephew visited a cliff house in Mancos Canyon. Fresh from publishing his most influential book, *Ancient Society* (1877), which presented his theory of cultural evolution, Lewis Henry Morgan sought to fit the Mesa Verde area into his theory. The "Village Indians," he concluded, had built the most impressive dwellings in North America, and he attributed to them remarkable influence. Not only did he think it likely they were the Aztecs' ancestors, he considered them the possible ancestors of the mound builders of the Mississippi Valley as well as the Indians of Yucatán, Central America, and other "historic tribes of Mexico."[35] Morgan's theory eventually faded away, along with his notions of cultural evolution, while Holmes's idea endured. Today, archaeologists identify the residents of Mesa Verde as Ancestral Puebloans, not Ancestral Aztecs.

The reports of the Hayden Survey sparked so much interest that as early as 1880 a small business in Animas City, about thirty miles east of Mesa Verde, thought it worthwhile to advertise "complete outfits, including tents, camp equipage, etc." for persons wishing to visit the cliff dwellings along the Mancos and "the far famed Aztec ruins" farther south on the San Juan River (the future Aztec National Monument).[36]

Drawn by the growing publicity and the completion in 1881 of a railroad connection to the newly founded town of Durango, increasing numbers of adventurers made their way to southwest Colorado. These included the improbable Virginia Donaghe, an easterner born to privilege who had moved to Colorado Springs in 1877 for her health.[37] In 1882, Donaghe crossed the mountains and persuaded the commanding officer of Fort Lewis, near Durango, to escort her into the Indian-controlled Mancos Canyon so she could do a story for the *New York Daily Graphic*. The first white woman to view the cliff dwellings, she was so inspired by the experience that she organized a return trip in 1886. This time she spent three weeks in Soda Canyon, where she saw the ruins of Balcony House, a spectacular cliff dwelling now encompassed within the boundaries of the national park. Donaghe went on to lead a movement to preserve the ruins at Mesa Verde, giving public lectures and publishing essays, the most influential reader of which was none other than Theodore Roosevelt.[38] Donaghe, later Virginia McClurg after her 1889 marriage to Gilbert McClurg, played a vital role in building public support for the eventual establishment of the national park.

At the time of Donaghe's visits, calls to preserve the ruins around Mesa Verde could already be heard. No law prohibited people from removing artifacts from prehistoric sites, and collectors of "antiquities" descended on Mancos Canyon in such numbers that the editor of a Denver newspaper feared that "vandals of modern civilization" would destroy the ruins. He asked Congress to set aside part of Mancos Canyon as a park and to appropriate funds to preserve its ruins.[39] The idea was a bold one, for the United States then had created only one national park (Yellowstone) and no national monuments. Such a declaration would also have required the consent of the Utes, whose reservation included Mancos Canyon. Congress failed to take the proposed action, but in 1889 the secretary of the Interior did something almost as revolutionary: he "withdrew" from the public domain a section of land a few miles west of Cortez to preserve a ruined pueblo. "Withdrawal" meant that the land was no longer eligible for homesteading, mining, or any other kind of claim. The site, known today as Goodman Point Pueblo, now constitutes the easternmost unit of Hovenweep National Monument. This early federal action seems to have had no precedent; it antedated the creation of Casa Grande, the nation's first formal archaeological reservation, by three years.[40]

The "vandals" whom the Denver newspaper editor hoped to discourage were mainly local residents—ranchers, farmers, and prospectors, and it would be "vandals" from one local family, the Wetherills, who discovered Mesa Verde's most spectacular cliff dwellings. A restless Pennsylvania-born Quaker, Benjamin Kite Wetherill had brought his family to Colorado in 1880. Near the new hamlet of Mancos and within sight of Mesa Verde, Benjamin and his wife Marion claimed a homestead and built a ranch they called the Alamo for its cottonwood trees. Their five sons had plenty of outdoor work, planting pastures and gardens and looking after livestock. In winter they moved the cattle into the lower, more protected environs of Mancos Canyon. Utes, with whom the Wetherill family enjoyed unusually good relations, perhaps not least because of their tolerant and humanitarian Quaker faith, offered no objection, so the young men established winter camps in the canyon, where they took turns watching their stock, exploring nearby ruins, and hauling out ancient artifacts, some of which they sold.[41]

In December 1888, the Wetherills' oldest son, Richard, and his brother-in-law Charlie Mason spotted Cliff Palace. One of Richard's younger brothers, Al, had seen it from a distance a few years earlier, but had not gone close enough to realize how fabulous it was. Soon after stumbling on Cliff Palace, the brothers-in-law found two other major ensembles in the cliffs, which became known as Spruce Tree House and Square Tower House. The new finds eclipsed all other discoveries both in size and architectural complexity. And they fascinated people everywhere. Cliff Palace alone, with its four-story buildings and towers, two hundred rooms, and twenty-one kivas, was enormous in comparison to the cliff dwellings found by Jackson and Holmes. It was also far more photogenic. "In the 1890s," one writer has noted, "no other Indian ruin so inspired the imaginations of people across the United States and Europe as did Cliff Palace at Mesa Verde."[42]

Cliff Palace became the icon of Mesa Verde and its discovery the iconic moment. Thereafter, in one form or another, the story of Richard Wetherill's and Charlie Mason's encounter with the ruins came to be remembered in popular accounts as the first impression of Mesa Verde, pushing Ingersoll's, Jackson's, and Holmes's earlier descriptions into the background.[43] Wetherill and Mason delayed writing down the story of their discovery for years, but Mason later remembered it this way: "In December, 1888, Richard and I went on a cruise of exploration. We followed the Indian trail down Chapin Mesa, between Cliff and Navajo canyons, and camped at the head of a small branch of the Cliff Palace fork of Cliff Cañon.... From the rim of the canon we had our first view of Cliff Palace just across the canon from us.[44] To me this is the grandest view of all among the ancient ruins of the Southwest. We rode around the head of the canon and found a way down over the cliffs to the level of the building. We spent several hours going from room to room, and picked up several articles of interest, among them a stone axe with the handle still on it. There were also parts of several human skeletons scattered about."[45]

The Wetherills continued to excavate and collect antiquities as they had before, but now it became their primary business. Paradoxically, they also added their voices to a growing chorus of demands that the government protect the ruins.

The decisive act of preservation finally came in June 1906. Soon after approving the Antiquities Act, which prohibited tampering with prehistoric and historic remains on government lands, President Theodore Roosevelt signed a bill creating Mesa Verde National Park. It was the country's fifth national park, after Yellowstone (1872), Sequoia and Yosemite (1890), and Mount Rainier (1899). Unlike those earlier parks, the legislation authorizing Mesa Verde did not mention timber or minerals. Rather, it called for the preservation of "ruins and other works and relics of prehistoric or primitive man" within the park's boundaries and adjacent Indian lands.[46] Inconveniently, Utes held title to Mesa Verde itself, not just to "adjacent" lands, until 1913, when the tribe, under heavy pressure from federal authorities, agreed to exchange waterless Mesa Verde for land on nearby Ute Mountain, which was equally dry and therefore deemed valueless by whites.[47]

With federal protection came both tourists and a small cadre of field researchers from the growing ranks of professional archaeologists. Mesa Verde was their magnet, their lodestone. They measured, excavated, described, and analyzed. As they deepened their understanding of ancient life on and around Mesa Verde, they confirmed the idea that ancestors of the present-day Pueblos, not Aztecs, built the ancient structures, and they credited Jackson and Holmes with sparking national interest in the area's exotic cliff houses. They also asserted that the pair's early work possessed lasting value. More than half a century after Holmes wrote his report, it was still regarded as the fullest and most reliable description of the ruins in the northern watershed of the San Juan River.[48]

Fast friends, William Henry Jackson and William Henry Holmes basked in the glow of their discoveries and watched scientific knowledge progress over the course of their very long lives. Holmes, who died in 1933 at age eighty-seven, credited his stint in the Mesa Verde region with introducing him to the "fascinating realm of archaeology."[49] He went on to play a leading role in the development of the science in America and was thought by some to be the "dean of American archaeologists."[50] Jackson, who died in 1942 at age ninety-nine, maintained a direct interest in Mesa Verde, returning to photograph it, publishing the story of his discoveries in several versions, and taking pride in his role in "revealing to the world, these 'cities that died.'"[51]

# 9 The Mohave Villages

As travelers cross the Colorado River on Interstate 40 at Topock, Arizona, they touch the southern end of the Mohave Valley, the heartland of the historic territory of the Mohave Indians.[1] Settlements of these Yuman-speaking Indians (the Pipa Aha Macav, or "The People by the River") once extended more than forty miles from the rocky spires called the Needles, below present Topock, up the valley of the Colorado River to lands that were inundated by Lake Mohave after completion of Davis Dam in 1953. The Mohaves also at various times controlled land and maintained settlements fifty miles to the south, on lands now included in the Colorado River Indian Reservation below Parker Dam, where many Mohaves reside today.[2] Mohaves acquired a well-earned reputation as a warlike people for their aggressive behavior toward other tribes in the nineteenth century, but like many Native American groups they offered hospitality to the first Europeans who visited their riparian oasis.[3]

Spaniards came late to the Mohave Valley. A Spanish expedition sailed up the Sea of Cortés and into the Colorado River in hope of supplying the Coronado expedition in 1540, but the fleet almost surely stopped short of Mohave territory. Coming from the east in 1604, Juan de Oñate, who established the first permanent Spanish colony in New Mexico, was probably the first Spaniard to encounter Mohaves. He apparently met them on the Colorado River below the mouth of the Bill Williams' Fork. The only detailed account of Oñate's journey to the Gulf of California says little about these "Amauacas," "Amavacas," or "Amacavas" beyond identifying their crops and pronouncing them "very friendly."[4] Not until 1776, when Fray Francisco Garcés followed the Colorado River northward from Yuma Crossing, did a European again enter the Mohaves' world.

Born in 1738 in Spain and ordained a Franciscan priest in Mexico, Francisco Tomás Hermenegildo Garcés arrived thirty years later at the frontier mission of San Xavier del Bac. With San Xavier as his base, Garcés explored the country to the west on horseback, usually with Indian guides, searching for new mission fields. One of his fellow Franciscans described him as uniquely suited to travel among Indians, for he could sit with them for hours around a campfire "with his legs crossed" and eat "nasty and dirty" Indian food with pleasure. "In short, God has created him, as I see it, solely for the purpose of seeking out these unhappy, ignorant, and rustic people."[5] Garcés's growing knowledge of the terrain between San Xavier and the Colorado River brought him to the attention of Spanish officials. In 1774, when Juan Bautista de Anza prepared to open an overland route from Sonora to the newly founded settlements on the California coast, he sought and received permission from the viceroy in Mexico City to take Garcés along as a guide.

After crossing deserts and mountains with Anza, from Sonora to the mission of San Gabriel in California and back again, Garcés set out in 1775 on a still more daunting venture. He hoped to find a direct route from San Gabriel and the nearby settlement of Los Angeles to the pueblos of the Moquis, or Hopis, and thence to Santa Fe. This quest took him into the lands of the Mohaves (as well as to the edge of the Grand Canyon, where we met him earlier). Once again setting out from his home mission at San Xavier and traveling with Anza, Garcés moved through familiar territory, which Apache raids had lately rendered dangerous. Along the Gila, O'odham villagers (known to Garcés as Pimas) presented Anza with the scalps of two Apaches killed in recent battle.

When the Spanish party reached the Yuma villages in early December, Anza and Garcés parted ways. Anza continued westward to California and ultimately to San Francisco Bay, while Garcés paused to explore the canyons of the lower Colorado River and learn whether the Indians who lived along it were disposed toward religious instruction, "which is what the Viceroy ordered me to do."[6] Encouraged by the friendly reception he received from the Yumas and other tribes, Garcés continued upstream on

February 14, 1776. He traveled unaccompanied by any other Spaniards, employing only Indian guides and interpreters, including Sebastián Taraval, a member of the Cochimí tribe, who had guided him and Anza to California the year before.[7] Two weeks from Yuma he reached his first destination, the villages of the Mohaves, whom he called the Jamajabs, near present-day Needles, California:

*I went seven leagues northnortheast and arrived at the Jamajab nation, having passed over a sierra that runs to the northwest and ends on the Rio Colorado River [the Mohave Range]. Having continued further, the rancherías of the Jamajab I saw were on the opposite bank of the river; these I called (Rancherias) de la Pasion. Here came soon all the Jamajabs, because the captain who was accompanying me [identified, two weeks earlier at Yuma Crossing, only as "an Indian of that nation who was there"] hastened on to inform them of my arrival. Those who came to see me that day remained to sleep in this place so that I could speak to them to my satisfaction on all subjects. To all that I set forth to them they replied that it was good; and added that license was given me to remain here to baptize them, because they knew that thus would result all sorts of good things.*

*I can say in all truth that these Indians are superior in many respects to the Yumas and the rest of the nations of the Rio Colorado. They are less molestful, and none are thieves; they seem valiant, and nowhere have I been better served.*

*I showed them the picture of the Virgin; it pleased them much; but they did not like to look at that of the lost soul. As I am the first Español who has been in their land they celebrated it beyond bounds (sobre manera) by their great desire to become acquainted with them (Españoles); and considering them to be very valiant, they manifested extraordinary joy at being now friends of a people so valorous.*[8]

The following day, February 29, 1776 (the added day of a leap year), Garcés remained with the Mohaves, receiving visitors and observing them closely:

*I tarried here, because there came successively many persons, and among them three captains, of whom one said that he was the head chief (el principal) of the nation, against whose will was naught determined; that he had come in order that I should tell him that which there was for him to do; that I should know him for what he was when I should see him do out of the goodness of his heart all that which I might propose; and finally he said that he would be baptized and married to one wife, adding other good things of like tenor. This is the captain general of them all (que ay) and lives in the center of this nation.*

*The female sex (el mugerio) is the most comely on the river; the male (la gente) very healthy and robust. The women wear petticoats of the style and cut that the Yumas (wear). The men go entirely naked, and in a country so cold this is well worthy of compassion. These say that they are very strong; and so I found them to be, especially in enduring hunger and thirst. It is evident that this nation goes on increasing, for I saw many lusty young fellows (gandúles), and many more boys; the contrary is experienced in the other nations of the river. There came together to visit me about two thousand souls. Abound here certain blankets that they possess and weave of furs of rabbits and nutrias [which probably refers to otters, but may include beavers] brought from the west and northwest, with the people of which parts they keep firm friendship. They have been also intimate friends of the Yumas. Their language is different; but through constant communication they understand the Yumas well enough. They talk rapidly and with great haughtiness (arrogancia). I have not heard any Indian who talked more, or with less embarrassment, than their captain general.*

*The enemies that they have are, on the northeast, the Cuercomache [a division of the Yavapais]; on the east, the Jaguallapais [Hualapais]; and on the south, the Jalchedunes [Halchidhomas]. During the harangues that they make they give smart slaps with the palms on the thighs.*

*Manifesting to these people the desires that I had to go to see the padres that were living near the sea [missionaries on the California coast], they agreed and offered soon to accompany me, saying that already they had heard of them and knew the way. But as now I had few provisions, I determined to depart immediately (quanto antes); and told them that on the return we would see each other at leisure (de espacio). I left here the greater part of my baggage and the interpreter that I had sent with the Indian girls (Inditas) that I had rescued; and in company with the Indian Sebastián [Taraval] and the Jamajabs I departed from this place.*[9]

The Mohaves had received Garcés generously. He reported them eager to receive baptism and adopt Christian lives—precisely the "disposition" for which he and his superiors had hoped. The accuracy of this judgment may seem questionable from a modern perspective, but Garcés appears to have been satisfied as he departed the Mohave Valley. Together with Sebastián Taraval and three Mohave guides, Garcés followed an Indian trade route westward across the Mohave Desert and the San Bernardino Mountains before descending into the Los Angeles basin and reaching Mission San Gabriel within a month. Having found the direct route he sought to Los Angeles, Garcés and his companions returned to the Mohave villages and from there continued eastward across the Colorado Plateau, guided successively by Hualapais and Havasupais. His route took him to the village of Supai and the rim of the Grand Canyon and continued on to the mesa-top pueblo of Oraibi, the largest of the Hopi villages. There his eastward progress stopped. Hopis, who had never resubmitted to Spanish rule after the Pueblo Revolt of 1680, refused to feed or shelter him. Unlike the Mohaves, the Hopis had had ample prior experience with Spaniards and had no desire for more. Fearing for his life, Garcés sent a letter via an Indian carrier to the governor at Santa Fe to let him know he had reached Oraibi. Then he saddled his mule and rode out of the pueblo on July 4, 1776, going back the long, laborious way he had come to return to San Xavier del Bac.

July 1781, five years after this remarkable journey, found Garcés among the Yuma Indians (the modern Quechan tribe). By then the Yumas had had enough of Spaniards, too, especially after a group of colonists bound for California brought large herds of livestock to Yuma Crossing and allowed their animals to trample and eat the Indians' crops. Garcés had just said Mass at a newly established mission when "rebels" burst into the church. Within days the Spanish garrison and nascent colony at Yuma were wiped out. With Garcés's death, viewed as a martyrdom by many of his compatriots, his dream of converting Indians on the Colorado River also perished. Spain never regained control of Yuma Crossing.

Farther upstream, the Mohaves remained undisturbed by outsiders for the next half century. Their happy isolation came to an end in 1826, when Anglo American trappers led by Jedediah Strong Smith arrived at the river. A twenty-eight-year-old New Yorker and the senior partner in the Rocky Mountain fur-trading company of Smith, Jackson, & Sublette, Smith had left the trappers' summer rendezvous—what he called the "deposit"—in the Cache Valley of northern Utah in mid-August. Accompanied by seven-

teen men and a number of Indian women, he made his way southwestward through Utah, following the basins of the Great Salt Lake and Utah
Lake and the valleys of the Sevier, Virgin, and Colorado Rivers in search of
beaver-rich streams. Early October found Smith at the northern edge of the
Mohave Valley, where Mohaves—whom he called Amuchabas—received
him and his party as hospitably as they had Garcés.

Smith, of course, had no interest in converting the Mohaves. His interest lay more in assessing their way of life and their resources. Here was a
place where one could find timber and establish small farms. In his journal, which he hoped one day to publish, Smith pragmatically described the
Mohaves' crops, foods, food preparation, pottery, weapons, games, clothing, and homes. Mohaves had little direct experience with Europeans, but
Smith makes clear that they had already adopted European-introduced
horses and wheat. Conscious of skin color, like other Americans of his day,
Smith noted with apparent approval that the Mohaves' complexions were
"not dark."

The day is October 9, 1826. Smith writes:

*I had lost a good many horses and some of those remaining were not able to
carry any thing. I got the Indians to assist me in moving down to where there
was several lodges. These Indians are quite a different nation from the Pautch
[Paiutes]. They call themselves A-muc-ha-ba's [Mohaves] and appeared quite
friendly bringing me corn beans dried pumpkins &c which I paid them for in
Beeds [beads] Rings vermillion &c. At this place there is considerable timber on
the river and the soil might admit of making small farms. There was but 3 or 4
horses among them but I did not succeed in purchasing them. verry little beaver
sign on the river. By enquiry I found that the principal part of this tribe were 30
or 40 miles down the river. I remained at this place 2 days during which time a
number of Indians came up from the village below. Among these were one or two
that could talk spanish and as I had a man that was able to speak the spanish I
could hold some conversation with them. I then moved on down the River accompanied by the Indians who had come up from the settlements below. The distance was upwards of thirty miles and the country barren. On my arrival at the
settlement I was treated with great kindness. Melons and roasted pumpkins were
presented in great abundance—At this time it was low water yet the Colorado
was 200 yards and in the shoalest [shallowest] place I could find 10 feet deep with*

*a smooth current. The timber in this vicinity consisting of the Cottonwood and a small species of Honey Locust [Mesquite] with some willow extends entirely along the river varying in width from ½ to 2½ miles in width the river winding through woodland from one side to the other alternately. Leaving the woodland which has a tolerable soil the sandy region commences producing nothing but sedge and prickly pear. On the East and West at the distance of ten miles a chain of Rocky hills run parallel with the river and about thirty miles south the Rocky hills close in to the River. This settlement of the Amuchaba's extending about 30 miles along the River appeared quite numerous and paying some considerable attention to agriculture they do not live in villages but are rather scattered over the country generaly whereever they find the most favorable situations. In person these Indians are tall and well formed complexion not dark. In abilities perhaps second to the Utas [Utes]. They do not appear much inclined to steal but are quite fond of gambling.*

*Their principal Game is conducted as follows. A piece of ground 30 or 40 feet long and 8 feet wide is made level and smooth. Each man has a pole ten feet long and one of them a hoop 4 inches in diameter. The hoop is set rolling from one end of the floor and at the instant both start and sliding their poles endeavor to intersect the hoop. The one that pierces the hoop or when hoop and poles stop is the nearest to the spot is the winner.[10] The women also gamble by tossing small colored sticks in a dish somewhat like throwing dice. The women are generally very fleshy with tolerable features.*

*The man when dressed at all have a Spanish Blanket thrown over the left shoulder and passing under the right arm it is pined on the breast with a wooden pin. They wear no head dress mocasins or leggings. The dress of the women is a peticoat made of a material like flax just Broken which is Banded with a plat on the upper edge like corn husks. It is fastened around the waist extending down to the knee and constitutes with whole of their clothing. They are in general much more cleanly that the Pautch. They make a kind of earthen ware and in large crocks of this they boil their beans corn pumpkins &c. The men appear to work as much in the field as the women which is quite an unusual sight among Indians. But few of them have bows and arrows. The bows are 5 feet long and the arrows verry long and made of cane grass with a wooden splice 6 inches long for a head. It is fashion with these indians to fill the hair full of mud and wind it around the head until the top resembles in shap[e] a tin pan. Their summer Lodges about*

*3 feet high are made of forks and poles covered with grass weeds and dirt flat on the top. The winter Lodges generally small are made in the woods but fronting to the south and where the trees are not sufficiently high to keep out the sun. As the rainy season approaches they throw dirt on the roof to give it a slope to carry off the water and also secure the sides with dirt leaving only a small aperture for a door. As they have not much clothing when the weather requires it they build a great many small fires sleeping in the intervals between them. When they become cold they draw the sand out from under fires and spread it where they sleep....*

*I found in this vicinity no beaver worth trapping for but remained here for the purposes of recruiting my men and horses. From the Indians I ascertained that below the rocky hills that came into the river and nearly down to the mouth of the Gila the country was barren and not inhabited. They also told me that it was about ten days travel to the spanish settlements in California. I swaped my poorest horses with the indians and endeavored to purchase others but without success\* (\*One morning an Indian came to me and said the Indians had killed one of my horses which on examination I found to be true. They had killed the horse to eat and took away every thing but the entrails. From this time I had my horses so carefully guarded that they had no chance to continue their depredations.) Believing it impossible to return to the deposit [the rendezvous] at this season and in my present situation I determined to prepare myself as well [as] possible and push forward to California where I supposed I might procure such supplies as woul[d] enable me to move on north. In that direction I expected to find beaver and in all probability some considerable river heading up in the vicinity of the Great Salt Lake. By this route I could return to the deposite. In pursuance of my plan I endeavored by all means in my power to procure a guide but could not succeed. I therefore got the best instruction I could in regard to the route and collected a supply of Corn, Beans, Locust Bread, and a little Indian flour.*[11]

Thus supplied, Smith crossed the Colorado in a raft and started west, but a lack of water and his suspicion that he might run into an Indian ambush drove him back. He recrossed the river and traveled some ten miles farther down the valley into the heart of Mohave country near present-day Needles. There he found himself in a more verdant country where Mohaves raised wheat and an abundance of melons and pumpkins, which they fed to horses that they kept tethered to keep them out of the crops.

*Melons were supplied in such numbers that I had frequently 3 or 400 piled up before my tent. A great many women and children were generally about us. Among the Amuchabas I did not find any verry influential chiefs. He that has the most wives and consequently the most numerous connexion is the greatest man. There was one chief which we called Red Shirt from the circumstance of his wearing a shirt made out of a piece of red cloth which I had given him. He was about 40 years of age and appeared to be a great favorite among the women. He frequently stayed at my tent and slept with any of the women he chose. No indians I have seen pay so much deference to the women as these. Among indians in general they have not the privilege of speaking on a subject of any moment but here they harangue the Multitude the same as the men.... It being a great object with me to procure a guide no means were left untried and finally I succeeded in engaging two Indians that lived in the vicinity of the Spanish Settlements.*[12]

The two Indians whom Smith recruited as guides were teenagers, "about 16 years of age," members of a small desert tribe whose territory lay well to the east of San Gabriel. Evidently, the boys had previously been residents of the mission but had fled from it, the proof being that, having successfully guided Smith across the Mojave Desert and reentered the Los Angeles basin, which was now under Mexican control, the boys were promptly imprisoned as runaways.[13] Smith, unfortunately, was in no position to help them. He had essentially retraced Garcés's route from the Colorado River to San Gabriel, but unlike Garcés, he was an interloper entering a foreign domain. As the leader of the first group of Americans to enter California by land, Smith aroused the suspicion of Mexican officials, who found it implausible that he—or anyone—would cross the continent in pursuit of beaver pelts.[14] Suspecting that Smith might be a spy, the governor of California briefly detained him, then changed his mind and ordered Smith to leave California by the route he had come.

Instead of complying, Smith charted his own course. He crossed the San Bernardino Mountains and trapped his way north up California's great central valley. He had hoped to find a great river that would lead him eastward, but ultimately his hope yielded to geography. The Sierras stood in his way, laden with snow in the spring of 1827. Smith made a bold and difficult choice. Leaving most of his men behind on the Stanislaus River, he and two companions crossed the still-frozen Sierras in late May, and then staggered

across the parched Great Basin of Nevada and Utah in June heat, a feat that
marked them as the first Euro-Americans to cross the Sierras and the first to
cross the Great Basin. On July 10, 1827, their epic journey came to an end
at the annual fur trappers' rendezvous at Bear Lake in the southwest corner
of today's Idaho, where they received the welcome of friends and acquain-
tances who had long assumed them to be dead. Resting for only ten days,
Smith set out again for California at the head of a party of eighteen men
and two Indian women, intending to rejoin the men he had left behind on
the Stanislaus. His first destination was the Mohave villages, but this time
he found the natives far less hospitable than before.

Shortly after Smith had departed Mohave territory the previous year, a
second group of American trappers appeared. Led by Ewing Young, this
party had worked its way upstream along the Colorado River, sparking a
series of disputes with various tribes along the way. An outright fight with
Mohaves erupted for reasons lost to us—although Mohave tradition has it
that the Indians deplored the wasteful carnage of the trappers taking beaver
pelts but leaving the carcasses to rot. One of Young's men, the unreliable
fabulist James Ohio Pattie, suggested that Mohaves attacked them for no
reason and that the Americans retaliated by killing a good many Indians
and hanging their bodies in trees "to dangle in terror to the rest."[15]

Whatever the truth may have been, when Smith returned to the Mohave
villages in 1827, he entered hostile terrain. The Indians' initial cordiality
screened a dangerous intent. As the Americans crossed the river, a process that rendered them vulnerable, the Mohaves attacked. Ten of Smith's
men and the two Indian women were killed. Smith and eight survivors
escaped with little more than their lives, surrendering their horses, traps,
supplies, munitions, and all but five of their guns to the Mohaves. Smith
had hoped to avoid the Mexican settlements on the Pacific and go directly
to the Stanislaus, but the Mohave attack forced him to seek supplies in the
California settlements.

For nine harrowing days the surviving trappers struggled across the
Mojave Desert and the San Bernardino Mountains, finally receiving succor
at a ranch in the San Bernardino Valley. Smith soon detoured to San José
for supplies and, although disappointed, was probably not surprised when
the Mexican authorities, still suspicious of his intentions, placed him under
arrest. After much difficulty and thanks to the crucial intervention of the

captain of an American ship trading at California ports, Smith slipped out of that predicament, as he would others yet to come. Four years later, however, his luck ran out. At age thirty-two, in a careless moment on the well-traveled Santa Fe Trail, Smith strayed from his companions in search of water. He soon came to the banks of the Cimarron River, where he found water but lost his life, for a group of Comanche hunters were lying in wait there for bison.[16]

Following the end of the U.S.-Mexico War in 1848 and the discovery of gold in California in 1849, Americans began to cross the Colorado River in increasing numbers Most of these "argonauts" and "forty-niners" arrived at the Colorado via the Gila River and crossed the big river at Yuma Crossing, well south of the Mohave villages. America's new sovereignty over the region, however, guaranteed increased interest in Mohave territory on the part of both civilians and the government. Survey parties began to visit the Mohaves in the 1850s, bringing new demands and new kinds of interactions. Where Francisco Garcés had sought to plant the seeds of Christianity among the Mohaves, Anglo American arrivals now sought horses, food, and safe passage across the Colorado River. Some of them, unsatisfied with the Indians' response, declared them to be unpredictable and untrustworthy.

Captain Lorenzo Sitgreaves of the Army Corps of Topographical Engineers, en route from Zuni, passed through the Mohave Valley in the autumn of 1851. Mohaves, eager to trade, greeted him warmly. The artist Richard Kern, who traveled with Sitgreaves, made the earliest known sketch of members of the tribe. "Their manner," he noted in his diary, "indicated they were quite used to Americans."[17] The only unpleasantness occurred after a wary Sitgreaves evicted the Indians from his camp as a security measure—early the next morning some Mohaves returned the favor by sending arrows flying toward his tents.[18] In 1854, another officer in the corps, Lieutenant Amiel Weeks Whipple, passed through with a survey party (Plate 7.) His guide, Antoine Leroux, who had accompanied Sitgreaves three years before, told Whipple that "no white party has ever before passed them without encountering hostility."[19] In fact, Whipple found the Mohaves generally helpful and hospitable.

R.H. Kern del    MOHAVE INDIANS (Big Colorado River N.M.    Ackerman Lith 379 Broadway NY

"Mohave Indians (Big Colorado River N.M.)," a lithograph based on a sketch by Richard Kern, was the earliest published graphic impression of members of the Mohave tribe. This view shows the elaborate tattooing and body paint that many travelers commented on, a custom that neither Garcés nor Smith had found worthy of mentioning. In his diary, Kern described Mohave men as "not only very tall but well formed.... Some tattoo their faces and breasts in thin lines or dots; black paint is the most used and red is the only other color." Some of the women, he said, "have their chins tattooed" (Weber, *Richard H. Kern,* 177–78). (From Lorenzo Sitgreaves, *Report of an Expedition Down the Zuni and Colorado Rivers,* 1853; courtesy DeGolyer Library, Southern Methodist University)

Since the diaries of Garcés and Smith were not published until the twentieth century, the accounts by Sitgreaves and Whipple, published in 1853 and 1855 respectively, gave the American reading public its first views of the Mohaves, both verbal and visual. These were followed in 1857 by the work of a Methodist minister, Royal B. Stratton, who seized upon the dramatic story of the captivity of Olive Oatman to offer American readers a presumed insider's view of Mohave society in a book that quickly became a best seller— *Captivity of the Oatman Girls.*

Yavapai Indians had killed Olive Oatman's Mormon parents and four of her siblings in the late winter of 1851 as her family made their way toward California along the Gila River. The Yavapais (Olive incorrectly believed they were Apaches) rode off with thirteen-year-old Olive and her eight-year-old sister, Mary Ann. In time, the girls' captors traded them to Mohaves. Mary Ann died in a famine in 1855; Olive survived to return to American society in 1856. Olive seems to have been well treated and may have left the Mohaves reluctantly. She was tattooed on the face in the Mohave fashion and some evidence suggests she had a Mohave husband and child, but the true story of her captivity will likely never be known.[20] In Olive's account, or what the Reverend Stratton presented as Olive's account, she remained a virgin ever eager to be rescued, never yielding to the natives, who treated her and her sister as slaves. Here, in words that Stratton gave her, Olive says:

> *For a time after coming among them, but little was said to us — none seemed desirous to enter into any intercourse, or inquire even, if it had been possible for us to understand them, as to our welfare, past or present. . . . Indeed, we were merely regarded as strange intruders, with whom they had no sympathy, and their bearing for a while towards us seemed to say, "you may live here if you can eke out an existence, by bowing yourselves unmurmuringly to our barbarism and privations."*

OLIVE OATMAN.

Olive Oatman, with the Mohave facial tattoos that fascinated the public when she went on the lecture circuit (From Royal B. Stratton, *Captivity of the Oatman Girls,* 1857; courtesy DeGolyer Library, Southern Methodist University)

*In a few days they began to direct us to work in various ways, such as bringing wood and water, and to perform various errands of convenience to them. Why they took the course they did, I have never been able to imagine, but it was only by degrees that their exactions were enforced. We soon learned, however, that our condition was that of unmitigated slavery, not to the adults merely, but to the children. In this respect it was very much as among the Apaches. Their whimpering, idiotic children, of not half a dozen years, very soon learned to drive us about with all the authority of an eastern lord. And these filthy creatures would go in quest of occasions, seemingly to gratify their love of command; and any want of hurried attention to them, was visited upon us by punishment, either by whipping or the withholding of our food. Besides the adults of the tribe, enjoyed the sport of seeing us thus forced into submission to their children.*[21]

Stratton frequently takes the liberty to enter the narrative in his own voice:

*Nothing during the summer of 1852 occurred to throw any light upon that one question to these captive girls — the all-absorbing one — one which, like an everywhere present spirit, haunted them day and night, — as to the probabilities of their ever escaping from Indian captivity. It was not long before their language, of few words, was so far understood as to make it easy to understand the Mohaves in conversation. Every day brought to their ears expressions, casually dropped, showing their spite and hate to the white race. They would question their captives closely, seeking to draw from them any discontent they might feel in their present condition. They taunted them — in a less ferocious manner than the Apaches, but with every evidence of an equal hate — about the good-for-nothing whites.*

*Many of them were anxious to learn the language of the whites; among these one Ccearekae, a young man of some self-conceit and pride. He asked the elder of the girls, "How do you like living with the Mohaves?" To which she replied — "I do not like it so well as among the whites, for we do not have enough to eat."*

*Ce — "We have enough to satisfy us — you Americanos (a term also by them learned of the Mexicans) work hard and it does you no good; we enjoy ourselves."*

*Olive — "Well, we enjoy ourselves well at home, and all our white people seem happier than any Indian I have seen since."*

*Ce — "Our great fathers worked just as you whites do, and they had many nice things to wear, but the flood came and swept the old folks away, and a white son of the family stole all the arts, with the clothing, etc., and the Mohaves have had none since."*

Olive — *"But if our people had this beautiful valley, they would till it and raise much grain. You Mohaves don't like to work, and you say you do not have enough to eat — then it is because you are lazy.*

*At this his wrath was aroused, and with angry words and countenance, he left.*[22]

Stratton's best-selling account tells us more about its author and the popular genre of the captivity narrative than it does about the Mohaves. It gave voice to the anti-Indian sentiments of many Americans of the day and seemingly affirmed the correctness of those attitudes toward Indians in general and Mohaves in particular. When Lieutenant Joseph Christmas Ives (with whom we traveled to the Grand Canyon) reported on his passage through the Mohave Valley on his paddle-wheel steamer *Explorer* in February 1858, he quoted a gruesome excerpt from *Captivity of the Oatman Girls* to describe Mohave cruelty, and he pronounced the Indians "lazy, cruel, selfish, disgusting in their habits, and inveterate beggars," notwithstanding their hospitable treatment of him and their "exactitude" in trade. Only the trusted guide Ireteba earns his complete approval, as "the only one that I have never known to beg for anything."[23]

The frequent vituperation of Indians by whites in times past raises the question of what Indians thought of the outsiders who came to their lands in those early years of contact. Unfortunately, the historical record is demonstrably one-sided, at least in time- and site-specific terms, for native people like the Mohaves stored up no "documents" against the inevitable erosion of memory. How did whites appear to them? Were they arrogant, prone to violence, preoccupied with possessing things? And how did Garcés, the Spanish priest, differ from Ives, the Anglo soldier, and in what ways were the two men seen as different from forlorn Olive Oatman, the captive? In historical terms, we lack the better part of half the story of these fraught encounters between cultures, and we are the poorer for it.

→→

In October 1857, a few months before Ives's visit to the Mohave Valley, Lieutenant Edward Fitzgerald Beale arrived from the east leading a pack string of camels. In one of the most unusual military experiments in the history of the Southwest, Beale was testing the practicality of using camels as beasts of burden, while also laying out a wagon road on Whipple's route along the 35th parallel. Mohaves, eager to trade, received Beale and his command in friendship. "Much astonished to wake up this morning and find my hair safe!" one young member of Beale's party, who apparently feared scalping, recorded in his diary.[24] Woefully short on rations, Beale traded with the Mohaves, resupplying fully, and ultimately swam his camels across the river laden with enough corn, beans, pumpkins, watermelons, and cantaloupes to make it to Los Angeles. Three months later, in late January 1858, Beale returned to the river to test both his wagon road and his camels in winter. As he approached the Colorado River he learned to his amazement that a steamship, the *General Jesup,* waited at the crossing to take him to the other side. He marveled that the ship should appear "in a wild, almost unknown country, inhabited only by savages," and he lamented the Mohaves' future, predicting that "the steam whistle of the *General Jesup* sounded the death knell of the river race."[25]

The opening of the wagon road brought emigrants from the eastern states. In August 1858, Mohaves attacked the first wagon train to approach the Mohave Valley over the Beale road, killing eight, wounding another dozen, and sending the survivors fleeing back to Albuquerque. The reasons for the attack have never been explained satisfactorily, but prior to the attack Mohaves repeatedly asked the emigrants if they intended to settle on the Colorado. One Mohave later recalled that some of the men urged the attack in order to stop the Americans from settling in their territory, taking their wives and children, and driving away the game.[26] Perhaps they had heard the "death knell" that Beale foresaw.

Predictably, the attack on the emigrant party brought a military response. The U.S. Army established Fort Mohave on a bluff on the east side of the river above the crossing of Beale's wagon road. In the inevitable ensuing confrontations, the soldiers soon dominated the Mohaves, the ranks of their warriors already badly diminished by heavy casualties from a battle two years earlier with Maricopas and Pimas.[27] Mohave independence had come to an end.

Demoralizing decades of poverty, disease, and dependence followed. A portion of the tribe, led by Ireteba, moved sixty miles south to the Colorado River valley, where they settled among Chemehuevis, a desert people

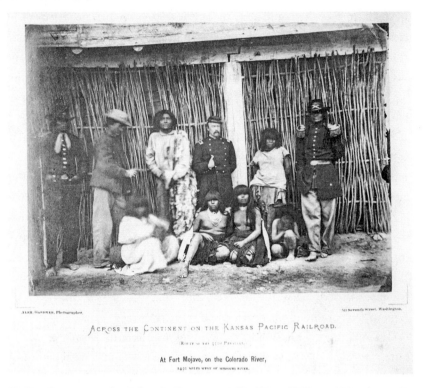

Across the Continent on the Kansas Pacific Railroad.

At Fort Mojave, on the Colorado River,

"At Fort Mojave, on the Colorado River, 1450 Miles West of Missouri River," one of three surviving photographs taken by Alexander Gardner at Fort Mojave in late 1867. These may be the first photographs of Mohave people. (From Alexander Gardner, *Across the Continent on the Kansas Pacific Railroad*; courtesy DeGolyer Library, Southern Methodist University)

who had moved to the river in the early nineteenth century. In 1865 this area was set aside as the Colorado River Indian Reservation, and in the 1940s Navajo and Hopi emigrants were also "resettled" there, joining the Mohaves and Chemehuevis to form the Colorado River Indian Tribes, or CRIT.

Other Mohaves remained in the Mohave Valley, where they came to be known as the Fort Mojave Tribe. Some found work on the Atlantic and Pacific Railroad when it came to Needles in 1883; others labored on riverboats or in mines or sold handicrafts to tourists. The Fort Mojave Indians were confirmed in at least a portion of their traditional territory when the government declared the Fort Mojave Reservation in 1880 and enlarged it in 1911. In the 1890s the government built a boarding school on the site of

Plate 1. Lieutenant James W. Abert, *Acoma N.M.,* watercolor on paper, October 1846. This is the earliest extant representation of Ácoma. (From James W. Abert, *Western America in 1846–1847: The Original Travel Diary of Lieutenant James W. Abert, Who Mapped New Mexico for the United States Army,* ed. John Galvin, 1966; courtesy DeGolyer Library, Southern Methodist University)

Plate 2. Timothy H. O'Sullivan, *Ancient Ruins in the Cañon de Chelle, N. M., in a Niche 50 Feet above Present Cañon Bed.* This image, taken in 1873 for Lieutenant George M. Wheeler's United States Geographical Surveys Beyond the 100th Meridian, became an icon in the history of photography. (Photograph by Timothy H. O'Sullivan; courtesy Library of Congress)

JIM WHITE, THE COWBOY, THE DISCOVERER, EXPLORER
AND FIRST PROMOTER OF CARLSBAD CAVERNS

Plate 3. Jim White on horseback (From *Jim White's Own Story,* 1943 edition;
courtesy DeGolyer Library, Southern Methodist University)

Plate 4. Casa Grande in 2008, showing the protective hip roof from 1932 designed by famed Boston architect Frederick Law Olmsted Jr. (Photograph by Marc E. Gottlieb, licensed courtesy of Artifract)

Plate 6. H. B. Möllhausen, *Mouth of Diamond Creek, Colorado River, View from the South,* transparent and opaque watercolor on paper, 1858. Ives mentioned that a sketch by Möllhausen depicts the grandeur of the canyon of the Colorado where Diamond River joins it, but neither this upstream view nor its downstream counterpart was included in the expedition report. (Courtesy Amon Carter Museum of American Art, Fort Worth, Texas, 1988.1.36)

Plate 5. "Spring at Inscription Rock," lithograph based on Richard Kern's sketch (From James H. Simpson, *Journal of a Military Reconnaissance . . . to the Navajo Country . . . in 1849;* courtesy DeGolyer Library, Southern Methodist University)

Plate 7. "Rio Colorado Near the Mojave Villages," a lithograph based on a drawing by J. J. Young from a sketch by A. H. Campbell (In Whipple, Ewbank, and Turner, "Report … upon the Indian Tribes" in 1853–54; courtesy DeGolyer Library, Southern Methodist University)

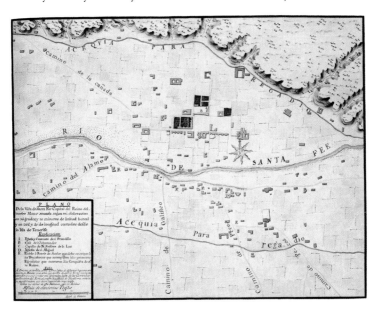

Plate 8. "Plano Dela Villa de Santa Fee." Santa Fe was still a village when Lieutenant José de Urrutia drew this map in 1766. Urrutia called attention to five of the town's special features: the church of San Francisco, the Palace of the Governors, the Chapel of Nuestra Señora de la Luz, the church of San Miguel, and the *barrio* of Analco. Urrutia's map was not published in its day and so made no impact on the reading public. (Fray Angélico Chávez History Library, New Mexico History Museum, Santa Fe)

Plate 9. Richard H. Kern, *La Parroquia, Santa Fe, New Mexico,* watercolor heightened with gum glaze over graphite on paper, 1849. Santa Fe's present cathedral was built around and over La Parroquia so as not to interrupt parish services. When the cathedral was finished, workers demolished La Parroquia and hauled out the rubble through the cathedral's doors. (Courtesy Amon Carter Museum of American Art, Fort Worth, Texas, 1975.16.9)

Plate 10. "Mission of San Xavier del Bac, near Tucson, Sonora," watercolor by Samuel Chamberlain, based on his "visit" while under arrest in 1848 (From a manuscript page in Samuel Chamberlain's memoirs; courtesy of the West Point Museum Collection, United States Military Academy)

Plate 11. Gustave Baumann, *Church—Ranchos de Taos,* 1919 (subsequent edition 1948), color woodcut, 9⅜ × 11¼ in. (Collection of the New Mexico Museum of Art, museum purchase with funds raised by the School of American Research, 1952, 1158.23G, © New Mexico Museum of Art; photograph by Blair Clark)

Plate 12. "Presidio of Tucson Sonora," watercolor by Samuel Chamberlain, 1848. At the time of this rendering, Tucson belonged to Mexico. While there (and still in chains), Chamberlain made this painting in his sketchbook, and also resolved to desert the army. In his autobiography, *My Confession,* he writes that with the help of the "lachrymal outlaw," Crying Tom Hitchcock, he soon made his escape and joined the infamous Glanton Gang. (From a manuscript page in Samuel Chamberlain's memoirs; courtesy of the West Point Museum Collection, United States Military Academy)

the old fort, where Mohave children were "instructed" to abandon their language, culture, and even their Mohave names. The school operated until 1931, and the buildings were destroyed in 1942, presumably little mourned by former students.

Today, the Mohave people remain divided between Fort Mohave and CRIT populations. Some enjoy comparative prosperity by leasing lands for large-scale irrigated agriculture or by participating in tribal businesses that include casinos, convenience stores, gas stations, RV parks, a golf course, and even an auto-racing track. All, however, face the economic and cultural challenges common to native people throughout the United States, but with a twist: the tribes control some of the most senior water rights along the lower Colorado River. By contrast, the rights belonging to the Central Arizona Project (CAP), which supplies water to the Phoenix and Tucson metropolitan regions, were subordinated (made junior) to all of California's Colorado River water rights when Congress authorized the CAP in 1968. When, not if, future shortages on the lower Colorado leave the CAP's rights unfulfilled, the Mohaves, whose senior rights will still be honored, may find themselves in the powerful position of brokering the reallocation of large quantities of a scarce and extremely valuable resource.[28]

# 10 Rainbow Bridge

Like Carlsbad Caverns, Rainbow Bridge escaped the notice of the wider world until the twentieth century. Unlike Carlsbad Caverns, Rainbow Bridge stood in plain sight—majestically so. It is the largest natural bridge in the world and, by at least one accounting, ranks as one of the "wonders of America."[1] Part of its attraction is its beauty. Viewed from any angle, the redrock sandstone arch is exquisitely graceful, an astonishing quality for a structure so massive and so large. The United States National Park Service, which administers Rainbow Bridge National Monument, measures the sandstone bridge's height at 290 feet and its span at 275 feet. A succession of writers have repeated the observation that the U.S. Capitol could fit under the arch with three feet to spare.

Despite its monumental proportions, Rainbow Bridge's remote location in the slick-rock canyon country of far southeastern Utah, wedged between the immensity of Navajo Mountain and the maze-like voids of the Colorado River's Glen Canyon, kept it out of sight of Spaniards and Anglo Americans until the nineteenth century. For questing trailblazers and fortune seekers, it lay on the path to nowhere. For the natives of the region, however, it was a destination in itself, a place of power and high holiness. The Navajos saw the bridge as a rainbow turned to stone, which formed the handle of the cradleboard of the Hero Twins, two of the most important figures in Navajo religious tradition. This one-sentence summary, however, barely scratches the surface of the significance of Rainbow Bridge and the canyon, known as Bridge Canyon, that contains it, in the cosmology and traditions of the Navajo people. Suffice it to say, one did not approach the place casually.[2]

Abundant evidence suggests that Anglo American trappers and miners visited Rainbow Bridge in the 1800s, but none called it to public attention. In the summer of 1909, however, two different parties, one led by Byron Cummings, a self-trained archaeologist and future president of the University of Arizona, and the other by William B. Douglass, a surveyor for the General Land Office, forged an uncomfortable partnership to "discover" Rainbow Bridge and to provide the first written impressions of this now iconic place.[3]

Byron Cummings captained what he termed the Utah Archaeological Expedition. Born and reared in upstate New York, Cummings had come to Utah in 1893 to teach Greek and Latin at the University of Utah. As he traveled the state, he took a serious interest in its prehistoric past, developing a course in American archaeology at the university. In the summer of 1907, two years before he found his way to Rainbow Bridge, he and a crew of student volunteers surveyed White Canyon, west of Blanding, Utah. There they discovered a series of beautiful natural bridges, and their report set the stage for the federal government to create Natural Bridges National Monument on April 16, 1908.[4] This was Utah's first national monument. (Rainbow Bridge never formed part of that preserve, but it became, instead, its own national monument in 1910.)

In the field season of 1908 Cummings returned to southeast Utah with his students, hiring an experienced Indian trader, John Wetherill, the brother of Al and Richard Wetherill of Mesa Verde fame, to outfit and guide his party. With his wife Louisa, John Wetherill had recently built a trading post in Oljeto Wash south of the San Juan River in one of Utah's remotest corners. (The names of the trading post and the community that exist there today are generally spelled *Oljato,* although the wash and its canyon usually appear as *Oljeto.* Either way, the spellings are corruptions of the Navajo word for "moonlight water.") In late summer 1908, Louisa Wetherill told Cummings that a Navajo elder had mentioned a large natural bridge in the area of Navajo Mountain.[5] As the season was late and classes were soon to begin, the professor proposed that he and the Wetherills search for it the next summer, 1909.

The leader of the other party to "discover" Rainbow Bridge, William B.

Douglass, also learned of its existence in the summer of 1908, but from a different source—a Paiute known to the Anglo Americans as Mike's Boy, Mike being his father, or Jim Mike, or simply Jim. Born in Indiana and trained as a lawyer, Douglass was new to the Southwest in 1908. He held the impressive title of examiner of surveys for the General Land Office (GLO), which was an agency of the Department of the Interior in Washington, D.C. The GLO, a precursor to today's Bureau of Land Management, bore responsibility for the administration of nearly all public lands, a task that was trimmed back by the creation of the Forest Service in 1907 and that would be further reduced by the creation of the National Park Service in 1916.

The GLO had sent Douglass to Utah to survey the newly declared Natural Bridges National Monument. Although Douglass's survey covered the same area that Cummings had reconnoitered the previous summer, he neglected to mention Cummings's work in his official report. Douglass, as events would prove, was not inclined to share credit with anyone. In October, his survey of Natural Bridges complete, Douglass set out for the Wetherill trading post at Oljato, where he hoped to procure provisions, animals, and information that would allow him to search for the bridge that Mike's Boy had described as "like a rainbow."[6] But it was late in the season and, like Cummings, Douglass felt compelled to put off the search until the next summer. Interestingly, he seems to have left Oljato in the autumn of 1908 convinced that the Wetherills knew nothing of the bridge until he told them about it. For their part, the Wetherills, who had already been informed of the bridge by the unnamed Navajo elder, apparently feigned ignorance in an attempt "to convince Douglass that Mike's Boy was either wrong about the existence of the bridge or misinformed about its location."[7] This subterfuge would later fuel Douglass's contention that he and Mike's Boy were the true discoverers of Rainbow Bridge.

In the summer of 1909, the task of finding the great stone bridge north of Navajo Mountain topped the agendas of both Douglass and Cummings, but first, other work demanded the attention of both men. Douglass had received orders to survey certain areas in southwestern Colorado, while Cummings needed to complete excavations in Arizona at Navajo National Monument, on land that the government had set aside for public purposes earlier that year. Cummings possessed a permit to conduct archaeological work at the site, but this did not stop Douglass, having identified a potential rival, from entreating government officials to revoke the permit and confiscate Cummings's artifacts. Douglass spread the view that Cummings was little more than a pot hunter and warned that the artifacts he unearthed would end up at the University of Utah rather than in the nation's capital.

In early August, John Wetherill appeared at Cummings's dig at the ruins of Keet Seel in Tsegi Canyon in the heart of the monument. By prearrangement Wetherill had brought supplies for their long-awaited search for the great stone bridge. Wetherill had also arranged to pick up a guide along the way—Nasja Begay, a Paiute who lived near Navajo Mountain and who claimed to have seen the bridge. Wetherill also brought surprising news. Douglass, he reported, was about to search for the bridge and was expected at Wetherill's Oljato trading post in four days to obtain provisions for his own expedition.

It stands to reason that, if Cummings had thought he was in a race with Douglass to discover Rainbow Bridge, he would have immediately forged ahead. He and Wetherill had a substantial head start on Douglass, and they had also obtained the services of a knowledgeable guide. But Cummings saw things in a different light. Against Wetherill's advice, he took a long detour to Oljato. There he hoped to talk with Douglass in person and learn his motives for trying to obstruct his archaeological work.

When Douglass and Cummings met at Oljato, Cummings was too polite to ask directly about Douglass's efforts to cancel the archaeological permit, and Douglass, perhaps aware that he was in the wrong, said nothing about it. Since both had the fabled stone rainbow in their sights, Cummings apparently proposed that the two men combine their parties. A "condescending" Douglass, as Cummings dryly remembered it, "said he was going to find the big arch he had heard about, that his Pahute [Paiute] guide, Mike's Boy, knew the country, had been to the bridge, and that we might go along if we wanted to. A wonderful privilege under the circumstances."[8]

So it was that the two men made the difficult desert journey from Oljato to Navajo Mountain, and beyond to Rainbow Bridge, together. Perhaps it was to be expected that they would remember, or at least report, the details

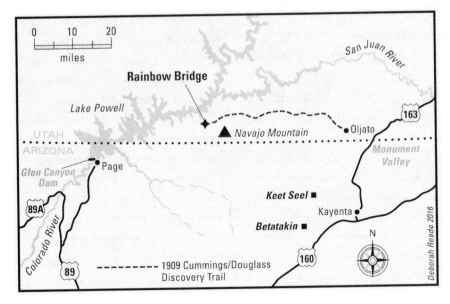

The location of Rainbow Bridge (Map by Deborah Reade)

of their mutual discovery quite differently. Let's begin with the official report that William Douglass submitted to the Government Land Office in the spring of 1910.

*I left Bluff, Utah, on August 9, 1909, on a hunt for the bridge with a party consisting of John R. English, head chainman; Jean F. Rogerson, 2d chainman; Daniel Perkins, flagman and packer; John Keenan, flagman, and Jim (Mike's Boy) as guide.*

*At Oljato, Utah, I met Professor Cummings of Salt Lake City, who with three students had been hunting relics in the interest of the University of Utah. He was preparing to start in search of the bridge, having learned of my proposed trip from Mr. Wetherell, whom he had employed as a guide. From this point we proceeded as one party all under the guidance of Jim. Later, we jointly employed an additional guide, a Paiute named Nasja Begay, supposed to have a better acquaintance with the local trails.*

*The route passed over a most interesting country but full of dangers and difficulties for the traveler, cut as it was with numerous box canyons, up the almost perpendicular side of which we clambered along crudely constructed Indian trails, passing over sloping sandstone ledges into which footholds had to be cut to support the horses. At night, camps were made in canyon bottoms where water and fuel were always to be had.*

*After two days of travel it became apparent that my pack horses could not make the trip so heavily laden, as the country was becoming more and more difficult to traverse. A halt was made and everything possible was thrown off, taking barely enough provisions to last during the survey should the bridge be found worthy.*

*On the morning of the last day's travel, when we were told by the Indian guides that the bridge would be reached by noon, the excitement became intense. A spirit of rivalry developed between Professor Cummings and myself as to who should first reach the bridge. The first 3 places of the single file line were of necessity conceded to the 3 guides. For 3 hours we rode an uncertain race, taking risks of horsemanship neither would ordinarily think of doing, the lead varying as one or the other secured the advantage over the tortuous and difficult trail.*

*Fortune favored me at the close, the Professor being some hundred feet in the rear when I reached the bridge. After him was an old gray pack horse who, assisted by Jean Rogerson, seemed anxious to be the first pack to arrive. The bridge was reached on Saturday morning August 14, 1909, at 11 o'clock. To Jim is due the*

The first photograph of Rainbow Bridge, August 14, 1909, taken by Stuart M. Young, a nineteen-year-old engineering student and grandson of Brigham Young (Northern Arizona University, Cline Library, Stuart M. Young Collection)

*credit of giving to the world the first knowledge of this remarkable monument; to the General Land Office belongs the credit for the discovery to civilization, and for its preservation as a National Monument.*[9]

In Douglass's apportioning of credit, Cummings, John Wetherill, and Nasja Begay receive none, which seems harsh treatment for trail mates whose labors contributed to the ultimate success of the expedition. In Chapter 3 we noted the considerable haggling over who might claim credit for first identifying the Carlsbad Caverns, but that dispute quickly cedes importance to Jim White's indisputable first entry into the bowels of the cave. Here the drive to be "first," at least in Douglass's mind, appears almost pathological. By his calculation, if he sees the bridge a half second before Cummings does, then he has earned all of "the credit for the discovery to civilization" and Cummings none. One marvels at the selfishness of such a view.

Douglass goes on to deliver the measurements of the bridge:

*Mr. Wetherell had succeeded in scaling the south walls of the cliff and re-turned with the information that the top of the bridge could be reached by means of a long rope. I dispatched my two chainmen and flagman with the necessary ropes. They lowered themselves over a 50-foot ledge to a point on the south arch of the bridge where sufficient footing was afforded to enable them to clamber to the top.*

*Two steel tapes having a combined length of 333 feet were lowered over the edge to the bed of the stream below. Later I was lowered to the bridge and made measurements as to width. We were the only ones to reach the top of the bridge....*

*It required more time to make the segregation survey than was anticipated. Our supply of food was exhausted. At the close of the last day of laborious cliff climbing, we ate our last food which consisted of one biscuit and a spoonful of boiled beans per man. For the next days we had nothing whatever, but we succeeded in finishing the survey and reaching the supplies we had left on the way....*

*Not only is this bridge the greatest known as to size, but it is more delicately proportioned than any of its rivals: A graceful, rainbow-like arch of buff sand-stone, with a span 278 feet, towers 309 feet above the bed of the small stream that winds its way through the rugged gorge below. The width is but 33 feet and the thickness of the arch only 42 feet.*

*Like the White Canyon Bridges, it was formerly a tongue of sandstone projecting from the south wall of the canyon, around the end of which the water surged, until long-continued wear undermined the rock. The stress of gravitation caused it to break[,] the arch formed[,] and weathering rounded it to the graceful rainbow outline.*

*Since the formation of the bridge, the water has cut a gulch 80 feet in depth through which runs a stream of clear water coming down from the Navajo Mountain. Almost under the arch, on the north side of the gulch is a pile of rocks which formed the wall of some small prehistoric structure in front of which slabs of sandstone set on edge outline an oval 3 × 5 feet—an altar, perhaps erected by the cliffdweller who no doubt viewed the great bridge with superstitious awe.[10]*

Douglass evinces no great curiosity about the ancestral Puebloan ruins in the canyon near the bridge, nor about the significance of the place in the Navajo worldview, except that on a second visit to the bridge two months later he derives amusement from the "superstition" of his guide Whitehorse Begay:[11]

*On my second visit to the bridge, I had with me a Navajo known as White Horse who after passing under the arch would not retrace his steps but invariably, at considerable personal inconvenience, would clamber around its north end. On being pressed for an explanation of his peculiar conduct he would only shake his head mysteriously and point to the sun.*

*Later, Mrs. John Wetherell, an accomplished Navajo scholar, obtained from an old Navajo the information that the arch represented the rainbow or sun path, and that he who passed under the arch could not retrace his steps without uttering a certain prayer under penalty of death. White Horse's trouble was he did not know the prayer, and was taking no chances.*

*Nothing could induce the old Indian to repeat the prayer for fear the "lightning snake" would bite him. This superstition and the shape of the bridge suggests as a name "The Rainbow," or "Barahoini," the Paiute equivalent.[12]*

Douglass's report was not immediately published, but Byron Cummings had a good idea of the attitude it would express because of the way Douglass had boasted about *his* discovery. Articles about the discovery had appeared in the regional press within weeks of the explorers' return, but Cummings soon had the satisfaction of bringing the bridge to the attention of a national audience.[13] After returning from the field that autumn he wrote an article titled "The Great Natural Bridges of Utah" for *National Geographic,* which appeared in February 1910. In it, he compared Virginia's much-visited Natural Bridge with Utah's little-known but larger bridges, three of which had spurred creation of Natural Bridges National Monument in 1908. Cummings, however, reserved his greatest praise for Rainbow Bridge, which he said was even more "marvelous" than any of the others. Here, from the *National Geographic,* is his description of Rainbow Bridge, to which he refers by one of its Navajo names, Nonnezoshi, or Nageelid Na'n'izoozhi, meaning Hole in the Rock Shaped like a Rainbow.[14] Cummings makes no mention of the role of the Indian guides or of the difficulties of the sometimes perilous journey from Oljato, but his focus is not on the finding of the bridge but on the character of the bridge itself.

*By going down the San Juan River from Bluff 25 miles to the new oil town of Goodridge and crossing the river over the new steel bridge now nearly completed, and then taking a southwesterly course of about 50 miles across the country, one may visit the recently discovered natural bridge known to the Indians as Nonnezoshi (the stone arch).*

*This is the largest natural arch yet found and measures 308 feet in height and 275 feet between the abutments.[15] It extends from a bench on one side across into a cliff on the other and hence spans the canyon in which it is found. This canyon, called by the Indians Nonnezoshi-boko, extends from the slopes of Navajo Mountain northwest and joins the Colorado River a few miles below the mouth of the San Juan. It is a deep, irregular gorge, in places so narrow that one has to walk in the stream in order to make his way along its course. The arch is situated about 6 miles above the mouth of the gorge in an exceedingly picturesque and beautiful part of the canyon.*

*This region formerly belonged to the Navajo reservation, then was segregated and held open to entry for a time, and now is included in that part of Utah recently set aside as a reservation for the Pahutes. It is seamed by deep gorges extending north and northwest toward the San Juan and the Colorado [Rivers] and broken by high cliffs and stretches of smooth, steep sandstone, so that it is almost impenetrable.*

*Few even of the Indians are well acquainted with this region. It is celebrated as the place where Hoskinimi, one of the most revered leaders among the Navajo, successfully evaded Kit Carson, in 1866, when the latter taught the Navajo such a terrible lesson; but not even Hoskinimi seems to have penetrated as far as the Nonnezoshi.[16] The members of the Utah Archeological Expedition and of [the] surveying party of the U.S. General Land Office, who visited the bridge together August 14, 1909, are evidently the first white men to have seen this greatest of nature's stone bridges. . . .*

*This remarkable freak in the earth's crust is hardly a bridge in the true sense of the term, but is more properly an enormous flying buttress that has been chiseled out by the ages and left as a specimen of the handiwork of the Master Builder. The surface formation of this section is the same thick bed of red and yellow sandstone found in the region of White Canyon, and Nonnezoshi has been cut out of the cliff in the same manner that the White Canyon bridges were formed. It is a graceful arch, looked at from any position, and is only about 20 feet thick in the narrowest part.*

*This slender arm of the cliff stretches out across the canyon like a rainbow. In its shadow on the bench at one side are the remains of what was probably an ancient fire shrine. One can easily imagine a group of cliff-dwellers gathered around the sacred fire with offerings to the Sun Father and the Earth Mother. The Pahutes look upon it with awe, and Mr. C.A. Colville, who took a party there in November, tells us that their Pahute guide, Whitehorsebiga, would not pass beneath the arch because he had forgotten the prayer that must be said before doing so.[17]*

Cummings's spare account avoided any hint of tension between the two parties. He shared credit for what he modestly described as an apparent discovery with a surveying party of the U.S. General Land Office, but he did not identify William Douglass by name as the head of that party. Cummings had good reason to overlook Douglass, for not only had the surveyor tried to stop his archaeological project, he had also behaved arrogantly and competitively throughout the expedition to Rainbow Bridge.

Neil Judd, Cummings's nephew and protégé who had been part of the joint expedition, showed none of his uncle's restraint. Soon after his return he wrote an article for a Salt Lake newspaper attacking Douglass head-on. Judd responded to Douglass's claim that he was the first to see the bridge and "that the Utah men attached themselves to his party and that his Indian, Jim's boy, was the real guide of the expedition."[18] Indeed, Judd's

The expedition at Rainbow Bridge. *Front row, from left:* Mike's Boy (Jim), John Wetherill, Byron Cummings, William Douglass, and Cummings's young son, Malcolm. *In the back row, far right:* Don Beauregard, who did the first sketch of Rainbow Bridge; next to him, partially visible, is Neil Judd. (Northern Arizona University, Cline Library, Stuart M. Young Collection)

article focused on Douglass more than on the bridge, and his partisan report provides an interesting counterpoint to Douglass's self-aggrandizing account. Neil Judd would go on to become one of the Southwest's premier archaeologists, remembered primarily for his work on Pueblo Bonito in Chaco Canyon, but in 1909 he was a twenty-two-year-old student telling readers of the *Deseret News* what his uncle refrained from revealing to readers of *National Geographic.* He titled his article "How W. B. Douglass, U.S. Examiner of Surveys, 'Discovered' the Big Bridge." After a paragraph and a half of preliminaries, Judd gets to the point:

*It is to correct the false impression that the Douglass reports would convey and to give Prof. Cummings the credit that is so justly his, that this article is written. The author has been with Prof. Cummings on his last three expeditions, is familiar with his work, and also that of W. B. Douglass in southern Utah during the past summer. These words have not been penned with an idea of starting another Cook-Peary controversy, but merely of giving the public the plain truth, that it may judge for itself.*[19]

*Failed to Find Bridge.*

In 1908 W. B. Douglass surveyed the three bridges in White canyon and repeated the recommendation of Dean Cummings, made in the summer of 1907, that the bridges, and the ancient ruins in their immediate vicinity, be set aside as a national monument. He outfitted at Bluff City, employing George Perkins as head packer and Jim, son of a Piute Indian called Mike, as guide. While the surveying was being done, Jim told the Douglass men of a larger bridge in the neighborhood of Navajo mountain. In turn, Douglass, who is very hard of hearing, was informed of this other arch by his men. He expressed his desire to visit the bridge and, for that purpose, engaged the services of Jim for this summer. The Douglass guide admitted, during the summer months, he had never seen the Navajo mountain arch but believed that he could take his employer to it from information given him by Nashja [Nasja], a Piute Indian living on the edge of the Navajo reservation.

Late last fall [of 1908], Douglass led his party into the Moonlight region for the purpose of visiting this great bridge and also some large cliff houses, the existence of which he had learned from John Wetherill of Oljato, Utah. He got no nearer the bridge, than the Oljato trading post, and could not find the ruins even after Mr. Wetherill had furnished him with an abundance of information concerning their location.[20]

*Douglass' Smallness.*

Upon reaching Bluff City this year, Douglass learned that Prof. Cummings was at the head of an expedition in the territory he wished to enter. He delayed his work six days in order that he might telegraph the information to Washington and issue orders to have the Utah party expelled from the field. He even went so far as to claim that Prof. Cummings was excavating without a permit. It was his opinion that the results of the university people should be confiscated and, in Bluff City, he threatened he would do it.

At the time of his visit to the Oljato trading post in the summer of 1908, Mrs. Wetherill had told Dean Cummings the Navajo story of the bridge near Navajo mountain. At that time she did not know its exact location but promised to gain all the possible information concerning it. During the winter Mrs. Wetherill learned that Nashja and his son Nashjabega [Nasja Begay] had both visited the bridge. She told the boy that she wanted him to go [as her guide], if she ever made the trip to the arch. The young Piute promised to take her to it when summer came again.

*After waiting three days at Oljato, in the hopes of meeting Douglass, Prof. Cummings and his party prepared to leave for the bridge on the morning of Aug. 10. The services of Mr. Wetherill, interpreter and head guide for the Utah people, were limited, and further delay was impossible. Two of the saddle horses had wandered away, so that it was 11 o'clock before everything was ready. While eating a hasty lunch, the party was informed by an Indian who had just arrived at the post that some white men were coming. It was Douglass. He reached the store shortly before noon.*

*Parties Unite.*

*He said that he proposed to visit the big bridge. Dean Cummings suggested that the two parties unite, a suggestion that was quickly accepted by Douglass. It was agreed to go on that afternoon and, while the Douglass horses rested, he and his men were fed at the Wetherill table. The start was made about 4 o'clock. During the 12 miles that were covered before sundown, the Utah party was forced to wait several times for the heavily loaded Douglass horses. During the afternoon Mr. Wetherill told Douglass that neither his guide nor the Navajo horse wrangler with Prof. Cummings knew where the bridge was to be found, but that he would pick up Nashjabega at his hogan in Piute canyon. Mr. Wetherill told Douglass that this Indian, and his father, were the only ones he knew of who had actually been to the bridge. When the party reached the canyon in question, it was learned that the young Piute had taken his goats out upon the mesa pastures. Mr. Wetherill pushed on, hoping to find the bridge from the information that his wife had secured in her talks with Nashjabega.*

*During the extremely rough traveling that the party encountered the next day, both the Piute with Douglass and the Navajo in our employ, wished to desert. It was only by subjecting the two Indians to much ridicule that Mr. Wetherill was able to keep them. Before daylight the next morning, Nashjabega caught up with the expedition and was fed at the Cummings stable [table]. He had heard that Wetherill was going to the bridge and had come on to join the party on the strength of his agreement with Mrs. Wetherill the winter before.*

*Bridge Discovered.*

*The bridge was reached just before noon the next day [August 14; Judd seems to have miscounted his days]. It lay in a network of box canyons through which it would have been impossible for one, not familiar with the country, to have gone. I, personally, was in the rear, with part of the pack train, when the bridge*

*was first seen so that I do not know to whom the "honor" of first sight really be-*
*longs. I do know, however, that Douglass had done his best to keep in front of the*
*guides during the entire morning, and that the owner of the horse he was riding*
*had complained to another member of his party that "the old man would kill the*
*little mare if he had to ride her much farther at that gait."*

*The next morning Douglass measured the bridge and said that he did not*
*want the Utah people to use his measurements....*

*This has been a hurried account of the doings of the Utah party during the*
*time in which Douglass was in the field. His suggestion to Dean Cummings,*
*that the Utah Historical society present his boy, Jim, with a gold medal for guid-*
*ing them to the bridge, makes one laugh. In regard to "the party of gentlemen*
*from Utah, who wished to get the benefit of his guide, Mike's boy," and their real*
*connection with the examiner of surveys, enough has been said when the truth*
*has been told. W. B. Douglass would have returned to Bluff City a second time*
*without seeing ... "this highest of all natural bridges" ... had it not been for the*
*courtesy of Prof. Cummings.*[21]

In later accounts, Judd would declare unequivocally that Cummings saw
the bridge before Douglass, and Cummings himself also made that case.[22]
In 1952, in an account apparently based on his diary, Byron Cummings told
the personal side of the story that he had omitted in his article for *National
Geographic*.[23] The story includes Douglass's ploy involving Cummings's
eleven-year-old son, Malcolm, who was a member of the expedition, to
beat Cummings to the bridge.[24] Douglass, whose name Cummings mis-
spells as "Douglas," emerges from this story as a petty manipulator.

*When we reached Beaver Creek, Mr. Douglas was sure Noscha [Nasja] Begay*
*would never overtake us, that we would get lost in that terrible country where*
*there were no trails. Mike's Boy plainly did not know the country and was be-*
*coming frightened. However, there was good grass and water for the horses, so*
*we let the animals rest the remainder of the day. Mr. Wetherill knew the general*
*direction we needed to travel and we told Mr. Douglas that while it would take*
*us longer to find the big arch without Noscha Begay, we were going to make the*
*attempt. But Noscha Begay rode into camp about ten o'clock that night so all*
*was well.*

*Mr. Douglas still fussed about getting lost among the rocks and his guide be-*
*came still more scared. After we had negotiated the difficult, narrow Red Bud*

*Pass, Mr. Douglas, Mr. Wetherill, Noscha Begay and I halted in the shade of a cliff to let the packs catch up with us. Mr. Douglas turned to me and said, "I should think you would go back and look after that boy of yours. I have a boy a little older than yours, but I think too much of him to bring him into a country like this. If you thought anything of your boy, you'd stay with him and look after him."*

*I replied simply, "You need not worry about him. He is on a sure-footed pony and the boys will take just as good care of him as I could."*

*It was soon evident why Mr. Douglas was anxious that I fall behind with the packs. Before long we were in Nonnezoshiboko (Big Arch Canyon). Noscha Begay suggested that I ride ahead with him, saying that when we rounded a certain bend ahead, we could see the big arch Nonnezoshie.*

*As we reached the point and I saw the object of our long trek just a little way ahead, I turned and shouted, "Eureka, here she is!" I was thinking of the tired boys behind us who had so patiently endured the long hard trip over cliffs and through canyons never before traversed by white men.*

*We had to climb a short slope to reach a bench along which we must travel to get to the arch. Our ponies were tired, so Mr. Wetherill and I jumped off to lead our horses up the slope; but Mr. Douglas put spurs to his horse and made it lope up the hill. Mr. Wetherill was too quick for him, however; springing on his pony, he reached the goal and passed under the arch first.*

*Thus, I was the first white man to see the Rainbow Bridge and John Wetherill was the first white man to pass under this great arch. Its real discoverers were the two Pahute Indians, Noscha and Noscha Begay.*[25]

Cummings's version of the events of August 14, 1909, supported by John Wetherill, has won the most adherents, but one scholar who has studied what he called the "race" to discover Rainbow Bridge has offered a tantalizing hypothesis.[26] Based in part on statements by Louisa Wetherill, Stephen Jett argues that John and Louisa Wetherill located the bridge months before its "official" discovery, but kept it a secret so that their client, Cummings, could claim credit. It was good for Wetherill's business to have his clients make "discoveries."[27]

The U.S. government, which created Natural Bridges National Monument in 1908, quickly recognized the significance of the rainbow arch. On

May 30, 1910, President William Howard Taft created Rainbow Bridge National Monument. The boundaries of the 640-acre monument were as Douglass surveyed them, and remain so today. Douglass was also responsible for selecting the name Rainbow, although he had recommended the Paiute word for rainbow, Barahoine.

Visitors began to come, and many left written accounts of their adventures because they found the journey itself as remarkable as the destination.[28] As the western novelist Zane Grey, who traveled to the Rainbow in 1913, put it: "It was not for many eyes to see. The tourist, the leisurely traveler, the comfort-loving motorist would never behold it. Only by toil, sweat, endurance and pain could any man ever look at Nonnezoshi. It seemed well to realize that the great things of life had to be earned. Nonnezoshi would always be alone, grand, silent, beautiful, unintelligible."[29]

John Wetherill continued to be the principal guide for visitors like Zane Grey. In December 1910 Wetherill moved his trading post thirty miles south from Oljato to Kayenta, in northeastern Arizona, and for the next fifteen years the trickle of visitors to the bridge went by way of Kayenta, some seventy miles on horseback each way.[30] In 1925, a new road and a new lodge shifted visitors away from Kayenta to Rainbow Lodge on the south side of Navajo Mountain, just thirteen miles from the bridge. In the late 1930s, visitors began to come by boat via the Colorado River, putting ashore on the beach at the mouth of Forbidding Canyon and hiking some six miles to the bridge. In the late 1950s, when the acerbic naturalist Edward Abbey made that journey, he observed that of the many who arrived at the mouth of the canyon by boat, few made the hike. Most tourists, he said, regarded a six-mile walk as a "semiastronomical" distance.[31] Abbey signed his name in the Rainbow Bridge register as visitor number 14,468, which he thought a small number to visit so great a site over the course of half a century.

Today, an equal number of people may visit the bridge in a single month, and more than two hundred thousand in a year. Even as Edward Abbey made his pilgrimage to the Rainbow, work on Glen Canyon Dam had begun.[32] After completion of the dam in 1963, the waters of newly created Lake Powell began to rise behind it, filling tributary canyons and enabling visitors to travel up Bridge Canyon by motorboat and come ashore at the foot of the Rainbow. The new water route, Abbey predicted, would transform "what was formerly an adventure into a routine motorboat excursion.

Those who see it then will not understand that half the beauty of Rainbow Bridge lay in its remoteness, its relative difficulty of access, and in the wilderness surrounding it, of which it was an integral part."[33]

In 1999, the last time Lake Powell was effectively full, forty-two feet of water stood in the canyon beneath the bridge. Since then, overuse and drought (consistent with climate change predictions) have shrunk the water reserves of the Colorado River system, so that in the autumn of 2015 the lake was only half full. By then the floating dock that accommodated motorboats at Rainbow Bridge had been moved down the canyon with the receding waters, and the walk up to the stone rainbow had necessarily lengthened. But still visitors come by the thousands, drawn by the graceful geologic marvel. A few hardcore desert rats, eschewing the boats, still make the trip to Rainbow Bridge on foot, circling Navajo Mountain as Cummings and Douglass once did, and logging more than seventeen miles of hard going to get there, plus seventeen more on the return.

Rainbow Bridge, however, has a far different resonance for many American Indians. For them Rainbow Bridge is not a new place but an old one. Traces of the passage of Paleo-Indians, as early as nine thousand years ago, have been found in Bridge Canyon, and modern Hopis, Paiutes, and Navajos continue to regard the canyon as a holy place, central to their understanding of their origins. The earliest Anglo visitors spotted a stone shrine close to the bridge, and Navajo ceremonies continue to be held there to the present day.

For Navajos, the waters of Lake Powell have undermined the sacredness of Rainbow Bridge. The tourists they carry to the holy place desecrate it with their presence and behavior, and they intrude on the privacy that is required for religious ceremonies. Because of this, in 1974, a group of Navajo religious leaders banded together to sue the secretary of the Interior and the heads of the National Park Service and the Bureau of Reclamation, which regulates the water level of Lake Powell, for violating their First Amendment religious rights, both as a result of the submergence of historic religious sites and because of infringements on Navajo religious practices caused by the influx of tourists. This was an unprecedented and glaringly public action on the part of the holy men, brought on by what they regarded as an exceedingly grave situation.

The case rose through the judicial system to the Federal Circuit Court of Appeals in Denver, which ruled against the Navajos in 1981. The decision was in interesting one, if disheartening to the plaintiffs. The court agreed that flooding Bridge Canyon violated the Navajos' religious rights, but it further reasoned that correcting the violation would jeopardize "the federal government's other compelling responsibilities of controlling water and producing power from Glen Canyon Dam."[34]

After the ruling, the National Park Service increased its efforts to accommodate Navajo ceremonies and honor the wishes of the tribe's spiritual leaders. Principally, it appealed to tourists to remain a respectful distance from the bridge. Although modest, this and other measures elicited lawsuits from non-Indians, which were bitterly contested. Sadly, it seems that while this iconic place gained new meaning in the late twentieth century as a site of touristic interest, it did so at the expense of those Navajos for whom it was an iconic spiritual site long before white men recorded their first impressions.[35]

# 11 Santa Fe

Today's Santa Fe, city and county combined, has a population of some 146,000, and it receives close to 2.5 million visitors a year. Its blue skies, striking vistas, high desert climate (at seven thousand feet), and nearby ski slopes and historic sites account for much of its popularity. Equally important, Santa Fe's picturesque architecture and streetscapes have endeared it to tourists. Its attractions are not accidental. The so-called Santa Fe style, an urban ensemble of adobe buildings that seem to rise organically out of the region's Spanish and Pueblo Indian pasts, was the product of invention. Influenced by the City Beautiful movement that swept across America, Santa Fe's boosters went a step further in the 1910s and characterized their community as "The City Different"—a motto used to the present day.

Before Santa Fe reimagined itself, generations of visitors had found it different, but far from beautiful. Indeed, most early visitors expressed disdain for the city's architecture, building materials, and streets. Alternately dusty or muddy, devoid of trees, and lacking in the amenities that one might find in more urbane places like Philadelphia or Mexico City, Santa Fe deserved some of that disdain. Yet the scorn that visitors expressed revealed as much about their biases and values as it did about the city itself. Early nineteenth-century Anglo Americans, for example, loathed Santa Fe for some of the same qualities that caused twentieth-century Anglo Americans to love it. The city had changed by the twentieth century, to be sure, but visitors' sensibilities had changed no less, and they did so in ways that helped shape the city's future.

Santa Fe's non-native origins date to 1608, if not before. North of today's Mexico, only two other European-founded communities have had a longer history of continuous occupation: Spanish St. Augustine (1565) and English Jamestown (1607). French Quebec had its beginnings in 1608, the same year as Santa Fe. Compared to Santa Fe, other important cities in the U.S. Southwest were late arrivals: Albuquerque was founded in 1706, Tucson in 1776, and Phoenix in 1868.

The beginnings of the Spanish capital are obscure. We know that Juan de Oñate traveled from central Mexico in 1598 to plant a permanent Spanish colony in New Mexico, settling in preexisting Indian pueblos on the Río Grande. A decade later, in 1608, it appears that a smattering of Oñate's colonists, led by Captain Juan Martínez de Montoya, established a small settlement at the foot of the Sangre de Cristo Mountains at a place uninhabited by Pueblo Indians. This village, which the Spaniards named Santa Fe for their holy faith, quickly came to the attention of the viceroy of New Spain, Luís de Velasco. In 1609 Viceroy Velasco dispatched a new governor to New Mexico with instructions to found a chartered town, or *villa,* at the site where Captain Martínez had established Santa Fe. When the new governor, Pedro de Peralta, arrived with a small military retinue and a few priests in late 1609 or early 1610, he apparently carried out the viceroy's instructions, establishing Santa Fe as New Mexico's capital and its only officially designated town.[1]

Located some fifteen hundred difficult and dangerous miles north of Mexico City, Santa Fe developed slowly. Spaniards failed to find anything of value that might mark New Mexico as a *new* Mexico possessing the kind of opulence that had enriched Cortez and other early conquistadors, and Spanish officials knew that a remote province lacking prosperous Indians and precious metals would drain rather than fill the royal coffers. Nonetheless, Spain's king, Philip III, supported New Mexico because Franciscan missionaries had baptized numerous Pueblo Indians and convinced the king that these converts needed to receive the Catholic sacraments or lose their souls to eternal damnation. It probably did not escape the king's attention that he would jeopardize his own chances for eternal life if he allowed the Pueblos to go to hell. Rather than abandon New Mexico as a profitless colony, Philip III gave it his support it as a center for maintaining and spreading the Catholic faith on the upper Río Grande.

Under these circumstances, it is not surprising that the first sustained description of Santa Fe came from a Franciscan, Alonso de Benavides. Fray Alonso had come to New Mexico in 1626 as the chief administrator of its missions. Three years later he returned to Mexico City with the triennial supply caravan and from there continued across the ocean to Spain. In a report published in Madrid in 1630, Benavides characterized his fellow Spaniards as instruments of a supernatural force and Franciscans' progress in New Mexico as miraculous. Infusing his statistics with hyperbole, Fray Alonso reported that he and his fellow friars had administered the sacrament of baptism to eighty-six thousand Indians—mostly Pueblos but also Navajos and Apaches—and he claimed that Spaniards had pacified five hundred thousand additional Indians who still awaited baptism. By comparison, current scholarship suggests that "the Puebloan population along the Río Grande and some of its tributaries in 1600 numbered about 50,000 people living in some eighty-one pueblos."[2] In an Age of Faith and scarce competing evidence, however, Fray Alonso's pronouncements elicited credence, as did his assertion that Santa Fe was the heart of a rich new field for missionary work that the Crown should support:

*The Villa of Santa Fé [is] head of this Kingdom, where reside the governors and the Spaniards, who must number as many as two hundred and fifty, though only some fifty of them can arm themselves, for lack of weapons. And though few and ill-equipped, God hath permitted that they should always come out victorious; and hath caused among the Indians so great fear of them and of their arquebuses that with only hearing it said that a Spaniard is going to their pueblos they flee. And to keep up this fear, when it is in order to punish some rebellious pueblo, they [Spaniards] use great rigors with them. Were it not for this, many times they [the Pueblos] would have tried to kill the Spaniards, seeing them so far from New Spain whence any succor might come to them. All the soldiers are well doctrinated [taught the catechism] and humble, and of good example, for the most part, to the Indians. Your Majesty supports this presidio [garrison], not with pay from your Royal coffers, but [by] making them [the Spaniards] encomenderos of those pueblos, by hand of the Governor.[3] The tribute which the Indians pay them is for each house one* manta, *which is one vara [thirty-three inches] of cotton cloth, and one* fanega *[roughly two bushels] of corn each year, wherewith the needy Spaniards sustain themselves. They must have in service seven hun-*

*dred souls; so that between Spaniards, half-breeds [mestizos], and Indians there must be a thousand souls [in Santa Fe]. And it is a folk so punctual in obedience to its governors that unto whatsoever fracas comes up they sally with their weapons and horses at their own cost and do valorous deeds. There lacked only the principal [thing], which was the church. The one they had was a poor hut, for the religious attended first to building the churches for the Indians they were converting and with whom they were ministering and living. And so, as soon as I came in as Custodian [in 1626] I commenced to build the church and monastery—and to the honor and glory of God our Lord, it would shine in whatsoever place. There already the Religious teach Spaniards and Indians to read and write, to play [instruments] and sing, and all the trades of civilization. Though cold, the spot is the most fertile in all New Mexico.*[4]

Father Benavides remained in Europe, traveling in Spain and Italy to gain support for the New Mexico missions and to elevate the ecclesiastic status of the province to a bishopric, which office he hoped to occupy. Although the bishopric failed to materialize and he never returned to New Mexico, Benavides eventually received an appointment as auxiliary bishop of Goa, a trading colony in Portuguese India.

Meanwhile, Santa Fe grew slowly. By 1660 its few residents inhabited thirty-eight adobe houses clustered around the *plaza principal* fronted by a parish church, town hall, and the *casas reales*—the building known today as the Palace of the Governors, which then housed government offices.[5] The neighborhood of San Miguel, with its chapel and modest homes, lay across the Santa Fe River. Removed from the center of town yet part of Santa Fe, San Miguel's residents were Hispanicized Tlaxcaltecan Indians from central Mexico who had accompanied the Spaniards northward. They were, like the Spaniards, tax-paying residents of Santa Fe—that is, *vecinos*.

If Pueblos initially feared Spaniards, as Benavides reported, fear eventually gave way to anger and courage. In 1680 many Pueblos united to force the Spaniards out of New Mexico. This unusual Indian victory over Europeans had been slow in coming, but in broad outline the causes of the conflict seem clear. Over the course of the 1600s the Spanish population had gradually risen while the Pueblo population, afflicted by deadly European-introduced diseases, had fallen. By 1680, a declining number of Pueblos were being forced to meet growing demands for tribute from their Spanish overlords. A prolonged drought worsened the situation. Crops withered, and Apaches, themselves suffering food shortages, increased their depredations. When Pueblos turned to traditional religious ceremonies to alleviate their suffering, Franciscans punished them for worshipping false gods.

In 1680, the Pueblos erupted. The revolt started in outlying areas, but Governor Antonio de Otermín soon found himself besieged in Santa Fe by some two thousand Indians, many armed with guns, lances, swords, and armor they had taken from Spanish victims. Of the thousand Spaniards who had gathered in Santa Fe, Otermín would later report, only one hundred were men-at-arms. The Pueblos tightened their siege. They cut off the water supply, sacked and burned homes, and forced the defenders to withdraw into the government buildings, their final redoubt. Faced with defeat and death if he held his ground, Otermín ordered a full-scale retreat. On August 21, the surviving Spaniards departed the charred remains of Santa Fe. The rebels (as Spaniards imagined the Pueblos, or freedom fighters, as the Pueblos might have described themselves) watched them go.[6]

Accompanied by a small number of Pueblos who remained loyal to them, the Spaniards fled three hundred miles down the Río Grande to the area of El Paso, not to return for a dozen years. During the Spaniards' absence, victorious Pueblo Indians occupied Santa Fe. They destroyed the church, government buildings, and other symbols of Spanish power, even as they strengthened the town's defenses. On a reconnaissance of New Mexico in 1692, Diego de Vargas reported that the Pueblos had expanded the old government buildings into a "fortress-pueblo."[7]

Santa Fe saw bloodshed and destruction once again when Spanish forces, led by Vargas, recaptured the town in 1693. With the aid of Pueblo allies (most of them drawn from the nearby pueblo of Pecos), Vargas's men broke through the gates, scaled the walls, and killed or seized the Pueblo defenders. Two Pueblo leaders committed suicide rather than be captured, and seventy others were executed.

Although the Pueblos failed to win permanent independence in 1680, their revolt marked a turning point in Spanish-Pueblo relations. Rather than risk another rebellion, Spaniards in eighteenth-century New Mexico made fewer demands on their Indian neighbors. They did not reestablish the *encomienda* nor did they forcibly suppress Pueblo religious ceremonies. In the 1700s new threats from Comanches, Apaches, and an expanding

French presence in Louisiana also encouraged coexistence between Pueblos and Spaniards, as they joined forces against common enemies. Their alliance won for the Pueblos a measure of freedom in the era that followed Vargas's reconquest of New Mexico. Through that time, Spain's military presence in New Mexico gradually strengthened, but even so, the garrison in Santa Fe lacked a barracks worthy of the name until 1791, and Pueblo auxiliaries remained essential to the success of Spanish arms.[8]

In designating Santa Fe a *villa* in 1609, the viceroy of New Spain had imagined that it would grow into a good-sized town, a settlement larger than a hamlet or village (*plaza* or *lugar*) but smaller than a city (*ciudad*). For the next two centuries, however, visitors described Santa Fe as a village (Plate 8). Certainly that was the view of the fastidious Fray Francisco Atanasio Domínguez, who produced the fullest description of Santa Fe in the eighteenth century. A Mexican-born Franciscan, Fray Francisco Atanasio was dispatched northward to report on the spiritual and economic condition of the New Mexico missions. Traveling over the *camino real* from Mexico City by way of El Paso (then part of New Mexico), the priest made it safely through lands controlled by Apaches and Comanches and arrived in Santa Fe in March 1776.

In the century and a half since Fray Alonso de Benavides's departure, New Mexico north of El Paso had grown to include three villas: Albuquerque and Santa Cruz de la Cañada (near present-day Española) now shared that status with Santa Fe. Nevertheless, in contrast to Fray Alonso's prediction of a rosy future in 1630, Fray Francisco Atanasio saw a province in decline, its sad condition exemplified by its capital: "Surely when one hears or reads 'Villa of Santa Fe,' along with the particulars that it is the capital of the kingdom, the seat of political and military government with a royal presidio, and other details that have come before one's eyes," one's expectations are dashed "as soon as its description is seen.... The location, or site, of this villa is as good as I pictured it in the beginning, but its appearance, design, arrangement, and plan do not correspond to its status as a villa nor to the very beautiful plain on which it lies, for it is like a rough stone set in fine metal."[9]

"In the final analysis," Domínguez wrote, Santa Fe "lacks everything. Its appearance is mournful because not only are the houses of earth [adobe], but they are not adorned by any artifice of brush or construction." To make matters worse, the population of the villa was too dispersed, its people living scattered among "many small ranchos at various distances from one another, with no plan as to their location, for each owner built as he was able, wished to, or found convenient, now for the little farms they have there, now for the small herds of cattle which they keep in corrals of stakes, or else for other reasons."

The town's sole street

*not only lacks orderly rows, or blocks, of houses, but at its very beginning, which faces north, it forms one side of a little plaza in front of our church [the parish church La Parroquia, which stood on the site of the present cathedral; Plate 9].[10] The other three sides [of the plaza] are three houses of settlers with alleys between them. The entrance to the main plaza is down through these. The sides, or borders, of the latter consist of the chapel of Our Lady of Light, which is to the left of the quasi-street mentioned, as has been said, and faces north between two houses of settlers.[11] The other side is the government palace, which, with its barracks, or quarters for the guard, and prison, is opposite the said chapel facing south. The remaining two sides are houses of settlers, and since there is nothing worth noting about them, one can guess what they are like from what has been seen. The government palace is like everything else here, and enough said.*

If the uninspiring adobe town did not merit further comment, the natural endowments of Santa Fe's location did:

*The sierra [the Sangre de Cristo Mountains] that lies to the east of this villa abounds in the firewood and timber needed by the population. There is a lake in it, from which a river with the most crystalline water takes its source.[12] Its current is so swift that in times of freshet it has done some damage, and although this was not extreme, measures have been taken to avoid further harm by installing a stone embankment. It runs from east to west, winding almost through the center of the villa, and although it carries enough water to be called a river, it is not overabundant. Indeed, it is usually insufficient, and at the best season for irrigating the farms, because there are many of them it does not reach the lowest ones, for the first, being higher up, keep bleeding it off with irrigation ditches, and only in a very rainy year is there enough for all. In such seasons ranchos 5 leagues downstream benefit as much as the rest. The water of this river runs three mills which are located from the foot of the sierra to just below our con-*

*vent. Although they do not grind large quantities, at least they lighten the labor of grinding by hand. There is trout fishing above in the canyon.*

As an emissary of Mexico City, steeped in the values of his time, Domínguez was acutely class-conscious, and he found little to admire in the comportment or speech of Santa Fe's residents. The worldly Domínguez thought the language of the locals old-fashioned and lacking in style:

*All the parishioners of this villa … speak the Castilian tongue simply and naturally among themselves, with the exception of the Europeans and other people from lands educated in speaking with courtly polish. This applies to the Spaniards, most of whom have servants of different classes, for only as a last resort do they serve themselves. … There are a number of* genízaro *Indians in this villa, who, after being ransomed from the pagans by our people, are then emancipated to work out their account under them.*[13] *Although they are servants among our people, they are not very fluent in speaking and understanding Castilian perfectly, for however much they may talk or learn the language, they do not wholly understand it or speak it without twisting it somewhat.*

For Domínguez, Santa Fe was a backward place, inhabited by rustics. He was not alone in this judgment. Anglo Americans, who approached Santa Fe from the east decades later, would view the town similarly. An army lieutenant and veteran explorer, Zebulon Montgomery Pike, was the first Anglo American to publish a description of Santa Fe based on a personal, albeit unintended, visit. Spain prohibited foreigners from entering its New World empire without special permission, so when Spanish troops discovered Pike in today's Colorado, in what was clearly Spanish territory, they arrested him as a spy (probably correctly) and brought him to Santa Fe on March 3, 1807. When he returned to the United States, Pike published an account of his adventures. It included a description of Santa Fe, which, however brief, was the only authentic account available to his English-speaking countrymen in the years before Mexican independence and the opening of the Santa Fe Trail.

Santa Fe, Pike wrote, "is situated along the banks of a small creek, which comes down from the mountains, and runs west to the Río del Norte. The length of the capital on the creek may be estimated at one mile; it is but three streets in width." From a distance, Pike thought that Santa Fe's flat-roofed adobe buildings looked like

*a fleet of the flat bottomed boats, which are seen in the spring and fall seasons, descending the Ohio river. There are two churches, the magnificence of whose steeples form a striking contrast to the miserable appearance of the houses. On the north side of the town is the square of soldiers houses, equal to 120 or 140 [feet] on each flank. The public square is in the centre of the town; on the north side of which is situated the* palace *(as the[y] term it) or government house, with the quarters for guards, &c. The other side of the square is occupied by the clergy and public officers. In general the houses have a shed before the front [by which he means a* portal, or covered porch], *some of which have a flooring of brick; the consequence is, that the streets are very narrow, say in general 25 feet. The supposed population is 4,500 souls. On our entering the town, the crowd was great, and followed us to the government house [the Palace of the Governors]. When we dismounted, we were ushered in through various rooms, the floors of which were covered with skins of buffalo, bear, or some other animal. We waited in a chamber for some time, until his excellency [Governor Joaquín Real de Alancaster] appeared.*[14]

Governor Real de Alancaster, courteous but firm, kept Pike in custody and sent him to Chihuahua for further questioning, an act that gave the putative spy a deeper and longer look at Mexico's interior than he might have obtained any other way. Pike had the further good fortune to be released in Chihuahua and escorted across northern Mexico and Texas to Louisiana. Other Americans who entered Spanish territory were not so lucky. Prison or house arrest awaited them.

Americans received a much different reception in New Mexico after Mexico won independence from Spain in 1821. Santa Fe, long the northern terminus for trade from Chihuahua, opened its doors to foreigners and became a western terminus for trade from Missouri, the nearest American state. Plying what came to be called the Santa Fe Trail, Mexican merchants headed eastward to the United States, and Anglo Americans went west to Santa Fe—a journey of some eight hundred miles. (Soon, as the Santa Fe market became saturated, they went even farther, trading deep into Chihuahua.)

Aware of the mines of northern New Spain, Anglo Americans initially supposed that Santa Fe was a wealthy place. Instead they found a humble frontier town constructed of mud bricks. One of those early visitors was Josiah Gregg, a medical doctor turned merchant, who recorded his impressions of the Santa Fe trade in a book, *Commerce of the Prairies*, that appeared in 1844 and went on to become a classic. Here he describes Santa Fe as he first encountered it in 1831:

*A few miles before reaching the city, the road again emerges into an open plain. Ascending a table ridge, we spied in an extended valley to the northwest, occasional groups of trees, skirted with verdant corn and wheat fields, with here and there a square block-like protuberance reared in the midst. A little further, and just ahead of us to the north, irregular clusters of the same opened to our view. "Oh, we are approaching the suburbs!" thought I, on perceiving the cornfields, and what I supposed to be brick-kilns scattered in every direction. These and other observations of the same nature becoming audible, a friend at my elbow said, "It is true those are heaps of unburnt bricks, nevertheless they are houses—this is the city of Santa Fé."*[15]

Gregg had ridden ahead with a dozen others and reached Santa Fe before the main body of his compatriots:

*Five or six days after our arrival, the caravan at last hove in sight, and, wagon after wagon was seen pouring down the last declivity at about a mile distance from the city. To judge from the clamorous rejoicings of the men, and the state of agreeable excitement which the muleteers seemed to be laboring under, the spectacle must have been as new to them as it had been to me. It was truly a scene for the artist's pencil to revel in. Even the animals seemed to participate in the humor of their riders, who grew more and more merry and obstreperous as they descended towards the city. I doubt, in short, whether the first sight of the walls of Jerusalem were beheld by the crusaders with much more tumultuous and soul-enrapturing joy.*

And then began the trading: "The arrival of a caravan at Santa Fé changes the aspect of the place at once. Instead of the idleness and stagnation which its streets exhibited before, one now sees everywhere the bustle, noise and activity of a lively market town. As the Mexicans very rarely speak English, the negotiations are mostly conducted in Spanish."

Like Domínguez and Pike, Gregg detailed the town's physical layout:

*Santa Fé, the capital of New Mexico, is the only town of any importance in the province. We sometimes find it written Santa Fé de San Francisco (Holy Faith of St. Francis), the latter being the patron, or tutelary saint. Like most of the towns in this section of country it occupies the site of an ancient Pueblo or Indian village, whose race has been extinct for a great many years. Its situation is twelve of [or] fifteen miles east of the Rio del Norte [Río Grande], at the western base of a snow-clad mountain, upon a beautiful stream of small mill-power size, which ripples down in icy cascades, and joins the river some twenty miles to the southwestward. The population of the city itself but little exceeds 3,000; yet, including several surrounding villages which are embraced in its corporate jurisdiction, it amounts to nearly 6,000 souls.*

*The town is very irregularly laid out, and most of the streets are little better than common highways traversing scattered settlements which are interspersed with corn-fields nearly sufficient to supply the inhabitants with grain. The only attempt at anything like architectural compactness and precision, consists in four tiers of buildings, whose fronts are shaded with a fringe of* portales *or corredores of the rudest possible description. They stand around the public square, and comprise the* Palacio, *or Governor's house, the Custom-house, the Barracks (with which is connected the fearful* Calabozo *[jail]), the* Casa Consistorial *of the* Alcaldes *[town hall], the* Capilla de los Soldados *or Military Chapel, besides several private residences, as well as most of the shops of the American traders.*

Although Gregg, like other Anglo Americans, lauded Santa Fe's cool, dry climate, he echoed Fray Francisco Atanasio Domínguez in dismissing the city and its structures as primitive. The town was so sleepy, Gregg supposed, that it required his fellow Anglo Americans to bring it to life. Where Fray Alonso de Benavides had seen the Christian deity and the Franciscans as the motor that made Santa Fe run, Gregg saw American commerce as the source of its energy. There was some truth to this view. By breaking the monopoly that merchants from Chihuahua had over local trade, Anglo Americans did make Santa Fe a more thriving commercial hub, but Gregg exaggerated. Santa Fe had possessed a vigorous local economy even before the arrival of *los americanos*.[16]

In the years between Mexican independence and the U.S.-Mexico War, Anglos arrived in significant numbers, some staying and others passing through, but familiarity did not increase their fondness for Santa Fe. The town remained as alien to the Protestants from across the plains as the darker-skinned, Spanish-speaking Catholics who inhabited it. With its low, flat-roofed, earth-colored houses, it reminded one visitor of an "assemblage of mole hills."[17] The American artist Alfred Waugh, who arrived in Santa Fe on June 24, 1846, just two months before its capture by U.S. forces at the outset of the U.S.-Mexico War, expressed the ethnocentrism typical of his place and time:

*Red granite abounds in the neighborhood, and although this fine building material is so convenient, yet for want of mechanical skill, or as is more likely, through pure laziness, the miserable beings who exist here, have not constructed their homes, or even their churches, of any other substances than sun-dried bricks. Their dwellings do not rise above the ground more than twelve or fifteen feet; they are flat-roofed and devoid of taste or ornament of any kind; the windows are small and placed low in the walls, and altogether present an appearance which is anything but pleasing to the eye. His Excellency, General Don Manuel Armijo, the present governor, dwells in a* palacio *whose externals differ very little from*

"La Ciudad de Santa Fé," lithograph based on a first-hand drawing by the West Point–trained topographical engineer Lieutenant James W. Abert, represents the first authentic artistic rendering of Santa Fe. An American flag flies over the plaza, and another atop a hill above town about six hundred yards northeast of the plaza, where the invading American army began to build Fort Marcy in 1846. (From *Report of Lieut. J. W. Abert of His Examination of New Mexico, in the Years 1846–'47,* 1848; courtesy DeGolyer Library, Southern Methodist University)

*those around it, only it has larger windows, is whitewashed, and a sentry keeps watch and ward at the entrance.... This building occupies one side of the Plaza, with the calabozo and guard-house at one end, and the office of the Secretary of State at the other. The Legislative Hall and the Custom-House occupy another side, while the remaining two contain the shops of the merchants and traders. All these are of the same general appearance, and are mean and dirty looking in an eminent degree. The whole is surrounded with portals, or as we could call them, piazzas, the supporting columns of which are rude trunks of trees, scarcely divested of their native roughness.*[18]

The American conquest of New Mexico did nothing to alter Anglo American attitudes toward the "mud town" of Santa Fe and its architecture. In 1866, for example, Colonel James Meline, a Union officer, readily dismissed Santa Fe's one-story adobe houses: "Nothing can be more sordid, monotonous, and un-architectural than the exterior of these buildings. They are built flush, as the carpenters say, with the street, presenting a naked wall with but one or two openings, surmounted with spouts which, in a rain, pour the contents of the roof some three feet into the street. Not a tree, shrub, paling [picket fence], or any thing for the eye's relief."[19]

In post–Civil War America, however, negative views of Santa Fe and its people began to fade. As the United States grew more urban and industrial, many Anglo Americans began to yearn for a simpler, agrarian past. They found it in Santa Fe, whose old, earthen structures conveyed a sense of permanence in a world fraught with change, and whose Spanish origins came to be regarded as evocative of a more romantic age.

When Lew Wallace came to Santa Fe to assume the governorship of New Mexico Territory in 1878, his wife, Susan, came with him. An aspiring writer like her husband (who famously wrote *Ben Hur* in his office in the Palace of the Governors), Susan Wallace produced a series of articles about New Mexico that revealed her contradictory reactions to Santa Fe. On the one hand she echoed Josiah Gregg and other early critics when she disparaged the town as resembling "an extensive brick-yard." Its adobe houses seemed as "comfortless" to her as the town itself, which was "older than the hills surrounding it, and worn out besides." Although Wallace found it "to the last degree disheartening" to travel its "narrow streets which appear mere lanes," she also anticipated the reactions of future visitors who

**Santa Fe Plaza,** circa 1855

"Santa Fe Plaza, circa 1855." This view of the southeast corner of the Santa Fe Plaza is among the first photographic representations of the city. As photographer William Stone has observed, "When photography was new, Santa Fe was old" (*New Mexico Then and Now,* 5). At right is the Seligman-Clever mercantile company; at left is the Exchange Hotel. In 1919 the Exchange was demolished and La Fonda Hotel, a prominent landmark today, replaced it on the same site. (Photographer unknown; courtesy Palace of the Governors Photo Archives, New Mexico History Museum [NMHM/DCA], negative no. 010685)

saw those same streets through a different lens: "Yet, dirty and unkempt, swarming with hungry dogs, it [Santa Fe] has the charm of foreign flavor, and, like San Antonio, retains some portion of the grace which long lingers about, if indeed it ever forsakes, the spot where Spain has held rule for centuries, and the soft syllables of the Spanish tongue are yet heard."[20]

On the wearying, jolting, seemingly endless journey to Santa Fe, Wallace had begun "to think the wayside crosses mark graves of travelers, murdered, not by assassins, but by the buckboard." But upon beholding the town, she was revived and found it "invested with indescribable romance, the poetic glamor which hovers about all places to us foreign, new, and strange.... At last, at last, I am not of this time nor of this continent; but away, away across the sea, in the land of dreams and visions, 'renowned romantic Spain.'"[21]

Clearly, Susan Wallace felt the beginnings of the spell that Santa Fe would cast over many tourists of the future, travelers seeking romance and respite. The spell affected men as well as women. A Kansas publisher, Noble Prentis, who visited Santa Fe shortly after Susan Wallace arrived, described its symptoms in a way that rings familiarly today: "If I was dyspeptic, worn out, a-weary of the world, tired of living and yet afraid of dying, I should come to Santa Fe in the summer-time and take some big, high, white-washed rooms in a Mexican house, with the fireplace in the corner. . . . I would . . . do nothing with great care and elaboration for awhile, and then I would return to the United States and join the 'march of progress,' which is doubtless a great thing, but which makes many people footsore."22

Susan Wallace had arrived in Santa Fe by buckboard, but Noble Prentis represented a new kind of visitor to Santa Fe—one who made the journey in comfort, by train—the very symbol of the progress that he sought to escape. Prentis had not, however, come to Santa Fe on the main line. Difficult terrain and Santa Fe's weak commercial potential had led the Atchison, Topeka, and Santa Fe Railway to bypass the town that bore its name and head directly toward larger markets in the rapidly developing Río Grande Valley. Albuquerque would be the big winner. The citizens of Santa Fe tried to offset the loss by raising money to bring a spur line from a depot at Lamy, eighteen miles to the east, but that did little to promote commercial development. To the contrary, the city's population fell from 6,635 in 1880, when the spur line arrived, to 6,185 a decade later. It declined further to 5,603 in 1900—even as New Mexico's population rose from 120,000 to nearly 200,000 during those same two decades.23 Despite Santa Fe's dwindling population, its position as territorial capital cushioned its economy (New Mexico was a territory from 1850 to 1912 rather than a state), as spending by politicians, civil servants, prison guards at the territorial penitentiary, teachers at a federal Indian school, and a trickle of tourists like Noble Prentis fueled its economy.

Although the spur line from Lamy never provided the commercial advantages that Santa Fe had enjoyed as a terminus of the Santa Fe Trail, the railroad did accelerate the Americanization of the town, a process made visible in Santa Fe's architecture. Logs and rough-hewn beams that supported the old *portales* were replaced with milled lumber, which was then whitewashed; adobe bricks were plastered over and the plaster stenciled to

"El Palacio, Santa Fé." The portal of Santa Fe's iconic Palace of the Governors, remodeled around 1855 and again in 1877–78, had its rough-hewn logs replaced by milled lumber and the addition of a decorative cornice. (Lithograph based on a drawing by Lew Wallace, in Susan E. Wallace, *Land of the Pueblos*, 1888; courtesy DeGolyer Library, Southern Methodist University)

look like stone; pitched roofs replaced flat roofs; brick coping and cornices, window and door moldings, and other elements added decoration. Before 1880, however, these innovations were confined largely to churches and to the buildings around the plaza, which began to resemble a Greek Revival town square somewhere east of the Mississippi.[24] After 1880 the arrival of iron rails and steam-powered transport made it easier to import machinery for milling lumber, cutting stone, and making brick, as well as cast-iron columns and other prefabricated building elements. With the availability of new tools and new materials, architectural styles from the East became commonplace on the streets that radiated from the plaza. Styles that had arrived before 1880 — Greek, Gothic, and Romanesque revivals — were joined in the 1880s by Italianate, Queen Anne, and Second Empire and later augmented by Colonial Revival and Neoclassicism in the 1890s.[25]

The new architectural fashions began inevitably to erase the vernacular style that had begun to charm tourists from the East, some of whom now lamented the loss. "Tourists who wish to visit the town should not delay," one visitor from Indiana gushed in 1892, "for the ruthless hand of progress will soon destroy the haloed glow of romance that broods with benign wings over the antique walls of this ancient city."[26]

Some of Santa Fe's leading citizens agreed, and resolved to put brakes on the local rush toward modernity. Foremost among these "anti-modernists" was a small group of writers, artists, archaeologists, and historians. By the early twentieth century Santa Fe had become popular, in the words of one guidebook, "as a summer residence for people from the South, and as a winter residence for people from the North, and as an all-the-year-round residence and sanitarium for people variously in search of health, comfort, pleasure, and business."[27] Through their writings and visual representations, the most creative of these newcomers celebrated the city's historic past, and some sought to use that past to shape its future. As the local newspaper reminded the citizenry in 1910, "The average man from the east ... does not come here to view Queen Anne cottages or factory chimneys. ... Old adobes which we despise are lodestones that help to make Santa Fe attractive to the traveling public."[28]

Other local leaders disagreed. They believed that Santa Fe would not progress until New Mexico achieved statehood and New Mexico would not become a state until it became less foreign and more American. Modernization, however, was failing to arrest the city's steady decline. Even as the population of New Mexico Territory rose, Santa Fe's population continued to fall, from 5,603 in 1900 to 5,072 in 1910, and economic activity weakened.[29]

The official prescription for ending this downward spiral arrived in 1912. Early that year, just months after New Mexico achieved statehood, the mayor of Santa Fe formed the City Planning Board and charged it with finding a way to turn the economy around. Fully aware of the economic potential of its vernacular architecture and inspired by the City Beautiful movement then sweeping the nation, the Planning Board, which included Edgar Lee Hewett, founder and first director of the Museum of New Mexico, and Sylvanus Morley, one of Hewett's most energetic acolytes, recommended "developing the town architecturally in harmony with its ancient character."[30] Winding streets, which once seemed in need of straightening, were now to be maintained as picturesque. Portales, once despised because they narrowed the streets, were now to be preserved precisely because they made the streets narrower and more visually interesting. Rustic, rough-hewn logs that had once supported portales but had given way to more refined milled lumber, were now to be restored because rusticity had become attractive. Humble sun-dried adobe bricks were to become, once again, the building material of choice, supplanting the stone and kiln-fired bricks that had supplanted them.

These were among the many ways that the Planning Board sought to express, if not invent, a regional architecture that drew from both the Pueblo and Spanish traditions. There was nothing inevitable about the adoption of this bicultural vernacular. The city might have echoed its Spanish architectural heritage alone, without Pueblo influences. The completion in 1912 of a Moorish-inspired Scottish Rite Masonic Temple, which copied features from the Alhambra, suggests one direction that the city might have taken. Instead of a Santa Fe style or Spanish-Pueblo Revival style, Santa Fe might have become known—or derided—for "Granada Revival."

Behind the Planning Board's turn toward the vernacular lay a credo to which Santa Fe has remained faithful to the present day: "We believe," the Planning Board declared, "that everything should be done to create a public sentiment so strong that the Santa Fe style will always predominate."[31] Happily for the Planning Board, Santa Fe's economic stagnation had left many of the town's older features intact, despite the forces of Americanization.

Although the plan of 1912 contained a blueprint for turning the results of stagnation into an asset, it met resistance from a number of quarters, brick makers not the least of them, and the city council rejected it. Undaunted, the plan's proponents, spearheaded by the New-Old Santa Fe Committee, kept up the pressure to create the Santa Fe that visitors wished to see. One of those visitors was E. Alexander Powell, a well-published travel writer who passed through the city at the time the Planning Board's recommendations were under debate. In the overwritten passage that follows, Powell lays out a vision for Santa Fe that echoes that of the Planning Board. He must have been familiar with the plan of 1912 as well as with the arguments against it, and he seems to have doubted that Santa Fe's leaders could bring it to fruition.

*Santa Fé, the capital of the State, is, to my way of thinking, the quaintest and most fascinating city between the oceans. Very old, very sleepy, very picturesque, it presents more neglected opportunities than any place I know. I should like to have a chance to stage-manage Santa Fé, for the scenery, which ranks among the best efforts of the Great Scene Painter, is all set and the costumed actors are wait-*

ing in the wings for their cues. Give it the advertising it deserves and the curtain could be rung up to a capacity house. Where else within our borders is there a three-hundred-year-old palace whose red-tiled roof has sheltered nearly five-score governors—Spanish, Pueblo, Mexican, and American? (In a back room of the palace, as you doubtless know, General Lew Wallace, while governor of New Mexico, wrote "Ben Hur.") Where else are Indians in scarlet blankets and beaded moccasins, their braided hair hanging in front of their shoulders in long plaits, as common sights in the streets as are traffic policemen on Broadway? Where else can you see groups of cow-punchers on sweating, dancing ponies and sullen-faced Mexicans in high-crowned hats and gaudy sashes, and dusty prospectors with their patient pack-mules plodding along behind them, and diminutive burros trotting to market under burdens so enormous that nothing can be seen of the burro but his ears and tail?

Though at present it is only a sleepy and forgotten backwater, with the main arteries of commerce running along their steel channels a score of miles away, Santa Fé could be made, at a small expenditure of anything save energy and taste, one of the great tourist Meccas of America. To begin with, it is the only place still left in the United States where Buffalo Bill's Wild West could merge into the landscape without causing a stampede. Those who know how much pains and money were spent by the municipality of Brussels in restoring a single square of that city to its original mediaeval picturesqueness, whole blocks of brick and stone having to be torn down to produce the desired effect, will appreciate the possibilities of Santa Fé, where the necessary restorations have only to be made in inexpensive adobe. Desultory efforts are being made, it is true, to induce the residents to promote this scheme for a harmonious ensemble by restricting their architecture to those quaint and simple designs so characteristic of the country, the Board of Trade [the City Planning Board] providing an object-lesson in the possibilities of the humble adobe by erecting a charming little two-room cottage, with an open fireplace, a veranda, and a pergola, at a total expense of one hundred dollars, but every now and then the sought-for architectural harmony is given a rude jolt by some one who could not resist the attractions of Queen Anne gables or Clydesdale piazza columns or Colonial red-brick-and-green-blinds.[32]

Set at the foot of the Sangre de Cristo Range, a mile above the level of the sea, with one of the kindliest all-the-year-round climates in the world, and with an atmosphere which is far more Oriental than American, Santa Fé has the making of just such another "show town" as Biskra, in southern Algeria, where Hichens

*laid the scene of "The Garden of Allah." If its citizens would wake up to its possi-
bilities sufficiently to advertise it as scores of Californian towns with not half of
its attractions are advertised; if they would restore the more historically important of the crumbling adobe buildings to their original condition and erect their
new buildings in the same characteristic and inexpensive style; if they would
keep the streets alive with the colourful figures of blanketed Indians and Mexican venders of silver filigree; and if the local hotel would have the originality to
meet the incoming trains with a four-horse Concord coach, such as is inseparably
associated with the Santa Fé Trail, instead of a ramshackle bus, they would soon
have so many visitors piling into the New Mexican capital that they could not
take care of them. But they are a* dolce far niente *["sweet doing nothing" or
"delicious idleness"] folk, are the people of Santa Fé, and I expect that they will
placidly continue along the same happy, easy, sleepy path that they have always
followed. And perhaps it is just as well that they should.*[33]

Of course, the "people" of Santa Fe did not follow that "sleepy path."
Santa Fe had already begun to remake itself into the "City Different" along
the lines that Powell and other romantic outsiders hoped it would. In 1913
an imaginative reconstruction of the façade of the Palace of the Governors
drew from the vernacular to give the building the solid, timeless appearance
it retains today. A block away and three years later, the doors opened to a
new Fine Arts Museum, a showy Spanish-Pueblo Revival building that borrowed features from several Franciscan missions, including Ácoma's. These
buildings became icons of the Santa Fe style—a style that spread through
Santa Fe and beyond.

From its humble beginnings in the early 1600s, Santa Fe had steadily
changed, as had the sensibilities of the many generations who recorded
their impressions of it. Ultimately, the impressions of observers proved so
powerful that they helped to reverse—or at least redirect—the Americanization of Santa Fe, creating a regional architectural identity that offers the
illusion of timelessness. By intention, Santa Fe became a tourist Mecca. The
costs of that transformation raise important questions. Have the advantages of tourism outweighed the negative impacts on longtime residents?
Has Santa Fe devolved into a theme park that caricatures itself?[34] These
issues were first debated early in the twentieth century, and the debate remains lively still.

# 12 San Xavier del Bac

Long ago, at the place called Wa:k, groundwater in the meandering, sandy bed of the Río de Santa María came reliably to the surface, or close to it, so that even in dry times, one could dig a hole and collect the precious fluid. Such an oasis was rare in the vastness of the Sonoran Desert, and a village took root whose people both gathered the wild fruits of the desert and grew corn nourished by the river's water. Things have changed since then, of course, as things have changed everywhere. The river has incised its channel, and the springs are gone, although the people are still there. The name of the river has changed, too, at least the name that was bestowed by people from far away. The name Santa María was forgotten, and Santa Cruz replaced it. On maps you will see that the Santa Cruz River, which is nearly always dry, "flows" from Nogales north through Tucson to lose itself in the Santa Cruz Flats near Casa Grande, just shy of the Gila, to whose watershed it belongs.

As you drive the interstate highway that parallels the river, your first sight of Wa:k, which Spanish missionaries wrote down as Bac, appears like a hallucination. Suddenly, amid the sweep of sun-bleached, thorny desert, you behold "a commanding building with a sensuous dome, elliptical vaults, sturdy bell towers, flying buttresses, and undulating parapets."[1] The edifice is so stunningly, brilliantly white, so sculpted in profile, and so anomalous to its setting that it has the look of a giant, unmelting ice cream confection, as cool as winter, as delicious as sugar.

This is the mission of San Xavier del Bac, which for a portion of its long and eventful history stood at the farthest limit of what a European then would have called the known world. It marked the very rim of Christendom.

*Rim of Christendom* is the title Herbert E. Bolton gave to his classic biography of the redoubtable Jesuit missionary Eusebio Francisco Kino, who was an Italian by birth and a geographer by instinct. In service to the Catholic Church of New Spain, Kino labored in northern Sonora and southern Arizona—the lands he called Pimería Alta—for a quarter century, preaching the Gospel, founding missions, encountering new peoples, and traveling without cease. The early days of the year 1691 found him pressing farther north than he had gone before. Across the divide at Nogales, he descended into the upper watershed of the Río de Santa María and stopped at a village of Sobaípuri Indians whose name he recorded as Tumagacori— today's Tumacácori. The Sobaípuris were part of the greater culture group we know today as the O'odham.[2] While Kino was there, as Bolton tells it, "Out of the north a band of warriors appeared at Tumacácori in full regalia. They were chiefs and headmen from the great Sobaípuri settlement of Bac, some forty miles beyond. They had come to urge the Black Robes [Jesuits] to visit their people also. Bac was a metropolis; Tumacácori a mere village."[3]

Kino wasn't immediately able to accept the invitation—he was already overdue to turn southward toward home—but he said he would return as soon as possible. He fulfilled this promise late in the summer of the following year, discovering a community of "more than eight hundred" souls centered at Wa:k, with more clusters of homes and fields scattered northward down the river. Kino preached to the natives "the Word of God, and on a map of the world showed them the land, the rivers, and the seas over which we fathers had come from afar to bring them the saving knowledge of our holy faith." He also explained "how in ancient times the Spaniards were not Christians, how Santiago came to teach them the faith, and how for the first fourteen years he was able to baptize only a few, because of which the holy apostle was discouraged, but that the most holy Virgin appeared to him and consoled him, telling him that Spaniards would convert the rest of the people of the world."[4] Surely Kino saw his own situation as similar to Santiago's.

Over the next eleven years, Kino paid at least seven visits to Wa:k, often passing through on journeys to more distant explorations, and by his own report, he was always warmly welcomed. No doubt the Sobaípuris held him in affection, but they also appreciated the things he brought with him. In January 1697, for instance, he and his party drove before them a small herd of mares and "*ganado mayor y menor*"—livestock large and small, which is to say cattle as well as sheep and goats.[5] Such animals would prosper in the virgin grasslands of the Santa Cruz Valley, and with their meat, muscle, and rawhide they would revolutionize the lives of the natives living there. Also revolutionary were the seeds and cuttings Kino brought to the valley, none more important than grains of wheat.

In April 1700 Kino came to Wa:k intending to continue his journey to the Gila, thence to the great Colorado River, and even to the fabled land of California which, according to the geography of the day, might or might not prove to be an island. Kino thought he might be able to settle this question, but at Wa:k he learned that his explorations would have to wait. Spanish soldiers were on the prowl not far away, and as their passage through the country sowed more discord than peace, the trails would be too dangerous for travel. Accordingly, Kino stayed put, but not idle. He lingered at Wa:k long enough to lay foundation stones for a mission church.[6]

Construction did not flourish. In the absence of a resident priest, the new church had still not risen far beyond its foundations when Kino died in 1711. Indeed, the "church" remained little more than a ramada (an open-air roof of poles to provide shade) more than two decades later, in 1734. When another ten years had passed, matters had seemingly worsened: a senior Jesuit, on a tour of inspection, made the following report: "There is a bad lot of Indians here and they are poorly instructed. Moreover, there are those who abandon the mission because pueblo life is not to their liking. There are many and powerful medicine men here and they slay one another. The missionaries who have resided here have become bewitched and it was necessary to withdraw them before they should die. This mission requires the assistance of soldiers who will force these Indians to live in the pueblo, since they are baptized, to labor in the fields, which are fertile, to punish the medicine men and, as a warning to others, to drive forth those who are most prejudicial to the common weal of the mission."[7]

Clearly, the optimistic early encounters of Padre Kino now lay far in the past. The missionizing at Wa:k had gone badly, and if one reads between the lines, it seems that the Jesuits no longer had anything to offer the Sobaípuris that they didn't already have. One might think things could not have worsened, but they did. In late 1751, in a manner reminiscent of the Pueblo Revolt of 1680, O'odham from throughout Pimería Alta revolted and drove out the Spaniards. The priest's house and the frail "church" at Wa:k were destroyed. Within a year, however, Spanish troops were back, and in due time the Jesuits followed.

Turmoil continued, but this time the missionaries were more successful in a material sense. With dogged determination, Father Alonso Espinosa, the most enduring Jesuit presence in Wa:k since Kino's time, succeeded in building "a substantial, flat-roofed, hall-shaped structure of sun-dried adobe bricks."[8] At last, the mission had a real church. But the success was short-lived: in 1767 King Carlos III decreed that all the Jesuits in New Spain should be expelled from the Spanish Empire, as they had previously been expelled from the empires of France and Portugal. The reasons were complex. The Jesuits represented a competing political and social power; the Crowns of Europe looked with envy on their vast properties and other sources of wealth; and rulers like Carlos saw the Jesuits as the embodiment of an old and confining worldview, even as Europe was swept by a new one called the Enlightenment.

If nature abhors a vacuum, so does a missionizing religion. Franciscans now hurried north to Pimería Alta to replace the departed Jesuits, and the friar posted to Wa:k was a true successor to Kino, at least insofar as he was equally peripatetic. Father Tomás Hermenegildo Garcés, whom we have met previously at both the Grand Canyon and the Mohave villages, was thirty years old when he arrived at San Xavier, and only fourteen more years of life lay ahead of him, most of which he would live in a state of motion. He seems to have used Wa:k more as a base than a home, but the man who filled in for him when he was traveling and who succeeded him after his untimely death at the hands of Quechan (Yuma) Indians on the banks of the Colorado would leave an indelible impact on the mission of San Xavier.

The assistant to Garcés, Father Juan Bautista Velderrain, was a Basque, and it was he who supervised the building of the present magnificent church. The date of the commencement of this project is somewhat uncertain, but if it was not 1783, it was close to it. Velderrain borrowed the considerable sum of 7,000 pesos, equivalent to twenty years of the pension he received for his own support, to finance construction, but it proved grossly inadequate. Even 40,000 pesos proved to be insufficient to complete the entire design, and the east bell tower remains unfinished to this day.[9]

During the years of church construction Wa:k suffered much from Apache raiders. Sited a hundred yards east of Espinosa's now crumbling mud-brick church, the new, more ambitious structure formed the north wall of a fortress plaza, with rows of houses lining the east, south, and west sides. An observer noted in 1780 that the plaza "lacks only a few small gates to be entirely enclosed," so some structures must have been removed to make way for the new church. At the corners of the plaza, the report continued, "they are in the process of building four rounded defense towers with gun ports facing in every direction. Even though it is in a spacious valley, the pueblo is placed squarely in the middle of the low hills known as the badlands of San Xavier. Using the hills as shelter, the Apaches appear suddenly from behind them."[10]

In spite of immense financial, military, and logistical difficulties—the frontier's poverty as well as hostile raiding kept it poorly supplied—one of the most splendid buildings in the American Southwest gradually rose from the desert. By 1797, when the "Father President" of the missions of Pimería Alta, Francisco Iturralde, arrived in Wa:k on a tour of inspection, the church, save for the missing cupola of its east bell tower, was complete. Iturralde found it to be well endowed with holy images, although humble in furnishings:

*I visited the church and sacristy which is a structure of two very good rooms whose construction is of burned brick [i.e., kiln-fired brick, not adobe] and lime. The roof is barrel-vaulted. The church is very large. It has five altars, four in the crossing and the High Altar: the High Altar has a reredos of burned brick and lime, and it is painted and gilded, and the other altars are only painted, and all are adorned with 32 statues of saints including the four that are in the four pillars in the body of the church, and all are very beautiful. Moreover, the walls of the church, the octagonal drum, the cupola, as also the choir are adorned with various images and mysteries in fine paintings which are applied on the wall,*

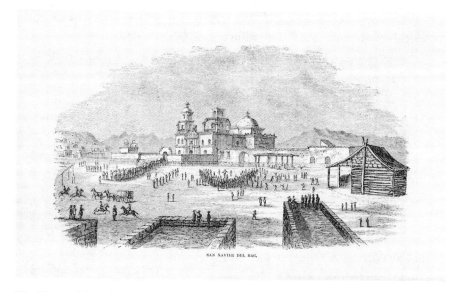

SAN XAVIER DEL BAC.

"San Xavier del Bac." This may be the earliest accurate published image of the mission, as Sam Chamberlain's painting (seen in Plate 10) remained in private ownership until much later. (From J. Ross Browne, *Adventures in the Apache Country*, 1869; courtesy DeGolyer Library, Southern Methodist University)

*but in such a manner that they appear to be on canvas. There are four windows in the drum of the crossing, all with glass. The church has two towers, one unfinished, but the only thing lacking is the dome. The pavement of the floor of the church is of mortar and well-polished. In one of the towers is the baptistry with its good font and a door. It has plenty of room and is enclosed by walls of burned brick and lime, and has a good door. It also has a new cemetery with walls of burned brick and lime and a door and a good chapel of the same material. All this structure is new. It was started by the deceased Father Juan Bautista Velderrain, and for the greater part it was finished by Father Preacher Juan Bautista Llorenz. It has only the necessary ornaments to celebrate the Holy Sacrifice of the Mass which are already well-used, and they are well-kept as are also the sacred vessels.*[11]

The use of "burned brick"—many thousands of them—raises an interesting question. If Velderrain, supervising native laborers, fired his bricks as Anglos and Mexicanos in the territorial period would later do, he preferred willow and cottonwood as fuel, and he would have needed a lot of it.[12] Cutting the necessary quantities of wood from the nearby bosques of the Santa Cruz River would have mightily reduced this vital element of the local environment. As the beautiful church was raised, perhaps the greenery along the river was brought low, with knock-on effects for local hydrology.

More than the landscape was being transformed. Apache raiding had grown so relentless and destructive that Pima communities along the San Pedro River retreated westward to resettle along the Santa Cruz. The Sobaípuris of Wa:k, meanwhile, had suffered badly from European diseases, which reduced their numbers drastically. The combination of immigration from without and loss from within meant that the world of San Xavier was changing rapidly.

Our best view of life during this period comes from a young Franciscan priest, Father Ignacio Joseph Ramírez y Arellano, who served the mission of San Xavier del Bac for the last three years of his brief life. His letters were wonderfully preserved by family members and came to the attention of a Franciscan historian in the early 1950s. In the first, Ignacio replies to a letter from his brother in which the brother complained of a sadness that had come over him:

> Get out of your enclosure and go on a trip. Get on a saddle some afternoon and come here for a ride and you will eat good watermelons and cantaloupes, peaches, grapes, pomegranates and a thousand other things for although we are poor, nothing is wanting to us. These things are ours because of good fortune and because of our labor for in order to eat a fig from the fig-tree, it is necessary to cover it with a protecting awning because of the severe frosts which spare nothing. The pomegranates are exquisite. What we never lack during the greater part of the year are the melons and watermelons, especially the latter which are very good ones. . . .
>
> The snowfalls came every year and water is scarce but not the storms which are many and terrible even though it does not rain. Now I am an everlasting exorcist for I have never anywhere seen the heavens so angry. What noises! What thunder! What wind! It appears that these elements wish to lift us and the house up to the stars. Thus there is no remedy but to take in one's hands the cross and the holy water. However, for your visit, choose a good afternoon, see the church and house and we will take a walk in the garden. . . . Here one passes the time in a continual battle and struggle in all matters so that much patience is necessary, not the patience of nature but the patience we call virtue.[13]

In a letter to his mother Ignacio expressed his sense of isolation and abandonment, the whole region being neglected by authorities to the south:

*Our labors here are the same as those of a pastor anywhere and to this is added the work of the temporalities. This work of conquest is quite different from what it is considered to be down there. The neglect on the part of the government, if not the calculated disregard, to work for any advance here, stupefies us. A long time ago many people here could have become Christians without any difficulty and these even asked for priests. But those gentlemen on whom devolved the duty of supplying them looked only to their own personal interests and this matter of founding missions does not bother them. Though they do not offer any opposition, yet without their help, what can we do? Nothing! As a result, the only conquests we make are a few among those who are faced with hunger or threatened by enemies who come from their lands and even then some of them flee after they are Christians and thus everything is lost. It is a shame to see so many Yumas coming here from their territory every day and still no advantage is gained. The Indians are of such a disposition that only by force of arms are they conquered and subjected and by force and fear are they settled in towns. Even then only as a matter of routine do they accept Christianity.*[14]

Of the Apaches, he wrote that they

*are mortal enemies not only of Christians but of everybody. They go about the whole area robbing and killing to get what they can. . . . They have nothing else to do or nothing else to think of nor are the many presidios which are located here for that reason only, of any avail to restrain them. For this reason the soldiers here are organizing a campaign against them . . . not only the soldiers but the mission Indians in recent days, those of San Xavier and Tucson which is a* visita *from here,*[15] *together with Papagos and Gilenos, went out against them. Though these latter are pagans they realize that the Apaches are their enemies. They set out and accomplished something because they brought back seven alive, women and youths, and killed eight. However, the alcalde of the town was killed and four more were wounded.*[16]

Wa:k and San Xavier are said to have been the site of more than a few miraculous events. One of them involved the death of Father Ignacio, who wrote to his mother that he suffered continually from rashes and fever and was extremely thin. When finally he succumbed, no more than thirty-five years old, "his death occasioned a prodigy. The day he died, being very flaccid and discolored, he appeared white and reddish as soon as he died, and he began to exhale a most sweet and delightful odor. Afterwards he began to sweat and this lasted for twenty-four hours so much so that when they were ready to bury him on the following day they decided not to but rather wished to defer the burial. Then they brought the remains again to his room. There the odor and sweat continued. They blessed him with holy water and then the sweating ceased and then only decided to bury him which they did. Everybody speaks of the prodigy which they observed and justly consider it fortunate." [17]

Fast-forward to 1848: the United States has won its war with Mexico and various military units are returning to the north. One of the units brings to San Xavier del Bac Sam Chamberlain, an artistically talented sometime-soldier, soon-to-be bandit, and full-time teller of tales. He is under arrest. As his company of dragoons made its way northwestward from Monterrey, Chamberlain fell out with his commanding officer, a Major Graham, who took such objection to Chamberlain's behavior that, as Chamberlain told it, "swearing to hang me, he ordered his orderly to bring me along as a prisoner." Thereafter Chamberlain, who had acquired the nickname Peloncillo Jack, walked while the rest of the mounted troop rode. He continued:

*One day while on our march near Tucson we emerged from a wilderness of mezquite and cottonwoods into an open space where, arising from the huts of an Indian village, was one of the grandest church edifices in Northern Mexico, the Mission of San Xavier del Bac, built in 1668.* [The source of his date would be interesting to know.]

*The village was inhabited by a tribe of Indians known as the Papagoes, with no white men or Mexicans nearer than Tucson. The buildings are in excellent condition, with a number of fine paintings and images well preserved. The Mission appeared to be unknown in Mexico, and is certainly a most remarkable edifice, standing as it does, in the midst of a desert, the home of wild savage Apaches.* [18]

The ensuing paragraph gives Chamberlain's account of "the earliest pictorial representation of Mission San Xavier thus far known": [19]

*I was sketching the place from my guard house, (a scaffold [ramada] used by the Papagoes to dry pumkin on) when Graham rode up and as the guard turned out, he saw me as a prisoner on their left with my sketch book in hand. "What in H——l have you got there?" was the polite inquiry of the Major. I respectfully replied "my sketch book Major." "Sketch book! you d——d hound, what in h——l do you know about sketching?" and riding up, the courteous West Pointer, snatched the book from my hands, and after glancing at its contents threw it in my face, and turning to the Sergeant said "tie Peloncillo Jack up for two hours, and then put handcuffs on him, and see if he can sketch then." "The mean! petty! malicious! tyrant!" I was accordingly tied up. Graham's tent was in plain sight, and he rode up to it, and dismounting, he took up a position where he could watch me. What dignity! a Major of the U.S. Dragoons, and commander of an important expedition, tormenting a poor boy, a citizen at that; and watching his guard to see if his brutal orders were carried out….*

*My two hours being up, I was cut down and ironed [placed in irons], but the pair was so large that I could slip them off and on with the greatest ease.*[20]

Exactly when Chamberlain executed his very creditable watercolor of San Xavier is unknown (Plate 10). No doubt his sketch or sketches, which Major Graham (who in fact was not a West Pointer) evidently refrained from destroying, provided a basis for the later painting, which doubles as a self-portrait. In it, you see Chamberlain himself, in the shade of his "guard house," making the picture, which in all respects appears to be true to the condition of the mission at the time of Chamberlain's ignominious visit.

A year later, gold having been discovered in California, a succession of forty-niners made their way through Wa:k. One of the most articulate among them was Benjamin Hayes, a native of Baltimore:

*This morning early went up to the village. Struck with the strange appearance of Indian wigwams on one side, and adobes on the other; still more with the splendid church of solid structure, whose dome and belfreys overlook the town and a wide extent of mountain and plain. Staid there till ten o'clock when finally succeeded in getting sight of the interior. Our first visit was to the church—the splendor of the outside and a glimpse of the beauty of the inside through a high window, exciting our curiosity to the highest. We asked a Mexican to admit us. He told us a Pimo had the key, pointing to the wigwam. On going there, he sent us another Pimo. Finally, for awhile, we abandoned the attempt, and I traded percussion caps for beans. Fired revolver, which seemed to please them, I mean, the Indians. A Pimo sent for a pistol; it would not stand cocked. Fired it for him, and then an old double-barrelled shot gun, nearly as bad to cock. At length a Pimo spoke in his language across the plaza to have us admitted, in Spanish, to send two of the mulieres [mujeres, Spanish for women] with us. They kept us waiting half an hour, meantime I examined the other premises. The delay itself seemed to have been made only to astonish & please us, the more.*

*Two belfreys, hexagonal base, the octagonal on it, then smaller dome-shaped with cross on top of the whole, whole height of the belfry finished perhaps 160 feet. Two bells in completed belfry, one in the other belfrey which seems never to have been completed. Dome back of the belfreys, over the altar. Terrace on top of the hole very pretty. Beautiful front, with niches for figures, some of them now defaced a good deal. High wall on the east, enclosing rooms with lofty ceilings, which may once have been a monastery; staircase view from interior gallery, and two galleries outside; floors solid cement, in square blocks, 3 altars. Light and airy appearance of ceiling over altar, with white, pink, and blue colors. Statues innumerable of saints, Apostles, Blessed Virgin, etc. 12 oil paintings by masters, sent no doubt from Europe; appear to be old, and to a connoisseur would be of great value. Besides, numerous fine paintings on the walls, some very large, of Scriptural scenes, and the colors fresh as if painted yesterday. Four old missals in a closet in the sacristy, which the girls, thinking doubtless that we would be interested in their treasures, unlocked for us. Oldest printed in 1762, another in 1769. Parish records of births, etc. Oldest date in the latter 1765. No seats. Side rooms, sacristy, etc., all highly finished. Splendid cornice. Gilded carved pilasters, making the altar, in the light of the sun's rays straying through a lofty window, glitter like a mass of gold. Girls showed us "San Antonio Chiquito," a very pretty little figure, on which she put a neat little cap of pink silk, and laughed at its beauty. The bier with a coffin. The Padre is to be here in 3 days. I was told by a Mexican that the church was built 200 years ago; a Pimo dissented, saying "mas."*[21]

In actual fact, the church visited by Hayes and Chamberlain was only a little more than half a century old. The older, far simpler church, built by Father Espinosa in the 1750s, would have been approaching its centenary, but it had been torn down decades earlier and its adobes and roofing material used to construct the *convento,* or parish residence.[22]

"San Xavier Church, Tucson, Arizona" (From Charles S. Gleed, ed., *Guide from the Missouri River to the Pacific Ocean,* 1882; courtesy DeGolyer Library, Southern Methodist University)

Young as the new church was, however, the domed and towered marvel that Father Velderrain had brought into existence was already suffering decay. Contrary to the assessments of Hayes and Chamberlain, the accumulating damage had even been the subject of official correspondence. In 1843 a Sonoran subprefect reported that seepage and humidity were damaging the elaborate interior murals of the church and, moreover, that in the absence of regular maintenance the church might soon fall into ruin.[23] And indeed there was no one to look after it, for San Xavier had lacked a resident priest since 1837. Through the rest of the nineteenth century, the mission would receive the transient attentions of a succession of overworked and underfunded priests and nuns, but it would not have a true and enduring caretaker again until the first decade of the twentieth century.[24] In the meantime, it would barely survive a shuddering earthquake in 1887, and

Timothy O'Sullivan, "San Xavier del Bar [Bac] Mission Near Tucson, Arizona,"
1871. Photo pairs like this one, when viewed via a stereoscope, produced a three-
dimensional effect and were a popular means for viewing photographs beginning
in the late nineteenth century. This image, by the Wheeler survey's redoubtable
Timothy O'Sullivan, may be the first photograph ever made of San Xavier.
(Courtesy National Archives and Records Administration, photo no. 106-WA-159)

for many years at a time, "the birds," according to a traveler in 1858, would
be the church's "only occupants and they sing praises from morning until
night. They build their nests on the heads of the saints and warble their
notes of joy while perched on their fingers. They do not respect the sacred
image of Christ for a noisy swallow has built her nest in the crown of thorns
that circles his brow and at this moment is perched on his bleeding hand
scolding loudly at my near approach. The door is always left open but the
property of the church is not disturbed. The natives look upon the structure
with a feeling of awe and could not be persuaded to deface or injure it."[25]

➤➤

That San Xavier today remains a wonder of the desert is no small marvel
in itself. The primary agent of this miracle was Henry Granjon, bishop of
Tucson, whose "love affair with Mission San Xavier del Bac, and it was certainly that, was its salvation."[26] He began his efforts in 1905, raising money

for the church, recruiting laborers and building experts, toiling long hours himself, and contributing what small fortune he personally possessed not only to the cause of protecting San Xavier from further damage, but to the restoration of its ornate and colorful glory.

More waves of restoration activity followed through the next hundred years, driven by the energy and dedication of scores of individuals, including many volunteers from Tucson, art conservators from Europe, craftsmen from Mexico, and new generations of Franciscan friars who reassumed the supervision of the mission from Bishop Granjon in 1912. More than a few O'odham members of the Wa:k community have added their efforts to the cause and have acquired the skills to carry on the delicate work of preservation. Today San Xavier del Bac remains an active parish church serving the people of the San Xavier District of the Tohono O'odham Nation, and members of the Franciscan Brotherhood administer it. Many agree that San Xavier constitutes the finest surviving example of Spanish Colonial architecture in the United States.[27]

No account of San Xavier can be complete without mention of Bernard Fontana, who, just as Bishop Granjon saved the physical church, has become the chief conservator of its history. His book *A Gift of Angels: The Art of Mission San Xavier del Bac* is an extraordinary piece of bookmaking. Fifteen years in the making and lavishly illustrated by the photographer Edward McCain, it painstakingly explores and explains the many hundreds of images, both sculptural and painted, that grace the interior of the church and embody its effusive ultra-baroque spirit. *A Gift of Angels* is itself a work of art and love, and there is no better source to provide the final words for this brief profile of a quintessentially iconic place of the American Southwest: "What strikes the first-time viewer of San Xavier is the incongruity of its setting. There is nothing else like it in its immediate presence, nor does it seem there should be. This great church is of another place and another time even as it is both timeless and universal. It doesn't belong here, but it does."[28]

# 13 Taos Valley

The beautiful Taos Valley, nestled at the foot of the Sangre de Cristo Mountains in northern New Mexico, is the home of three iconic places. Within a nine-mile stretch the well-watered valley supports the communities of Taos, Ranchos de Taos, and Taos Pueblo.

With a little over fifty-seven hundred inhabitants, the town of Taos resonates for modern-day Americans in ways far grander than its modest size might suggest. Like a handful of other small western mountain communities, such as Aspen, Colorado, and Jackson Hole, Wyoming, Taos has become a magnet for tourists. They come in summer to enjoy the cool, dry air of a town that stands at seven thousand feet, and in the winter they come to ski on mountain slopes a mile higher than the town. In any season, they come to see the striking scenery, the art galleries and museums, the charming adobe neighborhoods, and the two other iconic places in the valley—the multistoried Pueblo of Taos, a UNESCO World Heritage Site, located three miles north of the town, and Ranchos de Taos, a community four and a half miles south of Taos and half its size, which sprawls around the striking church of San Francisco de Asís. Like Taos Pueblo, the church at Ranchos de Taos has attracted the attention of legions of photographers and painters.

The earliest written mention of Taos Pueblo, the northernmost of the New Mexico pueblos, comes from one of Coronado's captains who led a small party up the Río Grande in 1540. Hernando de Alvarado, who also introduced us to Ácoma, was a military man, not especially given to literary or aesthetic considerations, and he had little to say about the pueblo's Tiwa-speaking residents. Even so, his terse report gives the sense of a curtain being raised, of a new and mysterious world being opened. Alvarado saw scores of native communities, all of them similar, as he followed the Río Grande northward from the vicinity of present-day Bernalillo. At Taos Pueblo, however, the similarity ended. There Alvarado encountered a community centered around immense apartment houses, or "sections," as high as six stories, each surrounded by a wooden portico:

*There are probably eighty towns of the sort I have [previously] told about. Among them [there is] one situated on some stream banks, [in which] there were twenty sections, which are something worth seeing. The houses consist of three stories made of mud walls and another three built of small planks of wood. Around the outside of each of those three stories made of mud there is a covered walkway made of wood. These [walkways] encircle the whole section, on the perimeter. Now, it seemed to us that there were probably as many as fifteen thousand persons in this town. It is a very cold land. Neither [turkeys] nor cotton is raised [there]. They venerate the sun and rain. Outside that place we found earthen mounds where [their dead] are buried.*[1]

The next year Captain Velasco de Barrionuevo, who had once served in the viceroy's personal guard, reached Taos Pueblo. We have only a secondhand account of his visit, which emphasized the town's chambers for religious ceremonies (kivas, or estufas, as the Spaniards called them) rather than its six-story architecture.

*Twenty leagues farther up the river there was a large and powerful . . . pueblo—called Braba, and which our men named Valladolid. The river flowed through the center of it, and the river was spanned by wooden bridges built with very large and heavy square pine timbers. At this pueblo were seen the largest and finest estufas that had been found in all that land. They had twelve pillars, each one two arms' length around and two estados high [an estado was the height of a man]. This pueblo had been visited by Hernando de Alvarado when he discovered Cicuye. This land is very high and extremely cold. The river [probably the Río Grande, as the Río Pueblo de Taos, which runs through the pueblo, is relatively small] was deep and had a swift current, without any ford. Captain Barrionuevo turned back from here, leaving all those provinces at peace.*[2]

Disappointed that he had not found a rich civilization or even Indian labor abundant enough to support a wealthy colonial regime, Coronado turned back to Mexico City in 1542. Nearly forty years more would pass before Spaniards reentered New Mexico and nearly sixty years went by before Spaniards under Juan de Oñate established a permanent colony among the Pueblos in 1598. That year Taos Pueblo got the name it is known by today, a Spanish adaptation of a Tiwa word meaning "in the village."[3] The names Braba and Valladolid vanished; Taos remained.

The Franciscans who accompanied Oñate established a mission at Taos Pueblo, as they did at other major pueblos in New Mexico, and pressed forward with efforts to evangelize the natives, meanwhile enlisting Indian labor to build their churches and friaries, or *conventos*. The first published impression of the Taos mission appeared in Madrid in 1630 (and in French, Latin, Dutch, and German editions between 1631 and 1634). Its author, Fray Alonso de Benavides, whom we briefly encountered earlier in Santa Fe, had served as chief administrator of New Mexico's Franciscan missions between 1626 and 1629, after which he returned to Spain to plead for more financial support for the conversion of New Mexico's natives to Christianity. He addressed his *Memorial*—a report on ecclesiastical conditions in New Mexico—to the king, Felipe IV. His account of pueblo after pueblo tells more about the achievements of the Franciscans than about the Indian residents, as may be seen in his report on Taos Pueblo, where, Benavides suggests, God himself intervened to support the Franciscans' work. The king, he boldly implies, should open his coffers and lend a hand as well:

*Taos Nation*

*Farther north another seven leagues, is the pueblo of the Taos, of the same nation as the foregoing [Picurís, another Tiwa-speaking pueblo], although the language varies somewhat. It has two thousand five hundred souls baptized; with its* convento *and church, which two Religious who have had charge of this conversion have founded with much care. These Indians are very well instructed. And in the bygone year of [One Thousand] Six Hundred and Twenty-seven, the Lord confirmed His Holy Word by a miracle among them. And it was [thus]: It went hard with them to give up having many wives as they used to have before [they were] baptized; and each day the Religious preached to them the truth of the holy Sacrament of Matrimony; and the one that most contradicted this was*

Joseph Horace Eaton, *Taos Pueblo, 1855,* watercolor (Private collection; courtesy Gerald Peters Gallery, Santa Fe, N.M.)

*an old Indian woman, a sorceress, who, under pretext of going to the country for firewood, took out four other women with her.*

*These were good Christians and married according to the rule of our Holy Mother Church; and going and coming, she kept persuading them that they should not consent to the method of marriage which the Father taught, for that which they used to use in their heathenism was better. The good Christian women always resisted this argument. And as they approached the pueblo, the sorceress not ceasing from her sermon, and the heavens being clear and serene, a thunderbolt fell and slew that infernal mistress of the Demon, right between the good Christians who were resisting her evil doctrine. And they remained very free from the thunderbolt and very much confirmed in the truth of the holy Sacrament of Matrimony.*

*Directly all the pueblo flocked thither; and seeing that rap [or "pounding on the door"] from heaven, all those who were living in secret concubinage got married, and believed very sincerely all which the Father taught them.[4] He promptly made them a sermon there, upon the event; and he preaches to them all the feast-days, as is done in the rest of the* conventos. *The glory be to God our Lord. It is a land very cold, and most abundant in provisions and flocks.[5]*

In his eagerness to assert that the Pueblos had warmly embraced Christianity—and that the missionizing of the Franciscans deserved increased support, Benavides omitted mentioning the natives' resentment of efforts to eradicate their religion and the Spaniards' demands for labor and tribute. In 1680 the Pueblos drove the Spaniards from New Mexico, with nearly simultaneous uprisings throughout the colony. At Taos, where the revolt was engineered and coordinated, the Pueblos killed the two Franciscans assigned to the mission and most of the colonists who had settled in the Taos Valley. Their number was small—about seventy Spaniards in 1680. They had little chance against the two thousand Tiwas who lived in the pueblo.[6]

In 1680, Spanish political authority was locally embodied in an "alcalde mayor and war captain of the jurisdiction of Los Taos," and it was he who sounded one of the early warnings of the impending Pueblo Revolt.[7] Some of his compatriots may have occupied the sites of the present-day communities of Taos town or Ranchos de Taos, but these settlements had not yet cohered into villages, and Taos Pueblo remained the only significant community in the valley.

The Pueblo Revolt forever changed the balance of power between Pueblos and Spaniards. After Spaniards reconquered New Mexico in the 1690s, they ruled their native subjects with a more respectful hand, lest what had happened in the past should happen again. Pueblos and Spaniards also increasingly recognized their need for common defense against Utes, Navajos, Apaches, and especially Comanches, who were new to New Mexico in the 1700s. In the Taos Valley, Pueblos and recolonizing Spaniards found themselves united in a paradoxical relationship with the mounted Indians, whose trade they welcomed but whose raids they feared. As the Comanches grew in wealth and power, dominating the southern plains, their raids increased. By the 1750s, many Hispanics, whose outlying ranchos were relatively defenseless, began to move into Taos Pueblo for protection, and, for their part, the Tiwas apparently welcomed the additional defensive manpower.

The Spanish authorities never established a garrison, or presidio, in the Taos Valley, and so we have no reports of military inspectors from this new era in Pueblo-Spanish relations. The most detailed descriptions come from visiting clergy, one of whom was the indefatigable sixty-three-year-old Pedro Tamarón y Romeral, Bishop of Durango. Tamarón visited Taos in 1760 in the course of a two-year tour of his vast bishopric. He describes the valley at the cusp of a difficult moment. Taos Valley was soon to host a lively and profitable trade fair, attracting natives from multiple tribes, but the fair was only prelude to calamity. Within a month after Tamarón's departure, one of the valley's best fortified but isolated households suffered a horrific Comanche assault, prompting even more Hispanics to move into the pueblo.

## Taos

*The titular patron of this Indian pueblo is San Jerónimo. To reach it we traveled through pine forests and mountains until we descended to the spacious and beautiful valley of Taos. In this valley we kept finding encampments of peaceful Apache Indians, who have sought the protection of the Spaniards so that they may defend them from the Comanches. Then we came to a river called Trampas, which carries enough water.*[8] *The midday halt was made at the large house of a wealthy Taos Indian, very civilized and well-to-do. The said house is well walled in, with arms and towers for defense. In the afternoon the journey through that valley continued. Three rivers of similar current and water were crossed. The first one in particular provides abundant ditches for irrigation. They are about a league and a half from one another. And, crossing the last one, we entered the pueblo of Taos, where a Franciscan missionary parish priest resides.*

*It is twelve leagues north of Picuris. It is the last and most distant pueblo of that kingdom. In this direction, it lies at the foot of a very high sierra and in latitude 40°. This pueblo has 159 families of Indians, with 505 persons. There are 36 families of Europeanized citizens, with 160 persons. There is a very decent and capacious church.*

*I also put forth every effort there to induce those best acquainted with Spanish to perform the act of contrition and confess. I therefore left this group until last, confirming the children first. And in fact some did confess, and, encouraged to contrition, were confirmed. But since they do not know the catechism except in Spanish, I did not feel as pleased and easy in my mind as I should have liked. [Tamarón was displeased that the Franciscans had not learned Tiwa and other Pueblo languages.] Therefore I reprimanded the mission father and duly reminded him of his duty, ordering him to continue receiving their confessions.*

*This pueblo is divided into three many-storied tenements. It would have been better, as I told them, if they had been kept together, for one is on the other side of the river about two hundred varas away. There is a wooden bridge to cross the river. It freezes every year, and they told me that when it is thus covered with ice, the Indian women come with their naked little ones, break the ice with a stone, and bathe them in those waters, dipping them in and out. And they say it is for the purpose of making them tough and strong.*

*When I was in the pueblo two encampments of Ute Indians, who were friendly but infidels, had just arrived with a captive woman who had fled from the Comanches. They reported that the latter were at the Río de las Animas preparing buffalo meat in order to come to trade. They come every year to the trading, or fairs. The governor comes to those fairs, which they call* rescates *[barter, trade], every year with the majority of his garrison and people from all over the kingdom. They bring captives to sell, pieces of chamois, many buffalo skins, and, out of the plunder they have obtained elsewhere, horses, muskets, shotguns, munitions, knives, meat, and various other things. Money is not current at these fairs, but exchange of one thing for another, and so those people get provisions. I left Taos on June 12, and a few days later seventeen tents of Comanches arrived. They make these of buffalo hide, and they say that they are good and well suited for defense; and a family occupies each one. And at the end of the said month of June seventy of these field tents arrived. This was the great fair.*

*The character of these Comanches is such that while they are peacefully trading in Taos, others of their nation make warlike attacks on some distant pueblo. And the ones who are at peace, engaged in trade, are accustomed to say to the governor, "Don't be too trusting. Remember, there are rogues among us, just as there are among you. Hang any of them you catch."* [9]

Tamarón has set the stage for presenting the dire news from Taos Valley that reached him after he departed the scene. He continues:

*In that year, 1760, I left that kingdom at the beginning of July. And on the fourth day of August, according to what they say, nearly three thousand Comanche men waged war with the intention of finishing this pueblo of Taos. They diverted, or provoked, them from a very large house, the greatest in all that valley, belonging to a settler called Villalpando, who, luckily for him, had left that day on business. But when they saw so many Comanches coming, many women and men of that settlement took refuge in this house as the strongest. And, trusting in the fact that it had four towers and in the large supply of muskets, powder, and balls, they say that they fired on the Comanches. The latter were infuriated by this to such a horrible degree that they broke into different parts of the house, killed all the men and some women, who also fought. And the wife of the owner of the house, seeing that they were breaking down the outside door, went to defend it with a lance, and they killed her fighting. Fifty-six women and children were carried off, and a large number of horses which the owner of the house was keeping there. Forty-nine bodies of dead Comanches were counted, and other trickles of blood were seen.[10]*

If Ranchos de Taos or Taos existed in 1760, neither village made an impression on Bishop Tamarón. The walled, fortified house of the prosperous Taos Indian on the Río Trampas, where Tamarón paused for an afternoon break, was probably on or near the site of Ranchos de Taos, which according to at least one account, was first settled not by Hispanics but by Taos Indians.[11]

The valley remained a dangerous place for ranching and farming. When the next ecclesiastical visitor arrived in 1776, he passed by the ruins of abandoned ranchos and reported that Hispanics continued to live in an apartment block in the pueblo. Their numbers had nearly doubled since Tamarón's 1760 visit, from 160 to 306.[12] Not until the late 1780s, when danger of Indian attacks diminished, did they begin to resettle the valley, consolidating their homes around small plazas for defense. The villages that then emerged included Don Fernando de Taos, which would change its name simply to Taos in 1885, and the village of Ranchos de Taos, which was also then known as the Plaza of San Francisco.[13]

Although the population of the Taos Valley continued to grow in the late Spanish colonial period, literacy was rare and no one seems to have written about Taos during the twilight of the Spanish Empire. With Mexican independence in 1821, however, the situation changed. Newly arrived outsiders from the United States began to record their impressions of the place, whose name they sometimes spelled phonetically as Tous, Taus, or Toas. Most Americans who entered New Mexico after Mexican independence followed the Santa Fe Trail directly to Santa Fe, without passing through Taos. Those who did otherwise often had special reasons to be in New Mexico's northernmost town, seventy miles north of Santa Fe over trails impassable by wheeled vehicles. They included fur trappers who chose to winter close to the vast expanses of the southern Rockies, and who also, like Ewing Young, became de facto smugglers, as they strove to avoid paying customs duties on their pelts, which the authorities in Santa Fe required. Some, like Charles Bent and Kit Carson, married into the Taos Valley and raised families there.

The Americans who commented on the Taos Valley almost uniformly remarked on its beauty. Dr. Josiah Gregg, who knew New Mexico as well as any of his American contemporaries and whose classic *Commerce of the Prairies* appeared in 1844, declared, "No part of New Mexico equals this valley in amenity of soil, richness of produce and beauty of appearance." El Valle de Taos, as he understood it, was the most important population center in New Mexico after Santa Fe, and the valley's largest Hispanic villages were Taos and Ranchos de Taos.[14]

Few of the Americans arriving in New Mexico were as worldly as Gregg, and initially the place seemed strange and exotic. Young James Ohio Pattie arrived in Taos Valley in the early autumn of 1825 with a party of trappers, who cached most of their trade goods on the east side of the mountains in order to avoid paying a tariff on them. Naively, Pattie had "expected to find no difference between these people and our own":

> On the evening of the 26th, we arrived at a small town in Tous [Valley], called St. Ferdinando [San Fernando de Taos], situated just at the foot of the mountain on the west side. The alcaide [alcalde] asked us for the invoice of our goods, which we showed him, and paid the customary duties on them. This was a man of a swarthy complexion having the appearance of pride and haughtiness. The door-way of the room, we were in, was crowded with men, women and children, who stared at us, as though they had never seen white men before, there being in fact, much to my surprize and disappointment, not one white person among them. I had expected to find no difference between these people and our own, but their language. I was never so mistaken. The men and women were not clothed in our fashion, the former having short pantaloons fastened below the waist with a red belt and buck skin leggins put on three or four times double. A Spanish knife is stuck in by the side of the leg, and a small sword worn by the side. A long jacket or blanket is thrown over, and worn upon the shoulders. They have few fire arms, generally using upon occasions which require them, a bow and spear, and never wear a hat, except when they ride. When on horse back,

*they face towards the right side of the animal. The saddle, which they use, looks as ours would, with something like an arm chair fastened upon it.*

*The women wear upon the upper part of the person a garment resembling a shirt, and a short petticoat fastened around the waist with a red or blue belt, and something of the scarf kind wound around their shoulders. Although appearing as poorly, as I have described, they are not destitute of hospitality; for they brought us food, and invited us into their houses to eat, as we walked through the streets.*

*The first time my father and myself walked through the town together, we were accosted by a woman standing in her own door-way. She made signs for us to come in. When we had entered, she conducted us up a flight of steps into a room neatly whitewashed, and adorned with images of saints, and a crucifix of brass nailed to a wooden cross. She gave us wine, and set before us a dish composed of red pepper, ground and mixed with corn meal, stewed in fat and water [possibly* posole*]. We could not eat it. She then brought forward some tortillas and milk. Tortillas are a thin cake made of corn and wheat ground between two flat stones by the women. This cake is called in Spanish,* metate *[certain grinding stones are called metates]. We remained with her until late in the evening, when the bells began to ring. She and her children knelt down to pray. We left her, and returned. On our way we met a bier with a man upon it, who had been stabbed to death, as he was drinking whiskey.*

*This town stands on a beautiful plain, surrounded on one side by the Rio del Norte, and on the other by the mountain, of which I have spoken, the summit being covered with perpetual snow.*[15]

If Pattie was surprised to observe differences between Taoseños and his Kentucky neighbors, his initial reaction soon gave way to a more disparaging point of view, which most visitors from the East who succeeded him tended to share. The Massachusetts poet Albert Pike arrived in Taos in 1831. Like Pattie, he believed he had entered "a different world." "To an American," he wrote, "the first sight of these New Mexican villages is novel and singular. . . . Everything is new, strange, and quaint." But newness did not guarantee Pike's approval. He derogated the town as nothing more than "a few dirty, irregular lanes, and a quantity of mud houses." The exteriors of the adobe houses, however, were "mica lime-washed to a dazzling degree of whiteness," not earthen-colored as today.[16] (Another visitor in the mid-

1850s noted that as he descended into the Taos Valley he "could plainly see the white houses of Taos, nearly twenty miles distant.")[17] Having attended a dance or fandango, Pike proved prudish, leaving in disgust after seeing "well dressed women—(they call them ladies)—harlots, priests, thieves, half-breed Indians—all spinning round together in the waltz."[18]

As war with Mexico approached in the 1840s and anti-Mexican propaganda flourished in the United States, American descriptions of the Taos residents, and of New Mexicans in general, became more stridently pejorative. Rufus B. Sage, a Connecticut-born trapper who visited Taos briefly in 1842, found much to like in the land but nothing to like in the people, his bigoted description of their character and traditions abounding in such adjectives as *miserable, despicable, squalid, degenerate,* and *abject.* The dyspeptic Sage even found the general happiness of New Mexicans objectionable:

*Taos proper embraces several fertile lateral valleys bordering upon the [Río Grande] del Norte, and three small affluents from the east and is supposed to contain a population of some ten thousand, including Indians, Moors, Half-breeds, Mulattoes, and Spaniards. It is divided into several precincts, or neighborhoods, within short distances of each other, among which Arroyo Hondo is the principal.*

*This section of country is very romantic, and affords many scenes to excite the admiration of beholders. It is shut in by lofty mountains, upon three sides, that tower to an altitude of several thousand feet, now presenting their pine-clad summits among the clouds, now with denuded crests defying the tempest; and then peering skyward to hold converse with the scathing blasts of unending winter.*

*The mountains are rich in minerals of various kinds. Gold is found in considerable quantities in their vicinity, and would doubtless yield a large profit to diggers, were they possessed of the requisite enterprise and capital. At present these valuable mines are almost entirely neglected,—the common people being too ignorant and poor to work them, and the rich too indolent and fond of ease.*

*The Mexicans possess large ranchos of sheep, horses, mules, and cattle among the mountains, which are kept there the entire year, by a degraded set of beings, following no business but that of herdsmen, or rancheros.*

*This class of people have no loftier aspirations than to throw the lasso with dexterity, and break wild mules and horses.*

*They have scarcely an idea of any other place than the little circle in which they move, nor dream of a more happy state of existence than their own.*[19]

Sage is more generous in characterizing Taos Pueblo, yet still he misreads the situation:

*A few miles to the southeast [northeast] of Taos, is a large village of Pueblos, or civilized Indians. These are far superior to their neighbors in circumstances, morals, civil regulations, character, and all the other distinguishing traits of civilization.*

*This race are of the genuine Mexican stock, and retain many of their ancient customs, though nominally Catholic in their religion.*

*Cherishing a deep-rooted animosity towards their conquerors, they only await a favorable opportunity to re-assert their liberty.*[20]

Sage was not alone in suggesting that the Pueblo Indians in Taos were more virtuous than the Hispanic neighbors, but if they had interest in reasserting "their liberty," it was not from Mexico but from the United States. This became clear during the war between the United States and Mexico, after American forces invaded New Mexico in 1846. Early the following year, in the Taos Revolt of 1847, Tiwas from Taos Pueblo joined many of their Hispanic neighbors in mobbing and killing the Americans in their midst, including the territorial governor Charles Bent. They also provided the backbone of resistance to fight against the troops who soon came to quell the uprising. They lost badly. The pueblo and its church were smashed by U.S. troops, and the ruins of the church can be seen at the pueblo to this day.

A glimmer of the attitude of Hispanics toward Anglo Americans during this time may be seen in an anecdote related by the English soldier of fortune George Frederick Ruxton, who visited New Mexico in 1846 and made note of the "bullying and overbearing demeanor" of Americans toward New Mexicans. He learned how this attitude was reciprocated one night when he lodged with a humble family near "Ohuaqui" [Pojoaque]: "The *patrona* of the family seemed rather shy of me at first, until, in the course of conversation, she discovered that I was an Englishman. 'Gracias á Díos,' she exclaimed, 'a Christian will sleep with us tonight, and not an American!'"[21]

→→

Joseph Heger, "Pueblo of Taos, 1859." This fanciful rendering shows, at left, the ruins of San Geronimo Church, which U.S. forces destroyed during the Taos Revolt of 1847. (From John Van Deusen Du Bois and Joseph Heger, illustrator, *Campaigns in the West, 1856–1861,* 1949; courtesy Palace of the Governors Photo Archives, New Mexico History Museum [NMHM/DCA], negative no. 031270)

The Taos Valley, like the rest of New Mexico, became part of the United States under the treaty that ended the war with Mexico in 1848. Its new status, however, did little to reduce its isolation. In the second half of the 1800s, as railroads knitted the new American territory to the rest of the nation, Taos remained distant and untouched. Finally, on the last day of 1880, completion of a branch of the narrow-gauge Denver and Río Grande Railroad, called the Chili Line, running between Española, New Mexico, and Antonito, Colorado, brought Taos somewhat closer to the rest of the world. A rail traveler, nevertheless, had to disembark the train at Caliente, a lonely stop in the midst of a sagebrush plain (its name was eventually changed to Taos Station), and then endure a bruising twenty-five-mile ride by stagecoach to Taos.[22] Few were the passengers who did not experience apprehension as the stage jolted down ledge-like switchbacks into the Río Grande gorge and then lurched up the other side along an equally narrow and boulder-strewn path. The stage remained in use into the early 1910s, when automobiles replaced it.[23]

Travelers who made the journey by stage to Taos, as the travel writer E. Alexander Powell did in the early 1910s, tended to be more impressed, as Rufus Sage had been, with Taos Pueblo than with the nearby town. Powell dismissed the town as "little more than a sun-swept plaza bordered on all

four sides by Mexican houses of adobe, while running off from the plaza
are numerous dim and narrow alleys, likewise lined by humble dwellings
of whitewashed mud." In Powell's view, the town would never again match
its better, earlier days when it was home to Kit Carson and other trappers
and traders. Only its young art colony offered an alternate kind of glory.
In prose as purple as a mountain nightfall, Powell asserted that in the foot-
steps of the frontiersman "have come another breed of men, who carry
palettes instead of pistols and who confront the Indian with brushes instead of bowie knives; for Taos, because of its extraordinary wealth of sun
and shadow, of yellow deserts and purple mesas, of scarlet blankets and
white walls, has become the rendezvous for a group of brilliant painters
who are perpetuating on canvas the red men of the terraced houses."[24]

The emergence of the art colony, which was firmly established by the
1910s, triggered a reversal of reputation, if not of fortune, for Taos. For the
painters and occasional writers and photographers who found their way
there, its isolation and its distance, physically and psychically, from the
rest of America became a virtue. To a degree that not even Santa Fe could
match, Taos offered refuge from industrial society. It was unmodern, un-

"Don Fernando de Taos, 1857," a rare early view of the Hispanic town (From
W. W. H. Davis, *El Gringo; or, New Mexico & Her People,* 1857; courtesy Palace
of the Governors Photo Archives, New Mexico History Museum [NMHM/DCA],
negative no. 071388)

hurried, steeped in tradition, and rich in elements of culture that seemed timeless. Artists seeking subjects that accorded with the "primitivist" values then esteemed in the salons of New York and the great cities of Europe found them in the landscapes, people, and architecture of both Indian and Hispanic northern New Mexico. Said the Canadian novelist Agnes Laut in 1913, "As Quebec is the shrine of historical pilgrims in the North, and Salem in New England; so Taos is the Mecca of students of history and lovers of art in the Southwest."[25]

The pueblo remained the valley's chief attraction for both tourists and artists, who described it in lavish terms: it was "the most ancient city in America," "the ancient capital of the Southwest," "as little changed as any Indian pueblo in all America," and "perhaps the most perfect specimen existing of Pueblo architecture."[26] But even as the fascination of the pueblo endured, the reputation of the town continued to improve. More and more visitors "found the Mexican town not without interest."[27] A guidebook from the early twentieth century termed Taos "one of the most charming places in America. It is in three parts. There is the outlying hamlet Ranchos de Taos; then the picturesque Mexican town Fernandez de Taos, famous in recent years for a resident artist colony whose pictures have put Taos in the world of art; and lastly, there is the pueblo of Taos."[28]

In the "outlying hamlet" stood a church that soon became an artistic as well as a religious shrine—the church of San Francisco de Asís, more widely known simply as the Ranchos de Taos Church (Plate 11). Art historians Sandra D'Emilio and Suzan Campbell suggest that it has been "portrayed more often, by more artists, than any other church in the United States, perhaps in the world."[29] Every artist and photographer who has passed through the Taos Valley appears to have rendered an image of it. The roster of its admirers includes Ernest L. Blumenschein, Gustave Bauman, Oscar Beringhaus, Paul Strand, Ansel Adams, Laura Gilpin, Georgia O'Keeffe, John Marin, and many more. They seem to have painted and photographed it from every possible angle, from the arched entryway beneath two bell towers to the massive buttresses on the back and sides. Its sphinxlike presence, built of massive, hand-shaped adobe volumes, has proved endlessly intriguing. The painter Alexandre Hogue may have identified a part of its magic when he said, "Those buttresses constitute a ready-made abstraction,

William Henry Jackson, "Taos Pueblo," probably 1881. Jackson's first pictures of Taos, made in 1877 using "Sensitive Negative Tissue," suffered the same fate as photographs he took that year of Canyon de Chelly and Chaco Canyon: none came out. Soon, however, Jackson returned to New Mexico, making stereo images for public consumption. (Photograph by William Henry Jackson, courtesy Palace of the Governors Photo Archives, New Mexico History Museum [NMHM/DCA], negative no. 086893)

an ever present challenge, a kind of outside-the-sanctuary place of silent visual worship."[30]

Writers describe the church in superlatives. As one architect put it, "For many people, the church at Ranchos de Taos is the quintessential adobe building of the Southwest." He continues, "No church shows more eloquently the sense of form that is the chief aesthetic attraction of the adobe churches of the Southwest."[31] Ultimately, the Ranchos de Taos Church can be seen as an iconic structure embodying an iconic place. Whatever genius loci one may sense in the Taos Valley, whatever distillation of sun, earth, culture, conflict, and serenity may seem to linger in its sweeping vistas, the qualities of this singular place may be thought to suffuse the great sleeping walls of San Francisco de Asís.

At one end of the Taos Valley stands the ancient and still-vibrant Pueblo of Taos, its great mud buildings as mountainous in shape as the actual mountains that rise behind them.[32] They remain as fascinating to us today as they undoubtedly were to the Comanches, Utes, and Apaches who came to trade in their shadows in the eighteenth century. At the other end of the valley stands San Francisco de Asís, which is equally a kind of architectural summation of the region. Between these structures spreads the Taos Valley, beautiful, enigmatic, and enduring.

# 14 Tucson

Modern Tucson began life in August 1776 as a Spanish military post, sited close to an O'odham village, and built by order of an Irishman. The walls of the Spanish military compound set the template for today's downtown, where visitors can still see evidence of their outline.

Spaniards chose the site of Tucson for several compelling reasons. First, the Santa Cruz River, an intermittent stream, offered springs, pasture, and woodlands, resources as rare as they were necessary in the Sonoran Desert. Second, the site stood strategically at the edge of the Apache frontier and shielded the mission of San Xavier del Bac, ten miles south. Through it ran the new route to California, recently opened by Captain Juan Bautista de Anza, the commanding officer of the garrison at Tubac, forty miles south of Tucson. Third, the nearby O'odham village provided Indian labor and allies. The O'odham, whose name means "People" in their Uto-Aztecan language, had welcomed a Spanish missionary as early as the 1690s, and although Spaniards had not established a presence closer than San Xavier, missionaries visited the village with some frequency thereafter. By the early 1770s Apache raiders gave the O'odham extra reason to make common cause with Spanish interests. Even before the Spaniards constructed their fort, the O'odham had begun to erect a defensive earthen wall around their village and to construct a chapel and residence for a Catholic missionary.[1]

For these reasons, when Lieutenant Colonel Hugo O'Conor — one of the many Irishmen who fled English-occupied Ireland to fight for

Catholic Spain—visited the site of Tucson in 1775, he thought it an excellent location for a fort. Operating in his capacity as inspector in chief of the garrisons, or presidios, of northern New Spain, O'Conor ordered the presidio at Tubac—the first Spanish settlement in what is now Arizona—to move north and reestablish itself on the east side of the Santa Cruz River, across from the walled O'odham village.

Following O'Conor's orders, the Tubac garrison founded San Agustín del Tucson in 1776, but the future of the new community was hardly secure through its early years. A revolt by Quechan (Yuma) Indians in 1781 closed the route to California, and Apache raiders continued to make life difficult on this northernmost edge of the province of Sonora. The unfortunate settlers who remained behind at Tubac, now bereft of its soldiers, lost their horse herds, cattle, and corn to marauders; Spanish officials countered by reestablishing a garrison there in 1787, this time with O'odham auxiliaries organized under Spanish officers.

By the century's end the Santa Cruz Valley began to enjoy a measure of prosperity. The fort at Tucson anchored a small community of Spanish speakers—civilians as well as soldiers—O'odham villagers across the river, and Aravaipa Apaches who had begun to settle north of the presidial walls in one of the *establecimientos de paz* (peace establishments) located near presidios on the northern frontier. After decades of raid and counterraid, some Apaches and Spaniards had begun to see peace as more advantageous than continual warfare. To encourage coexistence, Spaniards offered gifts, rations, and protection to Apaches who settled in the establecimientos.

Isolated Tucson remained Sonora's northernmost settlement until the end of the colonial period, seldom receiving literate visitors. Descriptions of the presidio in its first years are rare and brief. They offer glimpses of a military post surrounded by a dry moat and a log palisade, with soldiers and their families living inside as well as beyond its walls. In 1783, after a particularly devastating Apache assault, soldiers began to replace the palisade of upright logs with more a substantial masonry wall of sun-dried adobe bricks. Early descriptions of Tucson offer more statistics than prose: from them we learn that in 1783 sixty-two Spanish soldiers held the fort.

Captain José de Zúñiga, writing in the line of duty, penned the first substantial description of Tucson that has come down to us. In 1804, as commanding officer at Tucson, he received a questionnaire from the Vera

Cruz branch of the Real Consulado, Spain's board of trade. Sent to Spanish settlements throughout New Spain, the questionnaire asked for information about various aspects of local life. All related to the potential for economic growth.

Captain Zúñiga's response reflected deep knowledge and broad experience. Born in Cuautitlan, near Mexico City, in 1755, Zúñiga entered military service at the age of seventeen. He campaigned across northern New Spain with Hugo O'Conor, earning promotion to lieutenant in 1780. The next year he led a group of colonists from Guaymas to Loreto in Baja California, and then north to the Los Angeles basin. He remained in California, where he commanded the presidio at San Diego. A decade later, in 1792, he received promotion to captain and assignment to Tucson. He reached his new command in 1794 and thus drew from a decade of experience when he answered the Consulado's questions. During his tenure at Tucson, Apache raids had declined and prosperity increased throughout northern Sonora. In 1795, Zúñiga took advantage of this lull in Spanish-Apache warfare to blaze a trail from Tucson to Zuni in New Mexico, with the help of eight Apache guides. This was his most memorable achievement as commanding officer of the Tucson presidio.

In his reply to the Consulado's questionnaire, Zúñiga had much to say about Tucson's resources. He noted that his jurisdiction, which included over a thousand people, included the O'odham village across the river and the mission at San Xavier del Bac. Curiously, he made no mention of the Apache settlement to the immediate north, except to note that its residents received a subsidy of slaughtered cattle. He reported on local ranching, agriculture, and industry but consistently focused more on what Tucson lacked than what it had. His responses to the questionnaire reflect his position as a member of the Sonoran elite. Although born in New Spain, he was a pure-blooded Spaniard and a member of the nobility. Accordingly, he regarded the Indians and mixed bloods in his community as belonging to a lower caste. Condescension came easily to such a man; praise did not. Among Tucson's "public works," only the baroque church at nearby San Xavier del Bac elicited his approval.

*Tucson*

*August 4, 1804.*

*Geography*

*The soldiers, settlers, and Indians of Tucson live in an area less than two miles square. Their total population comes to 1015. Tucson's jurisdiction includes the Indian village of San Xavier del Bac, ten miles away, the Indian village at Tucson, and the presidio with its settlers and retired troops.*

*The rivers of the region include the Santa Catalina [today's Rillito], five miles from the presidio, which arises from a hot spring and enjoys a steady flow for ten miles in a northwesterly direction, but only in the rainy seasons. It is thirty-three feet wide near its headwaters. Our major river, however, is the Santa María Suamca [the Santa Cruz River] which arises ninety-five miles to the southeast from a spring near the presidio of Santa Cruz. From its origin it flows past the Santa Cruz presidio, the abandoned ranches of Divisaderos, Santa Bárbara, San Luis, and Buenavista, as well as the abandoned missions of Guevavi and Calabazas, the Pima mission at Tumacácori, and the Tubac presidio. When rainfall is only average or below, it flows above ground to a point some five miles north of Tubac and goes underground all the way to San Xavier del Bac. Only during years of exceptionally heavy rainfall does it water the flat land between Tubac and San Xavier.*

*We have no gold, silver, iron, lead, tin, quicksilver, copper mines, or marble quarries. Twenty-five miles from this presidio is an outcropping of lime which supplies us with all we need and whenever we need it for construction. We have no salt beds.*

*Public Works*

*Our major roads connect Tucson with San Xavier and Tubac. We have other trails which we use only for stock raising and chasing Apaches. No bridges have been built. We have no hostelries or inns.*

*The only public work here that is truly worthy of this report is the church at San Xavier del Bac, ten miles from this presidio. Other missions here in the north should really be called chapels, but San Xavier is truly a church. It is ninety-nine feet long, twenty-two feet wide in the nave, sixty feet wide at the transept, which forms two side chapels. The entire structure is of fired brick and lime mortar. The ceiling is a series of domes. The interior is adorned with thirty-*

*eight full-figure statues, plus three "frame" statues dressed in cloth garments, and innumerable angels and seraphim. The façade is quite ornate, boasting two towers, one of which is unfinished. The atrium in front extends out twenty-seven and a half feet. To the left of the atrium is a cemetery, with a domed chapel at the far end surrounded by a fired brick and lime-plaster wall, measuring eighty-two and a half feet in circumference. A conservative estimate of the expense incurred to date in the construction of all that has been mentioned, plus the sacristy, the baptistery, and other rooms, all of which are domed, would be 40,000 pesos. The reason for this ornate church at this last outpost of the frontier is not only to congregate the Christian Pimas of the San Xavier village, but also to attract by its loveliness the unconverted Papagos and Gila Pimas beyond the frontier. I have thought it worthwhile to describe it in such detail because of the wonder that such an elaborate building could be constructed at all out here on the farthest frontier. Because of the consequent hazard involved, the salaries of the artisans had to be doubled.*

*Military*

*We have no formal militia of cavalry or infantry, but the settlers here really do the same job. They are quite accustomed to using their own firearms and horses to help us defend the presidio and pursue the fleeing Apaches when we are short of troops. In fact, they are obliged to do so to hold title to land anywhere within five miles of the presidio. Their farmlands and the lots for their homes are given to them only under this condition, by order of the* Royal Regulation of Presidios. *In return for this military service, they are also exempt from personal taxes to the government and to the church and are entitled to the spiritual ministrations of the chaplain without the financial obligation to support a parish.*

*Two barracks are attached to this presidio, one for the resident garrison and another to house the troops here on detachment from other presidios. As to recruiting activities, we have five recruits attached to this company presently.*[2]

Few documents of the period give a better view of the frontier economy of New Spain. Zúñiga details the tax structure of his district, the market value of livestock, and the merchantable goods that were produced locally, as well as those that were imported at considerable cost from afar, even from China—although, probably more often, imported goods were only longed for because their cost was too high.

### Revenue

We pay no sales tax when we buy here at the presidio. I do not know what sales tax is charged elsewhere. That information is available through José Pérez, the sales tax administrator in Arizpe. We pay no tribute. In tobacco taxes, we have paid out 2210 pesos. We have no gold or silver mines and therefore are not subject to the royal twenty percent. No money is spent on the administration of fiscal activities. The presidio paymaster receives no extra pay for collecting the tobacco tax. The tobacco is sold either in the company store or directly by the paymaster. The paymaster also administers the revenue from the mails. No extra pay is received either by him or by the troops involved in carrying the mail from one military post to the next until it arrives in Arizpe.

### Commerce

The population here spends 5000 pesos a year at the company store on merchandise from Spain and 2500 pesos more for the same purpose with a private merchant. Five hundred pesos are spent annually on merchandise from Asia and China. Three hundred pesos a year are spent on wax and cocoa. Cocoa, however, is replaced here by commercial chocolate, since no cocoa is available. We receive no products directly from Vera Cruz, Acapulco, or San Blas. We have no smuggled goods.

### Agriculture

We produce 600 bushels of corn a year, and it sells at two and a half pesos a bushel. Wheat sells at two pesos a bushel, and our area harvests 2800 bushels annually. Beans and other vegetables sell at four and half pesos a bushel. About 300 bushels are produced annually. Cotton is raised only by the Indians. With it, they weave a domestic fabric for their own use. We grow no sugar, tobacco, cacao, vanilla, sarsaparilla, Tabasco pepper, Jalapa purgative, indigo, cochineal, Campeche wood for dyeing, or wood for fine lumber.

### Stockraising

We have some 3500 head of cattle, selling at three pesos a head. The sheep sell for half a peso a head, and we now have about 2600. We raise no pork and no goats. The horse herd stands at 1200 head, including the presidio, the settlers and the two missions. We have 120 mules and thirty burros.

*Industry*

*Animal slaughtering accounts for 300 beeves killed each year, including the 130 slaughtered at the expense of the royal treasury to maintain the peaceful Apaches. Two hundred sheep are slaughtered. A dressed beef sells at six pesos, a dressed sheep at one peso.*

*Soap making accounts for 1000 pesos spent annually by this population, including the soap needed to provision the garrison. It is difficult to estimate the quantity involved, since soap is sold here in bars and not by weight. Over half of this soap is made here in Tucson and at San Xavier. The rest is bought in Arizpe.*

*No brandy, whiskey or tequila is distilled. No gunpowder, chinaware or glass is manufactured.*

*Occupations*

*Four men here operate pack trains; there are no wagon trains. Two hundred are engaged full time in agriculture and stock raising, including the Indians who tend the fields and the livestock of their missions. Twenty men work at the ordinary industrial trades.*

Although decades of nearly constant warfare with Apaches had held back Tucson's economic development, Zúñiga sees opportunities. In his conclusion he becomes part pitchman, part scold, as he cannot seem to mention opportunities without also chastising the local population for failing to seize them.

*General Observations*

*In connection with government revenue, I observed that all connected directly with the presidio are exempt from all personal taxes. Why, then, do the privileged settlers not prosper more than they do? I believe this is their own fault. Since no demands are made on them, they lose all ambition. Even the most rustic Indian will double his efforts as the time approaches when his tribute is due. An artisan or laborer, whose wife is pregnant, will double his earnings to be able to pay for the approaching baptism celebration, or for the funeral celebration if his relative is dying. Since the royal regulations are in their favor, however, I am not saying that these settlers should be taxed.*

*Why, too, is there not even an attempt at the mechanical arts and trades? At least weaving should be carried on here, when even the coarsest woolen and cotton fabrics must be brought in from New Mexico or all the way from Mexico*

*City. I believe it is for lack of accomplished teachers in these arts and trades. Tucson desperately needs a leather tanner and dresser, a tailor, and a shoemaker. These people could support themselves very comfortably here. Perhaps even more important would be a saddle maker, who could vary his trade by making cinches, leather jackets, saddlebags, saddle pads, cruppers, pack saddles, gun sheaths, and cartridge belts. With his shop right here in the presidio, he could fashion these items to the exact specifications of his clientele. A professional weaver could do very well for himself by making artistic blankets and serge cloth, as could a hat maker by fashioning new hats and cleaning and blocking the used ones. These shops would not only offer the soldiers and settlers custom-made articles, but would also serve as schools for apprentices of these same trades.*

*I have also observed that there is very fertile land here. Why do the settlers not prosper when even neglected vineyards produce a bumper crop? They hardly allow the grape to mature properly before they are selling it, to say nothing of not experimenting with new vines and cuttings. All of this could be regulated by government control, and prizes could be offered to encourage both quantity and quality.*

Tucson enjoyed relative peace during the last years of Spanish rule, but with the coming of Mexican independence relations between the settlements and the Apaches deteriorated, and warfare resumed. In the 1830s and 1840s the little community that had grown up around the fort lost population and its economic activity declined, as was also the case at other presidios throughout Sonora. José de Zúñiga's son, Ignacio, blamed the region's decline on the government, which had ceased to pay soldiers regularly or provide adequate supplies. As soldiers deserted Tucson, civilians also left. Thus, he argued, "the Apache war is not nor has been the cause of the ruin and abandonment of the interested frontier settlements. To the contrary, the war is the result of the abandonment and decadence of the presidios."[3]

→→

The first Anglo Americans to describe Tucson arrived during or shortly after the U.S.-Mexico War. They found the place in a sorry state, thus confirming for many a stereotype of Mexican ineptness. The Mormon Battalion entered Tucson on December 17, 1846, without meeting resistance. Other military units, including that of Samuel Chamberlain (whom we

TUCSON.

"Tucson." J. Ross Browne had little good to say about Tucson, but the image he published shows an orderly, attractive town with an outsize U.S. flag waving above the old presidio parade ground. (From J. Ross Browne, *Adventures in the Apache Country*, 1869; courtesy DeGolyer Library, Southern Methodist University)

met at San Xavier), eventually followed, along with a considerable stream of forty-niners traveling the Gila Trail to the gold fields of California (Plate 12). Most of these visitors described Tucson as unremarkable at best, or contemptible at worst.

In 1854, when the U.S. Senate ratified the Gadsden Treaty, Tucson and the rest of today's Arizona south of the Gila River became U.S. territory. The United States officially took possession of Tucson in 1856, but did little to end hostilities with Apaches until long after the Civil War, which saw both Confederate and Union forces occupy the town. Tucson continued to languish and its inhabitants, three fourths of them Mexicans in the 1860 census, remained the object of Anglo Americans' derision.

One of the most biting and widely read accounts of Tucson appeared in the work of the popular traveler writer and humorist J. Ross Browne, who arrived in January 1864. He described Tucson in a series of articles that ran initially in the *San Francisco Evening Bulletin* and soon after in *Harper's Weekly* between October 1864 and March 1865. These articles became the basis of Browne's popular book, *Adventures in the Apache Country*, published in 1869. The book presents a classic statement of Anglo American contempt for Mexicans so common in the years before and after the U.S.-Mexico War, but it at least does so with a modicum of wit. Rather than accord the hearty residents of Tucson respect for adapting to a harsh desert environment on the dangerous edge of the Apache frontier, Browne mocks them and their poverty, clothing, and architecture. He fails to inform his readers that some of the city's Mexican residents were prosperous merchants like Leopoldo Carrillo, who was "one of the wealthiest men in Tucson, Anglo or Mexican."[4] Anglo Americans also came under Browne's acerbic gaze, for some of them were among the residents he characterized as "villains."

*I had no idea before my visit to Arizona that there existed within the territorial limits of the United States a city more remarkable in many respects than Jericho—the walls of which were blown down by horns; for, in this case, the walls were chiefly built up by horns—a city realizing, to some extent, my impressions of what Sodom and Gomorrah must have been before they were destroyed by the vengeance of the Lord. It is gratifying to find that travel in many lands has not yet fatally impaired my capacity for receiving new sensations. Virginia City came near it; but it was reserved for the city of Tucson to prove that the world is not yet exhausted of its wonders.*

*A journey across the Ninety-mile Desert prepares the jaded and dust-covered traveller to enjoy all the luxuries of civilization which an ardent imagination may lead him to expect in the metropolis of Arizona. Passing the Point of the Mountain, eighteen miles below, he is refreshed during the remainder of the way by scraggy thickets of mesquit[e], bunches of sage and grease-wood, beds of sand and thorny cactus; from which he emerges to find himself on the verge of the most wonderful scatteration of human habitations his eye ever beheld—a city of mud-boxes, dingy and dilapidated, cracked and baked into a composite of dust and filth; littered about with broken corrals, sheds, bake-ovens, carcasses of dead animals, and broken pottery; barren of verdure, parched, naked, and grimly desolate in the glare of a southern sun. Adobe walls without whitewash inside or out, hard earth-floors, baked and dried Mexicans, sore-backed burros, coyote dogs, and terra-cotta children; soldiers, teamsters, and honest miners lounging about the mescal-shops, soaked with the fiery poison; a noisy band of Sonoranian buffoons, dressed in theatrical costume, cutting their antics in the public places* to the most diabolical din of fiddles and guitars ever heard; a long train of Government wagons preparing to start for Fort Yuma or the Rio Grande—these are what the traveller sees, and a great many things more, but in vain he looks for a hotel or lodging-house. The best accommodations he can possibly expect are the dried mud walls of some unoccupied outhouse, with a mud floor for his bed; his own food to eat, and his own cook to prepare it; and lucky is he to possess such luxuries as these. I heard of a blacksmith, named Burke, who invited a friend to stop awhile with him at Tucson. Both parties drank whisky all day for occupation and pleasure. When bedtime came, Burke said, "Let's go home and turn in." He led the way up to the Plaza, and began to hand off his clothes. "What are you doing?" inquired his guest. "Going to bed," said Burke—"this is where I gen'rally sleep." And they both turned in on the Plaza, which if hard was at least well-aired and roomy. The stranger started for the Rio Grande the next day.

For various reasons Tucson has long enjoyed an extensive reputation. Before the acquisition of Arizona by the United States the Mexicans had a military post at this place, with a small command for the protection of the missions and adjoining grain fields against the Apaches. It then numbered some four or five hundred souls. Since 1854 it has been the principal town in the Territory, and has been occupied successively by the Federal and rebel troops.

As the centre of trade with the neighboring State of Sonora, and lying on the high-road from the Rio Grande to Fort Yuma, it became during the few years preceding the "break-up" quite a place of resort for traders, speculators, gamblers, horse-thieves, murderers, and vagrant politicians. Men who were no longer permitted to live in California found the climate of Tucson congenial to their health. If the world were searched over I suppose there could not be found so degraded a set of villains as then formed the principal society of Tucson....

... It will at once be seen that Tucson has greatly improved within the past two years, and offers at the present time rare attractions for visitors from all parts of the world, including artists, who can always find in it subjects worthy of their genius. The views of life, the varied attitudes of humanity that I, a mere sketcher, found in the purlieus of the town as well as in public places, will be valuable to posterity; but, as Dr. Johnson said when looking from an eminence over the road that led out of Scotland into England, it was the finest view he had seen in the country, so I must be permitted to say the best view of Tucson is the rear view on the road to Fort Yuma.[5]

The Tucson that Browne deplored slowly metamorphosed in the last decades of the nineteenth century. The town incorporated as a legal municipality in 1871, the Southern Pacific Railroad arrived in 1880, and the Apache wars effectively ended with the capture of Geronimo in 1886. John Gregory Bourke, an army officer who first visited Tucson in 1870, returned in 1882 to exclaim, "Tucson had changed the most appreciably of any town in the Southwest; American energy and American capital had effected a wonderful transformation: the old garrison was gone; the railroad had arrived."[6] Martha Summerhayes, an officer's wife who had lived there in 1874, returned on a Pullman car in 1886 to find that "the place seemed unfamiliar. … Everything seemed changed."[7]

Tucson residents were affronted when the legislature moved the capital of Arizona Territory from Prescott to Phoenix in 1889, failing to return it to Tucson, which had been the territorial seat from 1870 to 1877. Even lacking the industries of politics and patronage, however, Tucson thrived on an economy based on the three C's—copper, cotton, and cattle—and it enjoyed the prestige of a university town after the University of Arizona

"City of Tucson." Tucson grew rapidly once the Southern Pacific Railroad reached it in 1880. (From Patrick Hamilton, *The Resources of Arizona*, 1884; courtesy DeGolyer Library, Southern Methodist University)

CITY OF TUCSON.

opened its doors in 1891. With prosperity came people, particularly Anglo Americans, and the population swelled from 1,526 in 1864 to 13,193 in 1910.[8]

Arriving by train in 1915, one travel writer informed his readers, "Tucson is not by any means the frontier town that one would imagine it." He had come to a city of paved streets, well-kept shops, and attractive homes built in the bungalow or mission style, "smothered in masses of flowers and blossoming vines, and set on lawns shaded by pepper-trees, palms, and oleanders."[9]

Tucson of the early twentieth century was no longer the rude frontier town of J. Ross Browne's day, and Anglo American visitors no longer brought with them the same anti-Hispanic prejudices. Many now appreciated rather than deplored the city's Spanish past. The work of journalist Harry MacFadden, who visited the new Tucson by train in 1905, suggests that the city's Mexican residents, now outnumbered, lent a picturesque element to a community brimming with the bustle of the industrial age:

*It is full of vim, push and energy, and has all the modern improvements, with manufacturing plants, that many a larger city might be proud of. It is up at an elevation of 2,400 feet above the sea, and is a veritable oasis in the desert; a beauty spot in the sandy wastes. The early history of Tucson is full of romance, dating back to the days of the Spanish conquerors. The courageous Spanish padres, as early as 1649 [Jesuit missionary Eusebio Francisco Kino first visited in 1692], carried their religious banners into that country, and founded the nearby San Xavier Mission. A settlement soon sprang up, and later came the Spanish garrison to protect the settlers from the raids of the blood-thirsty Apache Indians. The place soon came to be known as Tucson, from the name given by the Indians to the waters in the Santa Cruz Valley, near the town. Later, in 1853, Tucson and the surrounding lands, by the Gadsden purchase, became United States territory.*[10] *The town later became an important station on the over-land coach mail route, and still later a hustling frontier town. Its future prosperity and growth was not fully assured until 1884 [the year was actually 1880], when the Southern Pacific Railroad was built into the town. Since that date the improvement [of] Tucson has been rapid and substantial, until she has become a modern city; a great business center; a metropolis of some very considerable importance. The city is full of modern homes and fine business houses, but it has still on it many of the marks of the Mexican domination—its narrow streets, lined with adobe houses, and large Mexican population, who still cling to all the customs of their Spanish ancestors. Even her newest buildings are built in beautiful Spanish and Aztec designs of architecture. It has its clubs, its churches and societies of the best secret orders to make life joyful and comfortable. With its important location and commercial enterprise, it presents many fine opportunities to the business man and capitalist.*[11]

Long before MacFadden made his visit, the growing town had begun to swallow its crumbling, century-old presidio. Section by section, the adobes of the fort's walls, which at their greatest extent encompassed eleven acres, were carted off for use in other buildings. In 1905 MacFadden might have glimpsed a remnant of the original presidio complex, as the last standing segment of the outer wall survived until 1918. Today, a partial reconstruction of the presidio stands at the northeast corner of the quadrangle of the original fort, at the corner of Washington and Church Streets. There visitors can explore a twenty-foot-tall *torreon,* a commissary, barracks, and other reimagined and reconstructed components of the former military post. The complex also includes a Hohokam pit house, a reminder that O'Conor and his contemporaries were not the first to deem the site a good one. From this assemblage of old and new historical elements a line of paving bricks follows the original outline of the presidio's peripheral wall. The El Presidio Park, along Pennington Street, occupies the site of the fort's Plaza de Armas, just outside the south wall of the quadrangle, where Spanish soldiers once drilled. The small, nearby Twentieth of August Park on Church Street commemorates the day in 1775 when Lieutenant Colonel Hugo O'Conor selected the site for Tucson and ordered the removal of the Tubac garrison to its new location, thereby setting in motion the development of one of the great cities of the modern Southwest.[12]

# 15 Zuni

Nestled amid stunning red sandstone buttes and mesas on the high Colorado Plateau, Zuni Pueblo (A:shiwi) consists of the village of Halona and its nearby "suburb," Blackrock. They lie thirty miles south of Gallup, on the western edge of New Mexico. Zuni is the largest and most populous of New Mexico's nineteen Indian pueblos. Including outlying farms and ranches scattered over more than 640 square miles of reservation lands, Zuni's total population numbers in the neighborhood of eleven thousand. The pueblo is best known today for its artists. A large majority of Zunis earn at least part of their income through the production and sale of pottery, stone fetishes, and silver jewelry.

Zuni occupies a special place in southwestern history. When Spaniards first arrived, Zunis occupied several villages, and it was at one of those, Hawikku, where Spaniards and Pueblos first met in decisive fashion in the summer of 1540. At Hawikku, as the Zuni tribe tells modern visitors, "history began."[1] The meeting between Europeans and Pueblos quickly deteriorated into violent conflict, as the Spaniards and their Mexican Indian allies assaulted the stone village. With commencement of that battle, Hawikku, from the vantage of modern scholarship, became "ground zero" for the "social cataclysm" that would attend all encounters between Indians and Spaniards throughout the Southwest.[2]

Spaniards arrived at Zuni as a result of a small deception with large consequences. The story begins with Alvar Núñez Cabeza de Vaca, who made a storied eight-year trek—ranking among the most famous journeys in American history—from the Gulf Coast of Texas across northern Mexico to the Pacific slope. When he reunited with fellow Spaniards in 1536, Cabeza de Vaca apparently made extravagant claims about the wealth to be found in the lands through which he had passed. As he told the king, "There are great indications and signs of mines of gold and silver."[3] His report deepened Spanish interest in the northern reaches of New Spain, as Mexico was then called. In the autumn of 1538, the viceroy of New Spain, Antonio Mendoza, dispatched a Franciscan priest, Fray Marcos de Niza, to investigate the northern lands. Cabeza de Vaca had returned to Spain to seek favors from the king and could not guide the friar, so Mendoza turned to one of Cabeza de Vaca's three companions, a black Arab slave known to history only as Esteban. Journeying well ahead of Fray Marcos and sending reports back to him, Esteban traveled as far as the Zuni villages. The Zunis killed him, perhaps because he had taken liberties with their women, as Spaniards later heard, or perhaps because the Zunis believed him a spy for Spanish slave hunters, as one Zuni historian has conjectured.[4]

Messengers brought back word of Esteban's death to Fray Marcos, who then retreated to Mexico City, where he reported to the viceroy. He had followed Esteban's trail, he said, and had seen one of seven rich cities in a place known to Indians as Cíbola (a Zuni word meaning buffalo). He did not enter the rich city, but kept at a distance lest Indians kill him as they had Esteban and thus prevent him from carrying the news of his fabulous discovery back to the viceroy.

Fray Marcos's claim was nonsense. He never saw the Zuni towns.[5] Nonetheless, Viceroy Mendoza accepted his story and authorized a large, costly expedition "to reconnoiter and pacify" the Tierra Nueva—the new lands to the north. Having discovered the great cities of the Aztecs and the Incas, credulous Spaniards had reason to suppose that other dazzling cities lay beyond the horizon. Moreover, the report of the Seven Cities of Cíbola had come from a man of the cloth and a presumed eyewitness, whom the viceroy had sent on a confidential mission to scout the new land.

In the spring of 1540 the expedition to Tierra Nueva marched northward under the leadership of the viceroy's protégé, Francisco Vázquez de Coronado.[6] The viceroy sent Fray Marcos along as a guide. The privately funded expedition gradually grew to include some 350 Spaniards, not counting their servants, black slaves, women, and children, and over 1,300 Indian allies recruited or conscripted from lands already under Spanish control. Certainly the Spaniards hoped to find gold and silver, as Cortés and Pizarro had done before but, more important, they hoped to find large numbers of prosperous Indians whom they might tax or enslave and whose labor would enrich them.

Leaving the northernmost settlements of New Spain behind, the expedition followed well-worn trade routes that took them close to the present Arizona–New Mexico border. Eighty hard and hungry days after departing the northern Mexican town of Culiacán, Coronado and an advance party consisting of about fifty Spanish horsemen and perhaps a thousand Indian allies reached Hawikku, the first of the Zuni pueblos. That day, July 7, 1540 (on the Julian calendar, not the Gregorian calendar used today), the Zunis were still celebrating ceremonies related to the summer solstice, and they ordered the strangers not to pass.[7] The Spaniards and their allies, for their part, were by then starving and intended to fight, if necessary, to acquire whatever food was stored in the village before them.

In strict observance of royal instruction, Coronado ordered the *requerimiento* read to the Zunis through an interpreter. That legal instrument — legal to Spaniards but at best opaque to the natives to whom it was shouted out — informed Indians that they must recognize the Spanish Crown as their sovereign or face destruction. Whether or not the Zunis understood even a particle of the no doubt inexactly translated *requerimiento,* they did not acquiesce. By one Spanish account, the Zunis responded that they "were not familiar with his majesty, nor did they wish to be his subjects."[8]

In the bloody battle that followed, Spaniards and their Indian allies prevailed. In addition to possessing overwhelming numbers, the intruders had the advantage of gunpowder and iron. In the summer of 2004, archaeologists wielding metal detectors in a survey of Hawikku were thrilled to find horseshoe nails and metal balls fired from Spanish arquebuses, confirming that Hawikku, whose ruins can be visited today with a Zuni guide, was the site of this battle.[9] It would be the first of many bloodlettings visited on Pueblo people by the Coronado expedition.

Coronado's victory at Hawikku cost him physical injury and worse, his hopes. He was hurt in the battle because of, not despite, his armor. Contrary to the popular image of metal-clad conquistadors, most of Coronado's men did not wear body armor. But Coronado did, and his golden helmet made him an obvious target for the defenders of Hawikku, who showered him with stones and knocked him unconscious. More disappointing, the rich city turned out to be a modest village. Devastated and angry at his Franciscan guide, Coronado told Viceroy Mendoza that Fray Marcos "has not spoken the truth in anything he said."[10] Too late, Coronado and the viceroy realized they had gambled their fortunes on a false tip.

Unwilling to write off the venture and heartened by new rumors of a people to the east who ate on dishes made of gold, Coronado continued into the Pueblo country along the Río Grande and thence onto the plains of central Kansas, where his disillusion deepened. In the spring of 1542, having discovered neither large settlements of well-to-do Indians nor precious minerals, the defeated conquistador withdrew empty-handed from Tierra Nueva. He returned to Mexico City, completing a two-year journey of four thousand miles.

What follows are excerpts from one of the many remarkable documents produced by the Coronado expedition. Coronado wrote his first report to Viceroy Mendoza from Tierra Nueva on August 3, 1540, less than a month after his arrival at Hawikku. He had not yet heard rumors of a wealthy people to the east, and his probing around Zuni had produced nothing. He despaired and spoke of "abandoning the enterprise." In his report he described what he could see—the houses, food, dress, animals, and the landscape. Unable to speak the language of the people he had vanquished and lacking a fully fluent interpreter, he had almost nothing to say about the Zunis' spiritual or social life or their political and religious organization, if indeed these subjects interested him at all.

Coronado's private report to Viceroy Mendoza first reached the reading public in Italian, published in 1556 by Giovanni Battista Ramusio; it reached English-language readers in 1600. The original Spanish letter was lost early on and all translations into other languages, including the English translation of 1600, have been based on the 1556 Italian version. Ramusio or his translator may have altered or embellished this document, but if so, the changes were minor; other documents corroborate the story that Coronado told the viceroy.[11]

*As soon as I arrived within sight of the* ciudad *[city], I sent* maestre de campo *don García López, fray Daniel, fray Luis, and Fernando Bermejo some distance ahead with some horsemen, so that the Indians might see them. [I ordered them] to tell [the Indians] that [the purpose of] our coming was not to do them injury but to protect them in the name of the emperor, our lord. The* requerimiento *was made intelligible to the natives of that land through an interpreter, in accordance with instructions [and] in the way His Majesty commands. However, [the Indians], being arrogant people, showed it little respect. [They acted this way] because it seemed to them that we were few in number and they would have no difficulty killing us. They struck fray Luis in his robe with an arrow, which it pleased God did him no harm.*

*At that [moment] I arrived with all the rest of the horsemen and footmen. I found a large portion of the Indians in the country outside the* ciudad. *They began shooting arrows at us. In order to comply with Your Lordship's advice, and that of the* marqués, *I did not want them to be attacked. So I prohibited the company from pursuing them, when they asked me if they could do so. And [I said] that what [our] enemies were doing was nothing and that it was not [right] to do battle with so few people.*

*On the other hand, the Indians, because they saw that we were not pursuing them, gained more courage and arrogance. So much so that they approached the horse's legs to shoot their arrows. When I saw there was no more time to stand in place, and it seemed the same to the ecclesiastics, [the company] attacked. [Then] there was little to do to them because some of them fled quickly to the* ciudad, *which was nearby and well fortified. And others [fled] into the countryside, to which chance led them.*

*Some Indians died, and more would have if I had allowed them to be followed. But I saw that little benefit could come from that. [That was] because the Indians who were outside were few in number and those who had retreated within the* ciudad, *together with those who had remained there before, were numerous. Because that was where the foodstuffs were that we needed so sorely, I gathered all my men and divided them as seemed best to me to do battle against the* ciudad. *Then I surrounded it.*

*Because the hunger we were suffering did not permit delay, I dismounted with some of those gentlemen and men-at-arms. And I ordered that the crossbowmen and arquebusiers make an assault and remove [our] enemies from the defensive structures, so that they could not do us injury. I attacked the wall on one side at a place where they told me a movable ladder was leaning. And I saw that an entrance was there. However, in short order the strings of the crossbowmen's weapons broke, and the arquebusiers accomplished nothing because they were so weak and debilitated that they could hardly stay on their feet.*

*Because of this, the people who were on the roof defending themselves had no difficulty at all inflicting the injury on us that they had power [to do]. With an infinity of large stones they hurled from the roof, they knocked me to the ground twice. If I had not been protected by the excellent helmet I wore, I think the result would have been grim for me. Even so, [the men] removed me from the field with two small wounds to the face, an arrow in one foot, and many blows from stones to my arms and legs. In this way I left the battle extremely worn out. I think that if don García López de Cárdenas had not, like an excellent* caballero, *sheltered me the second time they knocked me to the ground by placing his body on top of mine, I would have run much greater risk than I did. But it pleased God that the Indians surrendered. And Our Lord saw fit that this* ciudad *was captured. In it was found as great an abundance of corn as [we] were seeking [in] our necessity.*[12]

Coronado had bravely led the attack, but he did not have to find the hottest fighting, for it found him: "Because my armor was gilded and shiny, all [the Indians] assaulted me. [It was] for this reason that I was wounded worse than the others, not because I had done more and set myself ahead of the others, since all these *caballeros* and men-at-arms acquitted themselves very well, as was expected of them. I am now well, God be praised, although still somewhat battered by the stones."

The battle won, his wounds and those of a handful of other Spaniards enumerated, and without mention of any casualties among his Indian allies, let alone a tally of the enemy dead, Coronado proceeds to inform the viceroy of the little he can readily ascertain of the land of which he now finds himself the master. A reader might imagine that his mind was fairly spinning, and not because of the blows he had received to his head. He was in a land utterly new, unsure of his location in the world—he can only speculate about distance and direction to the ocean—and he eagerly remarks similarities between the alien, new *reino* (or kingdom) *de Cíbola* and familiar old Mexico and Spain, the better to make the new land intelligible to the viceroy and perhaps to himself. He is also deeply disappointed by the poverty of the villages now under his command, yet he strives to describe his situation in a positive light:

*It now remains for me to give an account of the seven* ciudades, *the* reinos, *and the* provincias *about which the father provincial reported to Your Lordship. So as not to beat around the bush, I can say truthfully that he [Fray Marcos] has not spoken the truth in anything he said. Instead, everything has been quite contrary, except the name of the* ciudad *and the large, stone houses. Although they may be decorated with turquoise, [they are made] from neither mortar nor brick. They are, nevertheless, very good houses, of three, four, and five stories. In them there are good lodgings, rooms with galleries, and some underground rooms [that are] very excellent and paved, which have been built for winter. They are almost like sweat baths.*

*The ladders they have for their houses are almost all removable and portable. They are raised and set in place when it suits them. They are made of two timbers with rungs like ours.*

*The seven* ciudades *are seven small towns, all consisting of the [sort of] houses I describe [here]. They are all located within close proximity, within four leagues [a league was roughly 3 miles, the distance one could walk in an hour]. All [together] are called the* reino *of Cíbola. Each one has its own name, and no single one is called Cíbola. Instead, all as a whole are called Cíbola. [To] this one that I call a* ciudad *I have given the name Granada. [I have bestowed] such [a name] because there is some similarity about it [and] in commemoration of Your Lordship.*

*In this one, where I am now lodged, there could be some two hundred houses, all encircled by a wall. It seems to me that together with the other [houses] that are not [encircled] in this way, they could reach [a total of] five hundred hearths [households]. There is another neighboring town, one of the seven [that] is somewhat larger than this one. [There is] another one the same size as this [one], and the remaining four are somewhat smaller. I am sending paintings of all this to Your Lordship, along with the route. The finely prepared hide on which the painting is was found here, along with other such hides.*[13]

*The population of these towns seems relatively large and intelligent to me, but I am not certain [that is] so. [That is] because it would seem to me that they have attained [sufficient] judgment and intellect to know how to build these houses in the way they are [built], [but] for the most part they go about completely* naked, with [only] their shameful parts covered. They also have mantas [shawls] painted in the way [the one is that] I am sending to Your Lordship.

They do not harvest cotton, because the land is extremely cold. However, they wear mantas, like the one you will see as an example. And it is true that some spun cotton was found in their houses. They wear the hair on their heads in the same way [the people] from [the Ciudad de] México [do]. And they are all very well brought up and tractable.

I think they have turquoise in quantity. By the time I arrived, this had disappeared, along with the rest of their possessions, except the corn. As a result, I did not find a single woman or any young men less than fifteen years old or [men] older than sixty, except for two or three elders who remained to command all the other youths and fighting men. Two bits of emerald were found in some paper, also some very worthless, small, red stones that tend toward the color of garnets, along with other [bits] of rock crystal, [all of] which I gave to a criado [servant] of mine to put away in order to send to Your Lordship. [But] according to what they tell me, he has lost them.

[Turkeys] were found, but only a few, although we have some. In all seven of these towns the Indians tell me that they do not eat them, but keep them only to avail themselves of the feathers. I do not believe them about this, because [the turkeys] are very excellent and larger than those from [the Ciudad de] México.

The weather in this land and the temperature of the air are almost like [those of Ciudad de] México, since now it is raining and hot. Up until now, however, I have never seen it rain heavily; rather, a little shower has come with wind, like those that customarily fall in Spain. The snow and the cold are usually very severe. [I report this] because the natives of the land say this, and it seems likely that it is so. And also because of the nature of the country, the type of rooms they have, and the hides and other things these people have to protect themselves from the cold.

There are no kinds of fruit or fruit trees here. It is all a land of plateaus, and in no direction are mountains visible, although there are some hills and a difficult pass. Birds are scarce here, which must be on account of the cold and because there are no mountains nearby. There are not many trees for making firewood here. They may obtain enough [wood] to burn for their own use [only by getting it] four leagues away, from a forest of very small juniper trees. Very good grass for our horses was located a quarter of a league from here, both for them to graze *and for being cut for hay. Of this we were in great need, because our horses had arrived there exhausted and worn out.*

*The food which the people of this land have consists of corn (of which they have a great abundance here), beans, and small game, which they must eat (although they say they do not), because many pelts of deer, hares, and rabbits were found. They eat the best tortillas I have seen anywhere. And generally everyone eats them. They maintain the finest order and cleanliness in grinding [their corn] that may be seen anywhere. One woman from among the people of this land grinds as much as four [women] from among the Mexica. They have excellent granular salt that they bring from a lake one day's journey from here [Zuni Salt Lake].*[14]

*No information has been supplied by them concerning the Mar del Norte or the one in the west. I cannot tell Your Lordship which we may be closer to, although logically they must be nearer to the one in the west. I imagine [I am] a hundred and fifty leagues away from it and that the one in the north must be much farther away. Your lordship may see how much the land widens here.*

Coronado next provides an accounting of the fauna of the region. The tigers and lions to which he refers are probably jaguars and mountain lions, although jaguars have been absent from the Zuni area for a considerable time. His "wethers" are desert bighorn sheep, and his "wild goats" may be bighorns as well, possibly immature ones with undeveloped horns, the actual habitat of North American mountain goats being far to the north. Coronado's wild boars are collared peccaries or javelinas. "Leopards" may again refer to jaguars, and "very large deer" suggest elk.[15] "There are many animals: bears, tigers, lions, and porcupines, and some wethers the size of horses, with very large horns and a small tail. I have seen the horns of these [animals], and their size is something to be marveled at. There are wild goats, heads of which I have also seen, and the claws of the bears and hides of the wild boars. There are game animals such as deer, leopards, [and] very large deer. Everyone has concluded that some may be larger than the beast [horse] that had belonged to Juan Melaz, which Your Lordship made me a gift of."

Coronado faces the difficult task of sorting fact from fiction in what the Zunis tell him. Given his situation, it is understandable if he was gullible in believing things that were pleasing for him to hear, including the idea that the Zunis had expected a conqueror like him to appear. About one matter he was certainly right: that the natives would tell him almost anything if they thought it would cause him to go away and never come back.

*They say they will bring their children, so that our ecclesiastics may teach them. And [further,] that they are anxious to know our laws. They assert that it was said among them more than fifty years ago that a people like us must come, from the direction we have come, and that they would subjugate this whole land.*

*According to what has been understood up to the present, what these Indians venerate is water. [I say this] because they say it generates their corn and sustains life. And they know of no other reason except that their forefathers did likewise.*

*I have made every possible effort to learn from the natives of these settlements whether they have information concerning other peoples,* provincias, *and* ciudades. *And they tell me about seven towns that are far from here and are like these. However, [those people] do not live in houses like these. Instead, they are small and made of earth. And much cotton is harvested among them. The first of these four places they know about they say is called Tucano [Hopi]. They are not being clear to me about the other ones. I believe they are not telling me the truth, thinking that in any case I would have to leave them soon and turn back from here. But they will soon be disabused about that.*

*I am sending don Pedro de Tovar to see it with his company and some other horsemen. I would not have dispatched this bundle of documents to Your Lordship as long as I had not learned what [that place] is, if I had thought that within twelve or fifteen days it would have been possible to have word from him. [But] because he will take at least thirty days, and when I considered that this information may be of little importance, and that already the cold and rains are approaching, it seems to me that I should do what your Lordship directed me [to do] in your instruction. Namely, that as soon as I was here, I should notify you. . . .*

*With this dispatch I would have liked to send Your Lordship many samples of things there are in this land, but the journey is so long and rough that it is difficult for me to do so. However, I am sending you twelve small* mantas *of the type the people of [this] land customarily wear and a garment that seems to me to be well made. I kept it because it appears to me to be very nicely embroidered [and] because I do not believe that anything has been seen [before] in these Indies embroidered with a needle, except since the Spaniards have been living there. I* am also sending you two cloths painted with [images of] the animals there are in this land, even though, as I say, the picture may be very poorly done. [That is] because the "master" took no more than a day to paint it. I have seen other paintings on the walls of the houses of this ciudad with much better proportions and better done.

I am sending you a [bison] hide, some turquoises, two ear pendants made of the same [material], fifteen combs the Indians [use], some tablets decorated with turquoise, and two small, decorated, wicker baskets, of which the Indians have a great abundance. I am also sending you two small [bearer's rings] that the women here customarily wear on their heads when they carry water from the spring, in the same way as [the women do] in Spain. One of these Indian women, with one of these rings on her head, will carry a jar of water up a ladder without touching it with her hands. In addition, I am sending you an example of the arms and armor the natives of this land fight with: a round shield, a club, and a bow with some arrows. Among the latter there are two with certain bone points, which, according to what the conquistadores who are here report, are different from those that have been seen before.

Having cataloged the various items—some of them impressive, some only odd or curious—that he was sending to the viceroy, Coronado delivers the bad news about gold and silver: "From what I am able to conclude, there does not appear to me to be any prospect of obtaining gold and silver, but I trust in God that if it exists here we will obtain it. And it will not remain [unlocated] for lack of seeking it."

And he continues with details pertinent to Spain's previous encounter with Zuni, wrapping up old business, so to speak:

The death of the Moor [Esteban] is a certainty, because many of the things he was carrying have been found here. The Indians told me that they [had] killed him here because the Indians from Chichilticale [had] told them he was a wicked man and not like the Christians. [That was] because the Christians did not kill anyone's women, but he did kill them. And [they killed him] also because he was touching their women, whom the Indians love more than themselves. Therefore they decided to kill him, but they did not do it in the way that was reported.

[I say this] because they did not kill any of those who had come with him. Nor did they wound the youth from the provincia of Petatlán who was with him.

*Instead, they took him prisoner and have held him closely guarded up until now. When I tried to get him back, they refused to give him up for two or three days, saying that he was dead. And other times [they said] that the Indians of Acucu [Ácoma] had led him away. But finally, when I told them I would become extremely angry if they did not give him to me, they turned him over to me. He is [now] acting as interpreter. Although he may not be fluent at speaking, he nevertheless understands [the language] well.*

At this point, Coronado contradicts himself. Previously he said gold and silver seemed to be absent from the region; now he says traces of the metals exist. Richard and Shirley Flint, scholars whose understanding of Coronado and his documents is unsurpassed, surmise that this inconsistency may indicate that Coronado wrote his report to Mendoza over the course of multiple days, incorporating new information as it became known to him.[16]

*In this place some gold and silver have been found. Those who understand mining have thought it not bad. To this point I have been unable to extract from these people where they dug it up. And I see that they refuse to tell me the truth about everything, imagining, as I have said, that soon I will have to depart from here. Nevertheless, I trust in God that they will not be able to avoid it any longer.*

*I beg Your Lordship to report to His Majesty about the outcome of this journey, because I have no more to say than I have [already] said. In the meantime, may it please God that we find that which we desire. May [the Indians] not do it [continue to obstruct us]. May God, Our Lord, protect and preserve Your Most Illustrious Lordship.*

*From the provincia of Cíbola and this ciudad of Granada, the third of August 1540. Francisco Vázquez de Coronado kisses Your Most Illustrious Lordship's hands.*

➤➤

Where we see one pueblo at Zuni today, Coronado and his men saw seven—or so they said. In 1540, some six thousand A:shiwi, as the Zunis call themselves yet today, lived in a cluster of farming villages scattered along the Zuni River. Archaeologists suspect that Zunis lived in at least nine pueblos at the time of Coronado's visit in 1540, but the number seven had special resonance for Spaniards.[17] Perhaps Spaniards saw only seven, as they said they did, or perhaps the number seven trumped the actual number.

From Coronado's visit in 1540 until Mexican independence in 1821, Spain claimed sovereignty over the Zunis. Spaniards initiated profound changes in Zuni life by introducing horses, mules, and sheep, and new crops such as wheat. Apart from missionaries, who began to work at Zuni in 1629 and who complained that Zunis were slow to embrace the new religion, Spaniards themselves rarely visited—and even more rarely lingered—in the Zuni towns.

In 1680, the lone Spanish missionary at Zuni disappeared for a generation. That year, along with most other Pueblos, Zunis rose up against the Spanish presence, and they may well have killed their missionary, as many other pueblos killed theirs. Several fascinating strains of Zuni oral tradition, however, tell the story of "Fray Juan Greyrobe," who was spared and absorbed into the life of the tribe, joining everyone else in the anxious months and years following the Pueblo Revolt atop the large mesa Zunis know as Dowa Yalanne or Corn Mountain, which towers a thousand feet above the surrounding countryside, east of present-day Halona. Expecting Spanish reprisals, the Zunis fled from their scattered villages and repaired to the mesa top, as they had done in previous times of danger. There they rapidly built new room blocks and refurbished structures already in place. They also built low defensive walls at the points where the few trails ascending the mesa reached the top. This was the first time that "the entire Zuni tribe gathered to live in a single settlement."[18]

Although life on Dowa Yalanne removed the Zunis from convenient access to farmland and water (atop the mesa, they built small reservoirs to capture runoff from rain and snowmelt), the mesa offered security from Apaches as well as Spaniards, *Apache* being the Zuni word for "enemy." Zunis remained atop the nearly impregnable mesa from the Pueblo Revolt in 1680 until 1699, when they made peace with the Spaniards, who had successfully reestablished themselves in New Mexico beginning in 1692. The Zunis came down off the mesa and resettled in the single village of Halona, where they might readily concentrate their numbers for defense.[19] Alliance with Spaniards now seemed wise, for the Spanish had the capacity to launch punitive campaigns against the pueblo's enemies. Accordingly, the Zunis allowed missionaries to return and build the church of Nues-

"Pueblo of Zuñi. Sept. 15." Although Coronado described Zuni in 1540, the first graphic image of Zuni did not appear in print until 1850. This lithograph, based on a wash drawing by Richard Kern, shows the pueblo of Halona and its church, looking east to Dowa Yalanne, or Corn Mountain, whose distinctive profile Kern failed to capture. (From J. H. Simpson, *Journal of a Military Reconnaissance ... to the Navajo Country ... in 1849*; courtesy DeGolyer Library, Southern Methodist University)

tra Señora de Guadalupe, which stands restored in the heart of the pueblo today.

With Mexican independence in 1821, the mission church at Zuni was abandoned and a new group of foreigners, Anglo Americans, began to visit the pueblo. First came trappers, like Old Bill Williams, in the 1820s and 1830s; then came U.S. troops during the U.S.-Mexico War; then came a stream of travelers crossing the country to California—gold seekers, home seekers, government surveyors, and military men. Located on a major east-west route, Zuni was an important oasis in a land otherwise empty of settlement.

Initially, Zunis profited from the traffic. They provisioned the visitors, and they sold corn and other produce to several U.S. military posts that were soon established in the region. They also extended their hospitality. The Anglo Americans did not always respond in kind. When Indian agent James S. Calhoun visited Zuni in 1849, he noted in a private letter that "wild Indians" like Navajos and Apaches raided the Zunis, "but what is shockingly discreditable to the american name, emigrants commit the grossest wrongs against these excellent Indians by taking, in the name of the United States, such horses, mules, and sheep, and grain as they desire, carefully concealing their true name, but assuming official authority and bearing. A wrong of this kind had been perpetrated a few days previous to our arrival there."[20]

Early American visitors to Zuni were often as disappointed with the pueblo as Coronado had been—but for different reasons. In 1851, medical doctor Samuel Woodhouse expressed pleasure at leaving "this dirty place," having spent three weeks at Zuni with a government expedition. "Living in an Indian pueblo is anything but agreeable," he wrote. "The atmosphere is strongly impregnated with all kinds [of] nauseous perfumes."[21] John Wesley Powell, the explorer who descended the Colorado River in 1869, further explored the canyon country the following year and stopped at Zuni en route to Albuquerque. He found little to like at Zuni: "Nothing can be more repulsive than the appearance of the streets; irregular, crowded, and filthy, in which dogs, asses, and Indians are mingled in confusion."[22]

Not all early Anglo visitors reacted negatively, but Zuni and the other pueblos inspired few to sing their praises.[23] By the first decades of the twentieth century, however, American sensibilities had begun to change, as more and more visitors found the pueblos agreeable.[24] Whereas Woodhouse and Powell had deplored Zuni as dirty, a later generation found it charming. One travel writer issued this backhanded compliment in 1918: "Dirt and picturesqueness were ever comrades, and Zuni is truly picturesque." From this new perspective, the narrow streets between multistoried houses opened out into small, enchanting plazas; beehive ovens suggested the Orient; and the typically open doorways of houses yielded the quaint sounds and smells of women grinding corn or of potters and weavers at work. Above all, visitors remembered Zuni as "the present-day representative of those Seven Cities of Cíbola, the fable of whose wealth led to the discovery of New Mexico."[25]

Anthropologists found another kind of treasure at Zuni in the form of ethnological and archaeological information. One of the first, the colorful, eccentric, and ultimately duplicitous Frank Hamilton Cushing, took up residence among the Zunis in 1879, at age twenty-two, and stayed for

"Buffalo Dance, Pueblo de Zuñi, N.M.," lithograph based on a drawing by Richard H. Kern. Americans had the opportunity to see more graphic images of Zuni in 1853 with the publication of an expedition report by Lorenzo Sitgreaves, with whom Kern had revisited the pueblo. (From Lorenzo Sitgreaves, *Report of an Expedition down the Zuni and Colorado Rivers*, 1853; courtesy DeGolyer Library, Southern Methodist University)

four years. He became a member of the tribe and, in the words of one scholar, "the world's first live-in anthropologist."[26] So many ethnologists and archaeologists have worked at Zuni in the years since that if it were possible to measure "words per capita," the pueblo might prove to be the most studied Indian place in America. Indeed, the anthropologists who have studied Zuni have themselves become objects of study.

Most engaging among these self-reflective works is *Zuni and the American Imagination* by Eliza McFeely, which recounts the careers of three early archaeologists who essentially looted Zuni of its religious treasures and secret knowledge: Frank Hamilton Cushing, Matilda Cox Stevenson, and Stewart Culin. Zuni, McFeely explains, was more than a laboratory for anthropologists and a rich repository of artifacts. In her view, anthropologists who studied Zuni revealed as much about themselves and the larger American society of their day as they did about Zuni. The pueblo served the "anthropologists and their audiences" as "a stage set on which they could play out their fantasies of pre-industrial wholeness and cultural superiority."[27]

Among modern studies of Zuni, none is more seemingly far-fetched than Nancy Yaw Davis's *The Zuni Enigma: A Native American People's Possible Japanese Connection,* which appeared in 2000. Davis suggests the possibility that Japanese Buddhists crossed the Pacific in the 1200s, landed on the coast of southern California, and followed well-worn Indian trading trails to New Mexico. There, in the mid-1300s, they joined with Native Americans on their own pilgrimage, according to Davis, and the two peoples merged and settled in the area that we know today as Zuni. Japanese influence, Davis suggests, would explain a number of Zuni anomalies: a language unlike that of any other Native American group, as well as unusual physical attributes. Davis also sees parallels with Japanese traditions in Zuni religion and decorative motifs, suggesting to her that Zuni culture developed in concert with a people who came eastward from the "ocean of

"Indian Weaving (Pueblo Zuñi)," lithograph based on a drawing by Richard H. Kern. In 1851, while Sitgreaves fumed that his expedition was delayed at Zuni awaiting a military escort, Kern set about recording aspects of Zuni life that had escaped him on his earlier visit with Simpson two years earlier. (From Lorenzo Sitgreaves, *Report of an Expedition down the Zuni and Colorado Rivers,* 1853; courtesy DeGolyer Library, Southern Methodist University)

INDIAN WEAVING
( Pueblo Zuñi )

ALEX. GARDNER, Photographer.                                                                    311 Seventh Street, Washington

ACROSS THE CONTINENT ON THE KANSAS PACIFIC RAILROAD.

(ROUTE OF THE 35TH PARALLEL.)

Ancient Pueblo Town of Zuni, Western New Mexico.

"Ancient Pueblo Town of Zuni, Western New Mexico," photograph by Alexander Gardner, autumn of 1867. This appears to be the first photograph of Zuni—and perhaps of any of the New Mexico pueblos. Below the print Gardner quoted from Coronado's description of Hawikku: "there may be some 200 houses" inside the walls, and all together "there may be some 500"; and "That which these Indians worship is the water, for they say it causeth their corn to grow." (From Alexander Gardner, *Across the Continent on the Kansas Pacific Railroad;* courtesy DeGolyer Library, Southern Methodist University)

the sunset world," as recalled in one Zuni migration story.[28] Recent DNA research, however, offers no hint of a Japanese connection.[29] If nothing else, Davis's work reminds us of the enigma Zuni continues to present to the rest of the world. Its many mysteries persist, as they always have.

No scholar of the Zuni past can adequately characterize the place without reference to the first written impressions of Zuni. The documents produced by the Coronado expedition mark the line between prehistory and history, which begins, by most definitions, with the accumulation of a documentary record. The first documents from Zuni open a remarkable window into the region's past and establish a baseline for measuring historical change within the region.[30] Coronado failed to find either precious metals or Indians whose labor he might profitably exploit, but posterity is far richer for the trove of descriptive literature that his expedition left behind.

# Notes

Epigraph: Price, *Dry Place*, xxii.

1. Sitgreaves, *Report of an Expedition Down the Zuni and Colorado Rivers*, 18; and Ives, *Report upon the Colorado River*, 19–20. Ives had with him Pedro de Castañeda de Nájera's narrative.

2. Charles Francis Saunders, *Finding the Worthwhile in the Southwest*, 1–2.

3. Anna Brown and Mark Hugo Lopez, "Ranking Latino Populations in the States," *Pew Research Center: Hispanic Trends*, August 29, 2013 (www.pewhispanic.org /2013/08/29/ii-ranking-latino-populations-in-the-states). In 2011 Hispanics constituted 46.7 percent of New Mexicans and 30.1 percent of Arizonans.

4. Brown, *Four Corners*, 7–8.

5. Ives, *Report upon the Colorado River*, 110.

6. Hernán Cortés to Queen Juana and her son, Carlos V, Rica Villa de la Vera Cruz, July 10, 1519, in Cortés, *Letters from Mexico*, 3–4. Emphasis added.

7. Coronado to the viceroy, Cíbola, August 3, 1540, in Flint and Flint, *Documents of the Coronado Expedition*, 252–62. Other accounts in the Flints' collection of documents, such as those by Fray Marcos de Niza and Pedro de Casteñeda, also fail to express positive emotions toward the land.

8. Thomas, *Man and the Natural World*, 254–60. Thomas writes principally about English attitudes, but they seem to apply to Spaniards as well.

9. Teague, *The Southwest in American Literature and Art*, 28–30, quoting Josiah Gregg and noting historian Barbara Novak's useful distinction between an "older sublime" and a "newer, more tranquil sublime."

10. Sitgreaves, *Report of an Expedition Down the Zuni and Colorado Rivers*, 5.

11. John Russell Bartlett, *Personal Narrative*, 1:247.

12. Cather, *Death Comes for the Archbishop*, 234–35.

13. Erna Ferguson, *Our Southwest*, 18–19.

CHAPTER 1. ÁCOMA

1. Minge, *Ácoma*, 1, notes the variant spellings of Ácoma and the meaning of that name, but García-Mason, "Acoma," 464, herself from Ácoma, asserts that Ácoma refers not to the place but only to "a person from Acoma pueblo." Minge's work remains the best one-volume history; he relied heavily on information provided him by Ácomas. Two popular guides to New Mexico place-names (Julyan, *The Places Names of New Mexico* and Pearce, *New Mexico Place Names*) each give the word Ácoma as meaning "people of the white rock."

2. The trail, which apparently paralleled the present Highway 53, had several variations. For a consideration of the possibilities, see Riley and Manson, "The Cibola-Tiguex Route," 353–56.

3. Flint and Flint, *Documents of the Coronado Expedition*, 661n23, tries to correlate Alvarado's account of these pueblos with ruins known today. For the rise and decline of settlements in the El Morro Valley, see Kintigh, *Settlement, Subsistence, and Society in Late Zuni Prehistory;* and LeBlanc, "A Cultural History of Cibola," 2–8.

4. Alvarado's original report has vanished, but a contemporary scribal copy remains. Flint and Flint, in *Documents of the Coronado Expedition*, 303–8, reproduce the Spanish text, translate it, and analyze it. Their treatment is followed here. Other transcriptions and translations of the text exist, but they are based on a copy made in the 1770s; the Flints' is closer to the original source.

5. The best translation of the anonymous *Relación del suceso* is in Flint and Flint, *Documents of the Coronado Expedition*, 499. A variant translation is in Winship, *The Journey of Coronado*, 355.

6. Castañeda's *Relación*, in Flint and Flint, *Documents of the Coronado Expedition*, 398–99. The original *Relación* has apparently disappeared; we know it from a copy made in Seville in 1596. It was not published until 1838, and then in French. Pinole is a mixture of cornmeal and other ingredients.

7. Flint and Flint, *Documents of the Coronado Expedition*, 401–2.

8. Gallegos's report on the Chamuscado-Rodríguez expedition, 1682, in Hammond and Rey, *The Rediscovery of New Mexico*, 107, and Espejo's report, October 1583, in ibid., 224.

9. Diego Pérez de Luxán's account of the Espejo expedition, in ibid., 182. Lummis, *Mesa, Cañon and Pueblo*, 197–200, identified the four prehistoric trails in some detail.

10. Diego Pérez de Luxán's account in Hammond and Rey, *The Rediscovery of New Mexico*, 201.

11. Gallegos's report in Hammond and Rey, *The Rediscovery of New Mexico*, 107.

12. Act of Obedience and Vassalage by the Indians of Acoma, October 27, 1598, in Hammond and Rey, *Don Juan de Oñate*, 1:355, which contains English translations related to the Oñate expedition. For a brief, vivid biography of Oñate, see Simmons, *The Last Conquistador*.

13. This story and others from the Oñate expedition appear in an epic poem written by one of the participants, which is available in two English-language editions: Villagrá, *History of New Mexico*, 197–98; and Villagrá, *Historia de la Nuevo México*. The latter contains the Spanish version and a translation in verse.

14. Oñate to the viceroy, March 2, 1599, in Hammond and Rey, *Don Juan de Oñate*,

1:485. By the early eighteenth century *maese de campo* equated to the formal military rank of *coronel,* or colonel.

15. By "Mexicans," he meant two Indians from central Mexico.

16. Juan Velarde's account of the proceedings at Ácoma, January 21–23, 1599, in Hammond and Rey, *Don Juan de Oñate,* 1:460–63. Like most of the documents of this era, this report did not make its way into print until the twentieth century, but Oñate's version of these events, written from New Mexico on March 2, 1599, was published in Rome in 1602 in a remarkable book by a Franciscan who had no first-hand knowledge of New Mexico but who did have access to archival sources. That publication of 1602 is reproduced in facsimile and translated in Hammond and Rey, *New Mexico in 1602,* 44–50, 89–97.

17. For the earlier view of conquistadores, see Peixotto, *Our Hispanic Southwest,* 151–52.

18. Matea to deBuys, personal communication, Ácoma, November 2, 2013.

19. Gilbert, quoted in *Dallas Morning News,* November 6, 2003. The statue was officially unveiled in April 2007.

20. Seefeldt, "Oñate's Foot," 169–70. Seefeldt uses this episode to ruminate on broader issues of historical memory in the Southwest.

21. Scully, *Pueblo,* 249. Interestingly, the mission of San Esteban at Ácoma would become a model for the general form of the New Mexico State Building at the 1915 Panama-California Exposition in San Diego, one of the first exemplars of the emergent Pueblo Revival architectural style of the early twentieth century. The exposition building was reproduced in the 1916 construction of what is today the St. Francis Auditorium at the New Mexico Museum of Art on the plaza in Santa Fe and, in circular fashion, the museum served as a model for the restoration of the San Esteban Mission, specifically the reconstruction of its towers, under the direction of John Gaw Meem in the 1920s. See Wingert-Playdon, *John Gaw Meem at Acoma,* 170–72. Wilson, *The Myth of Santa Fe,* 128, notes that the model for the towers of the exposition building was the mission at San Felipe Pueblo.

22. Abert, *Western America in 1846–1847,* 48. The U.S. government edited Abert's diary for publication in 1848, but Galvin has reproduced its original text and generously noted that his edition contains no copyright and that anyone may quote from it.

23. Arny, *Indian Agent in New Mexico,* 53, entry of October 7, 1870.

24. Lummis, *A Tramp Across the Continent,* 165–66, 169. Lummis based this book on letters he wrote to the *Los Angeles Times* while on his trek.

25. As pointed out by James Byrkit in Lummis, *Letters from the Southwest,* xiii–xiv.

26. Lummis, *The Land of Poco Tiempo,* 57.

27. Ibid., 58–61.

28. Ibid., 61. Lummis returned to the same theme thirty years later, continuing to insist, "Acoma is the most interesting rock in the world." *Mesa, Cañon and Pueblo,* 185.

29. A. Eugene Bartlett, *Least Known America,* 101.

30. Laut, *Through Our Unknown Southwest,* 87.

31. Ibid., 81, 83.

## CHAPTER 2. CANYON DE CHELLY

1. For debates, see, for instance, Mindeleff, "Cliff Ruins of Canyon de Chelly," 153–74.

2. Campbell Grant describes the traditional view that "warlike hunter-foragers" caused

most population shifts among Ancestral Puebloans in *Canyon de Chelly*, 54–67. The possibility of internecine conflict (although not in specific relation to Canyon de Chelly) is explored in deBuys, *A Great Aridness*, 74–89. The terms "Ancestral Puebloan" and "Anasazi" are discussed in deBuys at 68 and at 322n4.

3. Campbell Grant, *Canyon de Chelly*, 69–72. The possibility of a Hohokam link is speculation by deBuys. See *A Great Aridness*, 186–87.

4. Campbell Grant, *Canyon de Chelly*, 82. Brugge and Wilson, "Appendix 5: Chronology," in *Administrative History*.

5. Kelley and Francis, *Navajo Sacred Places*, 126.

6. Campbell Grant, *Canyon de Chelly*, 1.

7. Ibid., 133.

8. Antonio Narbona to Governor Fernando Chacón, January 24, 1805, translated by David M. Brugge and comprising appendix A in McNitt, *Navajo Wars*, 431–33. A second (presumably earlier) translation by Brugge appears in Campbell Grant, *Canyon de Chelly*, 86–88, and differs in important respects from this one. The original letter may be found in the New Mexico State Record Center and Archives, Spanish Archives, Document 1792, in Santa Fe.

9. Antonio Narbona to Governor Fernando Chacón, January 24, 1805, in McNitt, *Navajo Wars*, 432.

10. Ibid., 431.

11. McNitt, *Navajo Wars*, 43–44; Weisiger, *Dreaming of Sheep in Navajo Country*, 121–23; Campbell Grant, *Canyon de Chelly*, 84–85. Grant also reports a second version of the story in which a young man, thwarted from marrying a young woman from his own clan, betrays the location of the cave.

12. Antonio Narbona to Governor Fernando Chacón, January 24, 1805, in McNitt, *Navajo Wars*, 433.

13. Simpson, *Navaho Expedition*, l.

14. For a full appreciation of Richard Kern's eventful and too brief career, see Weber, *Richard H. Kern*.

15. Hughes, *Doniphan's Expedition*, 181.

16. McNitt, *Navajo Wars*, 62, mentions that the Navajo headman's name "was borrowed" from the Spanish colonel, but elaborates no further. Another possibility, helpfully suggested by Klara Kelley, is that the Navajo leader's native name may have involved the word *naabaahii*, meaning warrior, the sound of which Spanish speakers might have converted into the more familiar-sounding "Narbona."

17. Simpson, *Navajo Expedition*, 65–69. Editor McNitt's note 77 in this passage cites a biographer of Edward Kern to the effect that "both of the Kerns 'were later furious with themselves' because, in the excitement, they had failed to secure Narbona's head for their scientist friend and associate at the Philadelphia Academy of Natural Sciences, Samuel George Morton." For a contrasting account of Narbona's death, one that is informed by oral traditions known to his descendents, see Newcomb, *Hosteen Klah*, 30–43.

18. Simpson, *Navajo Expedition*, 75; Julyan, *The Place Names of New Mexico*, 239. As chair of the New Mexico Geographic Names Committee, Julyan played an important catalyzing role in bringing about the name change.

19. This and the following excerpts from Simpson's report are taken from J. H. Simpson, *Reports of the Secretary of War Communicating the Report of Lieutenant J. H. Simpson*, 102–5. Simpson's account is also available in the previously cited modern edition edited and richly annotated by Frank McNitt.

20. Simpson, *Navajo Expedition*, 86–87.

21. Dawdy, "The Wyant Diary," 258.

22. Clark, *Alexander Wyant*, 12.

23. Kelsey, "Photography in the Field," 1.

24. Dawdy, "The Wyant Diary," 266.

25. Arizona Territory was separated from New Mexico along present lines in 1863, and Canyon de Chelly lies in Arizona. The title O'Sullivan gave his photograph would seem to be a misnomer. This is not the only curiosity associated with the photograph's publication. Initially it was printed backwards, reversed left to right (Brugge and Wilson, *Administrative History*, chapter 1; see also Newhall and Newhall, *T. H. O'Sullivan*.

26. Kelsey, "Photography in the Field," 166.

27. This quote comes courtesy of photographer and photo historian David Scheinbaum, who is executor of the Newhall estate. It is drawn from material in Newhall's personal papers.

28. Dawdy, "The Wyant Diary," 258–60, 271–78.

29. Wheeler, *Photographs Showing Landscapes, Geological and Other Features.*

30. For the place of the O'Sullivan photograph in the MoMA exhibit, see Salvesen, "'Surrealistic and Disturbing,'" 164–66. Salvesen says Adams acquired the Wheeler booklet from his friend the mountaineer and writer Francis Farquhar. According to information drawn from Beaumont Newhall's papers, however, Adams himself acknowledged Bender as the source of the booklet in an introduction he prepared for an exhibit of O'Sullivan's work at the George Eastman House in Rochester, New York. (Thanks again to David Scheinbaum for providing materials that clarify this point.)

31. William Henry Jackson and Driggs, *The Pioneer Photographer*, 249–55. Jackson wrote his autobiography twice: the aforementioned volume and Jackson, *Time Exposure*. The first title has been reprinted in illustrated and annotated form as Jackson, *William Henry Jackson's "The Pioneer Photographer."* Hales, *William Henry Jackson and the Transformation of the American Landscape*, narrates Jackson's career and analyzes his photography; and Waitley, *William Henry Jackson*, offers a concise overview. Clarence S. Jackson, W. H. Jackson's son, offers another treatment in *William H. Jackson*.

32. William Henry Jackson and Driggs, *Pioneer Photographer*, 282.

33. William Henry Jackson, *Time Exposure*, 246. At least two Jackson photographs have mistakenly been catalogued and published as originating from Canyon de Chelly. The error originates from confusion over place-names. At various times, including in his official report at 421–25 in *Tenth Annual Report*, Jackson referred to Chinle Wash as "Rio de Chelly" and to its environs as "the cañon of the Chelly." Indeed, the wash drains the canyon, but it also flows, outside the canyon, more than sixty miles north to the San Juan River. In 1875 Jackson ascended this stretch of Chinle Wash, almost to the mouth of the canyon known today as de Chelly, photographing landscapes and ruins, including a large complex he called "Cave Town." The resulting photographs include some that have been misattributed to Canyon

de Chelly proper (see Waitley, *William Henry Jackson,* 167, 168; and Clarence S. Jackson, *William H. Jackson,* 226).

34. Brugge and Wilson, *Administrative History,* chapter 2.

## CHAPTER 3. CARLSBAD CAVERNS

1. These claims are chronicled in Bullington, "Who Discovered Carlsbad Caverns?"

2. Rothman, *Promise Beheld,* 144n17.

3. Nymeyer and Halliday, *Carlsbad Caverns,* 36–37.

4. We have left the occasional idiosyncratic spellings unchanged from the original sources, rather than interrupt the flow of the narrative with the repeated insertion of "[*sic*]." All quotations have been thoroughly checked against the originals for accurate transcription and subsequently proofread carefully.

5. White, *Jim White's Own Story.* This pamphlet, whose pages are unnumbered, bears the copyright date of 1932, by Jim White and Charley Lee White, who was no relation to Jim White. Reprinted here with permission of the Carlsbad Caverns Guadalupe Mountains Association.

6. Rothman, *Promise Beheld,* 144.

7. Long and Long, *The Big Cave.*

8. Rothman, *Promise Beheld,* 146.

9. Nymeyer and Halliday, *Carlsbad Caverns,* 42, quoting Carl B. Livingston, "Through the Carlsbad Cavern with Jim White," an article apparently published in 1926 (www.nps .gov/cave/his-carl.htm), 2.

10. MacVaugh, "Preserving the Underground," 161–68.

11. Caiar and White, *One Man's Dream,* 54–75. The quotation is on 74. Ruth Caiar was the sister of Jim White's daughter-in-law, Marguerite White. Jim White Jr. was Jim White's son. (MacVaugh, "Preserving the Underground," 9n9.)

12. Caiar and White, *One Man's Dream,* 76, 80. Caiar and White reproduce an article from the *El Paso Herald,* April 15, 1930, which is highly unfavorable to Nicholson.

13. Caiar and White, *One Man's Dream,* 86–102.

14. White to Major Richard Burges, Carlsbad, June 16, 1830, quoted in ibid., 71.

## CHAPTER 4. CASA GRANDE

1. Note that the name Kino gives here, Casas Grandes, is plural. He is referring to a place different from Casa Grande. Also known as Paquimé, Casas Grandes is today a UNESCO World Heritage Site. It is located south of Janos, Chihuahua.

2. Marcos de Niza's story of the Seven Cities had provided impetus for the epic exploration of Francisco Vázquez de Coronado a century and a half earlier.

3. Translated in Kino, *Historical Memoir of Pimería Alta,* 1:128–29, a work that Kino wrote over a number of years. In the classic biography of Kino by Bolton, *Rim of Christendom,* see 285–86.

4. Manje, *Unknown Arizona and Sonora,* 84–86.

5. Ibid., 86–87. Casas Grandes lies closer to thirty degrees of latitude and it is not clear what ruins at thirty-four degrees Manje might be referencing, but the 37th parallel marks the northern boundary of present-day Arizona and New Mexico and is one of the axes

of the Four Corners, an area famed for its multitude of ancient ruins. One wonders how Manje came by such information. Another officer, Lieutenant Cristóbal Martín Bernal, left a shorter but similar description in his diary, quoted in Fay Jackson Smith, Kessell, and Fox, *Father Kino in Arizona,* 41.

6. Manje, *Unknown Arizona and Sonora,* 288. Multiple Spanish-language versions of Manje's 1797 trip to Casa Grande are reproduced and ably explicated in Burrus, *Kino and Manje,* 333–84. Kino asserted the Aztec origins of the builders of Casa Grande in the statement reproduced here and also toward the end of his memoirs: *Historical Memoir of Pimería Alta,* 2:234.

7. Kino, *Historical Memoir of Pimería Alta,* 1:172–73.

8. Sedelmayr's Relación of 1746, in Sedelmayr, *Missionary, Frontiersman, Explorer,* 20–23, 46n33, quotation on 23.

9. Nentvig, *Rudo Ensayo,* 13. Nentvig knew of the observations of Father Ignacio Xavier Keller (5, 14.)

10. Font, *Font's Complete Diary of the Second Anza Expedition,* 35 (entry of October 31, 1775).

11. Garcés, *A Record of Travels in Arizona and California,* 6–7, 13, 74. Garcés traveled with Font. Anza, who led the expedition that included the two friars, noted that the house was "popularly but incorrectly called Casa de Moctezuma." Bolton, *Anza's California Expeditions,* 2:197.

12. Clavijero, *The History of Mexico Collected from Spanish and Mexican Historians,* 1:151. This work was first published in Italian in 1780–81, and the first English edition was published in 1787.

13. Arricivita and Espinosa, *Chrónica apostólica y seráphica,* 2:462.

14. Humboldt, *Political Essay on the Kingdom of New Spain,* 2:301.

15. Francaviglia, *Mapping and Imagination in the Great Basin,* 49–50, 80–82.

16. Mayer, *Mexico as It Was and as It Is,* 239.

17. Kingsborough, *Antiquities of Mexico,* 6:539–40. Volumes 1–7 of this nine-volume series appeared in 1831, the last two volumes in 1848.

18. Prescott, *History of the Conquest of Mexico,* 941.

19. The earliest of these conjectures apparently dates to 1820. Meltzer, introduction to *Ancient Monuments of the Mississippi Valley,* 46.

20. Emory, *Notes of a Military Reconnoissance,* 63 (October 22).

21. Houk, *Casa Grande Ruins National Monument,* 16.

22. Emory, *Notes of a Military Reconnoissance,* 64 (October 25).

23. Gregg, *Commerce of the Prairies* (1954), 187.

24. Mott, *Golden Multitudes,* 95; Johannsen, *To the Halls of the Montezumas,* 150.

25. Emory, *Notes of a Military Reconnoissance,* 68 (October 28, prior to his arrival at Casa Grande). Dr. John Griffin, a surgeon for the detachment, called the Great House "Casa Montezuma" and expressed no such doubts. Griffin, *A Doctor Comes to California,* 32. Nor did A. R. Johnston (Johnston, Edwards, and Ferguson, *Marching with the Army of the West*).

26. John Russell Bartlett, *Personal Narrative,* 2:274, quotations on 283.

27. Browne, *Adventures in the Apache Country,* 116. Browne visited in 1864. For similar questions at Casa Grande, see Conklin, *Picturesque Arizona,* 289.

28. Abraham Robinson Johnston, "Journal," in Emory, *Notes of a Military Reconnoissance.*

29. Lister and Lister, *Aztec Ruins National Monument,* chapter 1.

30. Bancroft, *History of Arizona and New Mexico,* 4.

31. For an overview of current scholarship, see Fish and Fish, *The Hohokam Millennium.*

32. Noble, *The Hohokam,* offers an accessible general introduction.

33. Suzanne K. Fish and Paul R. Fish, "The Hohokam Millennium," in Fish and Fish, *The Hohokam Millennium,* 5.

34. Wilcox and Shenk, *The Architecture of the Casa Grande,* 2.

35. Mark D. Elson, "Into the Earth and Up to the Sky," in Fish and Fish, *The Hohokam Millennium,* 52–53.

36. Reséndez and Kemp, "Genetics and the History of Latin America," 288–92.

37. The Bostonians' petition is reproduced in Lee, *The Antiquities Act of 1906,* 18–19. Repairs were made soon after Casa Grande's official designation as an archaeological reserve. See ibid., 20; Rothman, *Preserving Different Pasts,* 12. Later in 1889 the Department of the Interior withdrew the land around another ruin, Goodman Point Pueblo, from homesteading, although it apparently took no active measures to protect the site. See chapter 8, "Mesa Verde."

38. Dependable, handsomely illustrated, and brief, Houk, *Casa Grande Ruins National Monument,* is the best overview of the site for the general reader. Clemensen, *A Centennial History of the First Prehistoric Reserve,* is useful for the modern monument, but the discussion of early visitors to the site contains errors and should be used with caution.

CHAPTER 5. CHACO CANYON

1. R. Gwinn Vivian, "Puebloan Farmers of the Chacoan World," in Noble, *In Search of Chaco,* 13.

2. Brugge, "Vizcarra's Navajo Campaign of 1823," 227, contains a translation of Vizcarra's campaign journal. Brugge, "The Chaco Navajos," in Noble, *In Search of Chaco,* 64, observes that Vizcarra "recorded a full set of Spanish place-names with no suggestion that he was applying them for the first time."

3. Simpson, *Navaho Expedition,* 55. See also Fowler's review of Florence C. Lister's *Troweling Through Time,* 71.

4. This and the following excerpts from Simpson's report are taken from Simpson, *Reports of the Secretary of War Communicating the Report of Lieutenant J. H. Simpson,* 102–5. To facilitate reading, we have removed references to specific illustrations and divided lengthy paragraphs into shorter ones. Simpson's account is also available in McNitt's modern edition cited in the previous note, where the Chaco narrative may be found at 82–96.

5. Simpson has measured the outer boundary of the ruins complex, and the total length of the boundary comes to 403 feet. By the same method, perhaps devised on the spot, he will measure each of the ruined pueblos he examines, thereby enabling himself to compare their relative sizes.

6. A counterfort is a buttress on the thrust-receiving side of a wall.

7. National Park Service, U.S. Department of the Interior, *Pueblo Bonito* (www.nps.gov/chcu/planyourvisit/upload/CHCU-PuebloBonito.pdf).

8. By "the Silver Mountain," he means today's La Plata (Spanish for "silver") Mountains in southwest Colorado.

9. Joseph Hutchins Colton (1800–1893) was an American mapmaker. Simpson may be referring to his 1853 "Map of the United States of America, the British provinces, Mexico, and the West Indies."

10. Simpson, *Navajo Expedition,* 227–28.

11. William Henry Jackson, "Ruins of the Chaco Cañon," 431.

12. Ibid.

13. William Henry Jackson and Driggs, *Pioneer Photographer,* 284.

14. William Henry Jackson, "Ruins of the Chaco Cañon," 432.

15. William Henry Jackson and Driggs, *Pioneer Photographer,* 285.

16. William Henry Jackson, "Ruins of the Chaco Cañon," 432. In *The Pioneer Photographer,* Jackson gives the boy's name as Victoriana: "a bright boy, a worthy successor of his grandfather" (290).

17. The reader may recall from Chapter 2 that on Jackson's expeditions of 1877 to Canyon de Chelly and Chaco he experimented with a precursor of photographic film instead of using his usual (and cumbersome) wet-plate collodion process. (Transporting the equipment would have slowed him down and required at least one additional mule.) As matters turned out, Jackson grievously rued his decision to experiment with the new technology.

18. William Henry Jackson, "Ruins of the Chaco Cañon," 435.

19. Ibid., 446.

20. Ibid., 435.

21. Ibid., 434.

22. Ibid., 447.

23. William Henry Jackson and Driggs, *Pioneer Photographer,* 288–89.

24. William Henry Jackson, "Ruins of the Chaco Cañon," 448.

25. William Henry Jackson, *Time Exposure,* 246.

## CHAPTER 6. EL MORRO/INSCRIPTION ROCK

1. From *estanque* southwesterners get the word *tank* for a pond.

2. Villagrá, *Historia de la Nuevo México,* 180–81.

3. Oñate, "Expedition to the South Sea and the Salines," in Hammond and Rey, *Don Juan de Oñate,* 1:395.

4. There are, of course, variant translations. Here we follow Slater, *El Morro,* 7, which also provides a photograph of the original image (98, 44). Slater's book, with its historical introduction, transcriptions of inscriptions, photographs, and maps, is the most complete single source on El Morro, but most general readers will find Murphy, *El Morro National Monument* very satisfying.

5. Hammond and Rey, *The Rediscovery of New Mexico,* 183.

6. Vargas campaign journal, October 16 to December 27,1692, in Kessell and Hendricks, *By Force of Arms,* 545, and noted by Murphy, *El Morro National Monument,* 8. Vargas stopped again at El Morro on his return trip, in the afternoon of December 1, mentioning the stormy, freezing weather in his journal. Kessell and Hendricks, *By Force of Arms,* 584–85.

7. Slater, *El Morro,* 13.

8. Simpson, *Navaho Expedition,* 139; Weber, *Richard H. Kern,* 107.

9. Bernardo de Miera y Pacheco depicts El Morro and the nearby hoodoos, "Los Gigantes," on his famous 1778 map of New Mexico and the Great Basin. See the facsimile folded into Bolton, *Pageant in the Wilderness*. A reproduction of the map may also be found in Kessell's superb biography, *Miera y Pacheco*, 38–39.

10. See Slater, *El Morro*, 27–28, for the two inscriptions from August 1849.

11. The 1606 inscription he refers to is Juan de Oñate's. Its 1605 can easily be read for 1606.

12. This and the following excerpts from Simpson's report are taken from Simpson, *Reports of the Secretary of War Communicating the Report of Lieutenant J. H. Simpson*, 119–23. See also Simpson's account in the modern edition edited by McNitt (125 ff.), whose annotations greatly enrich the narrative.

13. Crampton, *The Zunis of Cibola*, 12.

14. T. J Ferguson and Hart, *A Zuni Atlas*, 23, 127.

15. See Frank McNitt's discussion of the ruins in Simpson, *Navaho Expedition*, 130n149.

16. These ruins have not been excavated.

17. Simpson cites Gregg, *Commerce of the Prairies* (1844), 1:284. The quotation can be found on 198 in the definitive modern edition edited by Moorhead.

18. Kern incised a similar inscription on the south face, and William Bird carved "W. Bird" just to the left of that inscription. Slater, *El Morro*, 62, 101 (plate 49), contains a transcript and a photograph.

19. See, for example, Murphy, *El Morro National Monument*, 6–7. For "written rocks," see Weber, *Richard H. Kern*, 109.

20. For example, Sherburne, *Through Indian Country to California*, 127; Stacey, *Uncle Sam's Camels*, 85.

21. Simpson, *Navaho Expedition*, 227–41, contains an account of Simpson's life after the Navajo expedition. The quotation is on 239.

22. For Kern's life and death, see Weber, *Richard H. Kern*.

23. Whipple, *A Pathfinder in the Southwest*, 132–33.

24. Möllhausen, *Diary of a Journey from the Mississippi to the Coasts of the Pacific*, 2:69–70. The title page of this volume uses the English spelling of Möllhausen's first name, Baldwin, which in German is given as Balduin. The reference to "mail-clad Spaniards" is more fanciful than historical. In fact, only a small number of Spanish explorers wore metal armor in the Southwest. See, for example, Flint and Flint, *Documents of the Coronado Expedition*, 138.

25. Edward Fitzgerald Beale, "Wagon Road from Fort Defiance to the Colorado River," 278. Like Whipple, Beale referred his reader to Simpson's account for a fuller description. Beale did not visit El Morro in 1857. He traveled west to Fort Defiance following the northern edge of the Zuni Mountains.

26. Stacey, *Uncle Sam's Camels*, 86 (entry of August 24, 1857). Stacey's name can no longer be found; other members of the Beale party can. See Slater, *El Morro*, 39–40.

27. Lummis, *Some Strange Corners of Our Country*, 166, 182.

28. On Lummis and Roosevelt, see Gordon, *Charles F. Lummis*, 11–21. Although Lummis advised Roosevelt about things western, he apparently did not raise the question of preserving El Morro or Lummis surely would have taken credit for it.

29. The act is reproduced in Lee, *The Antiquities Act of 1906*, 73.

30. Lummis, *Mesa, Cañon and Pueblo*, 483–84.

31. One of Vogt's daughters has written a delightful, well-illustrated history of the Vogt family: Mallery, *Bailing Wire & Gamuza*.

32. Lummis, *Mesa, Cañon and Pueblo*, 484. Slater, *El Morro*, 49–50, took a less benign view of the "sandstoning-out" of inscriptions: "Ironically enough, the greatest single act of damage to the rock took place after the establishment of the Monument. About 1924 an attempt was made to cleanse the rock of countless worthless signatures by rubbing them out with sandstone. In the course of this ill-advised project many valuable inscriptions were erased." For Vogt, see Rothman, *Preserving Different Pasts*, 112–16.

33. Saunders, *Finding the Worthwhile in the Southwest*, 95, 96.

34. Austin, *The Land of Journeys' Ending*, 231, called to David Weber's attention by Lawrence Clark Powell.

35. Lawrence Clark Powell, *Southwest Classics*, 4.

## CHAPTER 7. GRAND CANYON

1. Katharine Bartlett, "How Don Pedro de Tovar Discovered the Hopi and Don García López de Cárdenas Saw the Grand Canyon," 37–45.

2. Flint and Flint, in *Documents of the Coronado Expedition* (675n192), observe that the Grand Canyon is not twenty days from the Hopi villages and suggest that the author may have meant twenty leagues. It could also be that the Hopi guides went by a circuitous route in order to dismay and disorient the Spaniards. The distance represented by a league has been variously defined by different societies. It was meant to reflect the distance a person might walk in an hour and ranged from two and a half to four miles.

3. Cárdenas and his men probably viewed the canyon from near present-day Desert View, at the southeast corner of the national park. It is one of the few places where the river is visible from the rim and also one of the closest such points to the Hopi villages. Katharine Bartlett, "How Don Pedro de Tovar Discovered the Hopi and Don García López de Cárdenas Saw the Grand Canyon," points toward the Desert View site based on several clues. Bolton, *Coronado*, 139, cites Bartlett's article, but prefers Grand View, which Bartlett rejected because of its ponderosa pines, in favor of Desert View, where one finds the "low twisted pines"—piñon and juniper, not ponderosa—that Castañeda described. Pyne, *How the Canyon Became Grand*, 6, also favors Desert View.

4. Flint and Flint, *Documents of the Coronado Expedition*, 397–98. The next two extended quotations also come from this passage.

5. Ibid., 675n198. The Giralda was seventy-six meters high in 1540; with the completion of a new belfry in 1568, it rose to its present ninety-three meters.

6. Sheridan et al., *Moquis and Kastiilam*, 1:30–62; see especially 59.

7. Melchior Díaz reached the Colorado River by land from Sonora at about the same time that López de Cárdenas traveled to the Grand Canyon. In relating his account, Castañeda knew that Díaz named the river Tizón for the firebrands that Yuma Indians carried to warm themselves in cold weather. Bolton, *Coronado*, 172.

8. The anonymous account is the *Relación del suceso*, written in the 1540s. See Flint and Flint, *Documents of the Coronado Expedition*, 494–507.

9. Bolton, *Coronado*, 142. López de Cárdenas was the only member of the Coronado party found guilty of such crimes. See Flint, *Great Cruelties Have Been Reported*, 336–39.

10. Escalante, *The Domínguez-Escalante Journal*, 120.

11. Garcés, *On the Trail of a Spanish Pioneer*, 2:336.

12. Thanks to Christa Sadler, Greg Woodall, and Scott Thybony for illuminating this alternative.

13. Garcés, *A Record of Travels in Arizona and California*, 67; Pyne, *How the Canyon Became Grand*, 17–21.

14. Garcés, *On the Trail of a Spanish Pioneer*, 2:347–51. Parenthetical additions, including those preserving the original Spanish, are by translator Coues, whose spelling of Bucaréli differs from general usage by adding an accent to the penultimate vowel. Bracketed material was added by the present authors. Coues, who dedicated his translation and extensive annotation of the Garcés journals to his friend John Wesley Powell, explained his approach to translation with verve: "My aim has been to translate Garcés literally, punctually, even with scrupulosity," and further, "I knew that if I once gave myself loose rein in this matter, I should never have known where to stop; and Couesian English of 1899, however nice I might make it, would fit Garcés of 1775–6 as well as a modern swallow-tail coat on a seedy friar of more than a century ago" (1:xx–xxi).

15. Anderson, *Living at the Edge*, 18. Garcés never reached New Mexico. The Hopis received him with hostility, and so he turned back toward the Mohave villages.

16. Pyne, *How the Canyon Became Grand*, especially 2–3.

17. In the seventeenth century, James Ussher, archbishop of Armagh, Church of Ireland, famously pinpointed the creation of Earth to the year 4004 BCE, based on a close reading of the Bible and its recitation of Old Testament genealogies. In the nineteenth century, the development of the field of geology would render such a calculation absurd.

18. Goetzmann, *Army Exploration in the American West*, 375–79.

19. Ives, *Report upon the Colorado River*, 86.

20. The spelling of Ireteba, as given by Ives, is not universal. Whipple used Irreteba, and others Iretaba, which also attached to Arizona's Iretaba Mining District and Iretaba City, the main camp of the district. In the present instance Ireteba seems preferable, both for consistency with Ives and because it is used in such place-names as Ireteba Peak, Ireteba Wash, and the Ireteba Peaks Wilderness Area, all within traditional Mohave territory in extreme southern Nevada.

21. Pyne, *How the Canyon Became Grand*, 40.

22. Ives, *Report upon the Colorado River*, 99–100.

23. Ibid., 100–101.

24. Ibid., 107.

25. Garcés, *On the Trail of a Spanish Pioneer*, 2:336.

26. Ives, *Report upon the Colorado River*, 107–8.

27. Ibid.

28. The best short overview of the Ives's expedition, with guidance to other sources, remains Goetzmann, *Exploration and Empire*, 378–94. Huseman, *Wild River, Timeless Canyons*, is a fine study of Möllhausen's work on the Colorado.

29. Ives, *Report upon the Colorado River*, 19–21.

30. John Strong Newberry, "Geological Report" in Ives, *Report upon the Colorado River,* 55.

31. Ibid., 58.

32. Ives, *Report upon the Colorado River,* 5.

33. Ibid., 110. Writers on the Grand Canyon frequently point out the irony of this characterization and its misreading of the future of a place that millions of people now visit every year. In fairness to Ives, however, the passage can be interpreted to refer primarily to the portion of the plateau through with Ives withdrew from the rim, and those lands remain today nearly as inactive in economic terms as they were in Ives's day. Thanks to Brad Dimock for this insight.

34. Pyne, *How the Canyon Became Grand,* 48.

35. Ibid., 62. Those interested in reading about Powell's remarkable journey and career have many choices, among them: Stegner, *Beyond the Hundredth Meridian;* Worster, *A River Running West;* and deBuys, *Seeing Things Whole.*

36. Pyne, *How the Canyon Became Grand,* 57, notes that the name Grand Canyon appeared on a railroad survey in 1868 and that Samuel Bowles used the term in a book published in 1869. Powell himself used the term as he planned his journey. Worster, *A River Running West,* 299, suggests that Powell, more than anyone else, was responsible for popularizing the name Grand Canyon.

37. This is Sockdolager Rapid, said to have been named by Powell's group. In the vernacular of the day, a *sockdolager* was a powerful roundhouse punch.

38. John Wesley Powell, *Exploration of the Colorado River,* 80–83. This work has appeared in several modern editions.

39. Ibid., 102.

40. Ibid., 5.

41. Worster, *A River Running West,* 191–96, 212–15. A counter-theory holds that the two Howlands and Dunn were killed by Mormons, but Worster refutes this convincingly in the cited pages.

42. Pyne, *How the Canyon Became Grand,* 63–71.

43. Ibid., 93.

44. Worster, *A River Running West,* 156–61.

45. Anderson, *Polishing the Jewel,* 6–10. The struggle over the use of the canyon and the Colorado Plateau did not end with creation of the national park. Morehouse, *A Place Called the Grand Canyon,* traces the story through most of the twentieth century, and since then, controversies over river and recreation management, uranium mining, real estate development, aircraft overflights, and other encroachments on the canyon's integrity have rarely been absent from the news for long.

46. King, *Clarence King Memoirs,* 348, mentioned by Pomeroy, *In Search of the Golden West,* 159.

47. Pyne, *How the Canyon Became Grand,* 113.

CHAPTER 8. MESA VERDE

1. Lister and Lister, *Those Who Came Before,* 159.

2. A series of forty 39¢ U.S. postage stamps issued in 2005, "Wonders of America:

Land of Superlatives," included Mesa Verde. The best overview of Mesa Verde's story for the general reader is Houk, Marcovecchio, and Duane Smith, *Mesa Verde National Park.* It is handsomely illustrated and contains lengthy quotations that let readers hear voices from the past, but it lacks guidance to sources. For those, Smith, *Mesa Verde National Park,* remains essential.

3. The current state of archaeological knowledge at Mesa Verde is best summarized by the essayists in Noble, *The Mesa Verde World.* Particularly recommended are chapters by Richard Wilshusen, William Lipe, Mark Varien, and Catherine Cameron. Another accessible introduction, Lister, *Troweling Through Time,* 225–50, suggests the likelihood of wildfires in time of drought.

4. Leiby, "Borderland Pathfinders," 129. Rivera passed through the region twice in 1765, and Leiby believes the quoted passage was written near the Dolores River.

5. "Aqui se manifiestan las Ruinas de grandes Poblaciones de Indios antiguas"–so wrote Miera y Pacheco on his map of 1778. At least six originals of this famous map appear to have been made. We have used the facsimile folded into Bolton, *Pageant in the Wilderness.* Notation called to the attention of David Weber by Paul Nelson.

6. "Hubo antiguamente una población pequeña, de la misma forma que las de los indios del Nuevo Méjico, según manifiestan las ruinas que de intento registramos." Escalante, *The Domínguez-Escalante Journal,* 14, 139 (entry of August 13).

7. The letter first appeared in the *Missouri Intelligencer* of Franklin, Becknell's hometown, on June 25, 1825, and is reproduced in Weber, "William Becknell as a Mountain Man," 257–58.

8. Because Cliff Palace is so spectacular, some writers have made it the focus of the Mesa Verde story. See, for example, Elliott, *Great Excavations,* 2–23; and Houk, Marcovecchio, and Duane Smith, *Mesa Verde National Park,* 17. See, too, Lister and Lister, *Those Who Came Before,* 161, which says of Gustaf Nordenskiöld that "he wrote the first scientific description of the ancient remains."

9. Fowler, *A Laboratory for Anthropology,* 83.

10. Jackson, *William Henry Jackson's "The Pioneer Photographer,"* 117. For biographical treatments of William Henry Jackson, see chapter 2 (Canyon de Chelly), note 31.

11. Ernest Ingersoll, "Colorado Antiquities: Discoveries of Ancient Stone Houses and Remains of Indian Life," *New York Tribune,* November 3, 1874, 3.

12. William Henry Jackson, *The Diaries of William Henry Jackson,* 305.

13. William Henry Jackson, *Time Exposure,* 227–28. Jackson talked with the Ute, named Billy, on August 21 and 22, but Jackson did not record the episode in detail in his diary.

14. William Henry Jackson, *The Diaries of William Henry Jackson,* 307–8.

15. Ibid., 308–10.

16. Ibid., 312.

17. Ibid., 312–13.

18. William Henry Jackson, "Ancient Ruins in Southwestern Colorado" (1875), 25.

19. William Henry Jackson, *The Diaries of William Henry Jackson,* 314.

20. William Henry Jackson, "Ancient Ruins in Southwestern Colorado," 30 (1875).

21. William Henry Jackson, *Time Exposure,* 232–34, reproduces much of Ingersoll's newspaper account.

22. This and the following excerpts are taken from Ernest Ingersoll, Denver, Colorado Territory, October 25, 1874, "Colorado Antiquities," 3.

23. Jackson's initial report appeared as "Ancient Ruins in Southwestern Colorado," 17–30, in the 1875 *Bulletin of the United States Geological and Geographical Survey of the Territories* and then, because the print run was small, it was reprinted under the same title the next year, lightly edited and with some deletions, in *Annual Report of the United States Geological and Geographical Survey of the Territories,* 368–81. Jackson's report was summarized and many of its illustrations reproduced in "Ancient Ruins in Southwestern Colorado," *American Naturalist* 10 (1876), 31–37.

24. Jackson was told that *Hovenweep,* a Ute/Paiute word, meant "deserted valley," and so he applied it to the ruin-rich canyon.

25. William Henry Jackson, "A Notice of the Ancient Remains in Arizona and Utah," 25–45; Jackson, *William Henry Jackson's "The Pioneer Photographer,"* 148–68; William Henry Jackson, *Time Exposure,* 236–42.

26. Holmes, "A Notice of the Ancient Remains of Southwestern Colorado," 1–24; Holmes, "Report on the Ancient Ruins of Southwestern Colorado." The latter source expanded on the former as Holmes added new information from a short return trip to the area in 1876.

27. Fernlund, *William Henry Holmes,* 61, provides a fine description of the exhibit.

28. William Henry Jackson, *Time Exposure,* 243.

29. William Henry Jackson, "Ancient Ruins in Southwestern Colorado" (1875), 30; the paragraph was dropped from his report when it was reprinted in 1876.

30. This Hopi story, apparently told to Moss, who told it to Ingersoll, resonates with the findings of present-day archaeologists. The *New York Tribune* published it, as part of Ingersoll's larger story, on November 3, 1874, and it appeared again in Ingersoll, *The Crest of the Continent,* 156–64, which recycled some of the text from his initial newspaper article, with additional elaboration. "Savage Indian tribes," Ingersoll said, "the prehistoric Utes and Apaches and Navajos," had forced the ancient people to take up shelter in the cliffs. Their raids, combined with a drought, compelled the "Village Indians" to abandon the area and build new pueblos to the south (163, 164). Jackson reproduced it in "Ancient Ruins in Southwestern Colorado" (1875), 28–29, and in subsequent versions of that paper. The story has been reprinted recently as Ernest Ingersoll, "A Hopi Story about Castle Rock," in Noble, *The Mesa Verde World,* 137–38. See, too, Lister, *Troweling Through Time,* 218.

31. William Henry Jackson, *The Diaries of William Henry Jackson,* 316.

32. Holmes, "A Report on the Ancient Ruins of Southwestern Colorado," 383, 384, 408.

33. Hardacre, "The Cliff-Dwellers," 270.

34. Fossett, *Colorado,* 437, noted by Duane Smith, *Mesa Verde National Park,* 14, who provides guidance to early publications about the region.

35. Lewis H. Morgan, "On the Ruins of a Stone Pueblo," 556. Having been guided by a local rancher, Morgan's nephew published a report on a single site, but without theorizing about the builders' origins. William Fellowes Morgan, "Description of a Cliff-House on the Mancos River," 300–306. Alden C. Hayes, "Mesa Verde: A Century of Research," in Noble, *The Mesa Verde World,* 152, identifies the relationship between the two Morgans.

36. *La Plata Miner* (Silverton, Colo.), July 17, 1880, quoted in Duane Smith, *Mesa Verde National Park,* 14.

37. The description of Virginia Donaghe is based on a 1985 recollection by someone who knew her late in life. Writers have described her as obese, decked out in feather-adorned hats and excessive lipstick, but if that was true in her later life, there is no reason to project such descriptions back to the 1870s. Robertson, *The Magnificent Mountain Women*, was apparently the first to caricature Donaghe (61) and was then followed by others, such as Lister, *Troweling Through Time*, 8.

38. Tom Wolf, Ph.D., former Mesa Verde NP interpretive staff, personal communication, December 10, 2015.

39. Duane Smith, *Mesa Verde National Park*, 18, quoting the *Weekly Tribune-Republican*, December 1886.

40. On September 16, 1889, the secretary of the Interior withdrew a section of land (section 4, township 36 N and range 17 W) from homesteading. Mark D. Varien, director of research, Crow Canyon Archaeological Center, Cortez, Colorado, to David J. Weber, February 2, 2007. Efforts to protect Casa Grande also date back to 1889. Earlier that year Congress authorized setting it aside, although it took the executive branch three more years to act on that legislation.

41. Wetherill, *The Wetherills of the Mesa Verde*, 50–109, is the best account of the family's early years at the Alamo Ranch, and contains a photograph of the brothers' crude winter wickiup in Mancos Canyon. For the sale of artifacts, see Duane Smith, *Mesa Verde National Park*, 215n29. McNitt, *Richard Wetherill*, is a vividly written biography.

42. Elliott, *Great Excavations*, 5.

43. One highly fictionalized version of the story is Willa Cather's marvelous "Tom Outland's Story," which is sometimes presented independently as a novella, sometimes as the center section of Cather's 1925 novel, *The Professor's House*, of which a number of modern editions are available.

44. They were apparently standing at the site of the ruin known to today as Sun Temple. Lister, *Troweling Through Time*, 11.

45. Charles C. Mason, "The Story of the Discovery and Early Exploration of the Cliff Houses at the Mesa Verde" *Denver Post*, July 1, 1917, sec. 2, p. 6. A typed copy dated May 5, 1918 is in the Colorado Historical Society, signed by the four surviving Wetherill brothers (Richard was shot dead in Chaco Canyon in 1910), who "vouched for" its facts. David Weber transcribed the excerpt reproduced here from a photocopy kindly provided by Duane Smith. Richard Wetherill's version appeared in print in the *Mancos Times*, August 16, 1895. There is some disagreement between the two sources. Dates vary—Mason said December 18 and Wetherill said December 8. According to Mason, they were on a "cruise of exploration," but Wetherill stated that they were chasing stray cattle.

46. Lee, *The Antiquities Act of 1906*, 79–81. Specifically, the legislation protected adjacent Indian lands within five miles of park boundaries.

47. Houk, Marcovecchio, and Duane Smith, *Mesa Verde National Park*, 25.

48. Hewett, *Ancient life in the American Southwest*, 276, 285.

49. Holmes, "Random Records of a Lifetime," 1:130 (quotation), in the collection of the Library of the National Museum of American Art, Smithsonian Institution, Washington, D.C. Photocopy courtesy of David Meltzer. For an appreciation of Holmes as an archaeologist, see Holmes, *The Archaeology of William Henry Holmes;* and the fine biography: Fernlund, *William Henry Holmes*, 56, 59, 239n20.

50. Hewett, *Ancient life in the American Southwest,* 39.

51. William Henry Jackson, "First Official Visit to the Cliff Dwellings," 151–59; Jackson, *William Henry Jackson's "The Pioneer Photographer,"* 139, 147 (quotation); William Henry Jackson, *Time Exposure,* 228–35.

## CHAPTER 9. THE MOHAVE VILLAGES

1. The use of "Mojave" versus "Mohave" can be confusing. Most Arizona place-names use Mohave; across the river in California the preferred spelling is Mojave. Tribal members on the reservation of the Colorado River Indian Tribes use Mohave and those of the Fort Mojave Tribe use the alternate spelling, consistent with the name of the fort. We use Mohave except in reference to the Fort Mojave tribe and California's Mojave Desert.

2. Stewart, "Mohave," 69. Stewart provides an authoritative overview of Mohave history and culture. See also Stewart, "A Brief History of the Mohave Indians," 219–36.

3. Kroeber and Kroeber, *A Mohave War Reminiscence,* 1–5. The Kroebers note the scanty sources on Mohave culture prior to their contact with Americans and discuss the two schools of thought about the origin of Mohave warfare: ethnographers have found it deeply embedded in Mohave culture; ethnohistorians explain it as an outcome of contact with Spaniards, who gave Mohaves incentive to take slaves and steal horses. The Kroebers find the former explanation more convincing. See also Kroeber and Fontana, *Massacre on the Gila.*

4. Fray Francisco de Escobar briefly describes them in Sheridan et al., *Moquis and Kastiilam,* 107 ff. An older translation may be found in Hammond and Rey, *Don Juan de Oñate,* 2:1017. Additionally, Salmerón, *Relaciones,* has been used as a source for Oñate's journey, but Salmerón was not a member of the party. Forbes, *Warriors of the Colorado,* 102–3, unequivocally identified the Amauacas as Mohaves.

5. Pedro Font, quoted in Kessell, "The Making of a Martyr," 190.

6. Garcés, *A Record of Travels in Arizona and California,* 15. See also Elliott Coues's extensive notes in his older translation: Garcés, *On the Trail of a Spanish Pioneer.*

7. The home ground of the Cochimí tribe included much of Baja California.

8. With a few adjustments for clarity, we have followed Coues in Garcés, *On the Trail of a Spanish Pioneer,* 1:226–29. The parenthetical additions to the text are his, the comments in brackets ours. See also Garcés, *A Record of Travels in Arizona and California,* 33–34.

9. Garcés, *On the Trail of a Spanish Pioneer,* 1:229–33, with minor alterations.

10. Whipple, *A Pathfinder in the Southwest,* also describes this game, but said the hoops were six inches in diameter and the poles fifteen feet long. Robinson, *A Journal of the Santa Fe Expedition under Colonel Doniphan,* 47, described Navajos playing this game.

11. Reprinted from Jedediah Strong Smith, *The Southwest Expedition of Jedediah S. Smith,* 71–78. Smith's original journal has disappeared; what survives and is published here derives from a transcript of the original, to which we have added a few paragraph breaks for ease of reading.

12. Ibid., 83–85.

13. Ibid., 105. Quite likely, the teenagers were later flogged for their disobedience.

14. Alta California, along with the rest of the Southwest, had passed from Spanish to Mexican rule in 1821.

15. Quoted in Weber, *The Taos Trappers*, 125.

16. Word of Smith's demise reached his friends through New Mexican traders who did business with the Comanches. The classic biography of Smith is Dale Lowell Morgan, *Jedediah Smith*. Concerning Smith's extrication from San Jose, see 245–55, concerning his death, 329–30, 362–66. Barbour, *Jedediah Smith*, incorporates information unavailable to Morgan, including that found in Weber, *The Californios Versus Jedediah Smith*.

17. Quoted in Weber, *Richard H. Kern*, 177.

18. Sitgreaves, *Report of an Expedition Down the Zuni and Colorado Rivers*, 17–19; Andrew Wallace and Hevly, *From Texas to San Diego in 1851*, 145.

19. Whipple, *A Pathfinder in the Southwest*, 237.

20. McGinty, *The Oatman Massacre*; and Mifflin, *The Blue Tattoo*, cautiously reconstruct her story from shreds of evidence.

21. Stratton, *Captivity of the Oatman Girls*, 143–44. The book was so successful that the first edition, which bore a somewhat different title, sold out quickly. The revised and corrected second edition is used here.

22. Ibid., 144–46.

23. Ives, *Report upon the Colorado River*, 72–73.

24. Stacey, *Uncle Sam's Camels*, 114 (entry of October 20, 1857).

25. Beale, "Wagon Road from Fort Defiance to the Colorado River," 258–63; the quotation is on 262.

26. A detailed account of the Mohave attack on the emigrants, written from the emigrants' perspectives, appears in Baley, *Disaster at the Colorado*, 58–76. The Mohaves' repeated inquiries are discussed on 59, 61, 63, and 64. See Kroeber and Kroeber, *A Mohave War Reminiscence*, 11–14, for the Mohave point of view.

27. For a full account, see Kroeber and Fontana, *Massacre on the Gila*.

28. deBuys, *A Great Aridness*, 164–68.

CHAPTER 10. RAINBOW BRIDGE

1. A series of forty 39-cent U.S. postage stamps issued in 2005, "Wonders of America: Land of Superlatives," included Rainbow Bridge.

2. Sproul, *A Bridge Between Cultures*, chapter 5. This excellent treatment is also available online at www.nps.gov/rabr/learn/historyculture/upload/RABR_adhi.pdf.

3. The story of the discovery of Rainbow Bridge, its antecedents and aftermath, is well told in two books: Hassell, *Rainbow Bridge*, which features color images and reproductions of historic photographs; and Sproul, *A Bridge Between Cultures*. Hassell, 60–63, casts doubt on accounts by Anglo Americans who claimed to have seen Rainbow Bridge before 1909; we follow Sproul, chapter 2. Each book contains guidance to additional sources. Jett, "The Great 'Race' to 'Discover' Rainbow Natural Bridge," is deeply researched and sorts through variants of the story in detail. Jett, in contrast to Hassell, supports the idea of early Anglo American sightings of Rainbow Bridge (43–45). Chidester, "The Discovery of Rainbow Bridge," 209–30; and Babbitt, *Rainbow Trails*, reproduce primary sources, some not previously published.

4. Cummings's remarkable life as an archaeologist and administrator is the subject of a book-length biography, Bostwick, *Byron Cummings*.

5. Gillmor and Wetherill, *Traders to the Navajos,* 161–71. In this book, Louisa Wetherill does not take credit for telling Cummings the story of a natural bridge, but see Sproul, *A Bridge Between Cultures,* chapter 3, p. 1.

6. Quoted in Sproul, *A Bridge Between Cultures,* chapter 3, at n. 76.

7. Ibid., chapter 3, p. 9.

8. Cummings, *Indians I Have Known,* 41.

9. Douglass, "From the Field Notes of U.S. Deputy Surveyors," 9, 14.

10. Ibid., 14–15.

11. Douglass returned to the bridge for further surveying between October 12 and October 27. Jett, "The Great 'Race' to 'Discover' Rainbow Natural Bridge," 35. Douglass identifies his guide on this trip as Navajo but, as will be seen, Cummings asserts that "Whitehorsebiga" was "Pahute."

12. Douglass, "From the Field Notes of U.S. Deputy Surveyors," 15.

13. Jett, "The Great 'Race' to 'Discover' Rainbow Natural Bridge," 58, lists seven articles about the find, all written anonymously. See, too, Hassell, *Rainbow Bridge,* 54.

14. Linford, *Navajo Places,* 303.

15. Douglass had given 278 feet for the span and 309 feet for the height. The Park Service, agreeing with Cummings that the bridge spans 275 feet, measures its height at 290 feet, perhaps a reflection of a change in the terrain at the bottom of the canyon.

16. The Long Walk of the Navajo—their deportation to Bosque Redondo, as ordered by Kit Carson and his superiors—began in 1864 and continued through 1866, involving more than fifty forced marches of different groups. Hoskinimi is Hashké Neiniih, also rendered Hoskininni. For a brief biography and guidance to sources, see Jett, "The Great 'Race' to 'Discover' Rainbow Natural Bridge," 6–7. Hoskininni's photograph, taken in 1909, may be found in Hassell, *Rainbow Bridge,* 61.

17. Cummings, "The Great Natural Bridges of Utah," 165. Here he refers to Clyde Colville, the Wetherills' partner in the trading post at Oljato, who accompanied Douglass on his second trip.

18. This quotation comes a decade later, in a report to the National Park Service, July 30, 1919, published for the first time in Chidester, "The Discovery of Rainbow Bridge," 213. He names Douglass's guide incorrectly as Jim's boy; he was Mike's boy, or Jim. Apparently Judd's article in the *Deseret News* in 1909 was a response to a claim that appeared on or about September 20 in the *Salt Lake City Herald Republican* asserting that reports crediting the Utah Archaeological Society with the discovery of Rainbow Bridge were "entirely erroneous. The honor belongs to Mr. Douglas[s]." Quoted in Jett, "The Great 'Race' to 'Discover' Rainbow Natural Bridge," 35.

19. The Cook-Peary controversy would have been in the public eye when Judd was writing that year. Robert Peary reached what he believed to be the North Pole on April 6, 1909, but a physician-explorer, Frederick Cook, claimed to have reached it in April of the previous year. Cook continues to have defenders and detractors and the controversy persists.

20. On this point, Judd and Douglass contradict one another.

21. How W. B. Douglass, U.S. Examiner of Surveys, 'Discovered' the Big Bridge," *Deseret Evening News,* October 2, 1909, 17. The same issue of the *Evening News* carried a story by another of Cummings's students, Donald Beauregard.

22. See report of July 30, 1919, to the National Park Service, published for the first time in Chidester, "The Discovery of Rainbow Bridge," 213–14; and Neil M. Judd, "The Discovery of Rainbow Bridge," *National Parks Bulletin,* November 1927, 8–16, reprinted in Babbitt, *Rainbow Trails,* 3–18.

23. Part of this is reprinted in Chidester, "The Discovery of Rainbow Bridge," 210. Chidester knew Cummings and claimed to have heard him "recount the details [of the discovery] on numerous occasions."

24. Malcolm Cummings published his reminiscence, "I Finished Last in the Race to Rainbow Bridge," in *Desert Magazine* in 1940. It is reprinted in Babbitt, *Rainbow Trails,* 127–33.

25. Cummings, *Indians I Have Known,* 43.

26. Wetherill, quoted in Jett, "The Great 'Race' to 'Discover' Rainbow Natural Bridge," 26, also said that Cummings was the first to see the bridge and that he, Wetherill, was the first to ride under it. It appears that Wetherill was by Cummings's side when he first saw the bridge, but perhaps, as Neil Judd said, Wetherill was "too much of a gentleman deliberately to arrogate to himself the rights [of discovery] of his employer." Judd, "The Discovery of Rainbow Bridge," in Babbitt, *Rainbow Trails,* 3.

27. Jett, "The Great 'Race' to 'Discover' Rainbow Natural Bridge," 20–21, 40–43. Hassell, *Rainbow Bridge,* 63, dismisses Jett's argument too lightly, ignoring both Wetherill's motive, as explained by Jett, and Louisa Wetherill's statements.

28. Some of those accounts are reproduced in Babbitt, *Rainbow Trails.*

29. Zane Grey, "Nonnezoshi," an essay first published in 1922 and reprinted in Babbitt, *Rainbow Trails,* 27–36 (quotation on 36). Grey also published a novel called *The Rainbow Trail: A Romance.*

30. "Their desert post office, they boasted, was the farthest distant from a railroad of any in the United states." McNitt, *The Indian Traders,* 271. McNitt offers an engaging portrait of John Wetherill, and also reproduces a photograph of the ramshackle trading post at "Oljetoh."

31. Abbey, *Desert Solitaire,* 190.

32. The dam was authorized 1956, and Abbey's trip ended just short of the construction site.

33. Abbey, *Desert Solitaire,* 192.

34. Kelley and Francis, *Navajo Sacred Places,* 176.

35. Sproul, *A Bridge Between Cultures,* chs. 2, 5, and 7, is the best account.

CHAPTER 11. SANTA FE

1. Dating the founding of Santa Fe has required piecing together fragmentary sources. For a more extended discussion and guidance to sources, see Weber, "Santa Fe," 136–40.

2. Barrett, *The Spanish Colonial Settlement Landscapes of New Mexico,* 32.

3. Juan de Oñate had rewarded many of his followers with *encomiendas,* a traditional Spanish institution that made Spaniards trustees, or *encomenderos,* of Indians, responsible for their Christianization. Indians, in turn, paid tribute to their encomenderos. The system was almost universally abused, imposing crushing burdens of labor on the Pueblos as well as heavy assessments of goods of all kinds, especially corn.

4. Benavides, *The Memorial of Fray Alonso de Benavides,* 22–23.

5. Esquibel, "The Palace of the Governors in the Seventeenth Century," 25–26, 29. Esquibel, drawing from a report by Governor Bernardo López de Mendizábal of 1661, notes the existence of thirty houses in Santa Fe in the text of his article, but that is a misprint. His note on p. 29 says thirty-eight, and that is the correct number. Clarification courtesy of Mr. Esquibel.

6. Knaut, *The Pueblo Revolt of 1680,* provides an introduction. Liebmann, *Revolt,* delivers insights from the most recent research. Weber, *What Caused the Pueblo Revolt of 1680?* contains different historians' interpretations of the causes.

7. Diego de Vargas to the Conde de Galve, El Paso, January 12, 1693, in Kessell, Hendricks, and Dodge, *To the Royal Crown Restored,* 110.

8. Moorhead, *The Presidio,* 172–75.

9. This and the following quotations from Domínguez are drawn from Adams and Chávez, *The Missions of New Mexico,* 39–40, 42. Several other well-known visitors to Santa Fe in the 1700s are more laconic: Naylor and Polzer, *Pedro de Rivera and the Military Regulations for Northern New Spain,* 79; Adams, *Bishop Tamarón's Visitation of New Mexico,* 46–48; Lafora, *The Frontiers of New Spain,* 91.

10. The church of San Francisco, which Fray Alonso de Benavides directed to be built on this site in 1626, having been destroyed in the Pueblo Revolt of 1680, La Parroquia (*parroquia* means "parish church") rose from its ruins in 1714–17. When Bishop Jean Baptiste Lamy came to Santa Fe in 1851, he resolved to build what to his mind would be a proper cathedral on the same ground. Not wanting to disrupt the regular schedule of church functions, he instructed that Santa Fe's Saint Francis Cathedral be erected *around and over* La Parroquia. When the cathedral was finished in 1886, workers demolished La Parroquia and carried its rubble out through the cathedral's doors.

11. Our Lady of Light, the Capilla de Nuestra Señora de la Luz, a military chapel also known as the *castrense.* It stood on the south side of the plaza across from the Palace of the Governors, and was demolished about 1859.

12. The lake he refers to is Santa Fe Lake, not to be confused with the modern reservoirs McClure and Nichols, but a tarn lying at the head of the canyon.

13. New Mexicans employed the word *genízaro* to describe Indians from various tribes, such as Navajos and Comanches, who, as Domínguez says, were ransomed from other Indians and brought into Spanish households where they worked as servants. The word "ransom" suggests rescue, and from the Spanish point of view, any action that brought a nonbeliever to baptism and the teachings of the church was a form of rescue—and offered justification for the colony's lively trade in slaves. In economic terms, most of these transactions involved the straightforward purchase of a human being. In addition, many genízaros were captured by Spaniards in the course of military operations or kidnapped in unsanctioned raids. (See Hämäläinen, *The Comanche Empire,* 26–27.)

14. Zebulon Montgomery Pike, *An Account of Expeditions to the Sources of the Mississippi,* 211–12. The best modern edition is Pike, *Journals.*

15. This and the following observations by Gregg are taken from Gregg, *Commerce of the Prairies* (1844), 1:109–12, 113, 143–45. The best modern edition is Moorhead's (1954).

16. Frank, *From Settler to Citizen,* demonstrates how economic activity accelerated in New Mexico in the closing decades of the Spanish regime.

17. Sunder, *Matt Field on the Santa Fe Trail*, 202.

18. Alfred Waugh to John B. Tisdale, Santa Fe, July 14, 1846, in Waugh, *Travels in Search of the Elephant*, 120.

19. Meline, *Two Thousand Miles on Horseback*, 152.

20. Her published articles were gathered and published in book form: Susan Wallace, *The Land of the Pueblos*, 14.

21. Ibid., 13–14.

22. Prentis, *South-western Letters*, 66–67, quoted in Noggle, "Anglo Observers of the Southwest Borderlands," 129.

23. Tobias and Woodhouse, *Santa Fe*, 24.

24. Wilson, *The Myth of Santa Fe*, 42–53. This simplified Greek Revival came to be known in New Mexico as the Territorial Style.

25. Ibid., 63–71, 86.

26. Quoted in the *Daily New Mexican*, September 7, 1892, quoted in Wilson, *The Myth of Santa Fe*, 79.

27. Wood, *Over the Range to the Golden Gate*, 111–12.

28. *Santa Fe New Mexican*, April 23, 1910, quoted in Tobias and Woodhouse, *Santa Fe*, 74.

29. Tobias and Woodhouse, *Santa Fe*, 105.

30. Ibid., 75.

31. Portions of the board's plan, issued in December 1912, are quoted in ibid. Wilson, *The Myth of Santa Fe*, 122–23, provides additional context.

32. The cottage he refers to is the Roque Lobato house, restored in 1912 by Sylvanus Morley, a member of the Planning Board, and thus also known as the Morley House.

33. E. Alexander Powell, *The End of the Trail*, 16–18.

34. Lovato, *Santa Fe Hispanic Culture*.

## CHAPTER 12. SAN XAVIER DEL BAC

1. Fontana, *A Gift of Angels*, 3.

2. The O'odham people include a number of subgroups, among them the Tohono O'odham, or desert people (formerly known as Papago) and the Akimel O'odham, or river people (formerly Pima). The Sobaípuris of Wa:k suffered mightily from European diseases, and over the centuries their community received the influx of many desert and river O'odham so that Wa:k today bears the heritage of all three groups.

3. Bolton, *Rim of Christendom*, 265.

4. Kino, *Historical Memoir of Pimería Alta*, 1:122.

5. Sheridan, *Landscapes of Fraud*, 39–40.

6. Bolton, *Rim of Christendom*, 506–8.

7. Fontana, "Biography of a Desert Church," 7–10. The quote is from a longer passage reproduced by Fontana from Dunne, *Juan Antonio Balthasar*, 78–79. In 2015, Bernard Fontana and the Southwest Mission Research Center (www.southwestmissions.org) published a much expanded version of "Biography of a Desert Church," with photographs by Edward McCain, under the title *San Xavier del Bac: Portrait of a Desert Church*.

8. Fontana, "Biography of a Desert Church," 14.

9. Ibid., 24.

10. As quoted in ibid., 22.

11. Iturralde, as quoted in ibid., 24.

12. Bahre, *A Legacy of Change,* 144.

13. As quoted by Geiger, "A Voice from San Xavier del Bac," 8.

14. Ibid., 8–9.

15. A visita is a place of worship without a priest that is served by a priest based elsewhere, in this case San Xavier.

16. Geiger, "A Voice from San Xavier del Bac," 9.

17. Father Pedro Bringas to Jose Carlos Moreno, June 6, 1806, as quoted in ibid., 11.

18. Chamberlain, *My Confession: Recollections of a Rogue,* 295. The original Chamberlain manuscript is held at the West Point Museum and this excerpt is reproduced courtesy of the West Point Museum Collection, United States Military Academy. A better known but heavily redacted edition of *My Confession,* edited by Roger Butterfield, was published by Harper & Brothers (New York) in 1956.

19. Fontana, "Biography of a Desert Church," 31.

20. Chamberlain, *My Confession: Recollections of a Rogue,* 370.

21. Hayes, *Pioneer Notes from the Diaries of Judge Benjamin Hayes,* quoted in Fontana, "Biography of a Desert Church," 34.

22. Fontana, "Biography of a Desert Church," 41.

23. Officer, *Hispanic Arizona,* 166.

24. Fontana, "Biography of a Desert Church," 30, 39.

25. The writer is an Ohioan, Phocian Way, and the passage, quoted by Fontana in "Biography of a Desert Church," 37, may be found in Duffen, "Overland via 'Jackass Mail' in 1858," 147–64.

26. Fontana, "Biography of a Desert Church," 49.

27. Ibid., 52–56.

28. Fontana, *A Gift of Angels,* 3.

## CHAPTER 13. TAOS VALLEY

1. "Document 24. Hernando de Alvarado's Narrative, 1540: Report of What Hernando de Alvarado and Fray Juan de Padilla Found During Their Search for the Mar del Sur," in Flint and Flint, *Documents of the Coronado Expedition,* 306. The word given for turkeys is *gallinas,* which more commonly refers to chickens, an animal the Pueblo Indians of that era did not possess.

2. "Castañeda's History of the Expedition," in Hammond and Rey, *Narratives of the Coronado Expedition,* 244–45.

3. Bodine, "Taos Pueblo," 267.

4. The original Spanish for the "rap" from heaven appears to be *aldabada,* a knock on the door, delivered by an *aldaba,* a door knocker, which in Benavides's day would probably have been a heavy and substantial apparatus made of forged iron. The translators' choice of *rap* understates the emphasis Benavides intended. His aldabada was a loud banging on a thick and resonant door. God meant business! (Thanks to John Kessell for shedding light on this arcane term.)

5. Benavides, *The Memorial of Fray Alonso de Benavides*, 26–27, with minor revisions of the translation and added paragraph breaks to ease reading.

6. Hackett, *Revolt of the Pueblo Indians of New Mexico*, 1:xxx, 110. Blanche Grant, *When Old Trails Were New*, 10, mistakenly assumes that the presence of an alcalde indicated the existence of a town.

7. "Autos Drawn Up as a Result of the Rebellion of the Christian Indians, Aug. 9, 1680," in Hackett, *Revolt of the Pueblo Indians of New Mexico*, 1:3.

8. Trampas is an early name for the Río Grande del Rancho, which flows through the village of Ranchos de Taos, which in turn grew up around the Plaza de Nuestro Padre San Francisco de las Trampas (Blanche Grant, *When Old Trails Were New*, 18; Kessell, "Born Old," 115–16). This Trampas River should not be confused with the Río de las Trampas, which nourishes the village of Las Trampas, roughly forty winding mountain miles southwest of Taos.

9. Adams, *Bishop Tamarón's Visitation of New Mexico*, 56–58.

10. Ibid., 58–59.

11. Blanche Grant, *When Old Trails Were New*, 18.

12. Adams and Chávez, *The Missions of New Mexico*, 111–13, 251.

13. Baxter, *Spanish Irrigation in Taos Valley*, 17–19, offers an especially rich discussion of place-names.

14. Gregg, *Commerce of the Prairies* (1954), 104.

15. Pattie, *Personal Narrative*, 41–43. Pattie suggested that he arrived in 1824, but the correct year is 1825.

16. Albert Pike, *Prose Sketches and Poems*, 148.

17. W. W. H. Davis, *El Gringo*, 306. Garrard, *Wah-To-Yah and the Taos Trail*, 156, describes Taos in 1847.

18. Albert Pike, *Prose Sketches and Poems*, 148.

19. Sage, *Scenes in the Rocky Mountains*, 81–87. There is a modern edition in Sage, *Letters and Papers*. The quoted passages appear in 2:81–82.

20. Sage, *Letters and Papers*, 2:87.

21. Ruxton, *Ruxton of the Rockies*, 188.

22. Myrick, *New Mexico's Railroads*, 110, 122.

23. Guidebooks and travel accounts published in the mid-1910s advised travelers that they would have to take the stage. Laut, *Through Our Unknown Southwest*, 186; and E. Alexander Powell, *The End of the Trail*, 196.

24. E. Alexander Powell, *The End of the Trail*, 56, 57.

25. Laut, *Through Our Unknown Southwest*, 183.

26. Ibid., 196; A. Eugene Bartlett, *Least Known America*, 21, 59; Saunders, *Finding the Worthwhile in the Southwest*, 29.

27. A. Eugene Bartlett, *Least Known America*, 56.

28. Saunders, *Finding the Worthwhile in the Southwest*, 28.

29. Sandra D'Emilio and Suzan Campbell, "Mission of Beauty: The Art of Ranchos de Taos Church," in D'Emilio, Campbell, and Kessell, *Spirit and Vision*, 1.

30. D'Emilio, Campbell, and Kessell, *Spirit and Vision*, 49.

31. Drain and Wakely, *A Sense of Mission*, 73.

32. The theme of pueblo structures echoing the outlines of the mountains behind them is intriguingly explored in Scully, *Pueblo*.

## CHAPTER 14. TUCSON

1. For the early years of Tucson, see in particular Dobyns, *Spanish Colonial Tucson;* Kessell, *Friars, Soldiers, and Reformers;* McCarty, *Desert Documentary;* and Officer, *Hispanic Arizona.*

2. This translation of Zúñiga's report here and in the following quotations appears in McCarty, *Desert Documentary,* 86–92, and is reproduced here with permission of the Arizona Historical Society.

3. "La guerra de los apaches no es ni ha sido la causa de la ruina y abandono de las interesantes poblaciones de la frontera: al contrario la guerra es el resultado del abandono y decadencia de los presidios." Zúñiga, *Rápida Ojeada al Estado de Sonora,* 22.

4. Sheridan, *Los Tucsonenses,* 50–51.

5. Browne, *Adventures in the Apache Country,* 131–34, 138. Browne's classic, or portions thereof, has appeared in several modern editions. See, too, Goodman, *A Western Panorama.*

6. Bourke, *On the Border with Crook,* 450.

7. Summerhayes, *Vanished Arizona,* 223.

8. Census figures in Sonnichsen, *Tucson,* 91, 210.

9. Peixotto, *Our Hispanic Southwest,* 121.

10. The treaty was agreed in December 1853 and ratified by the U.S. Senate the following year.

11. MacFadden, *Rambles in the Far West,* 67–69.

12. Sonnichsen, *Tucson,* remains the best one-volume history of Tucson, and Sheridan, *Los Tucsonenses,* looks at its Hispanic community in modern times.

## CHAPTER 15. ZUNI

1. *Zuni 2006 Visitors Guide,* 1.

2. Kennedy and Simplicio, "First Contact at Hawikku (Zuni)," 63.

3. These words come from Cabeza de Vaca's account published in Spain in 1542, and apparently reflect what he told his countrymen in 1536. Cabeza de Vaca, *The Narrative of Cabeza de Vaca,* 162. See, too, 158.

4. Ladd, "Zuni on the Day the Men in Metal Arrived," 228–29.

5. Some historians have claimed that Fray Marcos did see one of the Zuni villages from a distance. David Weber reviewed the arguments in "Fray Marcos de Niza and the Historians," 19–32, suggesting that Fray Marcos did not see Cíbola, but also concluding that a definitive answer may not be possible. Since then, based on a close reading of the documents, Richard and Shirley Flint have come to the unequivocal judgment that Fray Marcos did *not* see Cíbola and they may have put the question to rest. *Documents of the Coronado Expedition,* 60–64. To assume that Fray Marcos saw one of the Zuni Pueblos from a distance does not give much credit to the Zunis, who, warned by Esteban's arrival that other strangers might follow, would have been on the alert.

6. For Viceroy Mendoza's appointment of Coronado, January 6, 1540, see Flint and Flint, *Documents of the Coronado Expedition,* 108–10.

7. Ladd, "Zuni on the Day the Men in Metal Arrived," 231–33. Ladd, himself a Zuni, also notes that the Zunis may have believed that Coronado led a Spanish slaving party.

8. See Flint and Flint, *Documents of the Coronado Expedition,* 654n53; and Flint, *Great Cruelties Have Been Reported,* 353. The Flints have found evidence of more Spaniards and more Indian allies on the expedition than previously supposed. For a biography of Coronado that includes up-to-date research and understandings, see Flint, *No Settlement, No Conquest.*

9. Damp, "The Summer of 1540," 4–5.

10. This quote from Coronado's letter to Viceroy Mendoza, as well as those that follow, are drawn from Flint and Flint, *Documents of the Coronado Expedition,* 257–62.

11. Ibid., 252–53.

12. Most of the language in square brackets was supplied by the Flints, with a few additions by David Weber. Other English-language versions of this letter exist, but the Flints are most faithful to the Italian translation that is the earliest known copy of the original and long-lost letter.

13. An artist, Cristóbal Quesada, accompanied the expedition and presumably made this painting.

14. Zunis regard this spring-fed lake, located about fifty miles south of present-day Zuni Pueblo, as a sacred place. In 2003, Zunis won a two-decades-long battle to halt strip mining near the lake, which they feared would drain the aquifer by which the lake is fed.

15. Flint and Flint, *Documents of Coronado Expedition,* 654–55nn77–81.

16. Perhaps also an early transcription of the document or its translation into Italian was faulty. Ibid., 655n102.

17. Anyone wishing to explore the current state of knowledge about the occupied sites that Coronado might have seen could do no better than to consult Kintigh, introduction to *Hemenway Southwestern Archaeological Expedition.*

18. T. J. Ferguson, "Dowa Yalanne," 33. Ferguson discusses the tradition of Fray Juan Greyrobe and gives a detailed picture of the Zunis atop Dowa Yalanne.

19. For historical background, see Crampton, *The Zunis of Cibola;* and T. J Ferguson and Hart, *A Zuni Atlas,* which are also excellent sources for the general reader.

20. Calhoun to Col. Medill, Comr. of Indian Affairs, Santa Fe, N.M., Oct. 1, 1849, in Calhoun, *The Official Correspondence,* 30. He describes Navajos and Apaches as "wild Indians" (32).

21. Samuel Washington Woodhouse, traveling with the Lorenzo Sitgreaves's expedition, diary entry for September 24, 1851, quoted in Weber, *Richard H. Kern,* 159. This passage was inadvertently dropped from the splendid published edition of Woodhouse's diaries: Andrew Wallace and Hevly, *From Texas to San Diego in 1851.*

22. John Wesley Powell, *Canyons of the Colorado,* 355.

23. For example, Whipple, *A Pathfinder in the Southwest,* 140–48; and Beale, "Wagon Road from Fort Defiance to the Colorado River," 188–89, offered dispassionate descriptions.

24. Frost, "Photography and the Pueblo Indians of New Mexico," 196–98.

25. Saunders, *Finding the Worthwhile in the Southwest,* quotations on 86 and 85.

26. Cushing, *Cushing at Zuni,* vii. For Cushing's published writing, see Cushing, *Zuni.*

27. McFeely, *Zuni and the American Imagination,* 17.

28. Nancy Yaw Davis, *The Zuni Enigma,* 21.

29. Malhi et al., "Native American mtDNA Prehistory in the American Southwest," 113, found "low levels of gene diversity" among the Zunis, suggesting little or no mixture with other groups—Japanese or other Native Americans.

30. See, for example, the manuscript of a lecture that Cushing gave in 1885, "From Discovery of Zuni or the Ancient Province of Cibola and the Seven Cities," published in *Cushing at Zuni,* 335–39.

# Bibliography

Abbey, Edward. *Desert Solitaire: A Season in the Wilderness.* 1968. Reprint, New York: Simon & Schuster, 1990.

Abert, James William. *Western America in 1846–1847: The Original Travel Diary of Lieutenant J. W. Abert, Who Mapped New Mexico for the United States Army.* Edited by John Galvin. San Francisco: J. Howell, 1966.

Adams, Eleanor B., trans. and ed. *Bishop Tamarón's Visitation of New Mexico, 1760.* Albuquerque: Historical Society of New Mexico, 1954.

Adams, Eleanor B., and Fray Angélico Chávez, trans. and eds. *The Missions of New Mexico, 1776: A Description by Fray Francisco Atanasio Domínguez.* Albuquerque: University of New Mexico Press, 1956.

Anderson, Michael F. *Living at the Edge: Explorers, Exploiters and Settlers of the Grand Canyon Region.* Grand Canyon, Ariz.: Grand Canyon Association, 1998.

———. *Polishing the Jewel: An Administrative History of Grand Canyon National Park.* Grand Canyon, Ariz.: Grand Canyon Association, 2000.

Arny, William F. M. *Indian Agent in New Mexico: The Journal of Special Agent W. F. M. Arny, 1870.* Edited by Lawrence R. Murphy. Santa Fe: Stagecoach, 1967.

Arricivita, Juan Domingo, and Isidro Félix de Espinosa. *Apostolic Chronicle of Juan Arricivita.* Translated by George P. Hammond and Agapito Rey. Edited by Vivian C. Fisher and W. Michael Mathes. Berkeley, Calif.: Academy of American Franciscan History, 1996. Originally published in Spanish in 1746.

Austin, Mary. *The Land of Journeys' Ending.* New York: Century, 1924.

Babbitt, James E., ed. *Rainbow Trails: Early-Day Adventures in Rainbow Bridge Country.* Page, Ariz.: Glen Canyon Natural History Association, 1990.

Bahre, Conrad Joseph. *A Legacy of Change: Historic Human Impact on Vegetation of the Arizona Borderlands.* Tucson: University of Arizona Press, 1991.

Baley, Charles W. *Disaster at the Colorado: Beale's Wagon Road and the First Emigrant Party.* Logan: Utah State University Press, 2002.

Bancroft, Hubert Howe. *History of Arizona and New Mexico, 1530–1888.* 1889. Reprint, Albuquerque: Horn & Wallace, 1962.

Barbour, Barton H. *Jedediah Smith: No Ordinary Mountain Man.* Norman: University of Oklahoma Press, 2011.

Barrett, Elinore M. *The Spanish Colonial Settlement Landscapes of New Mexico, 1598–1680.* Albuquerque: University of New Mexico Press, 2012.

Bartlett, A. Eugene. *Least Known America.* New York: Fleming H. Revell, 1925.

Bartlett, John Russell. *Personal Narrative of Explorations and Incidents in Texas, New Mexico, California, Sonora, and Chihuahua, Connected with the United States and Mexican Boundary Commission, During the years 1850, '51, '52, and '53.* 2 vols. London: George Routledge, 1854.

Bartlett, Katharine. "How Don Pedro de Tovar Discovered the Hopi and Don García López de Cárdenas Saw the Grand Canyon, with Notes upon Their Probable Route." *Plateau* 12 (1940): 37–45.

Baxter, John O. *Spanish Irrigation in Taos Valley.* Santa Fe: New Mexico State Engineer, 1990.

Beale, Edward Fitzgerald. "Wagon Road from Fort Defiance to the Colorado River." In *Uncle Sam's Camels: The Journal of May Humphreys Stacey Supplemented by the Report of Edward Fitzgerald Beale (1857–1858),* by May Humphreys Stacey. San Marino, Calif.: Huntington Library Press, 2006.

Benavides, Alonso de. *The Memorial of Fray Alonso de Benavides, 1630.* Translated and edited by Frederick Webb Hodge, Charles Fletcher Lummis, and Mrs. Edward E. Ayer. Chicago: privately printed, 1916.

Bodine, John J. "Taos Pueblo." In *Handbook of North American Indians,* vol. 9, *Southwest,* edited by Alfonso Ortiz. Washington, D.C.: Smithsonian Institution, 1979.

Bolton, Herbert Eugene. *Coronado, Knight of Pueblos and Plains.* Albuquerque: University of New Mexico Press, 1949.

———. *Pageant in the Wilderness: The Diary and Itinerary of Fathers Dominguez and Escalante into the Area Northwest of New Mexico.* Salt Lake City: Utah State Historical Society, 1950.

———. *Rim of Christendom: A Biography of Eusebio Francisco Kino, Pacific Coast Pioneer.* 1936. Reprint, Tucson: University of Arizona Press, 1963.

Bostwick, Todd W. *Byron Cummings: Dean of Southwest Archaeology.* Tucson: University of Arizona Press, 2006.

Bourke, John G. *On the Border with Crook.* 1891. Reprint, Lincoln: University of Nebraska Press, 1971.

Brown, Kenneth A. *Four Corners: History, Land, and People of the Desert Southwest.* New York: HarperCollins, 1995.

Browne, J. Ross. *Adventures in the Apache Country: A Tour Through Arizona and Sonora, with Notes on the Silver Regions of Nevada.* New York: Harper & Brothers, 1869.

Brugge, David M., trans. and ed. "Vizcarra's Navajo Campaign of 1823." *Arizona and the West* (1964): 223–44.

Brugge, David M., and Raymond Wilson. *Administrative History: Canyon de Chelly National Monument, Arizona.* National Park Service, January 1976. www.nps .gov/cach/learn/historyculture/upload/CACH_adhi.pdf.

Bullington, Neal R. "Who Discovered Carlsbad Caverns?" 1968. *CAVE History Update: A Newsletter from CAVE Cultural Resources Stewardship and Science Division,* February 25, 2004/ www.nps.gov/cave/planyourvisit/upload/CHU _20040225.pdf.

Burrus, Ernest J., trans. and ed. *Kino and Manje, Explorers of Sonora and Arizona: Their Vision of the Future.* St. Louis: Jesuit Historical Institute, St. Louis University, 1971.

Cabeza de Vaca, Alvar Núñez. *The Narrative of Cabeza de Vaca.* Translated and edited by Rolena Adorno and Patrick Charles Pautz. Lincoln: University of Nebraska Press, 2003.

Caiar, Ruth, "with Jim White Jr." *One Man's Dream: The Story of Jim White, Discoverer and Explorer of the Carlsbad Caverns.* New York: Pageant, 1957.

Calhoun, James S. *The Official Correspondence of James S. Calhoun While Indian Agent at Santa Fé and Superintendent of Indian Affairs in New Mexico.* Edited by Annie Heloise Abel. Washington, D.C.: Government Printing Office, 1915.

Cather, Willa. *Death Comes for the Archbishop.* New York: Knopf, 1927.

Chamberlain, Samuel E. *My Confession.* Edited by Roger Butterfield. New York: Harper & Brothers, 1956.

———. *My Confession: Recollections of a Rogue; An Unexpurgated and Annotated Edition.* Edited by William H. Goetzmann. Austin: Texas State Historical Association, 1996.

Chapin, Frederick H. *The Land of the Cliff-Dwellers.* Boston: Appalachian Mountain Club, 1892.

Chidester, Otis H. "The Discovery of Rainbow Bridge." *Smoke Signal,* no. 20. Tucson: Tucson Corral of the Westerners, 1969.

Clark, Eliot. *Alexander Wyant.* New York: privately printed, 1916.

Clavijero, Francesco Saverio. *The History of Mexico Collected from Spanish and Mexican Historians, from Manuscripts and Ancient Paintings of the Indians.* 3 vols. Richmond, Va.: W. Prichard, 1806. This work first appeared in a 1780–81 Italian edition, translated by Charles Cullen. The first English translation was published in 1787.

Clemensen, A. Berle. *A Centennial History of the First Prehistoric Reserve, 1892–1992: Administrative History, Casa Grande Ruins National Monument, Arizona.* Denver: U.S. Dept. of the Interior / National Park Service, 1992.

Conklin, Enoch. *Picturesque Arizona: Being the Result of Travels and Observations in Arizona During the Fall and Winter of 1877.* New York: Mining Record Printing Establishment, 1878.

Cortés, Hernán. *Letters from Mexico.* Translated and edited by Anthony Pagden. New Haven: Yale University Press, 1986.

Cozzens, Samuel Woodworth. *The Marvellous Country; or, Three Years in Arizona and New Mexico, the Apaches' Home.* Boston: Shepard & Gill, 1873.

Crampton, C. Gregory. *The Zunis of Cibola.* Salt Lake City: University of Utah Press, 1957.

Cummings, Byron. "The Great Natural Bridges of Utah." *National Geographic,* February 1910.

———. *Indians I Have Known.* Tucson: Arizona Silhouettes, 1952.

Cushing, Frank Hamilton. *Cushing at Zuni: The Correspondence and Journal of Frank Hamilton Cushing, 1879–1884.* Edited by Jesse Green. Albuquerque: University of New Mexico Press, 1990.

———. *Zuni: Selected Writings of Frank Hamilton Cushing.* Edited by Jesse Green. Lincoln: University of Nebraska Press, 1979.

Damp, Jonathan E. "The Summer of 1540: Archaeology of the Battle of Hawikku." *Archaeology Southwest* 19 (Winter 2005): 4–5.

Davis, Nancy Yaw. *The Zuni Enigma: A Native American People's Possible Japanese Connection.* New York: Norton, 2000.

Davis, W. W. H. *El Gringo; or, New Mexico & Her People.* New York: Harper & Brothers, 1857.

Dawdy, Doris O., ed. "The Wyant Diary: An Artist with the Wheeler Survey in Arizona, 1873." *Journal of the Southwest* 22, no. 3 (1980): 255–78.

deBuys, William. *A Great Aridness: Climate Change and the Future of the American Southwest.* New York: Oxford University Press, 2011.

———. *Seeing Things Whole: The Essential John Wesley Powell.* Washington, D.C: Island, 2001.

Dobyns, Henry F. *Spanish Colonial Tucson: A Demographic History.* Tucson: University of Arizona Press, 1976.

Douglass, William B. "From the Field Notes of U.S. Deputy Surveyors: The Discovery of Rainbow Natural Bridge, by William B. Douglass, U.S. Examiner of Surveys, April 28, 1910." *Our Public Lands* 5, no. 2 (1955).

Drain, Thomas A. (author), and David Wakely (photographer). *A Sense of Mission: Historic Churches of the Southwest.* San Francisco: Chronicle Books, 1994.

Du Bois, John Van Deusen, and Joseph Heger (illustrator). *Campaigns in the West, 1856–1861: The Journal and Letters of Colonel John Van Deusen Du Bois, with Pen-*

*cil Sketches by Joseph Heger.* 1949. Reprint, Tucson: Arizona Historical Society, 2003.

Duffen, William A. "Overland via 'Jackass Mail' in 1858: The Diary of Phocian R. Way," *Arizona and the West* 2, no. 2 (1960): 147–64.

Dunne, Peter M., S.J. *Juan Antonio Balthasar, Padre Visitador to the Sonoran Frontier, 1744–45: Two Original Reports.* Tucson: Arizona Pioneers' Historical Society, 1957.

Elliott, Melinda. *Great Excavations: Tales of Early Southwestern Archaeology, 1888–1939.* Santa Fe: School of American Research Press, 1995.

Emory, William H. *Notes of a Military Reconnoissance from Fort Leavenworth, in Missouri, to San Diego, in California, Including Part of the Arkansas, Del Norte, and Gila Rivers. Made in 1846–7, with the Advanced Guard of the "Army of the West."* 30th Cong., 1st sess., [House] Executive Document 41. Washington, D.C.: Wendell & Van Benthuysen, 1848.

Escalante, Silvestre Vélez de. *The Domínguez-Escalante Journal: Their Expedition Through Colorado, Utah, Arizona, and New Mexico in 1776.* Rev. ed. Translated by Fray Angélico Chávez. Edited by Ted J. Warner. Salt Lake City: University of Utah Press, 1995.

Esquibel, José Antonio. "The Palace of the Governors in the Seventeenth Century." *El Palacio* 111 (Fall 2006).

Ferguson, Erna. *Our Southwest.* New York: Knopf, 1940.

Ferguson, T. J. "Dowa Yalanne: The Architecture of Zuni Resistance and Social Change During the Pueblo Revolt." In *Archaeologies of the Pueblo Revolt: Identity, Meaning, and Renewal in the Pueblo World,* edited by Robert W. Preucel. Albuquerque: University of New Mexico Press, 2002.

Ferguson, T. J., and E. Richard Hart. *A Zuni Atlas.* Norman: University of Oklahoma Press, 1985.

Fernlund, Kevin J. *William Henry Holmes and the Rediscovery of the American West.* Albuquerque: University of New Mexico Press, 2000.

Fish, Suzanne K., and Paul R. Fish, eds. *The Hohokam Millennium.* Santa Fe: School for Advanced Research Press, 2007.

Flint, Richard. *Great Cruelties Have Been Reported: The 1544 Investigation of the Coronado Expedition.* Dallas: SMU Press, 2002.

———. *No Settlement, No Conquest: A History of the Coronado Entrada.* Albuquerque: University of New Mexico Press, 2008.

Flint, Richard, and Shirley Cushing Flint, trans. and eds. *Documents of the Coronado Expedition, 1539–1542: "They Were Not Familiar with His Majesty, nor Did They Wish to Be His Subjects."* Dallas: SMU Press, 2005.

Font, Pedro, O.F.M. "Font's Complete Diary of the Second Anza Expedition." Vol. 4 of *Anza's California Expeditions,* edited by Herbert Eugene Bolton. Berkeley: University of California Press, 1930.

Fontana, Bernard L. "Biography of a Desert Church: The Story of the Mission San Xavier del Bac." *Smoke Signal,* no. 3. Tucson: Tucson Corral of the Westerners, 1996.

————. *A Gift of Angels: The Art of Mission San Xavier del Bac.* Tucson: University of Arizona Press, 2010.

Fontana, Bernard L., and Edward McCain (photographer). *San Xavier del Bac: Portrait of a Desert Church.* Tucson: Southwest Mission Research Center, 2015.

Forbes, Jack D. *Warriors of the Colorado: The Yumas of the Quechan Nation and Their Neighbors.* Norman: University of Oklahoma Press, 1965.

Fossett, Frank. *Colorado: A Historical, Descriptive, and Statistical Work on the Rocky Mountain Gold and Silver Mining Region.* Denver: Daily Tribune, 1876.

Fowler, Don. *A Laboratory for Anthropology: Science and Romanticism in the American Southwest, 1846–1930.* Albuquerque: University of New Mexico Press / University of Arizona Southwest Center, 2000.

————. Review of *Troweling Through Time,* by Florence C. Lister. *Western Historical Quarterly* 37, no. 1 (2006).

Francaviglia, Richard V. *Mapping and Imagination in the Great Basin: A Cartographic History.* Reno: University of Nevada Press, 2005.

Frank, Ross. *From Settler to Citizen: New Mexican Economic Development and the Creation of a Vecino Society, 1750–1820.* Berkeley: University of California Press, 2000.

Frost, Richard H. "Photography and the Pueblo Indians of New Mexico, 1870–1930." *New Mexico Historical Review* 84, no. 2 (2009).

Garcés, Francisco. *On the Trail of a Spanish Pioneer: The Diary and Itinerary of Francisco Garcés (Missionary Priest) in His Travels Through Sonora, Arizona, and California, 1775–1776.* 2 vols. Translated and edited by Elliott Coues. New York: Francis P. Harper, 1900.

————. *A Record of Travels in Arizona and California, 1775–1776: Fr. Francisco Garcés.* Translated and edited by John Galvin. San Francisco: John Howell Books, 1965.

García-Mason, Velma. "Acoma." In *Handbook of North American Indians,* vol. 9, *Southwest,* edited by Alfonso Ortiz. Washington, D.C.: Smithsonian Institution, 1979.

Gardner, Alexander. *Across the Continent on the Kansas Pacific Railroad: Route of the 35th Parallel.* Washington, D.C.: privately printed, ca. 1868.

Garrard, Lewis H. *Wah-To-Yah and the Taos Trail.* 1850. Reprint, Palo Alto, Calif.: American West, 1968.

Geiger, Maynard, O.F.M., trans. and ed. "A Voice from San Xavier del Bac (1802–1805)." *Provincial Annals* 16, no. 1 (1953).

Gillmor, Frances, and Louisa Wade Wetherill. *Traders to the Navajos: The Story of the Wetherills of Kayenta.* 1934. Reprint, Albuquerque: University of New Mexico Press, 1953.

Gleed, Charles S., ed. *Guide from the Missouri River to the Pacific Ocean via Kansas, Colorado, New Mexico, Arizona, and California.* Chicago: Rand, McNally, 1882.

Goetzmann, William H. *Army Exploration in the American West, 1803–1863.* Lincoln: University of Nebraska Press, 1959.

———. *Exploration and Empire: Explorer and the Scientist in the Winning of the American West.* New York: Knopf, 1967.

Goodman, David Michael. *A Western Panorama, 1849–1875: The Travels, Writings, and Influence of J. Ross Browne on the Pacific Coast, and in Texas, Nevada, Arizona and Baja California, as the First Mining Commissioner and Minister to China.* Glendale, Calif.: A. H. Clark, 1966.

Gordon, Dudley. *Charles F. Lummis: Crusader in Corduroy.* Los Angeles: Cultural Assets, 1972.

Grant, Blanche. *When Old Trails Were New: The Story of Taos.* New York: Press of the Pioneers, 1934.

Grant, Campbell. *Canyon de Chelly: Its People and Rock Art.* Tucson: University of Arizona Press, 1978.

Gregg, Josiah. *Commerce of the Prairies.* Edited by Max L. Moorhead. Norman: University of Oklahoma Press, 1954.

———. *Commerce of the Prairies; or, The Journal of a Santa Fé Trader, During Eight Expeditions Across the Great Western Prairies, and a Residence of Nearly Nine Years in Northern Mexico.* 2 vols. New York: H. G. Langley, 1844.

Grey, Zane. *The Rainbow Trail: A Romance.* New York: Harper & Brothers, 1915.

Griffin, John S. *A Doctor Comes to California: The Diary of John S. Griffin, Assistant Surgeon with Kearny's Dragoons, 1846–1847.* San Francisco: California Historical Society, 1943.

Hackett, Charles Wilson, ed. *Revolt of the Pueblo Indians of New Mexico and Otermín's Attempted Reconquest, 1680–1682.* 2 vols. Translated by Charmion Clair Shelby. Albuquerque: University of New Mexico Press, 1942.

Hales, Peter B. *William Henry Jackson and the Transformation of the American Landscape.* Philadelphia: Temple University Press, 1988.

Hämäläinen, Pekka. *The Comanche Empire.* New Haven: Yale University Press, 2008.

Hamilton, Patrick. *The Resources of Arizona: Its Mineral, Farming, Grazing and Timber Lands; Its History, Climate, Productions, Civil and Military Government, Pre-historic Ruins, Early Missionaries, Indian Tribes, Pioneer Days, etc., etc.* San Francisco: A. L. Bancroft, 1884.

Hammond, George P., and Agapito Rey, trans. and eds. *Don Juan de Oñate: Colonizer of New Mexico, 1595–1628.* 2 vols. Albuquerque: University of New Mexico Press, 1953.

———. *Narratives of the Coronado Expedition, 1540–1542.* Albuquerque: University of New Mexico Press, 1940.

————. *New Mexico in 1602: Juan de Montoya's Relation of the Discovery of New Mexico.* Albuquerque: Quivira Society, 1938.

————. *The Rediscovery of New Mexico, 1580–1594: The Explorations of Chamuscado, Espejo, Castaño de Sosa, Morlete, and Leyva de Bonilla and Humaña.* Albuquerque: University of New Mexico Press, 1966.

Hardacre, Emma. "The Cliff-Dwellers." *Scribner's Monthly,* December 1878.

Hassell, Hank. *Rainbow Bridge: An Illustrated History.* Logan: Utah State University Press, 1999.

Hayes, Benjamin, *Pioneer Notes from the Diaries of Judge Benjamin Hayes, 1849–1875.* Edited by Marjorie T. Wolcott. Los Angeles: privately printed, 1929.

Hewett, Edgar L. *Ancient Life in the American Southwest, with an Introduction on the General History of the American Race.* Indianapolis: Bobbs-Merrill, 1930.

Holmes, William Henry. *The Archaeology of William Henry Holmes.* Edited by David J. Meltzer and Robert C. Dunnell. Washington, D.C.: Smithsonian Institution Press, 1992.

————. "A Notice of the Ancient Remains of Southwestern Colorado During the Summer of 1875." *Bulletin of the United States Geological and Geographical Survey of the Territories.* 2nd ser., vol. 2, no. 1, 1–24. Washington, D.C.: Government Printing Office, 1876.

————. "Random Records of a Lifetime, 1846–1931: Cullings, Largely Personal, from the Scrap Heap of Three Score Years and Ten, Devoted to Science, Literature and Art." 20 vols. In the collection of the Library of the National Museum of American Art, Smithsonian Institution, Washington, D.C.

————. "Report on the Ancient Ruins of Southwestern Colorado Examined During the Summers of 1875 and 1876." In *Tenth Annual Report of the United States Geological and Geographical Survey of the Territories … for the Year 1876,* edited by F. V. Hayden, 381–408. Washington, D.C.: Government Printing Office, 1878.

Houk, Rose. *Casa Grande Ruins National Monument.* Tucson: Southwest Parks and Monuments Association, 1987.

Houk, Rose, Faith Marcovecchio, and Duane Smith. *Mesa Verde National Park: The First 100 Years.* Mesa Verde National Park, Colo.: Mesa Verde Museum Association; Golden, Colo.: Fulcrum, 2006.

Hughes, John Taylor. *Doniphan's Expedition: Containing an Account of the Conquest of New Mexico; General Kearney's Overland Expedition to California; Doniphan's Campaign Against the Navajos; His Unparralleled March upon Chihuahua and Durango; and the Operations of General Price at Sante Fé: With a Sketch of the Life of Col. Doniphan. . . .* Cincinnati: J. A. & U. P. James, 1848.

Humboldt, Alexander von. *Political Essay on the Kingdom of New Spain.* 4 vols. Translated by John Black. 1811. 3rd. ed., London: Longman, Hurst, Rees, Orme, & Brown, 1822.

Huseman, Ben W. *Wild River, Timeless Canyons: Balduin Möllhausen's Watercolors of the Colorado.* Tucson: University of Arizona Press, 1995.

Ingersoll, Ernest. *The Crest of the Continent.* 1885. Reprint, Chicago: R. R. Donnelley, 1888.

Ives, Joseph C. *Report upon the Colorado River of the West, Explored in 1857 and 1858.* U.S. 36th Cong., 1st sess., 1859–60, Senate Executive Document [no number]. Washington, D.C.: Government Printing Office, 1861.

Jackson, Clarence S. *William H. Jackson: Picture Maker of the Old West.* New York: Charles Scribner's Sons, 1947.

Jackson, William Henry. "Ancient Ruins in Southwestern Colorado." *Bulletin of the United States Geological and Geographical Survey of the Territories,* 2nd ser., no. 1, 17–30. Washington, D.C.: Government Printing Office, 1875.

———. "Ancient Ruins in Southwestern Colorado." In *Annual Report of the United States Geological and Geographical Survey of the Territories ... for the Year 1874,* edited by F. V. Hayden, 368–81. Washington, D.C.: Government Printing Office, 1876.

———. "Ancient Ruins in Southwestern Colorado." *American Naturalist* 10 (1876): 31–37.

———. *The Diaries of William Henry Jackson, Frontier Photographer.* Edited by LeRoy R. Hafen and Ann W. Hafen. The Far West and the Rockies Historical Series 10. Glendale, Calif.: Arthur H. Clark, 1959.

———. "First Official Visit to the Cliff Dwellings." *Colorado Magazine,* May 1924, 151–59.

———. "A Notice of the Ancient Remains in Arizona and Utah Lying about the Rio San Juan." *Bulletin of the United States Geological and Geographical Survey of the Territories,* 2nd ser., vol. 2, no. 1, 25–45. Washington, D.C.: Government Printing Office, 1876.

———. "Ruins of the Chaco Cañon, Examined in 1877." In *Tenth Annual Report of the United States Geological and Geographical Survey of the Territories.* Washington, D.C.: Government Printing Office, 1878.

———. *Time Exposure: The Autography of William Henry Jackson.* New York: G. P. Putnam's Sons, 1940.

———. *William Henry Jackson's "The Pioneer Photographer."* Edited by Bob Blair. Santa Fe: Museum of New Mexico Press, 2005.

Jackson, William Henry, and Howard R. Driggs. *The Pioneer Photographer: Rocky Mountain Adventures with a Camera.* Yonkers-on-Hudson, N.Y.: World Book, 1929.

Jett, Stephen C. "The Great 'Race' to 'Discover' Rainbow Natural Bridge in 1909." *Kiva* 58, no. 1 (1992): 3–66.

Johannsen, Robert Walter. *To the Halls of the Montezumas: The Mexican War in the American Imagination.* New York: Oxford University Press, 1985.

Johnston, Abraham Robinson, Marcellus Ball Edwards, and Philip Gooch Ferguson. *Marching with the Army of the West, 1846–1848.* Edited by Ralph P. Bieber. Glendale, Calif.: Arthur H. Clark, 1936.

Julyan, Robert. *The Place Names of New Mexico.* Albuquerque: University of New Mexico Press, 1996.

Kelley, Klara Bonsack, and Harris Francis. *Navajo Sacred Places.* Bloomington: Indiana University Press, 1994.

Kelsey, Robin Earle. "Photography in the Field: Timothy O'Sullivan and the Wheeler Survey, 1871–1874." Ph.D. diss., Harvard University, 2000. ProQuest cat. 9988568.

Kennedy, Tom R., and Dan Simplicio. "First Contact at Hawikku (Zuni): The Day the World Stopped." In *Telling New Mexico: A New History,* edited by Marta Weigle, Frances Levine, and Louise Stiver. Santa Fe: Museum of New Mexico Press, 2009.

Kessell, John L. "Born Old: The Church of San Francisco at Ranchos de Taos." In *Spirit and Vision: Images of Ranchos de Taos Church,* edited by Sandra D'Emilio, Suzan Campbell, and John L. Kessell. Santa Fe: Museum of New Mexico Press, 1987.

———. *Friars, Soldiers, and Reformers: Hispanic Arizona and the Sonora Mission Frontier, 1767–1856.* Tucson: University of Arizona Press, 1976.

———. "The Making of a Martyr: The Young Francisco Garcés." *New Mexico Historical Review* 45, no. 3 (1970).

———. *Miera y Pacheco: A Renaissance Spaniard in Eighteenth-Century New Mexico.* Norman: University of Oklahoma Press, 2013.

Kessell, John L., and Rick Hendricks, eds. *By Force of Arms: The Journals of Don Diego de Vargas, New Mexico, 1691–93.* Albuquerque: University of New Mexico Press, 1992.

Kessell, John L., Rick Hendricks, and Meredith D. Dodge, eds. *To the Royal Crown Restored: The Journals of Don Diego de Vargas, New Mexico, 1692–1694.* Albuquerque: University of New Mexico Press, 1995.

King, Clarence. *Clarence King Memoirs: The Helmet of Mambrino.* New York: G. P. Putnam's Sons, 1904.

Kingsborough, Edward King. *Antiquities of Mexico, Comprising Fac-similes of Ancient Mexican Paintings and Hieroglyphics. . . .* 9 vols. London: Robert Havell & Conaghi, 1831.

Kino, Eusebio Francisco. *Historical Memoir of Pimería Alta: A Contemporary Account of the Beginnings of California, Sonora, and Arizona, 1683–1711.* 2 vols. Translated and edited by Herbert Eugene Bolton. Berkeley: University of California Press, 1919.

Kintigh, Keith W. Introduction to *Hemenway Southwestern Archaeological Expedition.* Vol. 6. of Frank Hamilton Cushing, *Selected Correspondence, June 1, 1888 Through 1889.* Edited by Curtis M. Hinsley and David R. Wilcox. Frank Hamilton Cushing and the Hemenway Southwestern Archaeological Expedition, 1886–1889: The Southwest Center series 6. Tucson: University of Arizona Press, forthcoming.

————. *Settlement, Subsistence, and Society in Late Zuni Prehistory.* Anthropological Papers of the University of Arizona. 44. Tucson: University of Arizona Press, 1985.

Knaut, Andrew L. *The Pueblo Revolt of 1680: Conquest and Resistance in Seventeenth-Century New Mexico.* Norman: University of Oklahoma Press, 1995.

Kroeber, Alfred L., and Clifton B. Kroeber. *A Mohave War Reminiscence, 1854–1880.* Berkeley: University of California Press, 1973.

Kroeber, Clifton B., and Bernard L. Fontana. *Massacre on the Gila: An Account of the Last Major Battle Between American Indians, with Reflections on the Origin of the War.* Tucson: University of Arizona Press, 1986.

Ladd, Edmund J. "Zuni on the Day the Men in Metal Arrived." In *The Coronado Expedition to Tierra Nueva: The 1540–1542 Route Across the Southwest,* edited by Richard Flint and Shirley Cushing Flint. Niwot: University Press of Colorado, 1997.

Lafora, Nicolás de. *The Frontiers of New Spain: Nicolás de Lafora's Description, 1766–68.* Translated and edited by Lawrence Kinnaird. Berkeley: Quivira Society, 1958.

Laut, Agnes C. *Through Our Unknown Southwest: The Wonderland of the United States.* New York: McBride, Nast, 1913.

LeBlanc, Steven. "A Cultural History of Cibola," In *Zuni and El Morro, Past and Present,* edited by David Grant Noble and Richard B. Woodbury, Santa Fe: Ancient City, 1993.

Lee, Ronald F. *The Antiquities Act of 1906.* Washington, D.C.: Office of History and Historic Architecture, Eastern Service Center, Department of the Interior, National Park Service, 1970.

Leiby, Austin Nelson. "Borderland Pathfinders: The 1765 Diaries of Juan María Antonio de Rivera." Ph.D. diss., Northern Arizona University, 1984.

Liebmann, Matthew. *Revolt: An Archaeological History of Pueblo Resistance and Revitalization in 17th Century New Mexico.* Tucson: University of Arizona Press, 2012.

Linford, Laurance D. *Navajo Places: History, Legend, Landscape.* Salt Lake City: University of Utah Press, 2000.

Lister, Florence C. *Troweling Through Time: The First Century of Mesa Verdean Archaeology.* Albuquerque: University of New Mexico Press, 2004.

Lister, Robert H., and Florence C. Lister. *Aztec Ruins National Monument: Administrative History of an Archaeological Preserve.* Santa Fe: National Park Service, 1990.

————. *Those Who Came Before: Southwestern Archeology in the National Park System.* 1983. Rev. ed., Albuquerque: University of New Mexico Press; Tucson: Southwest Parks & Monuments Association, 1994.

Long, Abijah, and Joe N. Long. *The Big Cave: Early History and Authentic Facts*

*Concerning the History and Discovery of the World Famous Carlsbad Caverns of New Mexico.* 1956. 5th ed., Long Beach, Calif.: Cushman, 1964.

Lovato, Andrew Leo. *Santa Fe Hispanic Culture: Preserving Identity in a Tourist Town.* Albuquerque: University of New Mexico Press, 2004.

Lummis, Charles F. *The Land of Poco Tiempo.* New York: Charles Scribner's Sons, 1893.

———. *Letters from the Southwest, September 20, 1884 to March 14, 1885.* Edited by James W. Byrkit. Tucson: University of Arizona Press, 1989.

———. *Mesa, Cañon and Pueblo: Our Wonderland of the Southwest, Its Marvels of Nature, Its Pageant of the Earth Building, Its Strange Peoples, Its Centuried Romance.* New York: Century, 1925.

———. *Some Strange Corners of Our Country: The Wonderland of the Southwest.* 1892. Reprint, Tucson : University of Arizona Press, 1989.

———. *A Tramp Across the Continent.* New York: Charles Scribner's Sons, 1892.

MacFadden, Harry Alexander. *Rambles in the Far West.* Hollidaysburg, Pa.: Standard Printing House, 1906.

MacVaugh, Frederick Earle. "Preserving the Underground: The Creation of Carlsbad Caverns National Park." M.A. thesis, University of Texas at El Paso, 2000.

Malhi, Ripan S., Holly M. Mortensen, Jason A. Eshleman, Brian M. Kemp, Joseph G. Lorenz, Frederika A. Kaestle, John R. Johnson, Clara Gorodezky, and David Glenn Smith. "Native American mtDNA Prehistory in the American Southwest." *American Journal of Physical Anthropology* 120, no. 2 (2003).

Mallery, Barbara Vogt. *Bailing Wire & Gamuza: The True Story of a Family Ranch Near Ramah, New Mexico, 1905–1986.* Santa Fe: New Mexico Magazine, 2003.

Manje, Juan Mateo. *Unknown Arizona and Sonora, 1693–1721: From the Francisco Fernández del Castillo Version of Luz de Tierra Incognita.* Translated by Harry J. Karnes. Tucson: Arizona Silhouettes, 1954.

Mayer, Brantz. *Mexico as It Was and as It Is.* New York: J. Winchester, New World, 1844.

McCarty, Kieran, trans. and ed. *Desert Documentary: The Spanish Years, 1767–1821.* Tucson: Arizona Historical Society, 1976.

McFeely, Eliza. *Zuni and the American Imagination.* New York: Hill & Wang, 2001.

McGinty, Brian. *The Oatman Massacre: A Tale of Desert Captivity and Survival.* Norman: University of Oklahoma Press, 2005.

McNitt, Frank. *The Indian Traders.* Norman: Oklahoma University Press, 1962.

———. *Navajo Wars: Military Campaigns, Slave Raids, and Reprisals.* Albuquerque: University of New Mexico Press, 1972.

———. *Richard Wetherill: Anasazi.* 1957. Rev. ed., Albuquerque: University of New Mexico Press, 1966.

Meinig, D. W. *Southwest: Three Peoples in Geographical Change, 1600–1970.* New York: Oxford University Press, 1971.

Meline, James F. *Two Thousand Miles on Horseback, Santa Fé and Back: A Summer Tour Through Kansas, Nebraska, Colorado, and New Mexico, in the Year 1866.* New York: Hurd & Houghton, 1867.

Meltzer, David J. Introduction to *Ancient Monuments of the Mississippi Valley,* by E. G. Squier and E. H. Davis. 1848. Reprint, Washington D.C.: Smithsonian Institution, 1998.

Mifflin, Margot. *The Blue Tattoo: The Life of Olive Oatman.* Lincoln: University of Nebraska Press, 2009.

Mindeleff, Cosmos. "Cliff Ruins of Canyon De Chelly." *American Anthropologist* 8, no. 2 (1895): 153–74.

Minge, Ward Allen. *Ácoma: Pueblo in the Sky.* 1976. Rev. ed., Albuquerque: University of New Mexico Press, 2002.

Möllhausen, Baldwin. *Diary of a Journey from the Mississippi to the Coasts of the Pacific with a United States Government Expedition.* 2 vols. Translated by Mrs. Percy Sinnett. London: Longman, Brown, Green, Longmans, & Roberts, 1858. [The title page of this volume uses the English spelling of Möllhausen's first name, which is usually given as Balduin.]

Moorhead, Max L. *The Presidio: Bastion of the Spanish Borderlands.* Norman: University of Oklahoma Press, 1975.

Morehouse, Barbara J. *A Place Called the Grand Canyon: Contested Geographies.* Tucson: University of Arizona Press, 1998.

Morgan, Dale Lowell. *Jedediah Smith and the Opening of the West.* Indianapolis: Bobbs-Merrill, 1953.

Morgan, Lewis H. "On the Ruins of a Stone Pueblo on the Animas River in New Mexico; with a Ground Plan." In *Annual Report of the Trustees of the Peabody Museum of American Archaeology and Ethnology.* Cambridge, Mass.: John Wilson & Son, 1880.

Morgan, William Fellowes. "Description of a Cliff-House on the Mancos River of Colorado." In *Proceedings of the American Association for the Advancement of Science, Twenty-Seventh Meeting,* edited by Frederick W. Putnam. Salem, Mass.: Permanent Secretary, 1879.

Mott, Frank Luther. *Golden Multitudes: The Story of Best Sellers in the United States.* New York: Macmillan, 1947.

Murphy, Dan. *El Morro National Monument.* Tucson: Southwest Parks and Monuments Association, 2003.

Myrick, David F. *New Mexico's Railroads: A Historical Survey.* Albuquerque: University of New Mexico Press, 1970.

Naylor, Thomas H., and Charles W. Polzer, eds. *Pedro de Rivera and the Military Regulations for Northern New Spain, 1724–1729: A Documentary History of His Frontier Inspection and the Reglamento de 1729.* Tucson: University of Arizona Press, 1988.

Nentvig, Juan, S.J. *Rudo Ensayo: A Description of Sonora and Arizona in 1764.* Translated and edited by Alberto Francisco Pradeau and Robert R. Rasmussen. Tucson: University of Arizona Press, 1980.

Newcomb, Franc Johnson. *Hosteen Klah: Navaho Medicine Man and Sand Painter.* Norman: University of Oklahoma Press, 1964.

Newhall, Beaumont, and Nancy Newhall, *T. H. O'Sullivan, Photographer.* New York: George Eastman House and Amon Carter Museum of Western Art, 1966.

Noble, David Grant, ed. *The Hohokam: Ancient People of the Desert.* Santa Fe: School of American Research Press, 1991.

————, ed. *In Search of Chaco: New Approaches to an Archaeological Enigma.* Santa Fe: School of American Research Press, 2004.

————, ed. *The Mesa Verde World: Explorations in Ancestral Pueblo Archaeology.* Santa Fe: School of American Research Press, 2006.

Noggle, Burl. "Anglo Observers of the Southwest Borderlands, 1825–1890: The Rise of a Concept." *Arizona and the West* 1 (Summer 1959).

Nymeyer, Robert, and William R. Halliday. *Carlsbad Caverns: The Early Years.* Carlsbad, N.M.: Carlsbad Caverns / Guadalupe Mountains Association, 1991.

Officer, James E. *Hispanic Arizona, 1536–1856.* Tucson: University of Arizona Press, 1987.

Pattie, James Ohio. *The Personal Narrative of James O. Pattie, of Kentucky.* Edited by Timothy Flint. Cincinnati: E. H. Flint, 1833.

Pearce, T. M. *New Mexico Place Names: A Geographical Dictionary.* Albuquerque: University of New Mexico Press, 1965.

Peixotto, Ernest. *Our Hispanic Southwest.* New York: Charles Scribner's Sons, 1916.

Pike, Albert. *Prose Sketches and Poems Written in the Western Country (with Additional Stories).* Edited by David J. Weber. Albuquerque: University of New Mexico Press, 1967.

Pike, Zebulon Montgomery. *An Account of Expeditions to the Sources of the Mississippi, and Through the Western Parts of Louisiana, to the Sources of the Arkansaw, Kans, La Platte, and Pierre Juan Rivers; Performed by Order of the Government of the United States During the Years 1805, 1806, and 1807; and a Tour Through the Interior Parts of New Spain, When Conducted Through These Provinces, by Order of thr Captain-General in the Year 1807.* Philadelphia: C. & A. Conrad, 1810.

————. *The Journals of Zebulon Montgomery Pike, with Letters and Related Documents.* 2 vols. Edited by Donald Jackson. Norman: University of Oklahoma Press, 1966.

Pomeroy, Earl S. *In Search of the Golden West: The Tourist in Western America.* New York: Knopf, 1957.

Powell, E. Alexander. *The End of the Trail: The Far West from New Mexico to British Columbia.* New York: Charles Scribner's Sons, 1914.

Powell, John Wesley. *Canyons of the Colorado.* Meadville, Pa.: Flood & Vincent, 1895.

————. *Exploration of the Colorado River of the West, and Its Tributaries: Explored in 1869, 1870, 1871, and 1872, Under the Direction of the Secretary of the Smithsonian Institution.* Washington, D.C.: Government Printing Office, 1875.

Powell, Lawrence Clark. *Southwest Classics: The Creative Literature of the Arid Lands.* Los Angeles: Ward Ritchie, 1974.

Prentis, Noble L. *South-western Letters.* Topeka: Kansas Publishing House, 1882.

Prescott, William H. *History of the Conquest of Mexico, with a Preliminary View of the Ancient Mexican Civilization, and the Life of the Conqueror Hernando Cortes.* 1843. Reprint, New York: Modern Library, 2001.

Price, Patricia L. *Dry Place: Landscapes of Belonging and Exclusion.* Minneapolis: University of Minnesota Press, 2004.

Pyne, Stephen J. *How the Canyon Became Grand: A Short History.* New York: Viking, 1998.

Reséndez, Andrés, and Brian M. Kemp. "Genetics and the History of Latin America." *Hispanic American Historical Review* 85, no. 2 (2005): 283–98.

Riley, Carroll, and Joni L. Manson. "The Cibola-Tiguex Route: Continuity and Change in the Southwest." *New Mexico Historical Review* 58 (October 1983): 353–56.

Robertson, Janet. *The Magnificent Mountain Women: Adventures in the Colorado Rockies.* Lincoln: University of Nebraska Press, 1990.

Robinson, Jacob S. *A Journal of the Santa Fe Expedition Under Colonel Doniphan.* Edited by Carl Leslie Cannon. 1848. Reprint, Princeton: Princeton University Press, 1932.

Rothman, Hal K. *Preserving Different Pasts: The American National Monuments.* Urbana: University of Illinois Press, 1989.

————. *Promise Beheld and the Limits of Place: A Historic Resource Study of Carlsbad Caverns and Guadalupe Mountains National Parks and the Surrounding Areas.* Washington, D.C.: National Park Service, 1998.

Ruxton, George Frederick Augustus. *Ruxton of the Rockies.* Edited by LeRoy R. Hafen. Norman: University of Oklahoma Press, 1950.

Sage, Rufus B. *Rufus B. Sage: His Letters and Papers, 1836–1847, with an Annotated Reprint of His "Scenes in the Rocky Mountains, and in Oregon, California, New Mexico, Texas, and the Grand Prairies."* 2 vols. Edited by LeRoy R. Hafen and Ann W. Hafen. Glendale, Calif: A. H. Clark, 1956.

————. *Scenes in the Rocky Mountains and in Oregon, California, New Mexico, Texas, and the Grand Prairies; or, Notes by the Way, During an Excursion of Three Years, with a Description of the Countries Passed Through, Including Their Geography, Geology, Resources, Present Condition, and the Different Nations Inhabiting Them.* Philadelphia: Carey & Hart, 1846.

Salmerón, Jerónimo Zárate. *Relaciones.* Translated by Alicia Ronstadt Milich. Albuquerque: Horn & Wallace, 1966.

Salvesen, Britt. "'Surrealistic and Disturbing': Timothy O'Sullivan as Seen by Ansel Adams in the 1930s." *Journal of Surrealism and the Americas* 2, no. 2 (2008): 162–79.

Saunders, Charles Francis. *Finding the Worthwhile in the Southwest.* 1918. Rev. ed., New York: Robert M. McBride, 1937.

Scully, Vincent. *Pueblo: Mountain, Village, Dance.* 1972. Reprint, New York: Viking, 1975.

Sedelmayr, Jacobo. *Missionary, Frontiersman, Explorer in Arizona and Sonora: Four Original Manuscript Narratives, 1744–1751.* Translated and edited by Peter Masten Dunne. Tucson: Arizona Pioneers' Historical Society, 1955.

Seefeldt, Douglas. "Oñate's Foot: Histories, Landscapes, and Contested Memories in the Southwest." In *Across the Continent: Jefferson, Lewis and Clark, and the Making of America,* edited by Douglas Seefeldt, Jeffrey L. Hantman, and Peter S. Onuf. Charlottesville: University of Virginia Press, 2005.

Sherburne, John P. *Through Indian Country to California: John P. Sherburne's Diary of the Whipple Expedition, 1853–1854.* Edited by Mary McDougall Gordon. Palo Alto, Calif.: Stanford University Press, 1988.

Sheridan, Thomas E. *Landscapes of Fraud: Mission Tumacácori, the Baca Float, and the Betrayal of the O'odham.* Tucson: University of Arizona Press, 2006.

———. *Los Tucsonenses: The Mexican Community in Tucson, 1854–1941.* Tucson: University of Arizona Press, 1986.

Sheridan, Thomas E., Stewart B. Koyiyumptewa, Anton Daughters, Dale S. Brenneman, T. J. Ferguson, Leigh Kuwanwisiwma, and Lee Wayne Lomayestewa, eds. *Moquis and Kastiilam: Hopis, Spaniards, and the Trauma of History.* Vol. 1, *1540–1679.* Tucson: University of Arizona Press, 2015.

Simmons, Marc. *The Last Conquistador: Juan de Oñate and the Settling of the Far Southwest.* Norman: University of Oklahoma Press, 1991.

Simpson, James H. *Navaho Expedition: Journal of a Military Reconnaissance from Santa Fe, New Mexico, to the Navaho Country Made in 1849.* Edited by Frank McNitt. Norman: University of Oklahoma Press, 1964.

———. *Reports of the Secretary of War Communicating the Report of Lieutenant J. H. Simpson of an Expedition into the Navajo Country in 1849....* U.S. 31st Cong., 1st sess., Senate Executive Document 64. Washington, D.C.: Union Office, 1850.

Sitgreaves, Lorenzo. *Report of an Expedition Down the Zuni and Colorado Rivers.* U.S. 32d Cong., 2nd sess., Senate Executive Document 59. Washington, D.C.: R. Armstrong, 1853.

Slater, John M. *El Morro, Inscription Rock, New Mexico: The Rock Itself, the Inscriptions Thereon, and the Travelers Who Made Them.* Los Angeles: Plantin, 1961.

Smith, Duane. *Mesa Verde National Park: Shadows of the Centuries.* Lawrence: University of Kansas Press, 1988.

Smith, Fay Jackson, John L. Kessell, and Francis J. Fox. *Father Kino in Arizona.* Phoenix: Arizona Historical Foundation, 1966.

Smith, Jedediah Strong. *The Southwest Expedition of Jedediah S. Smith: His Personal Account of the Journey to California, 1826–1827.* Edited by George R. Brooks. Glendale, Calif.: A. H. Clark, 1977.

Sonnichsen, C. L. *Tucson: The Life and Times of an American City.* Norman: University of Oklahoma Press, 1982.

Sproul, David Kent. *A Bridge Between Cultures: An Administrative History of Rainbow Bridge National Monument.* Cultural Resources Selections 18. Denver: U.S. Dept. of the Interior, National Park Service, Intermountain Region, 2001. Also at http://www.nps.gov/rabr/learn/historyculture/upload/RABR_adhi.pdf.

Stacey, May Humphreys. *Uncle Sam's Camels: The Journal of May Humphreys Stacey Supplemented by the Report of Edward Fitzgerald Beale (1857–1858).* San Marino, Calif.: Huntington Library Press, 2006.

Stegner, Wallace. *Beyond the Hundredth Meridian: John Wesley Powell and the Second Opening of the West.* Boston: Houghton, Mifflin, 1954.

Stewart, Kenneth M. "A Brief History of the Mohave Indians Since 1850." *Kiva* 34, no. 4 (1969): 219–36.

———. "Mohave." In *Handbook of North American Indians,* vol. 10, *Southwest,* edited by Alfonso Ortiz. Washington, D.C.: Smithsonian Institution, 1983.

Stone, William. *New Mexico Then and Now.* Englewood, Colo.: Westcliffe, 2003.

Stratton, Royal B. *Captivity of the Oatman Girls: Being an Interesting Narrative of Life among the Apache and Mohave Indians, Containing Also an Interesting Account of the Massacre of the Oatman Family, by the Apache Indians in 1851; The Narrow Escape of Lorenzo D. Oatman; The Capture of Olive A. and Mary A. Oatman; The Death by Starvation of the Latter; The Five Years Suffering and Captivity of Olive A. Oatman; Also Her Singular Recapture in 1856. . . .* 1857. Rev. ed., San Francisco: Whitton, Towne & Co's Excelsior Steam Power Presses, 1857.

Summerhayes, Martha. *Vanished Arizona: Recollections of My Army Life.* 1908. Reprint, Philadelphia: Lippincott, 1963.

Sunder, John E., ed. *Matt Field on the Santa Fe Trail.* Norman: University of Oklahoma Press, 1960.

Teague, David W. *The Southwest in American Literature and Art: The Rise of a Desert Aesthetic.* Tucson: University of Arizona Press, 1997.

Thomas, Keith. *Man and the Natural World: A History of the Modern Sensibility.* New York: Pantheon Books, 1983.

Tobias, Henry Jack, and Charles E. Woodhouse. *Santa Fe: A Modern History, 1880–1990.* Albuquerque: University of New Mexico Press, 2001.

Villagrá, Gaspar Pérez de. *Historia de la Nuevo México, 1610: A Critical and Annotated Spanish/English Edition.* Translated and edited by Miguel Encinias, Alfred Rodríguez, Joseph P. Sánchez, and Fayette S. Curtis. Albuquerque: University of New Mexico Press, 1992.

———. *History of New Mexico by Gaspar Pérez de Villagrá, Alcalá, 1610.* Translated by Gilberto Espinosa. Edited by F. W. Hodge. Los Angeles: Quivira Society, 1933.

Waitley, Douglas. *William Henry Jackson: Framing the Frontier.* Missoula, Mont.: Mountain Press, 1999.

Wallace, Andrew, and Richard H. Hevly, eds. *From Texas to San Diego in 1851: The Overland Journal of Dr. S. W. Woodhouse, Surgeon-Naturalist of the Sitgreaves Expedition.* Lubbock: Texas Tech University Press, 2007.

Wallace, Susan E. *The Land of the Pueblos.* 1888. Reprint, New York: John B. Alden, 1890.

Waugh, Alfred S. *Travels in Search of the Elephant: The Wanderings of Alfred S. Waugh, Artist, in Louisiana, Missouri, and Santa Fe, in 1845–1846.* Edited by John Francis McDermott. St. Louis: Missouri Historical Society, 1951.

Weber, David J., ed. *The Californios Versus Jedediah Smith, 1826–1827: A New Cache of Documents.* Spokane, Wash.: Arthur H. Clark, 1990.

———. "Fray Marcos de Niza and the Historians." In *Myth and the History of the Hispanic Southwest: Essays by David J. Weber.* Albuquerque: University of New Mexico Press, 1988.

———. *Richard H. Kern: Expeditionary Artist in the Far Southwest, 1848–1853.* Albuquerque: University of New Mexico Press for the Amon Carter Museum, 1985.

———. "Santa Fe." In *Jamestown, Québec, Santa Fe: Three North American Beginnings,* edited by James C. Kelly and Barbara Clark Smith, 136–40. Washington, D.C.: Smithsonian Books, 2007.

———. *The Taos Trappers: The Fur Trade in the Far Southwest, 1540–1846.* Norman: University of Oklahoma Press, 1971.

———, ed. *What Caused the Pueblo Revolt of 1680?* Boston: Bedford / St. Martin's, 1999.

———. "William Becknell as a Mountain Man: Two Letters," *New Mexico Historical Review* 46 (July 1971): 257–58.

Weisiger, Marsha. *Dreaming of Sheep in Navajo Country.* Seattle: University of Washington Press, 2009.

Wetherill, B. A. *The Wetherills of the Mesa Verde: The Autobiography of Benjamin Alfred Wetherill.* Edited by Maurine S. Fletcher. London: Associated University Press, 1977.

Wheeler, George Montague. *Photographs Showing Landscapes, Geological and Other Features, of Portions of the Western Territory of the United States. Obtained in Connection with Geographical and Geological Explorations and Surveys West of the 100th Meridian, Seasons of 1871, 1872, and 1873.* Washington, D.C.: U.S. Army Corps of Engineers, 1875.

Whipple, Amiel Weeks. *A Pathfinder in the Southwest: The Itinerary of Lieutenant A. W. Whipple During His Explorations for a Railway Route from Fort Smith to Los*

*Angeles in the Years 1853 & 1854.* Edited by Grant Foreman. 1941. Reprint, Norman: University of Oklahoma Press, 1968.

Whipple, Amiel Weeks, Thomas Ewbank, and Wm. W. Turner. "Report of Explorations for a Railway Near the Thirty-Fifth Parallel of Latitude, from the Mississippi River to the Pacific Ocean: Report upon the Indian Tribes." In *Reports of Explorations and Surveys, to Ascertain the Most Practicable and Economical Route for a Railroad from the Mississippi to the Pacific Ocean, Made under the Direction of the Secretary of War, in 1853–4.* Washington, D.C.: Government Printing Office, 1855–61.

White, James Larkin. *Jim White's Own Story: The Discovery and History of Carlsbad Caverns, New Mexico.* "Compiled for Jim White by Frank Ernest Nicholson." 1932. Reprint, Carlsbad, N.M.: Carlsbad Caverns Guadalupe Mountains Association, 1998.

Wilcox, David R., and Lynette O. Shenk. *The Architecture of the Casa Grande and Its Interpretation.* Archaeological series 115. Tucson: Cultural Resource Management Section, Arizona State Museum, University of Arizona, 1977.

Wilson, Chris. *The Myth of Santa Fe: Creating a Modern Regional Tradition.* Albuquerque: University of New Mexico Press, 1997.

Wingert-Playdon, Kate. *John Gaw Meem at Acoma: The Restoration of San Esteban del Rey Mission.* Albuquerque: University of New Mexico Press, 2012.

Winship, George Parker, ed. *The Journey of Coronado, 1540–1542.* 1896. Reprint, New York: Dover, 1990.

Wood, Stanley. *Over the Range to the Golden Gate: A Complete Tourist's Guide to Colorado, New Mexico, Utah, Nevada, California, Oregon, Puget Sound, and the Great North-west.* 1889. Rev. ed. by C. E. Hooper, Chicago: R. R. Donnelley & Sons, 1904.

Worster, Donald. *A River Running West: The Life of John Wesley Powell.* New York: Oxford University Press, 2001.

*Zuni 2006 Visitors Guide.* Zuni Pueblo, 2006.

Zúñiga, C. Ignacio. *Rápida Ojeada al Estado de Sonora.* Mexico: Juan de Ojeda, 1835.

# Index

Page numbers in *italics* refer to illustrations

# Credits

Extended quotations subject to copyright are reprinted herein with appropriate permissions. Copyright holders who have requested formal acknowledgement include the following.

Chapters 1, 7, 13, 15: *Documents of the Coronado Expedition, 1539–1542,* ed. by Richard Flint and Shirley Cushing Flint, republished with permission of the University of New Mexico Press; copyright © 2005 University of New Mexico Press, 2012.

Chapter 1: *Don Juan de Oñate: Colonizer of New Mexico, 1595–1628,* ed. by George P. Hammond and Agapito Rey, republished with permission of the University of New Mexico Press; copyright © 1953 University of New Mexico Press.

Chapter 8: *The Diaries of William Henry Jackson,* ed. by Leroy R. Hafen and Ann W. Hafen, republished with permission of Arthur H. Clark Company via Copyright Clearance Center; copyright © 1959 Arthur H. Clark Company.

Chapter 9: *The Southwest Expedition of Jedediah S. Smith: His Personal Account of the Journey to California, 1826–1827,* ed. by George R. Brooks, republished with permission of the University of Nebraska Press; copyright © 1977 Arthur H. Clark Company.

Chapter 14: *Desert Documentary: The Spanish Years, 1767–1821,* ed. and trans. by Kieran C. McCarty, republished with permission of the Arizona Historical Society; copyright © 1976 Arizona Historical Society.

*Recent Titles*

*Sovereignty for Survival: American Energy Development and Indian Self-Determination,* by James Robert Allison III

*George I. Sánchez: The Long Fight for Mexican American Integration,* by Carlos K. Blanton

*Growing Up with the Country: A Family History of Race and American Expansion,* by Kendra Field

*Grounds for Dreaming: Mexican Americans, Mexican Immigrants, and the California Farmworker Movement,* by Lori A. Flores

*The Yaquis and the Empire: Violence, Spanish Imperial Power, and Native Resilience in Colonial Mexico,* by Raphael Brewster Folsom

*Subverting Exclusion: Transpacific Encounters with Race, Caste, and Borders, 1885–1928,* by Andrea Geiger

*The American West: A New Interpretive History, Second Edition,* by Robert V. Hine, John Mack Faragher, and Jon T. Coleman

*Legal Codes and Talking Trees: Indigenous Women's Sovereignty in the Sonoran and Puget Sound Borderlands, 1854–1946,* by Katrina Jagodinsky

*Gathering Together: The Shawnee People Through Diaspora and Nationhood, 1600–1870,* by Sami Lakomäki